MAHAN, CORBETT, AND THE FOUNDATIONS OF NAVAL STRATEGIC THOUGHT

TITLES IN THE SERIES

Progressives in Navy Blue: Maritime Strategy, American Empire, and the Transformation of U.S. Naval Identity, 1873–1898

Learning War: The Evolution of Fighting Doctrine in the U.S. Navy, 1898–1945

Victory without Peace: The United States Navy in European Waters, 1919–1924

Admiral John S. McCain and the Triumph of Naval Air Power

Churchill's Phoney War: A Study in Folly and Frustration

COSSAC: Lt. Gen. Sir Frederick Morgan and the Genesis of Operation OVERLORD

The Emergence of American Amphibious Warfare, 1898–1945

U-Boat Commander Oskar Kusch: Anatomy of a Nazi-Era Betrayal and Judicial Murder

Warship Builders: An Industrial History of U.S. Naval Shipbuilding, 1922–1945

STUDIES IN NAVAL HISTORY AND SEA POWER

Christopher M. Bell and James C. Bradford, editors

Studies in Naval History and Sea Power advances our understanding of sea power and its role in global security by publishing significant new scholarship on navies and naval affairs. The series presents specialists in naval history, as well as students of sea power, with works that cover the role of the world's naval powers, from the ancient world to the navies and coast guards of today. The works in Studies in Naval History and Sea Power examine all aspects of navies and conflict at sea, including naval operations, strategy, and tactics, as well as the intersections of sea power and diplomacy, navies and technology, sea services and civilian societies, and the financing and administration of seagoing military forces.

MAHAN, CORBETT, AND THE FOUNDATIONS OF NAVAL STRATEGIC THOUGHT

KEVIN D. McCRANIE

NAVAL INSTITUTE PRESS
Annapolis, Maryland

Naval Institute Press
291 Wood Road
Annapolis, MD 21402

Library of Congress Cataloging-in-Publication Data

Names: McCranie, Kevin D., author.
Title: Mahan, Corbett, and the foundations of naval strategic thought / Kevin D. McCranie.
Description: Annapolis, Maryland : Naval Institute Press, 2021. | Series: Studies in naval history and sea power | Includes bibliographical references and index.
Identifiers: LCCN 2020036744 (print) | LCCN 2020036745 (ebook) | ISBN 9781682475744 (hardcover) | ISBN 9781682475751 (pdf) | ISBN 9781682475751 (epub)
Subjects: LCSH: Naval strategy—History—19th century. | Sea-power—History—19th century. | Mahan, A. T. (Alfred Thayer), 1840–1914—Influence. | Corbett, Julian Stafford, 1854–1922—Influence. | Naval historians—United States—Biography. | Naval historians—Great Britain—Biography.
Classification: LCC V25 .M39 2021 (print) | LCC V25 (ebook) | DDC 359/.03—dc23
LC record available at https://lccn.loc.gov/2020036744
LC ebook record available at https://lccn.loc.gov/2020036745

∞ Print editions meet the requirements of ANSI/NISO z39.48-1992 (Permanence of Paper). Printed in the United States of America.

29 28 27 26 25 24 23 22 9 8 7 6 5 4 3 2

CONTENTS

ILLUSTRATIONS

ACKNOWLEDGMENTS

The end of a journey results in disparate thoughts. Who to thank? What led to the book and determined the path it followed? And particularly, how and why did that journey ever occur? This is a project that has germinated for a quarter of a century and captivated me like few others in recent years. I still think back to my master's thesis on George Keith Elphinstone, Lord Keith, a British naval officer of vast experience in the American Revolution as well as the Wars of the French Revolution and Napoleon. At my thesis defense, Paul G. Halpern asked if Keith's career better epitomized Mahan's or Corbett's theories. Fortunately, I knew just enough to respond "Corbett" given Keith's involvement in joint and expeditionary warfare. Even then, I could not truly escape the shadow that Alfred Thayer Mahan and Julian S. Corbett cast across naval history, operations, and strategy.

Nearly a decade later, I began teaching for the U.S. Naval War College. I found Mahan and Corbett to hold a prominent place in the curriculum even though they wrote at the turn of the twentieth century. Though I had certainly seen their shadow and influence while completing my previous projects, teaching proved a stern awakening to just how little I actually knew. As I attempted to draw comparisons between their theories, I came up wanting. Search as I might, I could not find a major work that put their arguments into a comparative perspective.

This book has benefitted from my continual engagement with students and colleagues. Of the latter, John Maurer has my particular appreciation. As chair of the Strategy and Policy Department, he suggested I focus on Corbett's theories. Sally Paine and Jon O'Gorman deserve special thanks for reading the following pages in their entirety. Though I have already mentioned John Maurer's role as department chair, his successors—Michael Pavković and David Stone—were instrumental in creating a working environment that fosters faculty research and publication. I know they have innumerable competing priorities, yet each chair bent over backward to facilitate my research.

This work is not merely a comparison of Mahan's and Corbett's published writings. Both men were educators who engaged broadly with professional and academic communities, and their letters and lecture notes have proven invaluable. Much of Mahan's correspondence has been published, but Corbett's diaries, letters, and notes remain in archives. Particularly, I wish to thank the Trustees for the Liddell Hart Centre for Military Archives at King's College, London, for giving me permission to quote from the Sir Julian Stafford Corbett Papers. I also wish to thank the National Maritime Museum's Caird Library and Archives for permission to quote from several of their permanent collections, including the papers of Sir Julian Stafford Corbett, Kenneth Dewar, Michael Lewis, and Sir Herbert Richmond.

Archivists at the Naval War College were particularly helpful in finding documents and rare books. The Naval War College librarians provided essential assistance with myriad issues ranging from interlibrary loan requests to helping with temperamental microfilm machines. I am greatly in their debt. My thanks also to the U.S. Naval Institute, the U.S. Military Academy, the Naval History and Heritage Command, and the archives and museum at the Naval War College for generously providing the images in the text.

I owe the greatest debt to my wife, Tracy: her steadfast support allowed me to carve out the time I needed to make this book a reality. And I could not end this acknowledgment without thanking my sister for her expertise in graphic design. Though hardly interested in navies and history, she made the mistake of becoming a professional graphic designer. Her maps and diagrams made the critical difference in this book.

Turning finally to the two theorists on whom this work is based. Understanding their works has been especially grueling because neither wrote as systematically as I would have liked. Mahan is particularly guilty. The following pages contain my interpretation of century-old theories. My conclusions, like those of others who have studied Mahan and Corbett, are the product of a mindset, a time, and a worldview. The result remains an interpretation subject to counterarguments that will, I hope, advance our understanding of naval strategy and particularly the roles of Mahan and Corbett in its development.

The positions I am about to express are my own views. I do not represent the Naval War College, the U.S. Navy, the Department of Defense, or the U.S. government, and my views are not necessarily shared by them.

INTRODUCTION

Three-quarters of a century has passed since the last great naval war ended with the surrender of Imperial Japan in 1945. The long era of relative peace on the world's oceans has contributed to globalization and unprecedented economic development, yet during that time our institutional understanding of naval power has evaporated. Important knowledge about the purpose of a navy and what a navy can and, perhaps more important, cannot achieve has slowly sunk into the abyss.

At the turn of the twentieth century, a similar situation existed. The final defeat of Napoleon in 1815 had ushered in another long period of relative peace on the world's oceans. With the Napoleonic Wars a distant memory, the purpose of naval power appeared at best cloudy. Some even believed that their leaders had forgotten how to employ their warships for national political objectives. To remedy this deficiency, commentators and historians at the dawn of the twentieth century sought to reacquaint naval and government leaders with the basics of naval power and strategy to instill in them a sense of what was possible in the maritime domain. Though many on both sides of the Atlantic pushed forward theories, two individuals—Alfred Thayer Mahan and Julian Stafford Corbett—today stand head and shoulders above the rest.

A series of accidents, offers, and suggestions led Mahan and Corbett to develop enduring theories of naval power. Once the two began writing on the subject, they continued to publish related material until their deaths. Though both developed their theories over more than a quarter of a century, their seminal works straddle the period of their greatest activity. Mahan published his most enduring work, *The Influence of Sea Power upon History, 1660–1783*, in 1890, near the beginning of his literary career. He developed, evolved, and added to his theories over the next twenty-five years. Corbett began writing history at approximately the same time that Mahan wrote *The Influence of Sea Power upon History*, but his early writings were limited to biographical sketches. Over time, Corbett's writing became more analytical. His most significant theoretical study, *Some Principles of Maritime Strategy*, was published in 1911 following years of historical research and nearly a decade of direct association with the Royal Navy. Their arguments evolved. Thus, it would be a disservice merely to compare their seminal works. Moreover, both wrote in a rapidly evolving field. Historical scholarship was becoming ever more reliant on a wider array of sources, perhaps most notably archival documents, and new technology was revolutionizing navies.

Differences between the two men do not end with the trajectories of their literary output: their backgrounds also could hardly have been more dissimilar. Born in 1840, Alfred Thayer Mahan grew up in an environment steeped in military education. His father, Dennis Hart Mahan, taught engineering and military theory at the U.S. Military Academy at West Point. It is not surprising that the younger Mahan sought a career in the armed forces, but instead of the Army he chose the Navy, first attending the U.S. Naval Academy and then serving in the Civil War.[1] His father's background in military education along with his own long naval career in both war and peace provided a clear foundation for Alfred Thayer Mahan's theories.

Across the Atlantic in Great Britain, Julian Corbett epitomized the naval outsider. He did not come from a military family; nor did he ever serve in the Royal Navy. Born fourteen years after Mahan, Corbett attended Trinity College, Cambridge, then briefly practiced law, but the legal profession failed to captivate him.[2] His family's well-to-do status allowed him to work for personal fulfillment rather than necessity. Corbett dabbled in various pursuits, including the writing of fiction, but his was a life of leisure often enjoying outdoor activities. An acquaintance from these years noted, "His achievements in naval science and naval history must always seem the more remarkable to those who knew him in early and even middle life."[3]

Who the two men were is less important than what they wrote. Just four years after the publication of *The Influence of Sea Power upon History*,

The Times of London called Mahan "the greatest living writer on naval history."[4] In the same year, Theodore Roosevelt noted that Mahan "may be regarded as founding a new school of naval historical writing."[5] An 1893 article in *The Times* concluded: "Captain Mahan is more historical than the strategists, more strategical than the historians, and more philosophical than either."[6] Within five years of publishing *The Influence of Sea Power upon History*, Mahan was called by one reviewer the "Copernicus of naval history"; another compared the importance of his work with Adam Smith's *Wealth of Nations*.[7]

Even after his death in 1914, Mahan has remained influential among historians and commentators of the twentieth and early twenty-first centuries. Jon Sumida, who has written extensively on Mahan, claims that he "laid the foundations of modern naval history and strategy in his books on sea power."[8] Colin Gray describes Mahan's work as "timeless."[9] Paul Kennedy, the author of *The Rise and Fall of the Great Powers*, contends that "Mahan is, and will always remain, the point of reference and departure for any work upon 'sea power.'"[10] Others have asserted: "Taken all in all he was nothing short of a genius—perhaps one of the greatest, certainly one of the most original thinkers America has produced"; and he "singlehanded did for sea power what Jomini, Clausewitz, and Haushofer were never quite able to bring off for land power."[11] In 2009, almost a century after Mahan's death, Jeremy Black, a historian who has written widely on naval issues, labeled him "the most influential writer on naval power."[12]

Turning to Julian Corbett, the author of one paper on his theories remarked, "It is odd that so little is known of the man behind the work that is referred to as 'the standard work on naval strategy.'"[13] We must certainly look deeper to find statements extolling Corbett's significance. For this we can partially fault Corbett. Being well off, he did not rely on his writing for financial security and thus had no need to be as prolific as Mahan. Moreover, Mahan and Corbett had different underlying agendas. Mahan wrote to sell the U.S. Navy to a skeptical audience in the United States. He was a salesman, perhaps the best the U.S. Navy has ever had. Many of his writings were deliberately appealing. Corbett wrote for a narrower audience. He did not need to sell Britain on a navy; that argument had been made long ago. Rather, he interpreted Britain's grand strategic position in the early twentieth century and the Royal Navy's role in it.

Another factor influences this debate. During Corbett's lifetime, he was viewed as a historian of significant repute. Not long before his death, a review of the second volume of his official history of World War I attested: "Among naval historians in the English-speaking world Sir Julian Corbett now stands alone."[14] Only in the years following his death have his theoretical contributions become more evident. J. J. Widen notes that "Corbett's theory of maritime strategy is still the most sophisticated and eloquently written scholarly treatment of its subject."[15] N. A. M. Rodger, a leading historian of the Royal Navy, adds, "*Some Principles of Maritime Strategy* remains the foundation of all serious study of the subject."[16] Beatrice Heuser, whose writings assess the evolution of strategic thought, describes Corbett as "the key author who has formed our thinking about naval and maritime strategy to this day."[17]

A commentator comparing the contributions of the two men notes: "Thus if Mahan is to be remembered as having brought naval history to its proper, rightful place in history of international relations and economic affairs, Corbett is to be enshrined as the person who best understood the utility of sea power."[18] Perhaps Winston Churchill described their relative contributions best: "The standard work on Sea Power was written by an American Admiral. The best accounts of British sea fighting and naval strategy were compiled by an English civilian."[19]

Mahan and Corbett were aware of the other's works but viewed each other differently. Mahan saw himself as the senior partner in the relationship. He labeled Corbett's writings "extremely useful" and noted, "They deal with matter in itself interesting and the treatment is good and suggestive."[20] He even asked Corbett's permission to republish an article titled "The Capture of Private Property at Sea" in one of his edited volumes.[21] About the worst Mahan wrote about Corbett was a critique of *England and the Mediterranean* (1904) where Mahan concluded: "Like most men, Corbett's theory to some extent runs away with him."[22] As noted above, *The Influence of Sea Power upon History* appeared at approximately the same time Corbett began dabbling in historical writing. Over the next two decades Corbett took advantage of the flowering of interest in naval matters that Mahan's work had generated. In 1911 Mahan described the maturation of Corbett's works as "illustrations of the interesting change in the direction of naval thought." Mahan did not invariably agree with Corbett's views, but that seemed not to matter, for he asserted, "Any difficult military situation will give rise to difference of opinion."[23] He accepted that others would develop different conclusions. As evidenced by notes he took on several of Corbett's books, Mahan tended to consider him a historian rather than a theorist, and thus treated him as a source of information rather than a competitor. When Mahan did consider Corbett's theories, he seemed intrigued with how they compared with his own.[24]

Corbett's opinion of Mahan was a bit more complex. During Mahan's lifetime Corbett spoke well of him in published writings, noting that he was "distinctively at the head of a branch of literature" and was "a weighty critical authority."[25] Mahan's was "the best naval opinion there is," Corbett wrote, and he "above all men, by his genius and learning is entitled to give judgment."[26] He certainly gave Mahan credit for bringing naval theories to a wider audience.[27] In private, however, Corbett thought Mahan's work contained "unsound ideas" that were "shallow" and "unhistorical."[28] In a personal letter, he even argued, "Mahan has poisoned the whole field."[29] After Mahan's death in late 1914, Corbett's attacks became public.[30] One article, for example, includes a statement about "the attractive, if dangerous, works of Captain Mahan."[31] Corbett labeled Mahan's "historical synthesis" that resulted in his theory of sea power "undoubtedly premature."[32] It may be that such statements reflected the junior party in the relationship attempting to carve out his own place in the field.

Yet, what the two wrote about each other means little without comparing their actual theories; their contemporaries certainly did.[33] As early as 1898, one review of Corbett's *Drake and the Tudor Navy* noted, "His work . . . belongs to the same order of naval literature as the classical volumes of Captain Mahan."[34] Just three years later, Corbett was described as "one of the few English writers of our time who are entitled to take rank with Captain Mahan as authorities on naval warfare and naval history."[35] Such comparisons peaked in 1911 when both men published books on strategy: Mahan's *Naval Strategy Compared and Contrasted* and Corbett's *Some Principles of Maritime Strategy*. One review comparing the two described Corbett as Mahan's "rival in the field."[36] Another asserted that Mahan and Corbett were "the official exponents of naval strategy in their respective countries—Great Britain and the United States."[37] Corbett outlived Mahan by eight years. His obituary in *The Times* cemented Corbett's place in naval strategic theory by referring to him as "a naval historian of remarkable gifts, who combined with a profound and detailed knowledge of sea power with a breadth of view worthy to be compared with that of Mahan."[38]

More often than not, their theories complement or collide instead of diverge, requiring a finer and more thorough comparative analysis. One pre–World War I critic explained, "We have the interest of watching how, by different routes, they arrive at results essentially the same."[39]

This becomes even more important given their significance in naval and world affairs. Mahan's contemporaries and subsequent generations of historians have claimed that his writings helped rationalize naval expansion before World War I.[40] And both supporters and detractors thought Mahan's writings contributed to the outbreak of the war. Mahan, in prewar writings, chastised Norman Angell for claiming that economic integration made militarism and war a thing of the past. Angell responded that "Mahan's teachings" were "one of the causes, and not the least potent, of this war."[41] Fellow naval historian and Mahan's friend John Knox Laughton concurred: "It may be said without pardon, that they [Mahan's writings] are among the primary causes of the present war."[42]

Corbett also proved influential in that regard. The Royal Navy's failure to achieve a Trafalgar-like victory during World War I has been at least partially blamed on Corbett's prewar teachings.[43] Several years after the war, the British Admiralty issued a disclaimer to the third volume of Corbett's official history of the war: "Their Lordships find that some of the principles advocated in the book . . . are directly in conflict with their views."[44] It is telling that this volume of the official history contains the account of the 1916 Battle of Jutland. One commentator calls the disclaimer "perhaps the true indicator of how far Corbett's thinking in strategic matters had permeated the Royal Navy's upper reaches."[45]

Both men's theories were important during their lifetimes, and they continue to profoundly influence discussions on how states exploit the sea in a strategic sense. One needs only look to statements from Admiral Mike Mullen and Admiral John Richardson, each a former Chief of Naval Operations of the U.S. Navy. Mullen argues, "While much of Mahan's theory is dated, the questions he asked are not."[46] Richardson is even more explicit in *A Design for Maintaining Maritime Superiority*: "The essence of Mahan's vision still pertains. . . . What was true in the late 19th century holds true today." Richardson in fact argues that "the lessons of the masters—Thucydides, Clausewitz, Sun Tzu, Corbett, and, yes, Mahan—still apply."[47] Others agree. Robert Kaplan, a bestselling author and commentator on contemporary affairs, notes: "The best way to understand the tenuousness of our grip on 'hard,' military power (to say nothing of 'soft,' diplomatic power) is to understand our situation at sea. This requires an acquaintance with two books published a century ago: Mahan's *The Influence of Sea Power upon History, 1660–1783* . . . and Julian S. Corbett's *Some Principles of Maritime Strategy*."[48]

The significance of Corbett and Mahan to modern naval strategy is thus beyond question, but too often their theories are simplified or used without a real understanding of their fundamental bases. Labeling a strategy, operation, or even a navy "Mahanian" or "Corbettian" tells very little unless one knows what that actually means. "Although statesmen were supposed to have slept with his [Mahan's] books under their pillows," one commentator notes, "the evidence is that they merely made extracts, summaries, and highly selective formulations of his views, using these chiefly to justify the role of a navy in relation to such national interests and policies as they wished to develop."[49] Subsequent generations have likewise often referenced Mahan without fully understanding his theory.[50] The vastness of his work makes him a difficult subject to master, particularly because his views changed over the course of his career. Sumida contends that this "has resulted in a striking paradox: a body of famous work that has received a great deal of study but has been misunderstood completely."[51] Corbett is slightly less puzzling since his body of scholarship is smaller and *Some Principles of Maritime Strategy* provides a single-volume synthesis of much of his theory.

Anyone who has studied Clausewitz, Mahan, and even Corbett might long for simplicity, but that might not necessarily be a positive attribute. One commentator claims, "To be very straightforward in military writing . . . may leave one too easily understood, and hence soon enough passed over as 'pedestrian,' as offering something which 'we all knew already.'" Perhaps theoretical writing *should* be difficult to digest. "Becoming a classic of military strategic writing perhaps inevitably requires that conflicting interpretations be possible, so that opposing sides to an argument can quote an author back and forth, so that students can derive stimulation by puzzling over the exact meaning of one chapter or another."[52]

The following pages emphasize the theoretical concepts Mahan and Corbett developed while acknowledging that their intellectual output was multidimensional and stretched far beyond theories of war and international relations. Mahan remains particularly hard to characterize. He was president of the American Historical Association and wrote respected histories. He also acted as a political scientist by putting forward his theory of sea power and then supporting that theory through the remainder of his literary career.[53] Yet one cannot forget that his writings also include leadership studies, archival-based history, and opinion pieces regarding contemporary events. He even wrote of his religious beliefs.[54] In some cases, theory stands front and center, but often, deeply embedded theoretical constructs function as explanations within seemingly nontheoretical writings.

Corbett is easier to characterize. First, his training as a lawyer and his dabbling in fiction created a foundation for effective writing. Always more comfortable than Mahan with archival documentation, he was much more willing to deeply engage his sources. Corbett was already a well-respected naval historian when he was brought into naval circles as a subject matter expert. Although he continued to write histories, he, like Mahan, became more than a historian. He addressed contemporary policy debates at the behest of naval leadership and engaged deeply in professional military education.[55] Corbett found theory a necessary adjunct to historical exposition in order to make his subject relevant to often-skeptical naval audiences. Beginning with his introduction to navy circles and continuing to the outbreak of hostilities in 1914, Corbett developed ever more sophisticated theories of war. He then went on to apply his theoretical knowledge by assisting the Historical Section of the Committee of Imperial Defence during World War I and eventually becoming the primary author of the official history of the Royal Navy's role in that war.

No writer has the time, and no publisher the resources, to be entirely comprehensive. Every author makes decisions on what is relevant and necessary, and any critical reader must account for this and its effects on the product. Both Corbett and Mahan advocated and even overemphasized key issues in an effort to explain aspects of their contemporary environment. They grounded their research in frameworks, adopted the agendas of others, and based their theories on historical examples. Though both men wrote history, neither was a historian in the truest sense. Their association with British and American professional military education at the turn of the twentieth century made this impossible: their involvement with their respective navies forced them to develop tools of analysis that were relatable and relevant to contemporary conditions. Their success is exemplified in the fact that their theoretical concepts remain in professional military education curricula a century later.

Although there is no substitute for reading their actual words, that requires time—not just to read but, more important, to understand. Instead of peeling back the layers through careful analysis, commentators too often drop in quotes without context, latch onto selective concepts, or highlight partial truths that confuse, obscure, or even mislead. It is time for us to dive deeper, not only into Mahan's and Corbett's theories but also the environments in which they wrote.

CHAPTER 1

THE GRAND STRATEGIC FOUNDATIONS

Neither Mahan nor Corbett viewed navies as existing in a vacuum devoid of national policy considerations; rather, navies were created, nurtured, and employed to support a state's security interests. To explain how this occurred, both Mahan and Corbett found it necessary to stretch existing definitions of "strategy." Mahan developed the concept of "sea power" to place the U.S. Navy within the economic and security structures he desired for the United States, while Corbett sought to explain Britain's "maritime strategy" through a multiple instruments of national power approach. Their theories reflect the challenges their respective countries faced and the problems each man thought most needed analysis. The broad approaches they created to explain naval power resulted in their writings presupposing some of the central concepts of modern "grand strategy."

There is nothing simple about grand strategy. Hal Brands, who has written extensively on the subject, calls the term "one of the most slippery and widely abused terms in the foreign policy lexicon. The concept is often invoked but less often defined, and those who do define the phrase do so in a variety of different, and often contradictory, ways. The result is that discussions of grand strategy are often confused or superficial. Too frequently, they muddle or obscure more than they illuminate."[1]

Yet words are important for clarity and meaning to facilitate intelligent discussion. We cannot discuss grand strategy until we know what it is; without a description, confusion is almost inevitable.[2] Though any explanation will be incomplete, let us first come to a better understanding of grand strategy and how Mahan and Corbett presupposed the concept.

Paul Kennedy, a historian and the author of *The Rise and Fall of the Great Powers*, notes that "the crux of grand strategy lies . . . in *policy*, that is, in the capacity of the nation's leaders to bring together all the elements, both military and nonmilitary, for the preservation and enhancement of the nation's long-term (that is wartime *and* peacetime) best interests."[3] Corbett's theory likewise implores leaders to integrate different instruments of power in the pursuit of national political objectives.

Barry Posen, a leading political scientist and security studies expert, describes grand strategy as "a state's theory about how it can best 'cause' security for itself."[4] More simply, then, grand strategy is a theory of security. Mahan's sea power thesis is an example of a theory of security. Hal Brands expounds on the theory of security argument by claiming that grand strategy "provides the intellectual architecture that gives structure to foreign policy and helps nations find their way in the world." It "involves figuring out . . . how to make today's policies bring about tomorrow's desired end state." Again, Mahan's sea power thesis resonates, providing an aspiration to focus national ambitions through periods of peace and war.[5]

The above descriptions of grand strategy demonstrate, as one recent commentator argues, that "there exists not one evolving tradition of grand strategic thought, but numerous ones."[6] Recognizing such differences allows for more nuanced discussions of grand strategy, and in this case allows us to more fully understand the emphases, agendas, and arguments Corbett and Mahan advocated.

MAHAN AND THE SEA POWER THESIS

Mail had finally reached Commander Alfred Thayer Mahan in Guayaquil, Ecuador. One six-week-old letter would forever change his life, the future of the U.S. Navy, and accepted views on naval power. Written by Commodore Stephen B. Luce in September 1884, the letter invited Mahan to serve as a professor at the Naval War College in Newport, Rhode Island.[7] The college was Luce's brainchild: "a place where our officers would not only be encouraged, but *required*, to study their profession proper—war—in a far more thorough manner than had ever heretofore been attempted."[8]

"I should like the position," responded Mahan, "like it probably very much." It would be "a new, difficult and most needful work."[9] Mahan had served as an instructor at the Naval Academy in the late 1870s and in 1878 signaled an interest in educational reform when he entered a Naval Institute essay contest on the subject. His essay, which placed third, emphasized the need to better prepare officers when confronting complex problems, including war.[10] Five years later, in 1883, Mahan demonstrated a certain aptitude for scholarship with the publication of *Gulf and Inland Waters*, a book chronicling U.S. Civil War naval operations in the Gulf of Mexico and the connecting U.S. river systems. In Mahan, Luce had chosen an officer with an interest in education and history. Together, these would give him the background to be an effective war college instructor.

There was, however, a problem. When Mahan received Luce's letter, he held command of the *Wachusett*, a Civil War–era steam-sloop stationed on the Pacific coast of South America. He was not free to join the war college faculty. Two months later, Mahan anchored the *Wachusett* at Callao, the port for Lima, Peru, and went ashore to peruse the library of the Phoenix Club.[11] There, he chanced upon *The History of Rome* by Theodor Mommsen. "I was struck," Mahan later recounted, "by the non-recognition of the vital influence of sea power upon Hannibal's career." Mahan soon thought of other examples; one compounded upon the next, and each further solidified his views about the importance of what he labeled "sea power."[12]

Mahan worried that another officer would be appointed to teach at the war college in his stead, but he remained optimistic when writing Luce about several possible topics of instruction: "I would investigate coincidently the general history and naval history of the past two centuries, with a view to demonstrating the influence of the events of the one upon the other."[13] Specifically, Mahan wanted to address the role "of the sea as a highway for commerce . . . then consider sources of maritime power . . . [and] bring forward instances, from ancient and modern history, of the effect of navies and the control of the sea upon great or small campaigns." More than teach, Mahan told Luce, he hoped to conduct research and ultimately to write, convinced that by "the quiet evolution of a book I am stronger than in the teacher's chair."[14]

After finally being detached from command of the *Wachusett* in September 1885 at Mare Island, California, Mahan traveled east to begin in earnest his scholarly preparation. Given the challenging nature of the job ahead of him, he admitted possible failure.[15] Over the next few years, Mahan divided his time between teaching and writing, which proved mutually reinforcing. In effect, Mahan based his early sea power books on his lectures. This stirred some controversy because it was "a departure from the sound general rule of the College, not to print its lectures." By publishing these works, however, he would provide officers in his courses with another means of digesting his theory. That value, Mahan insisted, "exceeds . . . the harm done by parting with so much of our stock in trade."[16]

Mahan aimed at more than educating naval officers: he intended to change the conversation about the significance of the sea. By September 1888 he had completed the manuscript of *The Influence of Sea Power upon History, 1660–1783*. He later admitted to ending the history in 1783 for no other reason than "the necessity to stop and take breath."[17] He planned the book as the first volume of a larger work on naval history and sea power. *The Influence of Sea Power upon History* was but the first in a long list of books and articles that included "sea power" in their titles.[18] Rather than an afterthought, Mahan's writings on sea power constituted a concerted effort to develop a framework that linked what occurred at sea to broader security issues.

Mahan's sea power concept was a type of grand strategy written with a very specific purpose. He wanted to encourage the people of the United States to become ever more involved in global affairs. He noted that sea powers act in certain ways, creating a predictable structure within their foreign policy. Mahan applied his ideas to the United States to explain how sea power could provide his own country with a theory of security while seeking greater wealth through global engagement. While the specific actions of sea power were based on specific events, the underlying objectives of the sea power remained constant through both war and peace.[19]

Mahan described "two requisites of a strong sea power,—a widespread healthy commerce and a powerful navy."[20] He considered both elements crucial, and identified "sea power in the broadest sense of the word. On the one side sea power is represented by maritime commerce.

. . . On the other side it is by sea power in the military sense,—of navies."[21] Sea power thus comprises the interrelationship of commercial shipping, sea lines of communication linking markets, and warships that protect the system. Mahan identified a "logical sequence: industry, markets, control, navy, and bases."[22] Navies protect and extend the more important economic instruments spanning the peace–war continuum. Taken together, economic and naval power form a virtuous circle.[23] Commerce demands protection, leading to the development of a navy. The navy then enhances commercial security. Mutually dependent and self-reinforcing, one begets the other.

Though the term "sea power" is indelibly linked with Mahan's name, he was not the first to identify the intersection of naval power and commercial power. In Britain, earlier commentators on the subject included John Colomb, John Knox Laughton, and Edward Hamley.[24] And in America, eight years before *The Influence of Sea Power upon*

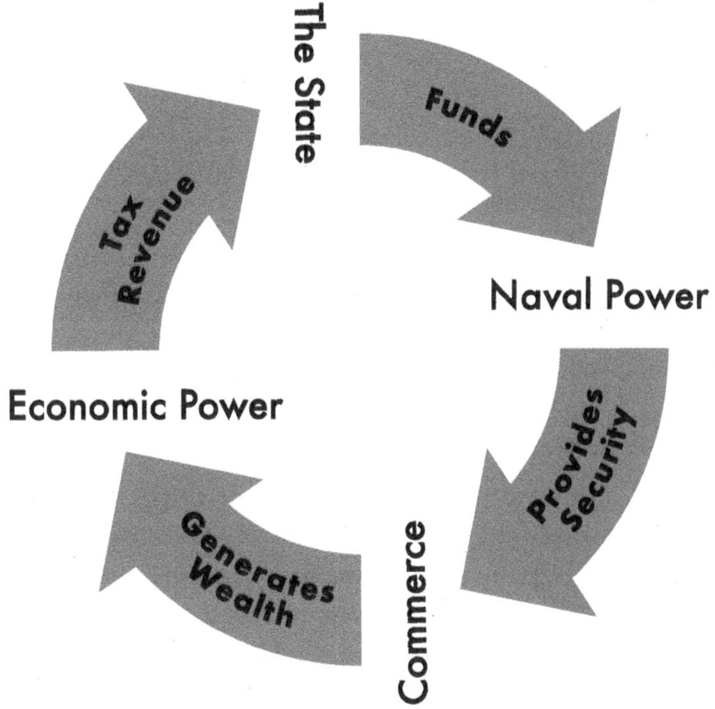

1.1. **Self-Sustaining Relationship of Naval and Economic Power**

History was published, a junior naval officer named William Glenn David submitted an essay titled "Our Merchant Marine" for a writing competition sponsored by the U.S. Naval Institute that was later published in its *Proceedings* magazine. David used the term "sea-power" as linking economic factors with "a proportionately strong navy." Though he never mentioned David's article, Mahan subscribed to *Proceedings*, and Mahan's chief biographer, Robert Seager II, asserts that he "almost surely read" the article.[25]

Even though the concept was already present in contemporary discourse when *The Influence of Sea Power upon History* went to print, it was Mahan who brought the importance of sea power to the modern consciousness. American naval officer Bradley Fiske, one of Mahan's contemporaries, wrote, "The book was so attractive, so complete, and so convincing, that it woke men suddenly to a perception of the truth, and at the same time to a realisation of the fact that this truth was of supreme importance to mankind."[26] Just as "Newton was not the first man to know, or to say, that things near the earth tend to fall to the earth," Fiske noted, ". . . he was the first to formulate and prove the doctrine of universal gravitation. In the same way, all through history, we find that a few master minds have been able to group what had theretofore seemed unrelated phenomena, . . . and became the guides of the human race."[27] Fiske considered Mahan such a mastermind.

Cyprian Bridge, a senior British naval officer at the turn of the twentieth century, wrote of Mahan: "We may regard him as the virtual inventor of the term. . . . He has made it impossible for anyone to treat of sea-power without frequent reference to his writings and conclusions."[28]

THE WORKINGS OF SEA POWER

Commerce, not naval power, drove Mahan's sea power thesis.[29] The world at the turn of the twentieth century was witnessing increased globalization and the movement of ever-larger quantities of goods across the oceans. Commercial shipping went beyond luxury goods to include key staples such as the grain required for daily life. Mahan was quick to recognize its importance, noting: "It is maritime commerce that has in all ages been most fruitful of wealth."[30]

Though Mahan certainly favored peaceful trade for the wealth it generated, he thought that commerce "has become the prize for which all the great states of the world are in competition."[31] By studying historical cases, he determined that "the history of Sea Power is largely, though by no means solely, a narrative of contests between nations, of mutual rivalries, of violence frequently culminating in war."[32] Mahan remained skeptical that long-term peaceful commercial competition was possible and was unable to divorce the potential for violence from his sea power thesis. He argued that sea power is neither a "cause" of increased global interaction nor the "result" of it. It is instead "the leading characteristic of activities which shall cease to be mainly internal, and shall occupy themselves with the wider interests that concern the relations of states to the world at large."[33] As a characteristic of a state's security structure sea power provided the framework for conceptualizing how a state attained its policy objectives.

Sea power entailed a competition with tremendous economic repercussions, and Mahan believed that governments should make every effort to influence maritime commercial activity with the object of gaining a larger portion of it. That was best accomplished by making "every effort . . . to exclude others, either by the peaceful legislative methods of monopoly or prohibitory regulations, or, when these failed, by direct violence."[34]

A more complex argument charts how naval and economic factors interacted to foster sea power over the long term. During the Wars of the French Revolution and Napoleon (1792–1815), Britain, the dominant sea power, slowly ground down France, the failed sea power. "There went on unceasingly that noiseless pressure upon the vitals of France, that compulsion, whose silence, when once noted, becomes to the observer the most striking and awful mark of the working of Sea Power."[35] "As everywhere and always," Mahan argued elsewhere, "the action of sea power was here quiet and unperceived." Sea power worked quietly because it did not require battle, but rather the monopolization of disparate commercial interactions on a regional or even a global scale. Mahan contended that other theorists had merely identified the effect of sea power without linking its effect to its cause.

Moreover, Mahan's concept of sea power reflected the concepts of Social Darwinism, a social theory popular at the turn of the twentieth century that predicted the survival of the fittest society. The struggle for survival had a zero-sum quality that played out in terms of economic competition and war.[36] "Irreconcilable differences of political and social systems, when brought into close contact," Mahan noted, "involve irrepressible conflict, and admit of no lasting solution except the subjugation and consequent submersion of one or the other."[37]

MAHAN'S HISTORICAL MODELS AND THE UNITED STATES

Mahan argued that "the world has long been accustomed to the idea of a preponderant naval power, coupling it accurately with the name of Great Britain."[38] Regarding Britain's naval and commercial might, he concluded, "It was in the union of the two, carefully fostered, that England made the gain of sea power over and beyond all other States." He dated Britain's ascendency to the War of the Spanish Succession (1701–14): "Before that war England was one of the sea powers; after it she was *the* sea power, without any second. This power also she held alone, unshared by friend and unchecked by foe. She alone was rich, and in her control of the sea and her extensive shipping had the sources of wealth so much in her hands that there was no present danger of a rival on the ocean."[39]

Mahan's use of Britain as his model sea power resulted in a positive reception among those associated with the Royal Navy. The British historian John Knox Laughton, for example, told of speaking with a member of Britain's Admiralty soon after the publication of *The Influence of Sea Power upon History.* The two spoke for more than a quarter of an hour, entirely captivated by the book. Laughton later explained that the book's "matter was not new: the historical details were often faulty, those of the battle inexact, but the picture of the influence, of the importance, of the effect of sea power was worked up [with] vividness and power of language, [and] wealth of illustration which was bound to carry conviction to an understanding mind."[40]

The Naval Defence Act of 1889 called for the expansion of the Royal Navy, and Mahan's book, which identified sea power as the factor behind Britain's international greatness, appeared at exactly the right moment to provide a rationale for the increased expenditures. Interest in the book "would always have been great," Laughton noted, "but is particularly so at the present time, when the conditions of naval strategy have been and are still being discussed among us with reference to the important problems of national defence."[41] Moreover, an American had developed the theory. While they might have been skeptical of one of their own extolling the virtues of sea power, Britons perceived Mahan as a disinterested foreigner whose thesis aligned exactly with what many wished to hear.[42]

One Mahan obituary noted, "His first book had made his reputation secure."[43] At the time it was published, however, Mahan worried that he had not done enough. Though he had written a groundbreaking study, it had stopped abruptly in 1783. He still had a great deal of his thesis to reveal. By the time *The Influence of Sea Power upon History* came out, Mahan had already begun research for his next book: *The Influence of Sea Power upon the French Revolution and Empire.* He considered this second volume "the one upon which my own reputation must rest."[44]

The second book spanned just one-fifth the period of the first, but it too appeared in England at just the right moment. Mahan's first volume was well regarded by those associated with the Royal Navy, but it had failed to attract a widespread popular audience. The same could not be said for the second volume. Published in 1892, it explained and justified what many in Britain witnessed at the Naval Exhibition of 1891. "People read it," explained Laughton, "because it appealed to their awakened sympathies."[45]

Of Mahan's first sea power volume, one reviewer noted, "The author's sympathies are very commonly with the French, even when his approval is with the English."[46] In that book, Mahan had asserted that

> France in its measure shows that a nation cannot subsist indefinitely off itself, however powerful in numbers and strong in internal resources. . . . With all her natural gifts France wasted away because of the want of that lively intercourse between the different parts of her own body and constant exchange with other people, which is known as commerce, internal or external. . . . So when the great strain came upon the powers of the nation, instead of drawing strength from every quarter and through many channels, and

> laying the whole outside world under contribution by the energy of its merchants and seamen, as England has done in like straits, it was thrown back upon itself. . . . The only escape from this process of gradual starvation was by an effectual control of the sea.[47]

Instead of pursuing sea power, France had become entangled in continental commitments. The draining attrition of land warfare followed.

Conversely, Britain rose to global dominance through the overwhelming economic advantages and naval strength of its sea power. "On the few occasions in which it is called to fight," Mahan observed, Great Britain's "superiority is so marked that the affairs can scarcely be called battles."[48] Even when Britain confronted a quantitatively superior coalition of opponents as the American Revolution evolved into a global maritime conflict against France, later Spain, and eventually the Netherlands, Britain leveraged its sea power and survived. France, in contrast, was caught between continental threats and maritime ambition.

Tension between the British model and French potential does much to explain the nature of sea power and served as a central theme in *The Influence of Sea Power upon History* but his later works increasingly focused on Britain as the model sea power. Though Britain possessed a smaller population and less fertile land than its French rival, sea power allowed it to punch above its weight. Because Britain controlled the global maritime commons, it took a leading position in European affairs.

Mahan's audience in England certainly devoured the sea power thesis, but he wrote, as Laughton noted, with "the circumstances of his own country definitely in view."[49] After all, Mahan admitted writing *The Influence of Sea Power upon History* for "the people of the United States in our own day" to question whether "the national character of Americans is fitted to develop a great sea power." Though later he would backtrack on his assessment, Mahan believed that France had faced a similar decision: "Of all the great powers she alone had a free choice; the others were more or less constrained to the land chiefly, or to the sea chiefly."[50] This led Mahan to speculate: "There is perhaps seen the prophecy of some other great nation in days yet to come, that will incline the balance of power in some future sea war . . . but that nation will not be the United States if the moment find her indifferent, as now, to the empire of the seas."[51]

Americans saw their country as a land power, and as a result, they awakened to Mahan's thesis more slowly than Britons.[52] One could even argue that the thesis needed to become fashionable on the other side of the Atlantic before Americans accepted it. Still, roots formed. President Benjamin Harrison in his 1891 Message to Congress noted, "We shall probably be in the future more largely a competitor in the commerce of the world, and it is essential to the dignity of this nation and to the peaceful influence which it should exercise on this hemisphere that its Navy should be adequate, both upon the shores of the Atlantic and of the Pacific."[53] Harrison's argument was in lockstep with Mahan's, but even with appropriations for warship construction, Mahan questioned whether the United States had the resolution to fund its navy through years of peace. On the answer to that question rested the long-term viability of U.S. sea power.[54]

Britain was Mahan's model, but when other countries, including the United States, differed from that model, he had to adapt his thesis. Twenty-one years after *The Influence of Sea Power upon History* Mahan wrote, "It seems reasonable to say that, where merchant shipping exists, it tends logically to develop the form of protection which is called naval but it is perfectly evident, by concrete examples, that navy may be necessary where there is no shipping."[55] Though he still preferred his original thesis linking commercial and naval endeavors to create sea power, he came to appreciate an alternative theory based on recent U.S. history. The United States developed naval power around the turn of the twentieth century even though it lacked both a substantial merchant marine and an overarching dependence on international maritime commerce. There were other reasons to develop a navy.

Moreover, Mahan wondered if the age of British naval supremacy was ending.[56] Even as early as 1894 he thought that Britain was "no longer supreme."[57] The decline of British sea power would eventually result in a power vacuum, leading toward global instability. Mahan's solution entailed Britain working with other powers to sustain its global sea power.[58] This would necessitate cooperation, preferably through an informal relationship between Britain and the United States, whom Mahan saw as natural partners. English-speaking with a common heritage and similar cultural outlook, the two together possessed the capability to exercise sea power in a manner that Britain could no longer do on its own. Mahan returned to Anglo-American cooperation in numerous writings.[59] "It would be to the interest of Great Britain and the United States, and for the benefit of the world," he concluded, "that the two nations should act together cordially on the seas."[60] He considered "formal alliance between the two . . . out of the question, but a cordial recognition of the similarity of character and ideas will give birth to sympathy, which in turn will facilitate a co-operation beneficial to both; for if sentimentality is weak, sentiment is strong."[61]

Mahan divided the nations' responsibilities so that the United States would act as the sea power in the Western Hemisphere and especially the Caribbean while Britain concentrated elsewhere.[62] Nor did he require an equal partnership, although the "American navy should be second to none but the British."[63] The cooperation between the two countries would situate America to inherit Britain's position, but this would be possible only if the people and government of the United States made use of their nation's favorable geography.

THE ELEMENTS OF SEA POWER

A state could obtain tremendous advantages from pursuing sea power, and even greater rewards if it became the dominant sea power. Mahan, however, recognized that not all states were equally positioned to benefit from sea power. To assess whether a state could develop and then be able to sustain sea power, Mahan outlined six "principal conditions affecting the sea power of nations."[64] These were:

1. Geographical Position: the location of a state relative to its neighbors and trade routes.
2. Physical Conformation: access between a country's interior and the sea lines of communication.
3. Extent of Territory: the nature of a state's coastline.
4. Number of Population: those employed in maritime occupations.
5. Character of the People: the willingness of the people to engage in commercial pursuits.
6. Character of the Government: the willingness of political leaders to support sea power.

The six elements can be grouped under three headings. The first deals with geographical factors; the second involves the population; and the third, the government. To make an analogy, the government is the brain that makes decisions about driving the state toward sea power; the people are the heart, pumping the lifeblood into the concept; and the geographic scope is the skeleton. Does a state, in other words, have the acumen, passion, and geographic body to pursue sea power? It is a question for leaders to consider when choosing to build a navy and becomes a test of the government and people for long-term sustainment.

Though many of Mahan's writings reference individual elements of sea power, they are most clearly outlined in the first chapter of *The Influence of Sea Power upon History*. Not Mahan's original intent, the first chapter was a late addition "to make the academic history of his main text more palatable to general readers." Oddly enough, this chapter is today the most recognizable of his writings.[65] It provides the clearest explanation of Mahan's grand strategy by explaining the underlying structure and architecture of sea power.

The six elements of sea power are not entirely Mahan's creation. It is likely that he drew extensively from William Glenn David's 1882 article, which noted the significance of geography, governments, and populations in developing and sustaining sea power.[66] There is no evidence, however, that Mahan read David's article immediately before writing his own version of the concept. Mahan had previously considered the elements of sea power as a teaching tool for students at the Naval War College. In January 1886, he proposed a lecture to Luce that would "naturally lead to . . . a consideration of the sources of Sea Power, whether commercial or military; depending upon the position of the particular country—the character of its coast, its harbors, the character and pursuits of its people, its possession of military posts in various parts of the world, its colonies, etc.—its resources."[67] Mahan investigated the elements of sea power while preparing to teach. Only at the publisher's request did he include the six elements in *The Influence of Sea Power upon History*.

The six elements provide a framework for designing or assessing a nation's grand strategy. The elements have nothing to do with the actual weapons employed or even warships in service; instead, the framework addresses underlying conditions of a state, be they potential enemies, allies, or even itself. Mahan created this tool by studying the seventeenth and eighteenth centuries and then applying what he learned to international relations in his own day. Whereas the six principles may remain largely relevant, they fail to provide a complete picture unless understood in the context of Mahan's environment.

The first three of Mahan's elements deal with geography. Devoting half the elements to geographic factors denotes its importance within his sea power thesis as well as a level of geographic determinism. An aspiring sea power's geography provides the bedrock on which the other elements rest. Mahan's emphasis on geography prefigured what would later be known as "geopolitics"—how geographical factors influence relations among states. Mahan's use of geography also bleeds into the concept of "geostrategy," or how its geography influences a country's strategy. It should be noted, however, that both "geopolitics" and "geostrategy" entered the English lexicon after Mahan published *The Influence of Sea Power upon History*. He presupposed the concepts rather than using the actual terms.

Mahan's first element of sea power entails geographic position: a country's location on a map, particularly in relation to other countries and marine trade routes. Island states have definite advantages because they cannot be invaded—or seek aggrandizement—across terrestrial borders. If island powers wish to expand, they must project power over water. Sea powers can thus use geography as a shield to protect the homeland while focusing on economic expansion. The latter is again facilitated through geography, and particularly a favorable location relative to oceanic trade routes.[68]

Geography, Mahan explained, gave Britain "one permanent advantage."[69] Its insularity made the possibility of invasion remote, thus allowing Britain to avoid fielding a large, costly army for defense. That same insularity forced Britain to develop a fleet to protect its merchant shipping, facilitating economic and industrial growth.[70] Britain was not just an island country, it was an island situated in the right location. Its position astride trade routes blocked the access of European states, including Germany, to global markets while simultaneously providing

Britain access to the global maritime commons. This put Britain in a central position to control both trade and naval action.[71]

Britain's geographic position contrasted sharply with those of continental states. Mahan noted, "History has conclusively demonstrated the inability of a state with even a single continental frontier to compete in naval development with one that is insular, although of smaller population and resources."[72] Continental states faced the prospect of overland invasion by powerful neighbors and lacked the freedom of choice possessed by insular states. Although that situation did not condemn the continental states to constant warfare, it did force their leaders to think strategically and act carefully to balance continental commitments against maritime development. Mahan cited France as the cautionary example: had France's leaders "chosen the path of sea power, she might both have escaped many conflicts and borne those that were unavoidable with greater ease."[73] Overall, a continental state lived in a tough neighborhood and had to consider landward threats. Confronting such threats often occurred at the expense of sea power. "Historically," Mahan concluded, "no nation hitherto has been able under such conditions to establish a supreme sea power."[74]

"Physical conformation," or the links between the interior of a country and its coast, is Mahan's second element. Traditionally, such links were the great rivers that act like highways penetrating into a country's interior and providing the routes to transport goods and resources between the coast and its hinterland.[75] The construction of canals and railroads made links to the interior more varied and changeable. Astute investments in such infrastructure could enhance a country's physical conformation.

The third and final geographic element encompasses the "extent of territory" and specifically the nature of a country's coastal frontier. "As regards the development of sea power," Mahan explained, "it is not the total number of square miles which a country contains, but the length of its coast-line and the character of its harbors that are to be considered." A coastline contributes to a nation's sea power through the nature of its harbors and the density of its population. Mahan reflected on his experience in the U.S. Civil War (1861–65) in that regard. The Gulf coast of the Confederacy should have been a source of great strength, with its many bays providing good harbors, but instead it weakened the Confederacy, for each inlet became a dagger into the interior. A potential strength became a vulnerability. "Dismay, insecurity, paralysis, prevailed in regions that might, under happier auspices, have kept a nation alive through the most exhausting war." The Confederacy's "population was not proportioned to the extent of the sea-coast which it had to defend."[76]

Geography thus encompasses factors ranging from where the people live, to the nature of a country's coastline and its harbors, to the links between a country's interior and its coastline, and finally to its actual location on the globe. People and governments can modify geography to some extent, but limits exist, particularly in terms of the country's position. Some states have geographic disadvantages that no people or government could mitigate.

"Number of Population" is the fourth element. "Sea Power, like other elements of national strength, depends ultimately upon population—upon its numbers and its characteristics," asserted Mahan.[77] "In point of population, it is not only the grand total, but the number following the sea, or at least readily available for employment on ship-board and for the creation of naval material, that must be counted."[78] A state needed a reserve maritime population that in peacetime worked in the merchant fleet, the shipyards, and related industries. In wartime, these reserves allowed for the fleet's rapid expansion. Mahan considered its maritime workforce to be one of Britain's great strengths.[79] Turning to the United States, he argued for the growth of its maritime population because "the strength of a merchant shipping lies in its men even more than in its ships."[80]

Mahan pondered whether "such reserve strength has now nearly lost the importance it once had, because modern ships and weapons take so long to make, and because modern States aim at developing the whole power of their armed force, on the outbreak of war." However, Mahan considered reserves absolutely necessary if the country survives the initial campaign, "the reserve strength will begin to tell; organized reserve first, then reserve of seafaring population, reserve of mechanical skill, reserve of wealth."[81] Mahan concluded that "preparedness for naval war therefore consists not so much in the building of ships and guns as it does in the possession of trained men, in adequate numbers, fit to go on board at once and use the material."[82]

Mahan's fifth element of sea power comprised people engaged in commerce. A risk-taking merchant was a prerequisite for the development of international commerce. Though the chance of failure was immense, the rewards were potentially greater. Mahan called this the "characteristic most important to the development of sea power" because it was not something that could be dictated by government leaders. It had to be inherent with the people. Thus, in Mahan's opinion, merchants were most productive when left to develop on their own.[83]

The government is Mahan's sixth and final element of sea power. This element worked differently than the other elements: "The history of seaboard nations has been less determined by the shrewdness and foresight of governments than by conditions of position, extent, configuration, number and character of their people."[84] Governmental leaders could provide positive or negative incentives, but the government was not a determining factor like geography or a national character that drove a state toward sea power. Even so, Mahan argued that the government should not be discounted. Indeed, he devoted almost as many pages in *The Influence of Sea Power upon History* to the government as to the previous five elements combined.

Not all types of government were equally adept at the long-term maintenance of a navy. After Britain concluded its last great war in 1815 with the final defeat of Napoleon, its government, in Mahan's words, "passed very much more into the hands of the people at large. Whether her sea power will suffer there from remains to be seen." This was particularly important because Britain's economy at the end of the nineteenth century relied even more on its control of the oceans than it had in 1815. "Whether a democratic government will have the foresight, the keen sensitiveness to national position and credit, the willingness to insure prosperity by adequate outpouring of money in times of peace, all which are necessary for military preparation, is yet an open question," he concluded. "Popular governments are not generally favorable to military expenditure, however necessary, and there are signs that England tends to drop behind."[85]

More than Mahan's other elements, the government was central to his grand strategy: how considerations respecting sea power stretched between periods of peace and war; how sea power involved a long-term competition for commercial gain supported by a powerful navy; and how leaders had to consider their state's geography and the disposition of their people toward maritime commerce. A government had a significant capability to foster sea power, but the reverse was equally true. A government unwilling to do so should invest its capital elsewhere.

Mahan's "sea power" comprises a multifaceted grand strategy aimed at a theory of security. It requires specific geographical, population, and governmental prerequisites and relies on a combination of economic and naval instruments. These emphases should not be surprising. Mahan was a propagandist, and his agenda was the growth of the U.S. Navy. Sea power provided the means of attaining that vision. Mahan had to place the navy front and center or he would undercut his argument. Linking the navy to economic factors strengthened his contentions about sea power given the capitalist mindset of American leaders at the dawn of the twentieth century.

CORBETT AND MARITIME STRATEGY

"We speak glibly of 'sea-power' and forget that its true value lies in its influence on the operations of armies," Corbett wrote in 1900.[86] Seven years later, he reflected on "the trite doctrine of the influence of sea power." Such statements called Mahan out in all but name. The implication was clear: "sea power" was not the cure-all that many believed it to be. More specifically, Corbett asserted, "Of late years the world has become so deeply impressed with the efficacy of sea power that we are inclined to forget how impotent it is of itself to decide a war against a great Continental state, how tedious is the pressure of naval action unless it be nicely co-ordinated with military and diplomatic pressure."[87] Mahan's theory of sea power explained only strictly naval wars. Though the Anglo-Dutch Wars of the seventeenth century fit this model, Corbett believed every major war that Britain had fought over the following two centuries did not. Each entailed significant land components, from campaigns of empire in distant regions to land operations in Europe.[88]

Corbett found the latter a particularly difficult puzzle given the asymmetry between British maritime power and continental nations' land power. His theory specifically aimed at answering how Britain could defeat a continental state. This had contemporary resonance during the early years of the twentieth century as Britain faced a new continental challenger in Germany.

As early as 1900, Corbett presented his own thesis, which highlighted "the limitation of maritime power."[89] Their opinions on the decisiveness of sea power are what differentiate Corbett and Mahan. The latter wrote to sell a navy to a skeptical American audience. The British found his argument appealing because it was what they wished to hear. After all, Britain was Mahan's model sea power. Corbett's audience did not need convincing about the importance of the navy or the link between naval and economic power: these arguments were already widely accepted in Britain. Rather, Corbett worried that Mahan's argument missed what in the present day would be described as a joint approach. Corbett explained, "We are accustomed, partly for convenience and partly from the lack of a scientific habit of thought, to speak of naval strategy and military strategy as though they were distinct branches of knowledge which had no common ground." He sought to spur a discussion of "a larger strategy which regards the fleet and army as one weapon" in which "no one service is master."[90] The union of multiple instruments of power created an organization stronger than its constituent parts. Whereas Mahan developed his sea power grand strategy as a theory of security, Corbett pioneered an alternative theory of grand strategy to address how maritime powers used all instruments of national power in the pursuit of policy objectives.

Just as Luce asked Mahan to teach at the U.S. Naval War College, Captain Henry J. May approached Corbett in 1902 to lecture to British officers attending the War Course taught at the Royal Naval College, Greenwich. Modeled on the U.S. Naval War College, the War Course sought to provide officers with a better understanding of the navy's role in imperial defense. May's invitation did not come as a complete surprise. In a letter written the previous year, Corbett had observed, "From what I hear there may soon be a boom in Naval History for educational purposes in the Navy. A lot of influential sailors are playing up hard for it."[91] Corbett implied that his background and connections would make him an ideal candidate to provide historical subject matter expertise to the Royal Navy. This was part of a larger trend emphasizing the intellectual preparation of naval officers through historical study that had been spearheaded by the likes of Mahan and Luce in the United States and by Colomb and Laughton in Britain.

Captain May asked Corbett to provide historical examples that student officers could take back to the fleet.[92] Corbett was particularly well qualified to do so. *Drake and the Tudor Navy* was published in 1898, and *The Successors of Drake* two years later. Both works demonstrated significant archival research as well as thoughtful analysis and placed Corbett high among Britain's naval historians. He was not, however, a naval propagandist in the vein of Mahan.

The first decade of the twentieth century witnessed a significant evolution of the War Course, which eventually became known as the Royal Naval War College. The curriculum was pared down to emphasize strategy, tactics, naval history, and international law; the length of the course was reduced; the size of the student body was expanded; and the location was moved to fleet concentration areas. The object was to educate the largest number of officers possible.[93]

Corbett's interaction with naval officers forced him to link real-world relevance to his research. In 1903 he went to sea as a guest on board a British warship. "I have dreamed of these things for so many years," he declared in a letter to his wife.[94] While Corbett had never served, he was certainly patriotic. When his naval obligations caused him to miss his wife's birthday, he explained, "I wish we could have been together but after all it is our country that calls us apart."[95] Corbett relished these naval connections. The assistance he provided the First Sea Lord, Admiral Sir John "Jacky" Fisher, was "a source of intense pride . . . to have helped to make a bit of history."[96] He taught future leaders and at the same time attempted to cultivate influence among the navy's current leadership. After a 1909 encounter with an admiral, Corbett wrote to his wife, "I found I knew him too (I seem to know them all)." Ultimately, he described his agenda of developing connections that "keeps me into close touch with . . . the Admiralty & I can indulge my fondness for having every spoke in the wheel."[97]

In a few short years, Corbett became quite busy. He continued to lecture, not just to the navy but also at the Army Staff College at Camberley. Moreover, he wrote documents in support of policy agendas, most notably for Fisher.[98]

His contribution to the War Plan of 1907 was particularly important in the development of Corbett's strategic thought. At Fisher's invitation, he wrote most of part 1, titled "Some Principles of Naval Warfare." Fisher asserted, "I can only repeat you will be doing the Navy a lasting service by giving us in the proposed preface an epitome of the art of Naval War."[99] Fisher believed that Corbett "could add most materially in their educational value."[100] Later, the First Sea Lord described "Some Principles of Naval Warfare" as "the finest bit of strategical exposition you have ever read."[101]

A disclaimer to the plans noted: "The opinions and plans herein . . . are not in any way to be considered as those definitely adopted, . . . but are valuable and instructive because illustrative of the variety of considerations governing the formation of War Plans."[102] Rather than an actual plan for making war, the War Plan of 1907 was intended to be educational; thus, it is not surprising that Corbett contributed to the section on general strategic principles. Admiral Charles Beresford, then commanding the Channel Fleet, described "Some Principles of Naval Warfare" as "an extremely clever Paper, containing facts that are A.B.C. to anyone who has ever studied war, with doctrines illustrated that apply to all Nations when discussing the primary matters connected with warlike operations. Take out the few references to Germany, and the sentiments may be accepted by any Nation as its own."[103]

A similar argument could be made for the Green Pamphlet, so called because of its cover. Corbett wrote the first edition in collaboration with Captain Edmond Slade, then president of the War College, and officially titled it "Strategical Terms and Definitions Used in Lectures on Naval History."[104] The confidential document was assigned to students and went through several editions.[105] The Green Pamphlet served as both an outline and a steppingstone toward Corbett's most important work: *Some Principles of Maritime Strategy*.[106]

Corbett contributed to documents such as the 1907 War Plan and the Green Pamphlet, but others edited, emended, and even added materially to them. It is probable that someone else, perhaps Fisher himself, wrote the section of "Some Principles of Naval Warfare" titled "Peace Preparations."[107]

In addition to his work for the navy, Corbett was "always writing a big book about the English Navy."[108] Though his books were available to the general public, historian Andrew Lambert argues that they were "purpose-made for service education."[109] Corbett left writing bestsellers to Mahan; instead, he wrote his books for those in the government and military who had roles in strategy and decision-making with the object of providing them with the equivalent of his War College lectures.[110]

His first manuscript written entirely after joining the War Course was a two-volume work titled *England and the Seven Years' War: A Study in Combined Strategy* (1907). In this work Corbett more than ever emphasized the mutual relationship of naval and land operations. Though such arguments had appeared in earlier works, they now more explicitly echoed contemporary policy debates about what "a small Army and a great Navy was able to accomplish."[111] Moreover, *England and the Seven Years' War* was not strictly a historical study, leading Corbett to admit, "It has been found unavoidable to introduce [a] certain amount of strategical exposition."[112] Corbett had transitioned from a historian to a strategist.

Corbett's work was not without controversy. He never followed the easier route of parroting popular arguments. Unlike Mahan, he was financially independent and could state what he believed rather than what would sell. He supported his conclusions with extensive historical research and did not care if others disagreed—and some did. Much of Corbett's strategic advice was out of step with the views of his contemporaries. His contentions about how navies served as strategic enablers put him at odds with navalists, and his arguments about the interdependence of land and sea forces offended those in the army who believed that war with Germany should be waged with a massive British army on the European continent.[113]

His argument for a joint approach, with the navy as an enabler, is the foundation of Corbett's grand strategic argument. Such theories would have caused few waves if he had been unconnected with the navy, but the title page of *England and the Seven Years' War* included the title "Lecturer in History to the Royal Naval War College" under his name. This led some to think that his writings were more influential than they perhaps were and eventually led him to jest, "I am busy perverting the ideas of naval officers as certain of my critics say."[114]

SOME PRINCIPLES OF MARITIME STRATEGY

In 1910 Corbett began writing the book that would become his calling card. Eventually titled *Some Principles of Maritime Strategy*, its exact origins are unclear. Corbett's diary indicates that Rear Admiral Lewis Bayly, while serving as president of the Royal Naval War College in 1910, suggested that he write it, but a close friend asserted that it was written at the behest of Fisher.[115] Corbett confirmed Fisher's interest by noting the gift of a blank notebook from the First Sea Lord in 1909 along with a cryptic, if humorous, note exhorting him to write a book on strategy.[116] Other evidence indicates that naval leaders wanted a textbook for the War College.[117] Corbett intended *Some Principles of Maritime Strategy* to fulfill that desire. The book also served as a capstone to his previous projects: it had incubated in his earlier books, taken shape in his lectures, and been given form in his contribution to the 1907 War Plan and the Green Pamphlet. Most telling, on the day Corbett started the book, he noted in his diary that he wanted to develop a "habit of thought" for naval officers.[118] *Some Principles of Maritime Strategy* thus clearly had multiple points of origin.

Corbett admitted that the project was "an experiment to see if it was possible to produce a useful book on the subject."[119] Several months later, he told a friend that he was "in the hard scientific mood putting through the press a difficult tasteless book on 'Maritime Strategy.'" Though Corbett might have written that in jest, he certainly had misgivings from the outset, noting to that same friend: "faintly in my ears are echoes of the jabber of these clever gentlemen who think they know other than Nelson how Trafalgar should have been fought."[120]

The writing went quickly. He began on 25 June 1910 and completed the final chapter on 15 February 1911.[121] This book differed from his earlier volumes intended for public consumption. Rather than address a single historical event, Corbett used history to inform broader strategic theories. His arguments were more in keeping with those in the confidential documents he had produced for the navy. Specifically, his book outlines considerations in the event of a conflict with Germany.

Fearing the book would divulge confidential information gleaned from his association with the Royal Navy, Corbett solicited the Admiralty's permission to publish it and was asked to submit the finished volume for scrutiny. This must have made him uneasy since naval leaders might decide to restrict the book's distribution. In the summer of 1911, however, the First Sea Lord, Sir Arthur Wilson determined, "There is no objection I believe to its publication."[122]

With *Some Principles of Maritime Strategy*, Corbett had taken a stand in the contemporary naval debate. Just days after its publication, an article in *The Times* assessed Admiralty decisions by quoting *Some Principles of Maritime Strategy* at length. Corbett declared to his wife, "That is better than the best review for anyone interested in the navy reads such articles."[123] Some reviews were quite enthusiastic. One explained, "In his previous works he has, however been but 'one of a group.' In his latest work he has achieved a position as distinct."[124] Others were less keen. An editorial ascribed to a naval officer noted, "We have all felt the want of some authoritative confidential book on naval warfare that would treat the subject on modern lines somewhat in the way that Clausewitz treated Land Warfare. . . . But in our wildest moments we never anticipated that our Mr. Corbett would sacrifice himself to us and satisfy our want (or attempt to do so) by writing a public volume of his own notions of naval or (as he calls it) maritime strategy." It was, this naval officer went on to write, "the crowning mistake of Mr. Corbett's literary career."[125] Corbett should have expected the divided response. He had weighed in on Britain's role in the contemporary environment, where strong opinions existed. Those who agreed raved about the book, while those who differed disparaged it.

Even so, Corbett found that officers at the War College "all want to talk about my new book about which they are very kind in spite of the criticism it has had," adding, "They seem to understand it better than the older men."[126] Perhaps their kindness was only the deference with which students sometimes treat their professors, but an alternate explanation could be that the War College had opened the mental aperture of its students.

Some Principles of Maritime Strategy was certainly Corbett's most controversial work to date.[127] Yet, of all his publications it is the most enduring, having "revealed him as a theoretical thinker on war of the first rank."[128] Indeed, the book has been described as "the seminal work on strategy in the English language."[129] It reads "like a well-designed lecture course," one reader noted, beginning with broad policy perspectives and ending with more specific aspects of naval strategy.[130] Above all else, *Some Principles of Maritime Strategy* gave decision makers outside the War College an education in British maritime security.

Near the beginning of *Some Principles of Maritime Strategy*, Corbett wrote, "Since men live upon land and not upon the sea, great issues between nations at war have always been decided—except in the rarest cases—either by what your army can do against your enemy's territory and national life, or else by the fear of what the fleet makes it possible for your army to do."[131] With wars decided on land, Corbett insisted that the navy enabled the army to obtain decisive results. It is unsurprising that he used the term "sea power" only once, noting "the vulnerability of a sea Power through its maritime trade."[132] Avoiding the term "sea power" was Corbett's conscious attempt to separate his theory from Mahan's.

Just as "sea power" expressed a distinct concept for Mahan, Corbett used "maritime strategy" to convey a message. He took the term "maritime" from Pitt the Elder, Britain's leading statesman in the Seven Years' War and, in Corbett's view, the "greatest war minister we have had."[133] He pointed out that Pitt described warfare involving naval and army cooperation as "maritime war."[134] While he outlined it as a historical concept in *England and the Seven Years' War*, Corbett linked maritime strategy to contemporary strategy in *Some Principles of Maritime Strategy*, describing maritime strategy as "what part the fleet must play in relation to the action of the land forces."[135]

The thesis of *Some Principles of Maritime Strategy* is perhaps more immediately apparent if one updates the title. A more apropos title for the present would be *Some Principles of the Navy's Role in Grand Strategy.* Though Corbett developed a grand strategy that used all of a nation's instruments of power, he focused particular attention on the navy. This should not be surprising given his association with the Royal Navy. The updated title, or something similar, does much to clarify the aim and subject matter of *Some Principles of Maritime Strategy*, and one could even argue that the updated title explains a focus stretching across Corbett's works.

MAJOR STRATEGY AND MINOR STRATEGY

Naval power by itself lacked the capability to achieve quick, decisive results. Corbett explained: "It scarcely needs saying that it is almost impossible that a war can be decided by naval action alone. Unaided, naval pressure can only work by a process of exhaustion. Its effects must always be slow, and so galling both to our own commercial community and to neutrals, that the tendency is always to accept terms of peace that are far from conclusive."[136]

Corbett favored naval action in combination with the other instruments of power to achieve more conclusive outcomes.[137] Based on this conclusion Corbett redefined "strategy" to include the relationship among diplomatic, land, economic, and naval instruments. Each element of power had limitations, but together, their weaknesses could be mitigated:

> No one of the three great national forces can rightly direct its efforts except hand in hand with the other two. Without knowledge of the probable limits and direction which diplomacy can set for a war, and without a clear conception of the political end in view, soldiers and sailors are alike without map or chart wherewith to trace their strategy; nor in like manner can diplomacy be rightly directed without a full grasp of the range and energy of the fighting pressure that can be brought to back it. And if this be true of the relations between diplomacy and the fighting forces, it is doubly true of the relations between the army and the navy.[138]

Elsewhere, he argued for "a constant aim—to widen the naval outlook till it embraces the diplomatic and military and even the financial and commercial points of view—every factor, indeed, that goes to complicate the great game of war."[139] Naval officers needed to work with those wielding the other instruments of power precisely because the naval instrument could not be decisive by itself.

Though Corbett used the terms "grand strategy" and "higher strategy" to identify the leader's role in coordinating all the instruments of national power, he most often identified such coordination as "major strategy."[140] Major strategy dealt "with whole theatre of war, with planning the war. It looks on war as a continuation of foreign policy. It regards the object of the war as the means of attaining it [the object]. It handles all the National resources. . . . It is the province of the Council of Defence."[141] Coordinating "the whole resources of the nation for war" was "a branch of statesmanship."[142] The political leadership had to determine how the instruments of power worked in conjunction while keeping the political objectives in perspective. This concept of political leaders coordinating the use of the nation's instruments of power remained the hallmark of Corbett's approach even after his experience in World War I. Following the war, he criticized the German military leadership: "Soldiers and sailors had come to be regarded as the supreme experts in the conduct of war. They of course could be no more than experts in military and naval operations. Of the other two main factors in war—foreign affairs and economics—they had no special technical knowledge. In these matters the statesmen were the experts."[143]

While major strategy involved the coordination of all the forces a nation could bring to bear, minor strategy focused on the individual instruments of power. Indeed, Corbett described "two kinds of strategy, as different from each other as tactics is from strategy."[144] Minor strategy "defines not ends but means."[145] It approximates Clausewitz's more restrictive definition of strategy as "the employment of the battle to gain the end in war."[146]

The term "minor" should not be seen as synonymous with "unimportant" or as a term of disparagement; minor strategy is a necessary component of major strategy.[147] "Every strategical problem must be considered in two separate ways," Corbett noted, first "from the point of view of its object," and second "from the point of view of the method, by which that object can be obtained."[148]

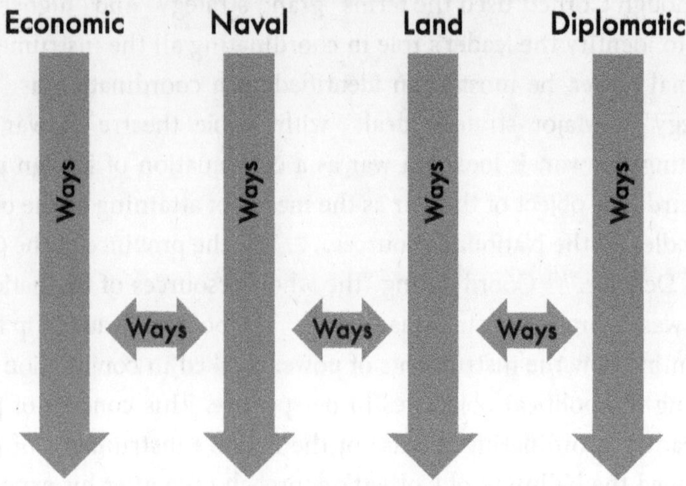

1.2. **Major and Minor Strategy**

Strategy is often described as the process of linking *ends*, *ways*, and *means*. Following this template, Corbett's minor strategy aims directly at the *means*: "the method of attaining the object of the war, rather than the object itself."[149] Major strategy addresses the *ends*: the desired objectives But where do the *ways* fit in this linkage? One could argue that Corbett developed multiple lines of minor strategy. These include naval, land, diplomatic, and economic means. Each specific means of minor strategy can be applied in specific ways to obtain desired major strategic ends. Thus, the *ways* link the minor strategies with the major strategy.[150]

Commentators have certainly recognized the importance of Corbett's "major strategy" concept. Hew Strachan, a noted authority in military history, argues, "Corbett had therefore begun to apply the word 'strategy' to policy and to see the two as integrated in a way that

Clausewitz had not. Corbett's title 'major strategy' prefigures what Britons came to call 'grand strategy' and Americans 'national strategy.'"[151] Moreover, Corbett's development of major strategy worked to expand the parameters of modern grand strategy to more fully account for the nonmilitary instruments of power.[152]

Corbett did not have a monopoly on the concept of major strategy. Mahan also addressed it, noting, "War upon the seas is not a subject that stands alone, by itself, without relations to other and kindred matters."[153] He wrote about "the inter-connection" of military, political, economical, and commercial considerations.[154] In 1908, Mahan even cited Corbett's study of the Seven Years' War when asserting, "Diplomatic conditions affect military action, and military considerations diplomatic measures. They are inseparable parts of a whole; and as such those responsible for military measures should understand the diplomatic factors, and vice versa. . . . The naval man should understand the military conditions, and the military the naval."[155] This was not a sea change on Mahan's part, however. He claimed to have developed these ideas himself in the final chapter of *The Influence of Sea Power upon the French Revolution and Empire*.[156] This built on previous statements in *The Influence of Sea Power upon History* where Mahan likened the prestige of the Dutch government to "the superiority of their fleet, the valor of their troops, the skill and firmness of their diplomacy." More broadly, Mahan recounted difficult tradeoffs in warfare by stating, "It becomes necessary to decide which shall be thus guarded and which neglected,—a question involving the whole policy of the war after a full understanding of the main conditions, military, moral, and economic, in every quarter."[157]

Though the above statements parallel Corbett's concept of major strategy, one must deeply engage Mahan's writings to locate them. He did not focus on the interplay among multiple instruments of power because his agenda aimed at popularizing the expansion of the U.S. Navy through the interplay of economic and naval factors.

Corbett's agenda emphasized a joint approach using all the nation's instruments of power. In effect, his argument was the opposite of Mahan's. Britons already looked at the navy as the figurative walls protecting the state. Corbett sought to explain that the navy alone could not win

Britain's wars. At best it enabled the other forces to operate freely. Britain waged war most effectively when utilizing multiple instruments of power. Britons loved their navy, however, and thus Mahan's arguments about sea power—which explains Corbett's remark about Mahan's writings: "It is not too much to say that my most arduous work has been pulling up the weeds he has sown."[158]

■ ■ ■

Each theorist had a different view of the role of the navy in a nation's grand strategy. Mahan's grand strategy was sea power, while Corbett developed maritime strategy and the overarching concept of major strategy to formulate his grand strategic argument. Those concepts led both men to broaden the existing definitions of strategy to anticipate foundational arguments for two schools of modern grand strategy. Mahan's sea power thesis is a theory of security. Corbett's focus on employing all instruments of national power places him at the foundation of an alternate description of grand strategy that tends to equate grand strategy with national strategy.

Though neither Mahan nor Corbett anticipated grand strategy in its modern guise, the complexity of naval warfare led both to expand the boundaries of strategy. Their differing emphases gave their theories unique strengths. Mahan applied his argument across the peace–war continuum while Corbett focused on periods of conflict. Corbett more fully considered the interplay of multiple instruments of national power while Mahan focused on a narrower set of economic and naval instruments. Corbett studied the past to understand how decision makers had developed a grand strategy tailored to Britain's maritime nature. For Mahan, the competition for sea power remained a constant in international relations, with the fittest state dictating the rules.

Their arguments anticipated arguments later generations have made about grand strategy, but this was not their intent. Mahan and Corbett had definite goals and specific audiences in mind when developing their arguments. As the French intellectual Raymond Aron poignantly contended, "Strategic thought draws its inspiration each century, or rather at each moment of history from the problems which events themselves pose."[159] Given this consideration, it is important to remember that

Mahan was a propagandist for the U.S. Navy. He wrote at the turn of the twentieth century with the goal of convincing Americans to seek wealth overseas, play an ever-larger role in the global economy, and develop a theory of security based on sea power. The interplay among geography, population, and government made sea power possible. Leaders in other nations found Mahan's argument appealing. Britain—Mahan's model—and rising naval powers such as Germany before World War I and contemporary China have all seen the value of sea power. This has expanded his popularity.

Corbett aimed at a narrow audience of British naval officers, their counterparts in the army, and the government officials involved in security decisions.[160] While British leaders understood the importance of sea power, Corbett worried that sea power was insufficient to defend Britain and its empire. Britain, in his view, waged war most efficiently as an insular maritime state utilizing all instruments of national power.

Mahan viewed sea power as having decisive influence. He argued that "sea power meant control of the issues upon the land, at least in regions distant from Europe." In a global contest, sea power would be instrumental in determining the results. Though that was true in peacetime competitions, the results could be even more significant in war. "In any coming war their permanency," meaning their outcome, as Mahan contended, "would depend wholly upon the balance of sea power, upon that empire of the seas."[161] In other words, sea power mattered in the global context more than land power.

Corbett countered that wars are decided on land. "Naval strategy is not a thing by itself," he insisted. A nation's "problems can seldom or never be solved on naval considerations alone, but that it is only part of maritime strategy."[162] Maritime strategy linked strategies at sea with those for the land, and the relationship between them created an argument that differed substantially from Mahan's theory.

Arguably, Mahan's work was a necessary prerequisite to Corbett's. Given the underdeveloped state of naval strategy, someone needed to provide a cogent argument about what navies did in isolation. Mahan's arguments on sea power created an intellectual ferment that resulted in counterarguments. Corbett found Mahan ineffective at explaining how an established maritime empire like Britain functioned. Britons understood and appreciated Mahan's thesis, but Britain already possessed the world's most powerful navy. Corbett maintained that Britain's leaders needed to learn how to use that navy as part of a grand strategy.

Oddly enough, Mahan contemplated using the term "maritime" instead of "sea power" when developing his thesis. He explained, "I deliberately discarded the adjective, 'maritime,' [as] being too smooth to arrest men's attention or stick in their minds." Mahan claimed that he "deliberately adopted" sea power "to compel attention."[163] In many respects, this contrast is Mahan and Corbett in a nutshell. Mahan was blunt, making forceful, impassioned arguments in favor of the decisiveness of navies. Corbett was subtler but no less passionate.

CHAPTER 2

THE USE OF HISTORY AND THE DEVELOPMENT OF THEORY

"I notice . . . that the moment shore historians touch salt water a mist comes over them, a mist and a haze which prevents their comprehending things which they see," Mahan lamented.[1] He meant that historians paid little attention to the sea, and those who did make their livelihood on the oceans wrote little about their environment. "It acts on an element strange to most writers," he explained, "as its members have been from time immemorial a strange race apart, without prophets of their own, neither themselves nor their calling understood." This ignorance needed redress given the sea's "immense determining influence . . . upon the history of the world."[2] Mahan was determined to kindle the conversation about the sea's significance with his writings.

Twenty-six years after *The Influence of Sea Power upon History* was published, Corbett noted Mahan's contribution, but people still possessed an incomplete understanding of maritime history. It particularly concerned Corbett that most historians failed to realize that the sea was "the main binding link that unifies world history. The general historian, then, cannot afford to neglect it, and he is the poorer for that link never having been fully forged for him." More specifically, he elaborated, "I fear it is too often regarded as having no wider significance. I mean that, speaking generally, it is a subject with which the general historian regards himself as but little concerned. I would submit that that is an error and the cause of much erroneous judgment, even in our best histories. . . . The tendency is to survey the field from the military and the political points of view," Corbett argued, "and to miss the striking and comprehensive new outlook which is almost always to be obtained from the sea." His own historical studies had demonstrated that "sometimes to view a European situation from the quarter-deck of a flagship at sea is little short of a revelation."[3] Corbett's argument echoed Mahan's in that regard.

Both Mahan and Corbett wrote to redress the deficiency in maritime history, but this was not history for its own sake. They wrote with a purpose that followed in the wake of the argument put forward in 1878 by the British naval historian John Knox Laughton, who claimed that the study of history could benefit the naval officer: "The wise man will learn from the experience of others: . . . so also will he learn the art of commanding ships or fleets from the history of his great predecessors."[4] Mahan likewise believed that "the salvation of a critical moment may come from such illumined knowledge of the past."[5] Both Mahan and Corbett considered history a relevant and essential component of professional military education. History provided the raw material, a trove of ready-made examples; however, both found that history meant little without theoretical frameworks to make their writings relevant to naval officers and decision makers. This chapter addresses how Mahan and Corbett developed historical content, how they constructed theoretical frameworks, and how they sought to make these relevant to their contemporaries.

HISTORY: THE FOUNDATION OF THEORY

Corbett thought that historians who provide only a mass of details "lose the sense of continuity, fail to seize any underlying principles, and sink bewildered in chaos of facts with no apparent connection and no defined progression."[6] Similarly, Mahan insisted that "facts, however exhaustive and laboriously acquired, are but the bricks and mortar of the historian. . . . It is not till they have undergone the mental processes of the artist . . . that there is evolved a picture comprehensible by the mass of men. . . . To attain to it, and to realize it in words, requires an effort of analysis, of insight, and of imagination."[7] The two understood that historical scholarship required focused organization: it was not as simple as dumping facts on the page or even narrating an event by providing all available details. Yet, they differed on how to develop and employ historical detail.

Mahan developed his sea power thesis before undertaking in-depth research. He recalled "that not only the general idea but the full leading outline of the whole story, from 1660–1812, was written down by me for Admiral Luce before I put pen to paper on the works themselves—before, in fact, I had acquired the knowledge necessary to the full treatment of the subject. This illustrates, I think, the fact that my strength lies not in abundance of minute knowledge but in quick perception and broad grasp of a matter." He added, "I attribute any success not to any breadth or thoroughness of historical knowledge but a certain aptitude to seize on salient features of an era."[8] He called seeking the big picture the "subordination of historical treatment." Minutiae meant little when dealing with large historical topics like sea power's influence on world history because "the fine dust of the balance rarely turns the scale."[9]

Some questioned Mahan's methodology and the rigor of his scholarship. One critic in 1918, for instance, wrote, "In order to make his points with extreme emphasis, he has sometimes tempted to overlook the plurality of causes."[10] More damning, a critic in 1910 complained, "Admiral Mahan has ignored every factor in the situation which does not fit in with his preconceived picture."[11] Later writers have noted similar issues. "Mahan knew what he wanted to prove before he set about proving it," one observed. "Consequently, Mahan's history is deliberately selective."[12] Such statements are unsurprising given the focus and intent of Mahan's writing: he wrote with an agenda to propagandize the significance of sea power. Mahan later claimed that he was, "of course, prepared to abandon my views if they proved erroneous."[13] This was at least somewhat disingenuous. Mahan believed that the main points of his sea power thesis were not topics for debate: "The subject lay so much on the surface that my handling of it could scarcely suffer materially for possible future discoveries. What such or such an unknown man had said or done on some back-stairs, or written to some unknown correspondent, if it came to light, was not likely to affect the received story of the external course of military or political events."[14]

Mahan's focus on the big picture meant that he was not entirely exacting with his use of historical evidence. In 1906, he wrote, "I have not taken myself very seriously as a historian, judged by the modern standards—with which I do not wholly agree." Those "modern standards" involved high levels of accountability based in original documentation, including letters and reports, often from archives. Why Mahan did "not wholly agree" with such diligent scholarship in part links to what he called "the subordination of historical treatment" where he accepted "ignorance of details as not material to the broad lines I wish to draw."[15] He reasoned:

> The complete and balanced narrative, which the modern historian rightly sets before himself as an ideal standard, is, however, a very different thing from the substantially accurate information which is demanded by the man of affairs, civil or military, called upon to keep abreast of the professional movement of his day, to be prepared himself to act in the light of the fullest accessible knowledge, but content also to accept, as an inevitable condition of all practical life, some degree of obscurity, of doubt, attaching to the problem he has to solve.[16]

Mahan aimed his argument at the naval officer who did not have time for nuanced discussion. He wanted the officer to grasp the centrality of the argument rather than become bogged down in the details.

Criticism of *The Influence of Sea Power upon History* led Mahan to reassess his methodology. He made better use of sources when completing the next installment to his sea power series: *The Influence of Sea Power upon the French Revolution and Empire.*[17] The books on Nelson and the War of 1812 that followed reflect ever-greater attention to original sources. Of *Sea Power in Its Relation to the War of 1812*, Mahan wrote, "In my own estimation, it is the best bit of historical writing I have ever done; superior by far in research, in treatment and in style."[18] Mahan took his time, mined the archives, and undertook painstaking research for that work, but he did not repeat this process in subsequent writings. Mahan wrote to make a living; it did not make financial sense to write an archive-based historical study. Moreover, he was aging. In his mid-sixties when he published *Sea Power in Its Relation to the War of 1812*, he lacked the time, finances, and inclination to write another in-depth study.

Corbett held vastly different views. He challenged Mahan's sudden sea power epiphany, arguing in 1904, "The great facts of strategy have always grown slowly to axiomatic solidity, by repeated example rather than sudden precept."[19] Two years after Mahan's death, Corbett gave a speech titled "The Revival of Naval History" in which he argued, "Mahan's work was premature because the facts on which his generalisations could have been securely based were not ascertained when he wrote." Significant scholarship, including Corbett's own, that appeared in the quarter century after *The Influence of Sea Power upon History* was published provided detailed studies of various aspects of the argument it presented. Corbett grudgingly admitted, "The wonder is that Mahan could build as well as he did on a foundation so insecure." He added, "Mahan almost miraculously succeeded. . . . Mahan with real skill and daring was building his castle on the sands."[20]

Unlike Mahan, Corbett matured into a historian steeped in the archives and original documentation. His path demonstrated progressive development, starting with the publication of his first historical work in 1889, a biography of George Monk (or Monck), the 1st Duke of Albemarle. The following year, his second biography appeared, this time of Sir Francis Drake. Corbett dashed off both biographies for popular audiences without resorting to archival sources or extensive research. But they whetted his appetite for naval history. Corbett's timing was fortuitous. The field stood poised to explode. Mahan's *Influence of Sea Power upon History* came out in print the same year as Corbett's biography of Drake. While Mahan served out the remainder of his naval career, wrote *The Influence of Sea Power upon the French Revolution and Empire*, and completed his biography of Nelson, Corbett spent much of the 1890s studying primary sources, often in the archives, to develop a base of knowledge. He later explained, "Until I had formed my own opinion to the best of my ability from the documents I should not consult any body."[21] His efforts came to fruition in 1898 with the publication of his first serious history, *Drake and the Tudor Navy*, which roughly applied Mahan's sea power thesis to an earlier period of British history. Corbett called the book "an attempt . . . to give a general view of the circumstances under which England first became a controlling force in the European system by virtue of her power upon the sea."[22] The book catapulted Corbett from obscurity to one of Britain's leading naval historians.[23]

In 1901 Laughton praised the "painstaking and costly research . . . which places Mr. Corbett high on the list of modern historians."[24] A more recent appraisal by Corbett's biographer, Donald Schurman, echoes Laughton and goes on to explain, "Corbett brought to his subject the training of the Bar, the temperament of a novelist and the charm of a cultured mind."[25] Corbett was well educated, trained as a lawyer, and dabbled in writing fiction, but this says nothing of the slow but progressive development of his historical research. By 1911 when *Some Principles of Maritime Strategy* was published, he had written complex histories of events ranging from the Spanish Armada of 1588 to the Trafalgar campaign of 1805. At the same time he was researching naval operations in the Russo-Japanese War (1904–5). Corbett could thus draw from varied examples when formulating his theory.

It has been argued that he saw the profession of history as a "guild" of sorts with its own values and obligations to provide the most accurate descriptions possible.[26] A scholar must not twist the past to make the tale lively or more interesting. Corbett considered such distortions "too glaring for the dignity of history." When applied to professional military education, such manipulations resulted in "rotten school boy stuff that bears no relation to the actualities of naval war."[27]

In the preface to the opening volume of his naval history of World War I, Corbett clarified his aim. He sought to develop an "intelligible view not only of the operations themselves but of their mutual connection and meaning, the policy which dictated them, their relation to military and diplomatic action, and the difficulties and cross-currents which in some cases delayed their success and robbed them of the expected results. Endeavour has thus been made to present the various naval movements, actions and individual exploits in their just relations to the course of the war as a whole."[28] He had refined this methodology over thirty years, blending naval operations into broader historical events while employing the most painstaking scholarship possible.

INDUCTIVE CORBETT, DEDUCTIVE MAHAN

Their use of history marks a vital distinction between the two men's respective theories. Corbett followed an inductive approach while Mahan leaned toward deduction. Those who followed the inductive method studied a subject across multiple relevant examples, sought out the details, and became experts on the subject before constructing theoretical generalizations. Those who used the deductive method followed the opposite approach, developing a hypothesis to explain various phenomena without having in-depth knowledge of the subject, then testing the hypothesis against other events.

Mahan, by his own admission, developed his sea power thesis before undertaking significant study. He then used the deductive method to prove the theories he already held. Conversely, Corbett emphasized the inductive approach, working up numerous historical case studies until he was confident enough to put his theories in writing. Comparing the inductive and deductive approaches, Corbett concluded, "The latter [deductive] method is by far the more difficult to handle and in inexperienced hands only too likely to lead to fallacious conclusions." He went so far as to state, "What is best is not to try the deductive method at all. Without training and discipline it is sure to lead astray. . . . Far better to stick to the inductive method. Collect and study the ascertained facts of war history, patiently build up your doctrine on the solid foundations they afford."[29] The deductive approach tended toward the selective use of history. An example could be found to support nearly any preconceived argument. Corbett, however, believed that this attitude was changing. No longer were people going "to history to prove they were right; now they go to it to find out where they are wrong . . . they go to history to search for principles, not to prove those which they believe they have already found."[30] The inductive and deductive approaches are thus competing methodologies for the student of war.

A third, related approach entailed using knowledge obtained from a noted authority. Mahan explained that the distilled information of an expert "serves better, perhaps, for starting upon his career the beginner who proposes to make war the profession of his life; for it provides him, in compact and systematic manner, with certain brief rules, by the use of which he can most readily apply, to his subsequent reading of military history, criteria drawn from the experience of centuries. He is thus supplied, in short, with digested knowledge." Mahan recommended that beginners consult the experts and accept their conclusions as a starting point. He warned, however, that "digestion by other minds can in no wise take the place of assimilation performed by one's own mental processes. The cut and dried information of the lecture room, and of the treatise, must in every profession be supplemented by the hard work of personal practice . . . the one school of progress for the soldier or seaman is to be found in the study of military and naval history." Mahan included his volumes on sea power and the lectures he gave at the Naval War College among the wisdom of the experts. The student of war should eventually graduate to something approximating the inductive approach, likened by Mahan to "an advanced course."[31]

Mahan and Corbett outlined three possible courses of action for those just beginning to study the history of war: (1) rely on expert opinions as a starting point before undertaking more in-depth studies; (2) follow the inductive approach from the outset; or (3) develop deductive conclusions before searching for evidence. Mahan's own career came closest to the third approach, the one Corbett thought the most dangerous. Corbett followed the second approach, but that required years of study. The students in their courses received the first method, but they became prisoners to their instructors' biases and agendas.

In 1911 Commander Kenneth Dewar of the Royal Navy dashed off a note to Corbett in which he recounted a conversation with a naval officer who had remarked on his preference for Mahan over Corbett. Dewar explained, "He lacked too a correct estimate of the research work in your books. . . . You have done great work but the N[aval] O[fficer] is brought up to look with suspicion on anything he cannot understand at a moment's notice & so one knows more of Mahan than Corbett." On the one hand, Corbett, the well-educated lawyer, developed arguments to stretch the minds of his students and readers, and many found his lectures difficult or even obtuse. On the other hand, Dewar noted "how superficial Mahan was in his treatment of applied strategical problems."[32]

THE ROLE OF THEORY AND THE INFLUENCE OF LAND WARFARE THEORISTS

History merely provided the data on which to base a theory; it did not impart relevance to the contemporary environment. "A naval historian is the last person in the world to belittle the value of naval history in clearing questions of to-day, but he cannot deny how misleading history may be if we look for guidance on the surface instead of seeking the underlying conditions which give that surface its conformation."[33] Mahan's conclusions aligned with Corbett's: he asserted that historical studies could be "most valuable for future guidance; but, when the attempt is made to utilize their teachings, contemporary conditions are found to differ so much from those preceding them that application becomes a matter of no slight difficulty, requiring judgment and conjecture rather than imparting certainty."[34]

Extracting lessons from history is an exercise fraught with peril. Not only does one need to determine the lesson, one must navigate through minefields of incomplete data, the biases of those who compile the historical record, and the fact that history does not repeat itself.[35] Corbett thought of history as a sort of fertilizer: it "comes in filling the mind with examples wh[ich] may disappear like manure." The fertilized mind can then approach problems more effectively.[36]

The theoretical frameworks Mahan and Corbett developed allowed them to apply history to contemporary events more effectively, but determining how Mahan and Corbett developed their frameworks is difficult given the evolution of their writings. Corbett began as a historian and developed into a strategist. Teaching officers led him to balance the practical against the theoretical.[37] As he matured, his historical writings became increasingly grounded in theory. This culminated with the first few chapters of *Some Principles of Maritime Strategy*, where he provided his most comprehensive explanation of theory's value. Mahan never wrote as systematically about theory, but his writings do provide many nuggets aimed at developing a "habit of thought" among leaders.[38]

Neither Mahan nor Corbett developed an entirely original theory; both used the writings of those who had come before them. Theories of naval warfare, however, were few and incomplete at that time. Mahan in various writings recognized the contributions of naval theorists such as Colomb and Corbett in England as well as Gabriel Darrieus and René Daveluy in France, at times comparing their historical arguments against his own theories.[39]

An inventory of Corbett's library reveals an extensive collection of theoretical works from both naval and military authors. Admittedly, having a volume and understanding it are not the same, but his library demonstrates at least an awareness of a broad range of sources. In terms of naval theory, Corbett's library included volumes by both Mahan and Colomb as well as various works by Reginald Custance, Cyprian Bridge, James Thursfield, Darrieus, Daveluy, and Raoul Castex.[40]

Given the nascent state of the field, these writers of naval theory were contemporaries of Mahan and Corbett. Theories of land warfare, however, were sources with enduring significance. In 1886, just as Mahan commenced research, he explained how he sought to integrate the theories of land warfare into his naval writings. He first attempted to find analogies between land warfare theories and his own, "and with an admirable system of one kind of war before me to contribute something to the development of a systematic study of war in another [naval] field." He wanted "to seek out any parallelism between weapons or branches of land forces and those of the sea."[41] Mahan took this methodology from Stephen B. Luce, who believed, "We must, perforce, resort to the well-known rules of the military art with a view to their application to military movements of a fleet."[42]

Corbett used land warfare theory differently. He considered its direct application to the maritime world fraught with peril and instead looked to its underlying methodologies. For example, Corbett took foundational aspects from Carl von Clausewitz, including the purpose of theory, the concept of principles, the use of critical analysis, and the primacy of political objectives. These provided points of departure for developing his theories of naval warfare.

In *Some Principles of Maritime Strategy*, Corbett acknowledged the influence of land warfare theorists such as Clausewitz and Antoine-Henri Jomini. Both fought in the Napoleonic Wars and wrote in the early decades of the nineteenth century, and both attempted to explain how land powers waged war against similar states. Though both Clausewitz and Jomini wrote with an eye to the same security environment, their approaches differed.

During the eighteenth-century Enlightenment, European intellectuals had begun to question nearly everything. They sought to advance the idea of progress by studying phenomena systematically. If the right questions were asked, answers could be found to even the most perplexing problems, including war. Jomini illustrated this school of thought, for his theories attempted to apply rules-based principles to warfare. Though Corbett described Jomini as one of the "apostles of the Napoleonic method," he thought his conclusions too absolute. They failed to reflect the true nature of war.[43]

By the Napoleonic era, the Enlightenment had begun to give way to Romanticism in Clausewitz's own Prussia. This movement emphasized human emotion, personality, and psychology over mere reason. Clausewitz's exposure to German Romanticism influenced him to take aspects from the Enlightenment and combine them with emotion and passion.[44] This merger stands at the heart of Clausewitz's theory: the intrusion of moral forces, including passion and emotion, challenged purely reasoned analyses. Corbett agreed with Clausewitz: war could never be more than an art given the human element and the interaction that takes place between belligerents. Though Clausewitz's seminal work, *On War*, was published incomplete, Corbett concluded that the "attempt [was] so sound that it remains the basis of all land strategy."[45]

Corbett seems to have discovered Clausewitz soon after he began lecturing for the War Course. The timing should not be surprising. Clausewitz's popularity increased in Britain following the Boer War (1899–1902).[46] The first of Corbett's books to benefit from Clausewitz was likely *England and the Mediterranean: A Study of the Rise and Influence of British Power within the Straits, 1603–1713*. This volume is significant in Corbett's intellectual development. The early chapters were written before or perhaps at the very start of his War Course experience. The writing style and the arguments are reflective of *Drake and the Tudor Navy* and the *Successors of Drake* and lack the analytical approach of his later writings. In the second volume of *England and the Mediterranean*, Corbett is a different writer, likely reflecting his interaction with naval officers and new habits of thought gleaned from reading works such as *On War*. In fact, the second volume of *England and the Mediterranean* includes such Clausewitzian terminology as "friction" and "centre of gravity" while emphasizing the primacy of policy in strategic calculations.[47]

Corbett's engagement with Clausewitz culminated in *Some Principles of Maritime Strategy*, which mimics *On War*, using Britain as the subject rather than Clausewitz's Prussia. Both works explain warfare as a continuation of politics from a specific national perspective, and both outline the author's methodologies in earlier parts of the book before advancing into more specific analyses. Finally, both focus on the use of violence to obtain political objectives after diplomacy fails.

Whereas Clausewitz most clearly affected Corbett's development, the land power theorist who most influenced Mahan is less clear. He often mentioned Jomini. In 1885, as Mahan broke ground on his own research, he explained, "At present my principal use of Jomini is as a model possibly suggestive of *manner* of treatment."[48] He also called him "the profuse writer on military art and military history—whose works, if somewhat supplanted by newer digests, have lost little or none of their prestige, as a profound study and exposition of the principles of warfare."[49] In the late nineteenth century, Jomini was widely acknowledged as a military authority, particularly in the United States.[50] Though Mahan referenced Jomini in his writings, his lecture notes demonstrate an even more pronounced influence. It is clear that Mahan studied Jomini closely and used his writings to ground many of his arguments.[51] Jomini served as a point of departure rather than an absolute guide, however, for Mahan was not afraid to express different conclusions.[52]

Sir Edward Bruce Hamley also influenced Mahan. Eventually rising to the rank of lieutenant general in the British army, he served as a professor and later commandant of the army's Staff College.[53] Though largely forgotten today, Hamley's writings were influential in the late nineteenth century. Mahan's association with the Naval War College, first as professor and later as president, paralleled Hamley's background in professional military education. In 1866 Hamley published *Operations of War Explained and Illustrated*, which went through several editions. As Mahan began work on what became *The Influence of Sea Power upon History*, Hamley's book was considered an essential treatise on the art of war, and Mahan acknowledged that he consulted it.[54]

The influence of Clausewitz on Mahan is more difficult to determine. Jon Sumida, who has written extensively on Mahan, notes that although he was "a Jominian by casual confession and to a degree in form, he was in substance, whether by direct or indirect inheritance or coincidence, a Clausewitzian." Specifically, both Clausewitz and Mahan viewed war as an art, noting its complexity and contingency "whose nature could not be encompassed by any system of theory."[55] Yet Mahan seems to have consulted Clausewitz only after completing his sea power series. In 1910 he read *The Reality of War: An Introduction to Clausewitz* by Stewart L. Murray. In approximately one hundred pages, Murray placed Clausewitz in context and provided a sort of "Cliffs Notes" of the Prussian's argument.[56] The book left an impression on Mahan, who in 1911 described Clausewitz as "one of the first authorities."[57]

Mahan's father, Dennis Hart Mahan, a professor at the U.S. Military Academy at West Point and a noted authority on military topics, may also have been an influence. Officers who went on to serve on both sides in the Civil War passed through Dennis Hart Mahan's classes, and he developed texts on topics ranging from engineering to theories of war. Though his writings could have aided his son, Robert Seager II, who has written the most detailed biography of the younger Mahan and edited his correspondence, is emphatic: "Surprisingly, there is no evidence that Alfred Mahan ever read any of D. H. Mahan's books." Sumida, however, who has delved deeply into Mahan's theories, claims that Mahan senior had greater influence than even Jomini given similarities in how the two Mahans addressed principles and leadership.[58]

THE MATERIAL SCHOOL AND THE HISTORICAL SCHOOL

Corbett, Clausewitz, Mahan, and Jomini had at least one thing in common: all used military history to inform their theories. Clausewitz explained, "Examples from history make everything clear, and furnish the best description of proof in the empirical sciences. This applies with more force to the art of war than to any other." Jomini added, "History, well studied and understood, is the best school."[59]

Grounding their theories in history was not easy for either Mahan or Corbett: history was an unpopular subject among late-nineteenth-century naval officers. The so-called material school held vast influence in the British and American navies. Its adherents thought "that under the circumstances of modern war—steam, torpedoes, rams, electricity, and so forth—the story of the past no longer held out any lessons for the future."[60]

Before arriving at the Naval War College, Mahan agreed with the "very common impression that naval conditions are so changed, that they [historical examples] are practically obsolete for present usefulness." His association with Luce along with his own studies caused him to reassess. It concerned Mahan that "there was danger of the art of war disappearing under a deluge of machinery."[61] He feared that "the idea of professional improvement in the United States Navy has fastened for its fitting subject upon the development of the material of war, to the comparative exclusion of the study of naval warfare."[62] Mahan wrote to Luce, "You know my general conviction that admission of questions of manufacture and material is most dangerous; not so much in themselves necessarily, perhaps, but because the whole drift of the navy is to put its trust in material development, rather than in strategic sagacity and tactical superiority."[63] Across the Atlantic, Corbett drew a similar conclusion. He worried that "in the absorbing task of changing and perfecting its weapons, the Navy had forgotten the art of war."[64]

Luce, the founder of the U.S. Naval War College, offered a striking counterargument against the material school: "Thus we arrive at a fundamental truth; and to disregard such teachings is not merely to commit a great blunder by shutting our eyes to the lessons of history, but it is to be unscientific in one's own profession, which these days is to be culpably ignorant, if not criminal."[65] Mahan developed similar arguments: "Naval History is, in every age the handmaid of Naval Warfare. . . . These experiences of Naval War give the foundation, upon which alone, in all ages, a sound theory of War must be built."[66] One naval officer who attended the college noted, "Luce, Mahan, and the others at the war college tried to make us see . . . that in the military and naval art the guns and other weapons used are tools, just as hammer and chisel are tools in the hands of sculptor or brush in the hands of painter."[67]

Though Mahan confronted the material school in his lectures, his writings were more influential in that regard. Indicative of his success, one journal editor in 1892 noted, "Another mistake is that of supposing that naval history . . . was of no present utility to us. Captain Mahan has so ably refuted this fallacy in his published volume that his views on this subject are already well known."[68] Mahan recognized his own achievement as well: "The disposition, so prevalent a few years ago as to be well-nigh universal, to look upon past naval history as a closed book, obsolete for all useful purposes, has in a large measure disappeared." Victory, however, remained incomplete. It was one thing for critics and commentators to agree with him: what truly mattered were the naval officers. Mahan admitted, "I question whether, even yet, naval officers in general have come to realize that in looking behind rather than before, in studying the past, near and remote, rather than in speculating upon the future, they will find the solid ground, . . . by whose clear and steady light they can best meet the conditions of the present—and of the future, when it in turn shall have become the present."[69]

Rather than engage in the distant past, some looked to recent events such as the Spanish-American War (1898) and the Russo-Japanese War (1904–5) as more relevant. Though both Corbett and Mahan wrote extensively on recent wars, there were only a few contemporary examples for them to consider.[70] Each entailed a regional conflict fought for limited political aims, and none involved the dominant naval power.[71] Specifically, Corbett worried that officers might mistakenly try and apply lessons from recent conflicts when making decisions. With so few examples, it remained unclear which lessons from these wars could be applied to future conflicts and which lessons were in fact outliers.[72] To avoid these traps, Mahan and Corbett considered the deep engagement of history imperative when developing theoretical frameworks of war.

CORBETT, CLAUSEWITZ, AND THEORY

Though some looked skeptically at the value of theory, Corbett claimed, "The truth is that the mistrust of theory arises from a misconception of what it is that the theory claims to do." Theory according to Corbett sought to separate "the fundamental constants . . . from what was merely accidental." It attempted to determine "how far the particular success was due to special conditions and how far it was due to factors common to all wars."[73] Theory organizes arguments "to cultivate correct habits of thought, not provide formulas."[74] "It does not pretend to give the power of conduct in the field," Corbett explained. ". . . Its main practical value is that it can assist a capable man to acquire a broad outlook whereby he may be the surer his plan shall cover all the ground, and whereby he may with greater rapidity and certainty seize all the factors of a sudden situation."[75]

The previous passage paralleled Clausewitz's explanation that theory "should educate the mind of the future leader in war, or rather guide him in his self-instruction, but not accompany him to the field of battle."[76] Corbett, like Clausewitz, used theory as a means of developing mental agility. When analyzing two courses of action, Corbett explained, "the theory of strategy advocates neither; it merely places the advantages of each before us & leaves the solution of each a practical problem to practical men, as it occurs. It offers no solution, but only the means of arriving at a solution."[77]

Moreover, Clausewitz asserted, "The first business of every theory is to clear up conceptions and ideas which have been jumbled together, and, we may say, entangled and confused."[78] This resonated with Corbett. His experience in teaching officers led him to develop a standard lexicon. The result was the formulation of the Green Pamphlet, a collaborative effort with then–War College president Captain Edmond Slade.[79] Before discussing strategy, Slade thought that "it was absolutely necessary . . . to fix the terminology . . . with which men talked about Strategy."[80] Corbett made a similar comment in the opening pages of *Some Principles of Maritime Strategy*. Terminology set the conditions for clear communication, whether it was at the highest levels of government or at the tactical point of contact. "Without such an apparatus no two men can even think on the same line."[81]

"How often," Corbett wondered, "have officers dumbly acquiesced in ill-advised operations simply for the lack of the mental power and verbal apparatus to convince an impatient Minister where the errors of his plan lay? How often, moreover, have statesmen and officers, even in the most harmonious conference, been unable to decide on a coherent plan of war from inability to analyse scientifically the situation they had to face, and to recognise the general character of the struggle in which they were about to engage."[82] Leaders had to explain objectives and intent clearly to their commanders in the field. Those in the field had to digest this information and provide applicable instructions to their subordinates. Only then could force be employed in a manner that was most likely to obtain the desired political objectives. Corbett's concept was not entirely his own. He borrowed from Clausewitz, who also noted the difficulty of communicating strategic concepts with clarity, especially "when it is a question, not of acting oneself, but of convincing others in consultation."[83] Each situation being unique, theory could not provide a tangible script for confronting real-world problems. Instead, Corbett, like Clausewitz, believed theory created the means for leaders to speak in the same vocabulary and to face challenges through a similar critical lens.

MAHAN: PRINCIPLES IN THE ABSTRACT

Though Mahan understood the importance of a common vocabulary as well, he considered another objective more important.[84] As early as 1886, Mahan hit at the crux of his quandary: "All naval history hitherto has been made by ships and weapons of a kind wholly different from those now in use. How to view the lessons of the past so as to mould them into lessons for the future, under such differing conditions, is the nut I have to crack."[85] How was he to "make the experience of wooden sailing ships, with their pop-guns[,] useful in the naval present?"[86] This puzzle led him to admit, "I am frankly still a little at sea . . . how to turn this into instructive material for the future." In a letter to Luce he worried, "If I confine myself to history the College would be blamed for not keeping me to things that were useful."[87]

Mahan had an epiphany in April 1886. "I think I have today had a first glimmering of how to hitch on the history of the past to the theory of the present."[88] He chose a methodology based on principles, or "controlling features," distilled from historical precedents.[89] War was by its nature uncertain, but a leader who understood its principles could "fasten on the broad general lines of action, which constitute the determinative features of military situations." Principles were distilled from historical study to provide guides or best practices. In Mahan's opinion, they were "essential for the ordering of our lives" because "no war, however singular in its origin and course, is an isolated fact, without links that bind it to the past, the present, and the future."[90]

Mahan did not create that concept. John Colomb had addressed "general principles" regarding maritime commerce in a groundbreaking 1867 work on the relationship between British naval power and merchant shipping. Colomb, however, did not effectively link his employment of principles to historical precedent.[91] This changed seven years later when Laughton wrote that "history, properly studied, teaches the principles on which battles have been won, or not won—have been lost, or not lost." Moreover, Luce had lectured in 1885 about "unerring principles" that existed "for our guidance."[92]

Though Colomb, Laughton, and Luce applied principles to naval issues, it was Jomini who made the concept a cornerstone of nineteenth-century military thought. Changes in land warfare led Jomini to note, "The new inventions of the last twenty years seem to threaten a great revolution in army organization, armament, and tactics." To make sense of these developments, Jomini argued for the existence of a small number of constants within warfare: "With few exceptions, the most brilliant successes and the greatest reverses resulted from an adherence to this principle in one case, and from a neglect of it in the other."[93]

This was just the framework that Mahan needed to make naval history relevant. Following Jomini, Mahan argued, "War has such principles; their existence is detected by the study of the past, which reveals them in successes and failures, the same from age to age."[94] Principles and history worked in conjunction. "Formulated principles, however excellent," Mahan explained, "are by themselves too abstract to sustain convinced allegiance; the reasons for them, as manifested in concrete cases, are an imperative part of the process through which they really enter the mind and possess the will. On this account the study of military history lies at the foundation of all sound military conclusions and practice."[95]

Jomini found principles most effective at the strategic level. Tactics depend on technology and the environment, but strategy is "independent of the nature of arms and the organization of the troops."[96] Jomini was not alone in this assertion; the utility of principles at the strategic level in land warfare was well known in the 1880s. Dennis Hart Mahan wrote that "the study of military history thus becomes very instructive in a strategical point of view, whilst, on the other hand, in endeavoring to apply the notions, gleaned from the same source, on tactics of the ancients, to our modern armies, errors of the gravest character might be committed."[97]

Such conclusions made sense to Alfred Thayer Mahan given the transformation of warfare in the maritime domain. Changes in weapons, propulsion systems, and material affected tactical action more than they affected strategy. Specifically, he claimed, "From time to time the superstructure of tactics has to be altered or wholly torn down; but the old foundations of strategy so far remain, as though laid upon a rock."[98]

MAHAN: PRINCIPLES IN APPLICATION

By focusing on strategic-level principles Mahan could minimize the significance of technological change. This allowed him to ward off attacks by the material school, but it also caused him to focus more fully on historical explanations for strategic-level principles. Some authors have interpreted that emphasis on history as meaning that Mahan looked "nostalgically" to the age of sail and that "when he did look at the present, it was often with the eyes of his eighteenth-century heroes."[99] Perhaps most damning, Harold and Margaret Sprout, who wrote widely on Mahan and U.S. naval power, have claimed that "nearly all his generalizations reflected judgments as to what would have been possible on the day of Trafalgar. . . . Essentially a conservative thinker, Mahan seems to have taken it for granted that the future would not be very different from the immediate past."[100]

Mahan's use of principles was in fact more dynamic than many authors credit. Rather than parrot Jomini, Mahan explained, "Jomini doubtless may be considered somewhat too absolute and pedantic in his insistence upon definite formulation of principles."[101] Thus, noting only Mahan's observation that "the old foundations of strategy so far remain, as though laid upon a rock" could very well miss the nuance of his argument.[102] A better quote to encapsulate the concept identifies principles "as guides which warn when it is going wrong."[103]

Principles were "living" agents rather than the repetition of past events, and Mahan admonished those who dogmatically adhered to principles regardless of the situation, because exceptions always existed. In 1888, even before he published *The Influence of Sea Power upon History*, Mahan wrote, "The conduct of war is controlled, not by cast-iron rules of invariable application immutable as the laws of nature, but by general principles." A skilled leader adapts the principle to the environment.[104] Mahan warned, "A man who has got hold of a sound principle, and has not breadth enough to recognize exceptions, there is more hope of a fool than of him. In war, nothing is more ruinous than blind adherence to rule, without first considering the qualifying circumstances."[105]

Principles comprise two components. There is first the underlying principle. This is constant: often it is a broadly generalized concept such as concentration of force or lines of communication. The second component entails its application, which varies according to time and circumstance.[106] "When we have correctly stated the principles," Mahan explained, "it by no means necessarily follows that the application of them will be the same, or superficially even much like those of previous generations."[107] In one instance he compared the bow and arrow with the rifle to note similar "fundamental principles" regarding their employment. The rifle merely provided "new illustrations of old and priceless principles." Though every war possesses unique characteristics, underlying similarities link military action. In effect, every "war is, like all others, a special case of a general problem, differentiated from the others by particular features, as one child of a strongly marked family is from another, but characterized yet more forcibly by the community of resemblance which results from identity of origin."[108]

Principles provide the promise of continuity, but the hazards of relying on past events when making decisions are immense. The student of war must consciously avoid drawing inappropriate conclusions from the past by understanding similarities but never forgetting that each situation is unique. Thus, Mahan warned, "In tracing resemblances there is a tendency not only to overlook points of difference, but to exaggerate points of likeness,—to be fanciful."[109]

CORBETT, PRINCIPLES, AND CRITICAL ANALYSIS

Corbett also utilized principles. As with Mahan, promoting the importance of principles allowed him to argue against the material school's contention "that the revolution which has taken place in naval material during recent years has put the old wars out of court."[110] More overt than Mahan, Corbett included the word "principles" in the title of his seminal volume on maritime strategy.

One must "determine the normal" before forming a coherent theory of war. "A careful collation of past events," Corbett noted, makes it "clear that certain lines of conduct tend normally to produce certain effects; that wars tend to take certain forms." He concluded, "Having determined the normal, we are at once in a stronger position. Any proposal can be compared with it, and we can proceed to discuss clearly the weight of the factors which prompt us to depart from the normal." He insisted that "every case must be judged on its merits, but without a normal to work from we cannot form any real judgment at all; we can only guess."[111]

Corbett based much of his argument about principles on his understanding of Clausewitz. Principles, according to the Prussian, provided no more than "aids to judgment" to assist in "an application of abstract truth to real events." Clausewitz went on to describe critical analysis (or examination) as "not merely the appreciation of those means which have been actually employed, but also of all possible means. . . . [T]he use of any particular means is not fairly open to censure until a better is pointed out."[112] Identifying the normal, comparing the normal not merely to what actually occurred but to all possible alternatives, and then attempting to determine if any of the alternatives would have yielded better results linked theory with applied history.

Assessing historical decisions proves quite difficult. In one instance, Corbett asked: "Was it or was it not good strategy?" His response was quite indicative of critical analysis: "No one but a beginner in the study of war would presume to answer the question with confidence."[113] Corbett understood that strategic problems were open to any number of interpretations, but assessing historical cases paled in comparison to decision-making in the present. When in the moment, fog, friction, and the lack of intellectual creativity will "obscure the true horizon. Such error can scarcely ever be eliminated, but by theoretical study we can reduce it, nor by any other means can we hope to approach the clearness of vision with which posterity will read our mistakes."[114]

Studying history allowed a leader to understand what normally occurred in a given situation. In real-world circumstances this knowledge heightened the leader's ability to see and analyze all potential courses of action. Leaders should also recognize that no event completely reflects the normal: every circumstance has unique attributes. The most effective leaders identified these attributes and then exploited departures from the normal. As Corbett explained, "Every case will assuredly depart from the normal to a greater or less extent, and it is equally certain that the greatest successes in war have been the boldest departures from the normal. But for the most part they have been departures made with open eyes by geniuses who could perceive in the accidents of the case a just reason for the departure." He saw great value in understanding the principles, but he agreed with Mahan that becoming wedded to them was perilous.[115] Rather than provide answers to the conduct of war, theory, in Corbett's opinion, provided the mental agility to analyze problems from multiple perspectives.

DOGMAS AND MAXIMS

Corbett thought that leaders tended to distort principles in two ways. Some refused to seek the normal and left everything to chance, believing victory in war came through hard fighting and risk. Others allowed principles to be perverted from guideposts to highways with well-defined lanes; this tended "inevitably to confuse the means with the end." Corbett concluded, "It would be wrong to claim that either school was right. In almost every department of life two such schools must always exist, and nowhere is such conflict less inevitable than in the art of war, whether by sea or land . . . it is probably only by the conflict of the two normal schools of naval thought that we can hope to work out the best adjusted compromise between free initiative and concentrated order."[116] Those who left it all to chance were not likely to read Corbett's works, while those who became wedded to principles tended to use strategy books as crutches. Corbett railed against this tendency in *Some Principles of Maritime Strategy*.[117]

Contemporary reviewers of that book noted Corbett's unwillingness to accept immutable theoretical truths. One commentator identified his "general thesis" to be "that circumstances alter cases so much that no fixed rules for anything can be laid down."[118] Another commentator observed that Corbett refused to accept "several hoary old nautical dogmas, such as 'Cruisers are the eyes of the fleet,' 'Attack is the best defence,' etc."[119]

Corbett attacked anything that reeked of a dogma. "Of all diseases from which strategical thought can suffer, dogma is the most fatal," he insisted. "When dogma steals in at the door, reason flies out of the window. Principle always has the tendency to ossify into dogma."[120] One reviewer of *Some Principles of Maritime Strategy* claimed, "We are left in confusion. No comforting dogma is laid down . . . we are left with preconceived ideas shattered and nothing substituted for them." But, this reviewer concluded, "This is the all-excellent merit of the book: it is designed to cause thought, not to enunciate a pet dogma. One clear idea only emerges. The course of the next naval war will be uncertain."[121]

Maxims also riled Corbett. Clausewitz explained the difference between a principle and a maxim: "Principle is objective when it is the result of objective truth, and consequently of equal value for all men; it is subjective, and then generally called *Maxim* if there are subjective relations in it, and if it therefore has a certain value only for the person himself who makes it." Jomini put it more succinctly: "every maxim has its exceptions."[122] Corbett agreed with both, asserting that a maxim "conveys a truth with a trail of error in its wake."[123] He warned, "A strategical maxim without the profoundest knowledge of its meaning is certain to trip you straight into the pit."[124] Relying on the maxim rather than the underlying principle leads toward distortion.[125] Corbett concluded, "Nothing is so dangerous in the study of war as to permit maxims to become a substitute for judgment."[126]

Corbett addressed maxims and dogmas to a much greater extent than Mahan did, yet the latter did not turn a blind eye to the subject. Mahan described dogmas along the same lines as Corbett, calling them "a fetish—which involves the danger of becoming 'doctrinaire.' Now of all dangerous conditions a military doctrinaire is one of the worst. He is a quick match and gunpowder."[127] Moreover, he cautioned, "How absurd it is to lay down rules for war—to think you can bring it under hard and fast dogmas like those of science." Like Corbett, Mahan understood that exceptions existed for every principle.[128]

In his earlier works Mahan seemed to blend maxims and principles; but in later works he differentiated them. Thus, in 1911, Mahan admitted that "maxims of war . . . are not so much positive rules as they are developments and applications of few general principles." A maxim is "generally correct under the conditions; but the teacher must admit that each case has its own features—like the endless variety of the one human face."[129] Maxims created in one era did not necessarily apply in others. The longer Mahan engaged the topic of strategy, the more nuanced his understanding of maxims became. By the 1910s, he and Corbett largely agreed on maxims and dogmas.

■ ■ ■

How Mahan and Corbett thought informed what they thought. Without understanding their theoretical methodologies it is impossible to truly understand their grand strategic formulations or their more narrow concepts of naval warfare. Both used land power theory as a foundation. Mahan looked to several sources, while Corbett relied extensively on Clausewitz. Neither drew broadly on earlier theories of naval war; when Mahan began writing, few sources existed. Corbett could have relied on Mahan and a host of others who published works in the 1890s, but he did not. Though Corbett drew snippets from naval theorists, including Mahan, he did not trust their historical foundations.

Both Mahan and Corbett found "principles" an effective counterargument against the material school. Mahan examined an array of historical cases looking for constants that could serve as guideposts, while Corbett sought the "normal"—how certain actions often led to similar results. Neither was dogmatic in the application of principles, and this factor does much to explain why neither organized his argument around a specific set of principles or even identified a master list of principles.

CHAPTER 3

WAR, POLICY, AND CIVIL-MILITARY RELATIONS

Both Mahan and Corbett aimed their writings at men of action, including the statesmen who guided nations and the officers who commanded the instruments of force. These individuals faced real, urgent situations that required quick action, not lofty theoretical debates. The theories Mahan and Corbett developed had limited utility for those addressing specific conditions and events, especially situations requiring the use of force. Yet both theorists claimed that grand strategy and theoretical methodologies are indeed useful for those tasked with taking action. Theory, for example, defines vocabulary and contributes to clear and effective communications. This chapter focuses on how Mahan and Corbett defined "war," "policy," and "strategy" to create a common understanding among military and civilian leaders that is necessary in the formulation of major strategy and the implementation of sea power as a grand strategy.

"War," "policy," and "strategy" are challenging concepts, as is their resulting impact on the relationship between civilian and military leaders. Neither Mahan nor Corbett wrote about these concepts systematically, and what we know of their views is often derived from snippets and sometimes even quips made within the larger bodies of their scholarship.

To understand the environment in which the theorists nested their theories, it behooves us to consider how Mahan and Corbett defined "war." Corbett took his definition directly from Clausewitz's dictum: "*War is only a continuation of state policy by other means.*"[1] Corbett claimed that this description had gained widespread acceptance in the early twentieth century.[2] Likewise, Mahan, in 1897, explained that "war is simply a political movement, though violent and exceptional in its character."[3] Both men agreed that wars are fought over political issues.

Mahan went further, however, in adding, "War in modern conception and practice is business, not fighting." He explained, "In short, it should be an accepted apothegm . . . that 'War is business,' to which actual fighting is incidental. As in all businesses, the true aim is the best results at the least cost." Mahan increasingly believed that war was, at least in part, an economic venture that did not necessarily involve actual violence, although its potential could serve as a cost-effective method for compelling an opponent. In describing one of the crises that occurred before World War I, Mahan for example asserted, "There was again war, but no bloodshed. Results were accomplished; but by force, however disguised. . . . Again force, war in all but striking."[4] He preferred to avoid violence to minimize risk and expense. To continue the business analogy, war should be used to seek objectives at the least risk and cost. Linking war to business highlighted the competitive nature of his thesis and the financial rewards obtainable from sea power. War, for Mahan, was another way to accrue wealth. To twist Clausewitz's dictum: war was a continuation of economic activity by other means. Moreover, Mahan's definition blurred the lines between peace and war.

Mahan even cited Corbett for support. After reading *England and the Seven Years' War*, he concluded, "Corbett makes another excellent point: that for a military establishment the distinction between a state of war and a state of peace is one of words, not of fact."[5] He was likely referring to the following passage:

> In modern times we have acquired the habit of regarding such problems as if there were two entirely different and contradictory states in the relations of nations, the one a state of war and the other a state of peace, or, in other words, as though there were always a point where intercourse or diplomacy ended, and severance or strategy began. Now Clausewitz, with all the experiences of the Revolutionary and Napoleonic wars to guide him, long ago pointed out that this conception of international relations was false both in theory and practice.[6]

Arguing that war was a continuation of existing policies allowed Clausewitz, and by extension Corbett, to contend that policy objectives are not created at the start of a war but exist beforehand. They remain in flux throughout the conflict and even beyond, just as questions of strategy transcend the continuum of peace and war.

Both Mahan and Corbett thought war involved an act of force to obtain political results. The American added a wrinkle by drawing an analogy between war and business. This allowed him to extend war beyond violent action to account for sea power's competitive nature. Their definitions of "war" informed other concepts, including "policy" and "strategy."

STRATEGY

Though both Mahan and Corbett took their understanding of strategy from land power theorists, neither was content to parrot the conclusions of those theorists. Corbett, for example, thought Clausewitz's statement, "Strategy is the employment of the battle to gain the end of the war" necessary but incomplete.[7] More issues were at play. Unlike the Prussian theorist, who considered land armies the determining factors in war, Corbett saw strategy through a joint, maritime lens: "There are no such things in the broader sense as naval strategy and military strategy, but one simple strategy of war in which naval and military considerations are inextricably intertwined."[8] From a joint approach to warfare Corbett spearheaded the concept of major strategy, which accounted for "the whole resources of the nation," connecting economic, diplomatic, and military means into a national strategy.[9]

Corbet insisted that every war is unique. In one lecture, Corbett chided the officers in his audience: "So we discuss a sort of abstract plan of war, as if wars were all much the same—whatever their object & whatever the means at the disposal of the belligerents. But they are not so & until we know [the] ends of war & means, we can't know what we are talking about."[10] Strategy involves linking the *ways* to attain a unique *end* with available *means*. One could not understand strategy without an appreciation of all three factors, which are specific to every conflict.

Mahan used Jomini as a point of departure for understanding strategy. Jomini claimed, "Strategy directs armies to the decisive points of a zone of operations, and influences, in advance, the results of battles." He added, "Strategy decides where to act" and, specifically, "Strategy is the art of making war upon the map."[11] Strategy, for Jomini, was limited to the preparation and planning aspects of a campaign. Mahan agreed with Jomini on the importance of strategy: "As in a building, which, however fair and beautiful the superstructure, is radically marred and imperfect if the foundation be insecure, so, if the strategy be wrong, the skill of the general on the battlefield, the valor of the soldier, the brilliancy of victory, however otherwise decisive, fail of their effect." He went further than Jomini, however, in emphasizing the continued importance of strategy throughout the campaign. Strategy, he wrote, "originates . . . in a mental process, but it does not end there . . . it is practical."[12]

Mahan called strategy "a game of wits," while Corbett described it as the "choice of lesser risk."[13] For both, strategy involved decision-making. Mahan added scope by distinguishing strategy from tactics: "The tactician deals with circumstances immediately before him and essentially transient, while the strategist has to take wider views of more lasting conditions . . . to glance over the whole board, to view the wider field."[14] Thus, strategy concerned "the conduct of campaigns."[15] Similarly, Corbett wrote, "The end of strategy is victory and not the destruction more or less complete of any section of the enemy's forces."[16] For both Mahan and Corbett, successful strategy was the path to achieving national policy objectives.

THE POLITICAL OBJECT

Corbett followed Clausewitz in explaining that the political object guides the war effort: strategy supports policy, never the reverse.[17] The maritime ambitions of eighteenth-century France failed because its leaders were not "careful to distinguish policy from strategy." The problem was not with French strategy or what French admirals did at sea so much as it was with government policies. Corbett concluded, "Seeing that she was a continental Power with continental aspirations, it was often a policy from which her military exigencies permitted no escape."[18] Continental policies placed the French navy in conditions where its admirals could not develop effective strategies. Policy, that is, placed the navy in an untenable position. Failed strategy, in Corbett's view, was often a symptom of incoherent or unobtainable policy. In no way did this provide a pass to those responsible for strategy: it merely highlighted the primacy of the political object.

Even before his exposure to Clausewitz, Mahan had arrived at a similar conclusion. "War now is never waged for the sake of mere fighting, simply to see who is the better at killing people," Mahan wrote. "The warfare of civilized nations is for the purpose of accomplishing an object."[19] He explained, "A navy is not an end, but a means. He who wills the end—the policy—wills the means."[20]

Mahan and Corbett agreed regarding the relationship of policy to strategy. Violence or the potential use of violence needed regulation and direction to differentiate it from criminal thuggery. This view also reflected the nature of their respective states. In both Britain and the United States, civilians provided leadership at the very highest level. Tradition dictated this in Britain while the U.S. Constitution required it.

CIVIL-MILITARY RELATIONS: MAHAN

Merely identifying the political objective and the means of obtaining it are insufficient. Political and military leaders must interact to achieve it. It would be too simplistic to suggest that the statesman established policy objectives and the military officer executed strategies to obtain them, for neither Mahan nor Corbett considered the policy-strategy relationship a linear process. Instead, there existed a dynamic, yet convoluted, interplay between policymakers and uniformed military leadership.

Mahan tilted the civil-military partnership in favor of civilian authority: "The military arm waits upon and is subservient to the political interests and civil power of the nation."[21] This reflected the oath he took as an officer of the U.S. Navy, grounded in the Constitution, which appointed the president commander in chief of the armed forces. Though Mahan clearly thought military leaders must submit to political authority, he argued, "It is a grave mistake to think that military and political considerations can be dissevered practically, as they can logically."[22] This is critical. In theory it appeared simple: the political leader decides on the policy and the military leader executes it, but Mahan recognized that political and military factors intrude on each other, tangling the civil-military relationship: "I cannot too entirely repudiate any casual word of mine, reflecting the tone which once was so traditional in the navy that it might be called professional,—that 'political questions belong rather to the statesman than to the military man.' I find these words in my old lectures, but very soon learned better, from my best military friend, Jomini."[23] Elsewhere, Mahan explained, "From Jomini also I imbibed a fixed disbelief in the thoughtlessly accepted maxim that the statesman and general occupy unrelated fields."[24] The best results, that is, occurred when the statesman and the commander cooperated.

Such cooperation aligned with Jomini's description of "Military Policy" as being "exclusively neither to diplomacy nor to strategy," for he saw an "intimate connection between statesmanship and war." There were, however, clear boundaries. Jomini extended this cooperative relationship to the "preliminaries"—the planning and opening of the war. Once the battle was joined, he argued, "Political objective points should be subordinate to strategy, at least until after a great success has been attained."[25] The statesman decided on the war while working in consultation with the uniformed leadership; military leaders then executed operations according to the principles of war. After the military obtained the objective, the statesman exploited the gains. This, to Jomini, was the proper division of authority between the statesman and the commander.

Mahan agreed. The statesman determined national interests and decided when protecting or defending these interests required the use of force. When force was required, the military leader needed to account for the following: "The methods by which the military force will proceed to the ends thus indicated to it—the numbers, character, equipment of the forces to be employed, and their management in campaign." These were "technical matters, to be referred to the military or naval expert by the statesman."[26] Mahan strongly entreated the statesman to avoid technical and operational issues relating to the employment of force. "To interfere thus with the commander in the field or afloat is one of the most common temptations to the government in the cabinet, and is generally disastrous."[27] Overall, Mahan concluded, "It is fair to assume, where not otherwise proved, that for the general direction of the war the government is responsible, and that in particular management of military movements the advice of professional men has had just weight." Mahan did admit, however, "It is not likely that such a division of labor, between the statesman, the soldier, and the seaman, is ever formally made."[28] A certain amount of tension was beneficial in the civil-military relationship, but in the end, the civilian and military leadership needed "to work together harmoniously and efficiently; to complement, not to antagonize each other."[29]

Mahan drew these lessons from his historical studies coupled with his naval career, including his experiences in the U.S. Civil War. He understood that the statesman and the commander occupy "related fields" that cannot be entirely separated. Without outlining a clear division of authority, the relationship could become murky with the potential for either the statesman or the commander inadvertently to step into the other's sphere.

The military side of the civil-military relationship intrigued Mahan both as a naval officer and as an educator. Political leaders tended to lack detailed knowledge of what the instruments of war could accomplish. As a result, he thought, "Military and naval men, from their habit of mind and their acquirements, should be the most competent advisers to the statesmen of country, to indicate to them what positions are most profitable to obtain by the conduct of diplomacy, . . . or as the result of successful war." This could occur only if senior officers were educated. Not only should they have a clear understanding of the principles of war, "every naval officer who respects himself and his profession should be well informed as to international conditions, for not otherwise can he form sound military judgment or give adequate counsel when called upon."[30]

Mere knowledge was insufficient. Evoking a statement from Nelson, Mahan insisted, "An officer should have political courage," which, "to be well based, requires political knowledge as well. That you may more effectually concentrate upon this necessary knowledge, avoid dissipating your energies upon questions interior to the country; questions financial, sociological, economical, or what not. The sphere of the navy is international solely."[31] With limited time to study, the officer should focus on international relations. Given the whole of Mahan's sea power thesis, it is odd that he steered officers away from financial and economic issues. Even at the domestic level, such economic and financial questions tended to spill into the international environment, potentially leaving the officer unprepared.

Since the "sphere of the navy" was international, then it was a naval officer's duty to be involved in influencing the international environment: "It is this which allies it so closely to that of the statesman. Aim to be yourselves statesmen as well as seamen."[32] Mahan expected the naval officer to do more than follow orders: the officer had to think critically about foreign policy and provide the best professional advice. His broader theory made it clear, however, that officers served the country's political leadership because "all this responsibility is civil and executive; the military adviser may contribute sound military opinion, but decision rests elsewhere."[33] Officers had to walk a difficult tightrope providing informed advice and even acting as statesmen while never forgetting to remain subservient to political leaders.

THE DEFLECTION OF STRATEGY BY POLITICS

The most effective military course of action often has unacceptable political repercussions. A certain choice might bring a neutral into the conflict or bolster the resolve of an opponent, increasing the cost and length of the war. Decisions based only on the most effective use of available force tend toward counterproductive results. Strategy does not exist in a vacuum: it must align courses of action with political objects and considerations. As a result, numerous factors twist, pull, and distort every strategic decision.

"To condemn details without having first considered what should be the leading outlines of a great design, is as unsafe as it is unfair," wrote Mahan, "for steps indefensible in themselves may be justified by the exigencies of the general policy."[34] Mahan likened war to a game of cards in which "the state of the score must at times dictate the play; and the chief who never takes into consideration the effect which his particular action will have on the general result, nor what is demanded of him by the condition of things elsewhere, both political and military, lacks an essential quality of a great general."[35]

In the best of all possible worlds, strategy rests on the time-tested principles of war, because that provides the best chance of victory at the most acceptable cost. One could describe this as pure strategy. But in Mahan's view, pure strategy did not win wars: "the means must be adapted to the conditions and to the end desired."[36] Strategy must be modified, even in ways that contradict established principles, to achieve the political object. And so, Mahan concluded, "political conditions may rightly be allowed at times to overweigh military prudence or to control military activity. This is eminently true, for, after all, war is political action."[37]

Across the Atlantic, Captain Henry J. May, the director of the War Course at the Royal Naval College, Greenwich, read Mahan's works and was struck by the influence of political factors on strategy. May worried that many of the officers attending the War Course were unaware of policy's influence on strategy. To educate them, May invited Corbett to provide lectures "to remind Naval Officers that expediency & strategy are not always in accord. An Admiral may have the force on the spot but may be restrained by political considerations from striking at the right time & place."[38] May described this as the "Deflection of Strategy by Politics." Corbett later explained that this involved teaching officers that "they were always hedged in by political and diplomatic considerations, which prevented them following purely strategical lines."[39]

Accepting May's invitation to lecture led Corbett to a very close reading of Clausewitz, whose theories helped him frame the relationship between strategy and policy. Eventually, Corbett provided a lecture titled "The System of Clausewitz." In it he explained, "It is useless to study Strategy apart from Politics 'on a clean slate,' & there will always be preexisting lines which we cannot efface." Officers needed to understand government policies so they could frame their assessments and develop effective strategies. Though officers grumbled over political restrictions, they "should never complain of the prejudicial effects of policy in the conduct of war."[40] War is a tool of policy; it is subservient to the political objective and should not drive the government's objective. Officers had to step outside their comfort zone and acknowledge political objectives when providing strategic advice. Their desire to develop the most effective strategy could not supersede the demands of policy.

The arguments seeped into Corbett's writings. *England and the Seven Years' War* is particularly suggestive: "One of its most valuable lessons, [is] how military and naval strategy are confused and deflected by political considerations."[41] The civilian leader was the master, and the political object both dominated and controlled strategy. "Take, now, the ordinary case of a naval or military Staff being asked to prepare a war plan against a certain State and to advise what means it will require," he later wrote. "To any one who has considered such matters it is obvious the reply must be another question—What will the war be about?"[42]

War, or the possibility of war, did not occur in a vacuum. Corbett had firsthand experience with this. His involvement with the Royal Navy occurred under the shadow of rising German antagonism, and in 1907 he helped develop a war plan against Germany.[43] His participation in the process led him to become an even stronger acolyte of Clausewitz, for the Prussian argued, "The political object, as the original motive of the war, will be the standard for determining both the aim of the military force, and also the amount of effort to be made."[44] Corbett, like Clausewitz before him, believed that strategic choices had to support policy objectives.

His association with the Committee of Imperial Defence during World War I allowed Corbett to witness how political decisions deflected strategy. He then had an opportunity to analyze these decisions while writing the official history of the naval war. Assessing the decision to intervene at Salonika in 1915, for example, Corbett explained, "So far the strategical problem was fairly simple, but its political deflections could not be ignored. Politically the most desirable way was to persevere at Salonica [*sic*], but naval and military considerations all condemned it."[45]

Though Corbett recognized that officers would find his admonition galling, he made no excuses; Mahan, however, took a different path. Though he understood that politics would intrude on operations and even deflect strategy, he also understood that statesmen might err in their decisions because they were uninformed or too far away.[46] Mahan called it "one of the commonest and most deplorable experiences of war—the hands of a commander-in-chief, present on the scene of operations, tied by the positive instructions of a man, or set of men, at a distance." Mahan entreated civilian decision makers to "beware of too particular directions, and, above all, of absolute orders, fettering the discretion of the commander-in-chief. If the man *on the spot* cannot be trusted, he should be removed; but no one at a distance from the scene of operations can effectively direct them."[47]

When the most effective strategic combinations and the desired political objective did not align, Mahan resolved the dilemma with his preferred methodology: he argued both sides simultaneously. On the one hand, the policy dominated, and under normal conditions emerged victorious; on the other, Mahan assessed the decision through the prism of pure strategy. If there was a divergence between pure strategy and the policy demanded by the government, Mahan was less apt to accept the deflection of strategy by politics. "While military operations must take account of political conditions," Mahan believed, "the latter should not be allowed to overbalance elementary principles of the military art."[48] As a naval officer, he did not trust the civilian to make correct choices and asked the officer to find the way out.

In contrast to Mahan, Corbett placed the onus on the statesman to find a better policy: "If there is a divergence between policy and strategy, it is either: (a) because the policy is not well aimed at the object; or (b) because Statesmen misapprehend the probable affect of the operations they favour."[49]

CIVIL-MILITARY RELATIONS: CORBETT

What Corbett said and wrote about the responsibilities of senior officers largely paralleled Mahan's argument and sheds great light on how they viewed the civil-military relationship. Their association with their respective war colleges provided both men with similar catalysts to explore the civil-military relationship, and both used historical cases to provide officers with vicarious experiences. Corbett explained, "In the higher grades of the service the most important thing is not obeying, but giving, orders and advising a Government what orders to give."[50] Again, this paralleled Mahan. Both theorists maintained that a naval officer should be able to give political leaders expert advice while still functioning as an officer.

Addressing one incident from the Seven Years' War, Corbett noted, "The incident is a striking example of two vital considerations in making war: one is the importance of admirals fully understanding the political significance of their orders, and the other the importance at headquarters of familiarity with the elementary principles of strategy." In another case Corbett wrote of an officer being "'minister' enough to understand" the political context.[51]

It is telling that Corbett addressed civil-military relations in the introduction to *Some Principles of Maritime Strategy* by linking that relationship with the purpose of theory. Being able to communicate clearly was key.[52] The global nature of the British Empire meant that decisions and discussions among leaders had to occur at great distances. Discussions might be between commanders in chief of adjacent stations, between naval and military officers, between civilian representatives and uniformed leaders, or between those on station and the heads of government in London. If all these people shared a common vocabulary, it was less likely that they would talk past or over the others. "Conference is always necessary," Corbett noted, "and for conference to succeed there must be a common vehicle of expression and a common plane of thought. It is for this essential preparation that theoretical study alone can provide; and herein lies its practical value for all who aspire to the higher responsibilities of the Imperial service."[53]

But what happened when the professionals disagreed or lacked necessary knowledge? If the object was deemed important enough, Corbett placed the onus on the policymakers to make the call: "When expert opinion differed it was they, and they alone, who must judge the extent of the risk involved, and they, and they alone, who must judge whether the probable advantages of success justified the acceptance of the risk."[54]

Political leaders had to understand when they should intrude on the military decisions and when such intrusions were unnecessary interference. As an example Corbett described Pitt's enlightened leadership in the Seven Years' War: "We have seen that in the offensive areas of the war, where results depended upon the intimate co-ordination of naval and military action, the admirals were receiving their orders direct from him, but in this case it was different. Nothing is more eloquent of Pitt's grasp of war than his frank recognition that here his interference was uncalled for. Having determined the function of the navy in the home area [Pitt] gave it a perfectly free hand, and the whole of the operations for discharging that function were left to the judgment of Lord Anson and his colleagues on the Board of Admiralty."[55] The civilian policymaker walked a fine line between too much interference and too little.

▪ ▪ ▪

War serves a purpose, and that purpose, according to Mahan, "is not to kill men, but to carry a point; not glory by fighting, but success in result." Corbett amplified Mahan's point, claiming the "goal is peace."[56] Yet Corbett did not provide much comfort when he described how "governments limp and stumble to vital decisions when their path is encumbered by a tangle of political and strategical considerations."[57] Both Mahan and Corbett attempted to untangle the knot through education, and that involved setting a vocabulary common to both officers and political leaders. Moreover, both theorists agreed that political considerations took precedence over military considerations in any discussion necessitating the use of force. Their divergence was in the "deflection of strategy by politics." On this subject their variance was in the degree to which political considerations should influence strategy.

Both Mahan and Corbett grounded their thoughts in the conclusions of the land power theorists of the early nineteenth century. Corbett drew extensively on Clausewitz's views on civil-military relations. Especially at the highest levels, the statesman and the commander had to establish a dialogue, or in Corbett's words a "conference," that sought agreement. Whereas Corbett took Clausewitz as a model, Mahan used Jomini as a point of departure. Mahan's argument, however, went further than Jomini insinuated in his writings. Like Jomini he remained leery of civilian involvement, or what might even be called interference, in military operations; however, he was more willing than Jomini to consider the effectiveness of a political-military dialogue throughout the campaign, and this brought his conclusions more closely in line with Corbett's methodology.

CHAPTER 4
INTRODUCTION TO NAVAL STRATEGY

"It was, of course, impossible for the people generally to understand the situation," Corbett wrote of the British populace during the early months of World War I. "They had no basis of appreciation, except a vague impression that the old naval wars were a succession of rapid and brilliant victories, which rendered a cowed and impotent enemy incapable of interfering with our control of the seas." Far from the public eye and popular knowledge, the Royal Navy had to undertake the "patient and arduous preparation which made these victories possible and the no less toilsome work of reaping their fruits."[1] Navies serve as an integral cog in advancing national policy, but most people do not understand how navies accomplish their essential mission. Explaining this in all its complexities was a prime objective of Mahan and Corbett. They grounded their work in historical examples and used theory to stretch those historical examples into applications for the present.

THE RELATIONSHIP BETWEEN THE THEORIES OF LAND WARFARE AND NAVAL WARFARE

"The study of naval strategy, systematically, began here at the Naval War College," Mahan recounted. Rather than create naval strategy, the War College provided an environment where officers learned to apply logic and method to understand the complexities of that subject. Without study, officers' understanding of naval strategy was limited to "the common sense of some, and the genius of others." Corbett noted a similar conundrum in Britain: "Naval Strategy consists of unconnected principles, often misapplied because their true theoretical value is misunderstood."[2]

Someone needed to identify principles for naval warfare: both men were determined to be that someone.

Both Mahan and Corbett integrated naval history and land warfare theories to develop concepts of naval strategy. The underdeveloped state of the field made this a challenging subject. They had to wade through historical examples to uncover and generate the data that supported their analyses of naval warfare. Theories of land war formed the second half of the equation. If strategic principles from land warfare translated perfectly to the employment of navies, there would have been little need for either Mahan or Corbett; the work of Clausewitz and Jomini would apply seamlessly to the maritime domain. But this was not the case. Conversely, naval theory and land war theory were not diametric opposites. Mahan and Corbett had to wrestle with the extent and nature of the overlap.

Both men concluded that naval strategy was a more expansive subject than terrestrial strategy. Clausewitz's dictum of strategy comprising "the employment of the battle to gain the end of the war" was simply not enough.[3] Mahan explained, "The definitions usually given of the word 'strategy' confine it to military combinations embracing one or more fields of operations . . . always regarded as actual or immediate scenes of war. However this may be on shore, a recent French author is quite right in pointing out that such a definition is too narrow for naval strategy." By using an unnamed "French author" to insulate his argument, Mahan could claim that he was only echoing another's contention that naval strategy was a broader subject than strategy in land warfare. Naval strategy stretched well beyond the battlefield to the entire maritime commons and even transcended the line between peace and war.[4] Mahan's conception of naval strategy drove his arguments about sea power into the realm of grand strategy.

Corbett followed a similar trajectory to reach his concept of major strategy. He concluded that a maritime state like Britain needed to link naval, land, diplomatic, and financial elements of national power to attain its desired political objectives.[5] Major strategy resides in the hands of the political leader who seeks national objectives by directing all instruments of power. The ways and means of using these instruments are what Corbett labeled "minor strategies." To delineate the nature of the relationship between major strategy and minor strategy, Corbett explained, "The major strategy of the war controls the minor strategy of the fleet."[6] It is the method of employing the fleet as a minor strategy that serves as the focus of this chapter.

Corbett and Mahan disagreed about the extent to which the same fundamental principles governed land warfare and sea warfare. Corbett lamented "the fallacy—against which I am always preaching—of arguing directly from military to naval conditions."[7] One could neither blindly nor directly apply principles of land warfare to the naval domain, yet he found this often occurred.[8] As a result, he borrowed very carefully from the land power theorists. From Clausewitz, for example, he took underlying frameworks and methodologies, including the primacy of policy, the purpose of theory, and the importance of critical analysis; but when addressing fleet operations, he distanced himself from the land power theorists.

Mahan, in contrast, wrote, "Warfare, the conduct of war, . . . is in its comprehensive sense a single form of human activity, one in its fundamental principles wherever, or whenever, waged."[9] He went on to state that "military war . . . and naval war, are two great principal subdivisions,—specializations,—of the military art."[10] Mahan's willingness to use military strategic theory to explain concepts of naval warfare reflects Luce's influence. As early as 1886 Luce emphasized a "comparative method" using land warfare theory to assist in the study of naval warfare.[11] Mahan agreed, claiming, "In the first place, land warfare has much more extensive narrative development, because there has been very much more land fighting than sea; and also, perhaps because of this larger amount of material, much more effort has been made to elicit the underlying principles by formal analysis." The painstaking work of military writers was a useful foundation for his theory of naval war. "We shall find differences enough," he wrote; "no one will mistake the new house for the old when it is finished yet the two will have strong resemblance, and the most marked contrasts will but bring out more clearly than ever the strong features common to both."[12]

Mahan used an analogy to explain why naval officers should study the great generals of land warfare: "The works of a great artist do not merely supply models for a copyist; on the contrary, that is far from being their chief service. By familiarity with the master-pieces . . . you become imbued with his spirit, enlightened by his intelligence, enkindled by the fire that burns in him; and, thus quickened, you may rise from the mere copyist to be yourself an artist." The great general was akin to the artist, and the naval officer the aspiring student. Rather than copy what the great general had done, the naval officer needed to use his deeds as a point of departure. "For this reason great land campaigns are so fruitful to the sea strategist, and I have no hesitation in saying that, if I have been able to contribute anything to the Art of Naval War, I owe such ability to the critical study of military warfare."[13]

Corbett would have none of this. He focused on differences between land warfare and naval warfare and labeled them the "continental" and the "maritime" schools. The continental school provided a model for states with contiguous great power rivals—France and Germany, for example. This was the method Clausewitz and Jomini adapted from the Napoleonic style of warfare. Corbett identified a combination of four principles that made Napoleonic warfare unique: (1) having the entire nation at war, (2) pressing the enemy until absolutely defeated, (3) taking the offensive, and (4) seeking battle with the opposing army. Though Corbett thought that Napoleonic warfare and the principles behind it had a place in military theory, he argued for the existence of other schools of warfare as well.[14] Rather than copy the continental models put forward by Clausewitz and Jomini, Corbett wrote for Britain, an island nation possessing a global empire. He reminded his readers that "the country we have to travel is radically different from that in which they acquired their skill."[15]

Instead of drawing a clear distinction between the Napoleonic school of continental warfare and his own naval theories, Mahan sought to apply general principles of land warfare to naval war.[16] He thus tended to draw analogies between the fleet and the army, going so far in one lecture to call the navy a "Sea-Army." In a similar vein, he wrote in *The Influence of Sea Power upon History* of the "navy, which may be accurately called the army in the field." Elsewhere, he compared "a light corps" of cavalry and fast-moving infantry with warships protecting the sea-lanes. He even related the choice between attacking the enemy's main fleet and seizing an enemy naval base as similar to the distinction between attacking an army and attacking its outposts.[17]

Though Mahan's analogies are neither overly pervasive nor illogically forced, Corbett found them less than compelling. "You cannot conquer sea because it is not susceptible to ownership," he insisted. He developed three "general principles" of all warfare to demonstrate the profound implication of this statement:

- There is the idea of concentration of force, that is, the idea of overthrowing the enemy's main strength by bringing to bear upon the utmost accumulation of weight and energy within your means.
- Secondly, there is the idea that strategy is mainly a question of definite lines of communication.
- Thirdly, there is the idea of concentration of effort, which means keeping a single eye on the force you wish to overthrow without regard to ulterior objects.

He maintained that each of the above points applied to naval and land warfare differently.[18]

While Corbett attempted to differentiate the naval and land domains, Mahan's focus on fundamental principles led him toward parallels between them. Mahan's position can, however, be easily misconstrued. He did not contend that land warfare and naval warfare were identical. While the underlying principle such as concentration or lines of communication was the same on land and at sea, "the methods of application will not be so, owing to the differences of conditions."[19] The student of war must differentiate the principle that is constant across the domains of war from its employment, which differs by domain and time.

If we look to the last hundred years of naval warfare to vindicate either Mahan or Corbett, we find much to support both; and oddly enough, many historical examples seem to sustain both. As much as Corbett wished to distance himself from Mahan, his arguments were not always as original as he wanted his readers to believe they were. For example, both theorists agreed on the importance of concentration of force, concentration of effort, and lines of communication, but they largely talked past one another. They agreed on the principle, and even on how it applied differently to land warfare and naval warfare. The difference resides in their methods of application. Mahan accepted concepts of land warfare and then asked how naval warfare differed; Corbett avoided conflating naval strategy with what occurred on land.

In the end, Corbett's arguments are generally more nuanced. This should not be surprising: he worked from a more solid foundation. Sometimes that nuance makes his arguments quite distinct from Mahan's, but elsewhere the similarities predominate, with Corbett emphasizing different points but arriving at similar conclusions. A comprehensive assessment of their naval strategies clarifies their similarities and differences. This begins at the macro level to identify the navy's role within national strategy and proceeds to more specific theoretical concepts relating to naval and maritime power.

THE NAVY'S ROLE IN NATIONAL STRATEGY: AN ENABLER OR THE DECISIVE INSTRUMENT?

Both Mahan and Corbett identified the navy's purpose within national strategy as "the function of the fleet." Corbett explained, "Reaching higher and wider than what is usually understood by naval strategy, it [the function of the fleet] is a branch of the art as vital for statesmen as it is for sailors, for diplomatists as it is for soldiers, and by history alone can it be mastered."[20] Neither entirely a branch of statesmanship nor fully the realm of the naval officer, the function of the fleet required input from both the political and the uniformed leadership.

The two naval theorists created divergent arguments about the navy's role within national strategy. Mahan considered the navy the indispensible instrument, the lynchpin of his entire theory on sea power. Conversely, Corbett asserted the impotence of any single instrument of power, arguing instead that the fleet was one part of a larger package of instruments. Given this difference, it should not be surprising that Mahan and Corbett diverged on the decisiveness of naval power. Corbett argued that a navy enabled other aspects of national power while Mahan viewed naval power as decisive in its own right.

Identifying what Mahan considered the object of naval strategy provides a point of departure for clarifying his views on the navy's role within national strategy: "Naval strategy has indeed for its end to found, support, and increase, as well in peace as in war, the sea power of a country."[21] His concept highlights "sea power," which he identified as a combination of naval and economic elements. Mahan added context elsewhere: "So in the permanency of the function of the Sea which identifies it with the communications of nations, with the interchange of commodities and the increase of wealth, whereby the support and advance of mankind is forwarded, . . . is to be found the unchangeable condition which underlies Naval Strategy."[22] Mahan came close to conflating naval power and economic power, but this should not be surprising given his definition of sea power and his view that war was business.

Mahan contended that navies "had the casting vote" in both the American Revolution and the U.S. Civil War. He identified "two great decisive moments of the [Revolutionary] War." First, Benedict Arnold's operations on Lake Champlain thwarted the British advance from Canada in 1776; and second, the French navy sealed Cornwallis' fate at Yorktown in 1781. Turning to the Civil War, Mahan asserted, "To the Navy also, beyond any other single instrumentality, was due eighty years later the successful suppression of the movement of Secession." Here, he highlighted the Union blockade that contained the Confederacy by severing it from international support. He concluded, "At these two principal national epochs control of the water was the most determinative factor."[23] It is important to consider why Mahan thought naval power had such influence on the outcome of both wars. Why were other factors like the population and the industrial base of the North not more significant in the outcome of the Civil War, or the will of the patriots in the American Revolution? Quite simply, Mahan had a thesis to prove. He needed naval power to be the factor that made the compelling difference in national strategy.

Before proceeding further, we must understand how Mahan defined "decisive." This is important given the charged nature of this term in the strategic lexicon. Mahan considered the decisive element to be the one necessary to *ensure* the outcome rather than *directly lead* to the outcome. Naval power was decisive in this sense because it set the stage for the other pieces to fall into place.[24] Navies created the conditions for land or even diplomatic power to attain the greatest effect. Sea power made other events possible. Though some might argue that land power was the decisive factor in the Civil War because the success of the Union Army directly brought an end to the fighting, Mahan considered the Union's success on land possible only because the naval blockade had set the conditions for the victory.

Mahan tended to address the navy in combination with commercial factors because he was attempting to sell the U.S. Navy to a skeptical capitalist audience in the United States. When he did link naval power and ground power, he did not develop a joint approach; instead, he argued that naval power provided the prerequisite for the successful employment of land power. Otherwise he would undercut his argument by placing the navy in the subordinate role of enabling operations on land. He needed the fleet as the essential facilitator of national strategy. This is particularly true in how he described the outcome of the Civil War.

Corbett's argument differed. He thought naval leaders tended to overemphasize the actions of naval forces and forgot to consider how naval forces interacted with the other instruments of power. By focusing too heavily on their own instrument of war, naval leaders tended to miss the navy's true role within national strategy. One only needs to consider the title of *Some Principles of Maritime Strategy* to understand how Corbett interpreted the function of the fleet. He asserted, "By maritime strategy we mean the principles which govern a war in which the sea is a substantial factor. Naval strategy is but that part of it which determines the movements of the fleet when maritime strategy has determined what part the fleet must play in relation to the action of the land forces."[25] A navy was part of a larger whole. This does not mean that naval strategy was unimportant or undeserving of study, but naval power had to be understood in a broader national security context.

The officers who read Mahan often focused narrowly on the navy, as Mahan intended them to do. Corbett provided a counterargument critiquing "sea power" by noting how "impotent it is of itself." He believed that wars are in almost all cases decided on land, with diplomacy and land power exerting more decisive leverage than naval forces. That did not mean the navy of a maritime state like Britain lacked a purpose, but "it must remember its functions are many besides defeating an enemy's fleet."[26]

He entreated leaders to avoid "confusing the functions of the fleet with the method of performing those functions."[27] While naval officers needed to understand how to employ the fleet, defeat the opposing navy, and leverage command of the sea, these aspects of naval strategy only provided the methods of obtaining the larger grand strategic functions of the fleet. As Corbett maintained, "The main war plan will determine the functions of the fleet."[28] This is critical: the fleet's function was to fulfill the navy's role in the war plan. It extended well beyond what Corbett labeled "the distorting influence of the enemy's main fleet"—the quest for a fleet-on-fleet engagement—and aspects of pure naval strategy. Rather, the function of the fleet was to integrate naval power with other instruments of national power. Corbett concluded: "The function of the fleet, the object for which it was always employed, has been threefold: firstly, to support or obstruct diplomatic effort; secondly, to protect or destroy commerce; and thirdly, to further or hinder military operations ashore."[29]

The fleet's function would "differ very greatly according to the geographical conformation and distribution of various states, and to their international characteristics." Its function would vary by country, historical period, and the nature of the belligerents. In assessing Britain in the early years of the twentieth century, when Germany was its greatest threat, Corbett asserted, "I think . . . the control of home waters is beyond shadow of doubt the primary function of our fleet."[30] Not only did the control of home waters ensure the defense of the homeland and protect Britain's commercial links with the remainder of the world, it created the conditions to stifle the commerce of Britain's most dangerous rival—Germany. Britain's geographic location gave it the opportunity to sever Germany's communications with the world. Control of home waters, moreover, supported Britain's budding entente with France and allowed for secure lines of passage to the European continent as an essential prerequisite for the projection of land forces.[31] According to Corbett's argument, the function of the fleet served as a means to attain the end. In his British example, the navy served as a necessary enabler for gaining the greatest effect from economic, diplomatic, and military instruments of power.

The function of the fleet can either enable other instruments of power or be decisive on its own. Corbett presented the navy as the key enabler for a maritime state to achieve national objectives, while Mahan presented the navy as the lynchpin that made the achievement of national objectives possible.

We should perhaps ponder whether the two theorists were partially talking past one another. Corbett, as we have said, considered the navy the critical factor that enabled land and diplomatic efforts to attain victory. Without its navy, Britain was impotent. In effect, this is what Mahan argued as well. He merely placed greater emphasis on the navy's role and tended to imply that land and diplomatic actions would fall into place if the navy were successful. Thus, the difference between the theorists lies not in the navy's position to assist the other instruments but in what that assistance means for national strategy.

Mahan told naval audiences at the dawn of the twentieth century what they wished to hear, and he sold books as a result. Conversely, Corbett asked naval officers to accept a less prominent role in national strategy. From budget battles to the naval establishment, this made Corbett less appealing but perhaps more relevant because he forced naval officers to think creatively about naval strategy.

CHAPTER 5

COMMERCE, THE SEA LINES OF COMMUNICATION, AND NAVAL POWER

Among the functions of the fleet is the support it provides to the national economy. Naval and economic instruments form a symbiotic relationship in both peace and war. This relationship is a necessary component within Corbett's major strategy and sits at the heart of Mahan's sea power thesis.

Mahan advocated a "perfectly legitimate and unobjectionable form of commercial competition, in open field without favor."[1] In the best of all possible worlds, a peaceful economic contest would occur, with the players seeking the greatest profits. The high value of the commercial objects meant that "all maritime nations more or less, depend for their prosperity upon maritime commerce, and probably upon it more than any other single factor."[2] Mahan's views reflected the increased importance of global trade in the international environment during the nineteenth century: "The vast increase in rapidity of communication, has multiplied and strengthened the bonds knitting the interests of nations to one another, till the whole now forms an articulated system, not only of prodigious size and activity, but of an excessive sensitiveness, unequalled in former ages. . . . The preservation of commercial and financial interests constitutes now a political consideration of the first importance, making for peace and deterring from war."[3]

Though Mahan extolled free trade, he worried that some nations would not allow it.[4] "While commerce thus on the one hand deters from war," Mahan noted, "on the other hand it engenders conflict, fostering ambitions and strifes which tend towards armed collision."[5] Since numerous factors could upset peaceful commercial competition, Mahan advocated for a powerful fleet to protect merchant commerce. A navy provided security in peacetime and was a powerful deterrent from war. If war became necessary, the navy stood poised to protect friendly commerce and deny commerce to the enemy.

Corbett implicitly agreed with nearly every one of Mahan's points. He did not object to free trade in peacetime. After all, he lived in and wrote about a British state that benefited from the free movement of international commerce; it was the basis of Britain's economic model and critical to its prosperity. Moreover, Corbett came from a well-to-do background: his family's investments brought him into direct contact with the global financial system.[6]

The difference between the two men is one of perspective. Corbett wrote for Britain, the global maritime trading empire whose leaders already understood the importance of international commercial enterprise. What Britain did in peacetime did not need belaboring; however, nearly a century had passed since it last fought a major war. The long peace had distorted views of the function of the navy in war. Clarifying the navy's wartime role became Corbett's mission. Mahan, for his part, wanted to change the mindset of Americans by arguing for the United States to develop sea power through building a strong navy, first to foster overseas commercial wealth in peacetime and then to protect it in war.

ECONOMIC, COMMERCIAL, AND FINANCIAL POWER

Economic power includes industry, commerce, and finance. The latter allows governments to manage the large sums required for the state to function. Without a solid financial footing, a maritime state's strategic position would collapse. "Wars are not decided exclusively by military and naval force," Corbett noted. "Finance is scarcely less important. When other things are equal, it is the longer purse that wins." He added, "It is commerce and finance which now more than ever control or check the foreign policy of nations."[7] As a historian, Corbett had studied wars from the period of Sir Francis Drake to Napoleon. England's major wars tended to become protracted struggles in which its insular position provided sanctuary and the seas the highways to victory. The longer the war, the more costly it became and the more important the state's finances.

Mahan also wrote extensively about the link between finance and a nation's ability to protract war. "Money, credit, is the life of war; lessen it, and vigor flags; destroy it, and resistance dies." And it is "financial potency that determines the issues of war."[8] A major theme in his study of the War of 1812 juxtaposes the strength that sound finances provided Britain with the limitation weak financial standing imposed on the United States.

Naval power provides integral support to state finance. "It protects the economical processes which sustain national endurance," Mahan explained, "and thus secures the foundation on which the vigor of war rests."[9] To underscore the link between naval power and economic power, consider how governments obtain funds. The majority derives from two basic sources: money collected in the form of duties on trade and tax revenues, and loans. Commerce is a critical component in both. "The public revenue of maritime states is largely derived from duties on imports," Mahan explained, and ". . . a large source of wealth, of money—ready money or substantial credit—is proverbially the sinews of war."[10] The wealth generated by commerce builds prosperity that portends a stable tax income. When taxation proves insufficient, the ability to raise money through loans is critical. The wealth generated by trade can purchase government debt, and a healthy national economy makes the state appear a better investment.

Maritime commerce is an extremely valuable cog in a nation's economy because it reaches beyond the nation's borders and allows industry to obtain raw materials from abroad and to expand markets. Maritime commerce, however, requires naval protection. Commerce and the navy form a virtuous circle (see diagram 1.1 in chapter 1). The greater the nation's wealth, the more revenue is available to fund the fleet; the larger the fleet, the safer the maritime commerce. "You may even go farther," Corbett argued, "for much naval history at least depends upon economic conditions. A deeper study of the subject often reveals that operations, which at first sight appear to be what is technically called eccentric, were dictated by the commercial and financial needs upon which the nourishment and vigour of our Fleet and Army depended."[11]

The Napoleonic Wars provided both theorists with an example of a high-stakes, multi-theater, great power, protracted war with a large maritime component. In *The Influence of Sea Power upon the French Revolution and Empire*, Mahan sought to explain Napoleon's defeat. He could not claim the great sea battle of Trafalgar ended the war: it occurred in 1805 but the war continued for another decade.[12] Instead, Mahan asserted, "I gained my conviction that the Continental System was the determinative factor in Napoleon's fortunes."[13] The Continental System, a means of economic warfare premised on preventing commercial exchange between Britain and its largest trading bloc—continental Europe—accelerated numerous points of conflict. Its enforcement drove a wedge between Napoleon and his potential allies on the European continent and led Napoleon into costly military campaigns in the Iberian Peninsula and Russia. Mahan argued, "It is enough to say that it [the Continental System] nearly ruined Great Britain, but it entirely ruined Napoleon."[14]

Mahan considered the Royal Navy to have made the critical difference in the failure of the Continental System because it fostered friendly commerce while preventing French commerce. No matter how hard Napoleon tried to stop it, British trade trickled into the continent. Mahan explained, "The downfall of Napoleon was due to the fact that for a series of years he had been wasting his armies, the manhood of France, her human capital, in unsuccessful attempts to restore her finances and compel Great Britain to cease from capturing private property at sea."[15] Moreover, he contrasted France's financial disaster with Britain's resilience: "Behind her stood the history and prestige of a Sea Power which men knew had met many a heavy reverse, yet had never failed. . . . She had credit, he had none."[16] The navy protected British trade, nurtured its economy, and forced Napoleon into a series of self-defeating actions. Thus, Mahan explained how Britain leveraged its sea power "to exert the decisive influence upon the result of the war."[17]

In the introduction to *England and the Seven Years' War*, Corbett attacked Mahan's conclusion: "It is evident that we require for the guidance of our naval policy and naval action something of wider vision than the current conception of naval strategy, something that will keep before our eyes not merely the enemy's fleets or the great routes of commerce, or the command of the sea, but also the relations of naval policy and action to the whole area of diplomatic and military effort." Corbett did not entirely dismiss Mahan's economic warfare thesis, but he did argue that it was insufficient to explain outcomes. He emphasized diplomatic and joint elements, stretching his argument beyond Mahan's economic focus.[18] "For a great part of the [Napoleonic] period it turned on a mortal commercial struggle, the issue of which for many exhausting years hung in the balance." The struggle became one of economic warfare, and Britain endured "by protecting and fostering our trade."[19] Commercial and financial factors gave Britain staying power essential for its survival, but not the way to ultimate victory. That could only occur when the international and military situations improved.

"And, be it remembered," Corbett noted, "it was the retention of our financial position that eventually enabled us to beat Napoleon down; it was our sole hope of securing allies."[20] That is, the economic-naval relationship sustained Britain and provided the foundation for potentially war-winning coalitions. Mahan offered a slightly different argument regarding Britain's role in the war: "It was economically wiser, for the purposes of the coalitions, that she should be controlling the sea, supporting the commerce of the world, making money and managing the finances, while other states, whose industries were exposed to the blast of war and who had not the same commercial aptitudes, did the fighting on land."[21]

Though both theorists believed that Britain's financial power was a critical element of its national power, they differed on the nature of that advantage. Mahan contended that a strong economy was essential for obtaining allies and funding armies. Without it Britain lost its comparative advantage. Corbett thought that the economic instrument enabled Britain to protract the war and perhaps achieve a better outcome, but land power and diplomatic power provided the difference.

Neither Mahan nor Corbett argued specifics relating to economic issues, and neither provided detailed statistics or other documentary support. They presented broad, general financial and economic frameworks to inform what really mattered to their theories: the navy's role in commercial interactions.

THE SIGNIFICANCE OF MARITIME COMMERCE IN NAVAL WARFARE

Both theorists considered the effects possible from waging war against maritime commerce. Corbett argued: "Anything . . . which we are able to achieve towards crippling our enemy's finance is a direct step to his overthrow, and the most effective means we can employ to this end against a maritime state is to deny him the resources of sea-borne trade."[22] Mahan concurred: "On the military side, the *general* question is; Does the interruption of his trade sap the resources of a belligerent, diminishing his power to fight? As to this, there can be little doubt."[23]

At the turn of the twentieth century, powerful interests argued for stronger protections for maritime commerce in wartime, in particular by narrowing the definition of what constituted contraband and giving neutral commerce greater rights; some even sought to make commercial vessels immune from capture on the high seas. Maritime belligerent rights were considered at the 1899 Hague Convention and were an even more prominent issue at the 1907 Convention.[24] Neither Corbett nor Mahan agreed that commercial ships should be off-limits to belligerents. Public opinion in the United States tended to side against Mahan. Though Corbett had the support of the Admiralty, elements in the Liberal government then in power considered limiting maritime belligerent rights.[25] In an effort to shape opinion, both Mahan and Corbett penned articles on the subject in 1907 at the time of the Second Hague Convention.[26] This point of solid agreement between the theorists led to one of Corbett's greatest compliments to Mahan: "Turning now . . . to America, we find that the best naval opinion there is entirely with us. . . . Let us see how it is treated by Captain Mahan, who above all men, by his genius and learning is entitled to give judgment."[27] Though Corbett had serious reservations about much of Mahan's theory, he was not above using the American's popularity to bolster his own argument. Mahan returned the favor by including Corbett's article "The Capture of Private Property at Sea" in an edited volume titled *Some Neglected Aspects of War.*

Those who supported restrictions on the capture of merchant shipping tended to use the term "private property" to describe bulk cargoes. Neither Mahan nor Corbett considered this a fair descriptor since maritime commerce included the resources that fed populations, drove economies, fueled militaries, and indirectly financed wars. Mahan explained, "There is fallacy, for the term private property is misleading. Goods embarked for the purpose of trade are undoubtedly the property of individuals, and in so far, private property; but in a very important sense they differ from private property which is not being used for purposes of exchange." He maintained, "It is against commerce only that the present practice of seizing the merchant ships and cargoes of an enemy is directed. The strictly private property of the individuals on board them for purposes of trade is inviolate."[28] Mahan in 1906 explained, "You probably know that our Government has proposed for the next Hague Conference (as it did at the last) the freedom from capture of 'private property,' so called, at sea. I believe that to do this would be to surrender much of that control in which Sea Power consists."[29]

The effects of limiting the capture of merchant commerce would be far reaching: "A government . . . would do well before surrendering existing powers . . . to consider rather the geographical position of the country, its relation to maritime routes—the strategy, so to say, of the general permanent situation—and the military principles upon which maritime capture rests."[30] A navy's primary means of exerting political pressure entailed economic warfare because it could regulate merchant commerce. Mahan knew of no other means of applying similar pressure.[31] Maritime commerce equated to "money in circulation. It is the life-blood of national prosperity, upon which war depends; and as such is national in its employment." Elsewhere he expressed the belief that "to stop such circulation is to sap national prosperity; and to sap prosperity, upon which war depends for its energy, is a measure as truly military as is killing the men whose arms maintain war in the field."[32] Mahan went so far as to claim that by limiting or preventing the capture of commerce "you will have removed one of the most efficient preventatives of war."[33] The crippling economic effects resulting from the elimination of merchant commerce deterred war and made sea power a potent weapon.

Whereas Mahan protested against using the term "private property" to describe merchant cargo, Corbett indirectly attacked the concept of restricting a belligerent's ability to take merchant ships. Denying the capture of maritime commerce assumed "that war consists entirely of battles between armies or fleets." This view was fallacious because "it ignores the fundamental fact that battles are only the means of enabling you to do that which really brings wars to an end—that is, to exert pressure on the citizens and their collective life."[34] Corbett argued,

> This becomes clear so soon as we fix the fact that naval warfare has for its end and its means the control of sea communication. That is to say, control of sea communication afloat has exactly the same value as conquest of territory ashore. You cannot conquer sea, for it is not the subject of ownership. You cannot subsist upon it, and you cannot exclude neutrals from it. All you can do is to appropriate the value which it has in the political system of the world as between you and your enemy.[35]

Corbett agreed with Mahan that commerce deterred war and that the financial cost resulting from the capture of merchant shipping during wartime tended to cause states to question the value of their wartime objectives.[36] Given Britain's naval dominance, Corbett attempted to enhance Britain's strategic position in the opening years of the twentieth century by making its potential opponent, Germany, more vulnerable to attacks on its commerce. To this end, Andrew Lambert, a historian who has written widely on Corbett, claims that he tried to manipulate the legal frameworks relating to the capture of commercial shipping to amplify naval power.[37] Assessing Britain's potential opponents, Corbett explained, "So long as the right of private capture at sea exists, they stand to lose in every maritime war immediately and inevitably whatever the ultimate result may be."[38]

Seizing a nation's maritime commerce, Mahan claimed, "touches every member of the hostile community, and, by thus distributing the evils of war, as insurance distributes the burden of other losses, it brings them home to every man, fostering in each a disposition to peace."[39] War had to be terrible. "The furor of war needs all the chastening it can receive in the human heart, to still the mad impulses toward conflict," Mahan insisted.[40] He had seen this firsthand during the U.S. Civil War: "To the downfall of the Confederacy, no single cause conduced more than did the entire destruction of its commerce. . . . The destruction of the Confederacy's commerce was but one cause in the result, and it was indirect in action; but, like some deep-seated local disease, it poisoned the springs of life, spreading with remorseless certainty through innumerable hidden channels into every part of the political frame, till the whole was faint unto death."[41] The destruction of its trade rots a society from within, leaving it vulnerable to the direct actions of military force.

Corbett agreed. Dominant naval powers had two choices: they could enable other instruments of power such as the land force or diplomacy, or they could act alone. If the latter, a navy's most important effects derived from waging war on commercial shipping.[42] Corbett even went so far to assert, "The reason why naval officers urge with heart and soul the retention of the old right of capture is because they know not how to make war without it, nor can any man tell them."[43]

Naval power has limited capability to terminate war when employed in isolation, largely because people live on land and warships operate at sea. An army can occupy territory or threaten the places where people reside; navies cannot generate the same effect. Instead, navies must coerce indirectly by seizing commerce. Acting against commerce to generate political effects does not result in a clear line of causality between the action and the result. This makes naval power unpredictable and often slow to take effect.

THE ABSTRACT CONCEPT

Naval Action — yields → Political Object

HOW NAVIES ACTING WITHOUT OTHER INSTRUMENTS OF POWER OBTAIN EFFECTS IN THE REAL WORLD

5.1. **The Employment of Naval Power in Isolation**

Given the interconnectedness of global commerce, attacking trade tends to affect parties beyond the intended target, including allies and neutrals. The tendency for neutrals to seek financial gain in times of war by attempting to trade with all belligerents adds complexity and increases the points of friction in commerce warfare. As neutrals take on more and more international commerce, all the belligerents fail to benefit equally. The dominant maritime state relies less on neutral shipping because it generally controls significant maritime commerce under its own flag. Weaker maritime states are less successful at protecting their own commerce and thus find neutral shipping a valuable way to shield their commercial interactions. Moreover, dominant sea powers need to be wary of wartime commercial gains by neutrals because these might become permanent.[44]

"It may be taken as a law of maritime warfare, which cannot be omitted from strategical calculation with impunity, that every step towards gaining command of the sea tends to turn neutral sea powers into enemies," Corbett cautioned. "The prolonged exercise of belligerent rights . . . becomes more and more oppressive. But the process is usually accelerated as the sense of power inclines the dominating belligerent to push its privileges beyond admitted limits."[45] By labeling this a "law" Corbett took a definitive stance, for a "law" is considered universally correct. It was quite rare for him to elevate a concept to that level of certainty. But this wording underscores its significance within Corbett's argument.

Both theorists also contended that the seizure of commerce was among the most humane ways of waging war. Mahan claimed, "It conduces directly to the ends of war by producing a bloodless exhaustion, compelling submission, and that at the least expense of life and suffering."[46] Corbett added, "No form of war indeed causes so little human suffering as the capture of property at sea. It is more akin to process of law, such as distress for rent, or execution of judgment, or arrest of a ship, than to a military operation."[47] Both men, however, failed to account for the suffering ashore when states were unable to trade. Before World War I, Britain and Germany had become increasingly dependent on maritime food imports. British naval leaders certainly understood both their own vulnerability and Germany's. Thus it is not surprising that Britain attempted to restrict Germany's trade during World War I, or that doing so contributed to starvation.[48] Though it caused significant suffering, it had the desired effect by weakening Germany's population. In the century since World War I, this type of vulnerability has only increased with globalization.

THE SEA LINES OF COMMUNICATION

We have yet to consider the medium through which maritime commerce flows. Just as today, the majority of people at the turn of the twentieth century had difficulty conceptualizing events that took place at sea. This is particularly true of the sea lines of communication: Mahan found that even naval officers had difficulty determining their significance, for he claimed, "The question of communications does not appeal as strongly to the naval mind as to the military."[49]

The sea's "greatest value to mankind is that it furnishes the most copious means of communication and traffic between peoples," Mahan observed.[50] He explained,

- Nothing unites as does the sea; through it nations most easily communicate with one another.
- The first and most obvious light in which the sea presents itself from the political and social point of view is that of a great highway; or better, perhaps, of a wide common, over which men may pass in all directions, but on which some well-worn paths show that controlling reasons have led them to choose certain lines of travel than others. These lines of travel are called trade routes.
- In itself the sea is a barren tenure; only as the great common, the highway of commerce, the seat of communications, does it possess unique character and value. The concrete expression of this singular importance of the sea is the merchandise in transit, the increment from which constitutes the material prosperity of nations. Surrender control of that, and the empire of the sea is like unto Samson shorn of his hair.[51]

Similarly, Corbett noted, "The only value which the sea has in international relations is as a means of communication between states and parts of states. Whatever our strength, we can secure no more than this." And "when, therefore, we have gained control of communications we have gained everything there is to gain."[52]

During their lifetimes, the sea was valuable for other reasons as well, of course, including fisheries, but compared with commerce these other factors were insignificant.[53] Today, the sea has worth that Mahan and Corbett never conceived, but even so, its significance as a commercial highway should be weighed against all else. Even oil pumped from the ocean floor must often be transported across the water to be refined and consumed.

Sea lines of communication played an essential role in both theorists' strategic calculations. Corbett asserted, "The whole theory of maritime warfare . . . is a mere question of communications."[54] He added, "This view that true naval warfare, as opposed to coastal operations, means nothing but the control of lines of passage and communication, though it is not always clearly recognized, is of the utmost importance." He went on to label his argument "the communication theory of naval warfare."[55] Mahan agreed: "Water being the greatest, simplest, and easiest mode of communication between countries, imparts to naval warfare its most determinative feature."[56] Describing the lines of communications, he claimed, "As an element of strategy they devour all other elements"; navies were "the guardians of the communications."[57] Most significantly, Mahan argued, "They are the most important single element of strategy, political or military. In its control over them has lain the pre-eminence of sea power."[58] Navies influence what occurs on the sea lines of communication in peacetime and control communications in times of war.

The denial or protection of the sea lines of communication prevents or allows the movement of information, commerce, and even armies. Neither theorist thought that securing control of the sea lines of communication would by itself yield victory; instead, it served as an intermediate objective and, for a maritime state, the prerequisite to victory.

Both believed that the lines of communication at sea differ from those ashore. Consider the most obvious physical characteristics: the sea is as much a barrier as it is a means of communication. On the one hand, it requires specialized equipment to cross, particularly in comparison with a road that can be traversed by foot. On the other hand, physical geography tends to restrict mobility ashore. Rivers, swamps, forests, and mountains impede and channel movement. At sea, Corbett concluded, "neither roads nor obstacles exist" if one possesses a ship. Mahan agreed: "By nature, the land is almost all obstacle, the sea almost all open plain."[59]

Mahan realized that he could not blindly apply what Jomini wrote about lines of communication ashore to naval warfare. While Jomini emphasized "communication between the army and its base," Mahan emphasized "the maintenance of communications between these depots and the home base."[60] By substituting "depots" for "the army," Mahan signaled a prime difference between naval warfare and land warfare. Rather than link the fleet with its base, Mahan linked the homeland with areas of the globe where the state engaged in commercial exchange. The fleet protected these links. Moreover, the fleet, unlike an army, could operate for considerable periods independent of its bases of resupply.[61] "In this respect the navy is essentially a light corps," argued Mahan; "it keeps open the communications between its own ports, it obstructs those of the enemy; but it sweeps the sea for the service of the land, it controls the desert that man may live and thrive on the habitable globe."[62] Using the desert as an analogy, Mahan noted that sea lines link settlements much as trade routes link oases.

Both theorists maintained that the sea lines of communication could be common to all states.[63] Corbett explained, "On land the respective communications of the two belligerents start from widely separated bases and approach each other from more or less opposite directions . . . at sea they are usually parallel, if not identical."[64] Corbett labeled this "the key note of Naval Strategy," and claimed, "This condition never occurs ashore."[65] Corbett's argument, however, had a great deal to do with geography. At the time he wrote, Britain's most likely opponents were on the European continent. Britain's proximity to these states and the nature of their overseas trade routes led him to focus on the commonality of the sea lines of communications. Though Mahan recognized this factor, the geographic position of the United States resulted in different conditions. The sea lines of communication tended to stretch from the United States toward its potential opponents, and vice versa. Thus, Mahan saw sea lines of communication as being similar to lines of communication ashore.[66]

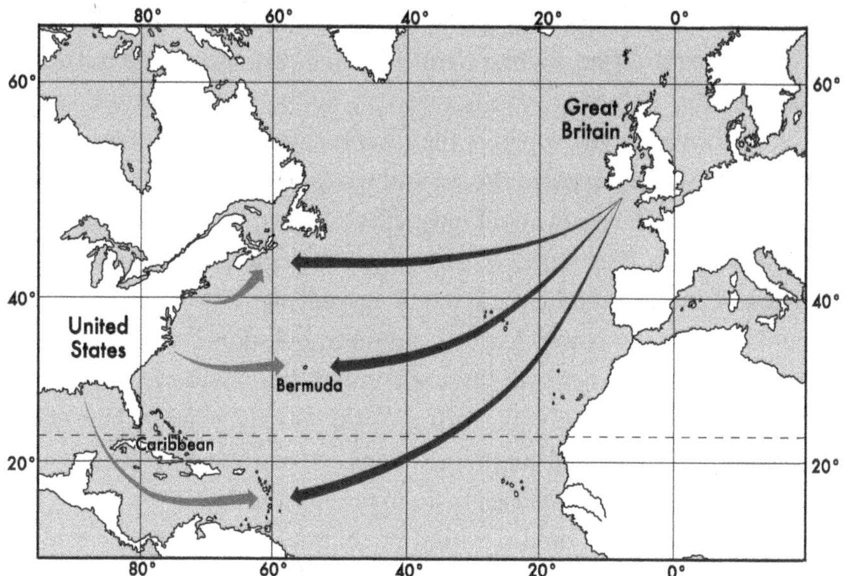

5.2. **Converging Sea Lines of Communication between Great Britain and the United States**

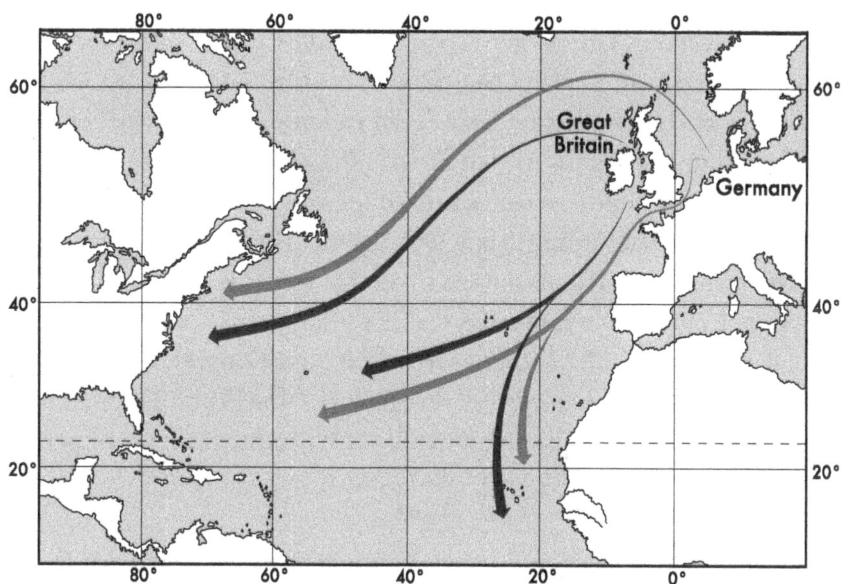

5.3. **Parallel Sea Lines of Communication between Great Britain and Germany**

Historically, water communications were far more efficient than their terrestrial equivalents. Mahan claimed, "Land carriage, always restricted and therefore always slow, toils enviously but hopelessly behind, vainly seeking to replace and supplant the royal highway of nature's own making."[67] States with access to the sea and navigable waterways penetrating deep into their interiors could most effectively exploit the lines of communication. In that sense, America's geostrategic position—including its coasts, harbors, and river systems—gave it significant advantages in the pursuit of sea power. Corbett, however, questioned the continuing superiority of sea lines over lines of communication ashore. Much had changed since the age of sail. During World War I he pondered the effectiveness of German land communications and concluded, "We can't beat him by sea carriage as we used to do in pre-railway days."[68]

While Mahan tailored the lines of communication argument to fit the United States, Corbett did the same for Britain. Unlike the United States, whose size and resources made defending the sea lines of communication a choice rather than a necessity, Britain was a small, insular state with limited resources and a global empire accessible only via maritime communications. One writer explained in 1884 that "two-thirds of all the bread eaten in England has come to be grown over the sea." If the sea lines of communication were "even endangered, our existence is at stake." Those in Britain who dealt with the national defense were well aware that maritime commerce carried the very food that Britons relied on to survive.[69] According to one 1908 report, "The margin within which all trades are carried on is now so small that very slight losses will mean ruin, not only to the trade affected, but also to a vast number of others dependent on it." Another government report from the years before World War I painted an even starker picture: "The British Empire floats on the British Navy. It is our all in all. . . . We must win at sea or perish as a nation."[70]

▪ ▪ ▪

Both theorists developed economic arguments, beginning with foundational concepts about finance and trade. Statements on these subjects informed more specific assertions about the sea lines of communication. At the broadest levels, Corbett and Mahan largely agreed on the importance of economics and finance. While Mahan focused more broadly across the peace–war continuum, Corbett described the functions of economics and finance in war. This paralleled what each thought his respective nation needed to learn. Mahan argued for the decisive importance of economic and financial power in national security while Corbett thought the same factors enabled state policies.

The latter appears to be a major point of disagreement between the two theorists, but the difference might be less than it first seems. Mahan considered a focus on economic issues to be critical for a maritime state, because economic strength attracts allies and forces opponents into self-defeating actions. Corbett saw the economy as an integral tool for furthering a maritime state's diplomatic actions and operations ashore. Remove the power a maritime state accrues through its economic strength and the state lacks the finances to support diplomatic, land, or even naval action. This was in effect Mahan's argument.

Thus, both men saw economics and commerce as critical. Both agreed that a strong economy insulated the maritime state from defeat and enhanced the effects of its other instruments of power. The issue of agency is where they disagreed. Mahan provided greater agency to the navy: if a state succeeded at sea, everything else tended to fall into place. Corbett believed a state needed to use all of its instruments of power effectively to first enable and then obtain victory.

As the two developed their economic arguments, their theories converged even more. Their views on maritime trade in wartime are virtual copies of one another. In respect to the sea lines of communication, both theories illustrate what Corbett labeled "the communication theory of naval war."[71] One must dig deeply to find divergences in their theories. These are not so much disagreements as differences resulting from national perspective.

CHAPTER 6
COMMAND OF THE SEA

In 1910, Cyprian Bridge, a retired British admiral, asserted, "The expression 'Command of the sea,' . . . in its proper and strategic sense, is so firmly fixed in the language that it would be a hopeless task to try to expel it; and as, no doubt, writers will continue to use it, it must be explained and illustrated."[1] Two years later the problem remained: "The true meaning of the phrase 'command of the sea' which is constantly in every one's mouth is still very little comprehended in many quarters. Yet there ought to be no room for misconception concerning an idea which lies at the root of all maritime strategy." This writer pleaded, "If we do not clearly understand what is meant by command of the sea and still more what is not meant by it, we cannot even begin to think profitably about maritime strategy at all."[2] But what is "command of the sea"? According to the statements above, it is both central to naval strategy and often misunderstood. We cannot proceed until its meaning is clear, because the concept is also central to the theories of both Mahan and Corbett.

As an idea, "command of the sea" dates to at least the fifth century BC when Thucydides implied the concept in writings about the Peloponnesian War. Sir Francis Bacon used the term in the early seventeenth century as he reflected on the role of navies from antiquity to the Battle of Lepanto (1571).[3] In the late nineteenth century, several writers reengaged the concept, among them Theodore Roosevelt, Sir John Colomb, and especially Vice Admiral Philip Colomb.[4] The latter published *Naval Warfare* nearly concurrently with Mahan's publication of *The Influence of Sea Power upon History*. Much like the works of Mahan, Philip Colomb's writings informed a generation of naval commentators.[5] He explained, "The control of the sea, or what I shall now and hereafter call by its established title, the 'Command of the Sea,' was henceforth to be understood as the aim of naval war."[6] Though Colomb cemented "command of the sea" as part of the modern strategic lexicon, he failed to define it clearly. Donald Schurman contends that Colomb's description "virtually declared that naval war was an end itself and not the means to an end."[7] Both Corbett and Mahan endeavored to make sense of the concept.

The unique character of the sea framed Corbett's understanding of command of the sea. He did not believe that the ocean was subject to conquest in the same way that land could be occupied.[8] His argument mirrored a concept of international maritime law dating back to at least the early seventeenth century when Hugo Grotius claimed, "The sea . . . cannot become subject to private ownership."[9] Corbett explained, "The utmost, then, that we can acquire at sea is something wholly different from the conquest of territory ashore, and to argue from the one to the other is to lay course to certain error."[10]

Even though Corbett did not believe that the sea could be conquered, a navy can still regulate movement across its surface. In the Green Pamphlet, Corbett argued that command of the sea meant "establishing ourselves in such a position that we can control the maritime communications of all parties concerned."[11] His definition of "all parties" encompassed friends, foes, and even neutrals. "The object of naval warfare," he wrote in *Some Principles of Maritime Strategy*, "must always be directly or indirectly either to secure the command of the sea or prevent the enemy from securing it."[12]

Corbett maintained that naval power, when acting alone, could influence the outcome of a war only through its ability to command the sea; regulating what occurred at sea influenced events ashore. The importance of controlling the sea lines of communication depended entirely on the degree to which a state relied on the sea.[13] The more essential maritime commerce and movement was to a state's economic and security systems, the greater the significance of command of the sea.

Like Corbett, Mahan used his understanding of the nature of the maritime environment to inform his views, and his argument parallels Corbett's in significant ways. "The value of the Sea to nations is as a means of communication, the greatest, the easiest and the best," Mahan explained.

"To control the communications, therefore, to one's own use, and to exclude the enemy from them is the strategic aim, the one thing to which all naval movements tend, and in which they find their unity."[14] Mahan did not develop his arguments as systematically as Corbett did; nor was he as consistent with his terminology: Mahan used the phrase "control of the sea" interchangeably with "command of the sea."[15] This should not be surprising, for Colomb in contemporaneous writings also linked the terms. In *The Influence of Sea Power upon History,* Mahan more frequently used "control of the sea," but in his final major work, *Naval Strategy Compared and Contrasted,* he used the terms in similar proportions.[16]

Mahan described control of the sea as "the one supreme decisive object of her [a nation's] naval operations," "the great object of naval warfare," and "the one clear and necessary aim of naval warfare."[17] Mahan's evaluation of the importance of command of the sea in effect aligned with Colomb's argument that command of the sea was the aim of naval warfare. Mahan also linked control of the sea to his view that certain principles of war remained the same from age to age: "Methods of fighting, like methods of motion, change; the object, the command of the sea, the control of the great system of highways, by which ships traverse it, remains the same."[18] Once again Mahan argued that technologies affect tactical applications but not the underlying strategic principle.

For Mahan, however, command of the sea was the object of naval operations, not the object of national strategy: "The mere command of the sea is a barren acquisition except as leading to something more."[19] Mahan asked his readers not to become infatuated with obtaining command of the sea; leaders should always keep the political objective clearly in view. In this area, his argument and Corbett's overlap.

There are levels of command of the sea. Both Mahan and Corbett agreed that it could be local or general, temporary or permanent. As a rule, local command tends to be temporary, and general command is more likely to be permanent.[20] "The control of the sea," Mahan wrote, "even in general, and still more in particularly restricted districts, has at times and for long periods remained in doubt; the balance inclining now to this side, now to that."[21] Mahan took the concept further than Corbett in linking "overwhelming control of the sea" to "making it [the sea] as

One could conceptualize command of the sea as a spectrum, with disputed command in the middle and each side in a conflict attempting to pull command to its side of the spectrum.

6.1. **Command of the Sea as a Spectrum**

it were its own territory."[22] With such control, Mahan argued, one side could reach a level of command that nearly corresponded to occupation of an opponent's country. Corbett refused to go that far.

Both men were careful to explain that even permanent command did not equate to absolute security; ships would be lost and setbacks would occur. Mahan claimed, "Absolute immunity from injury, occasionally even grave, is a vain dream of those who would fain wage war without running risks. In sober conception, 'control' means such use of the water as a man has of a well-established business; not liable to failure, but also not exempt from reverses."[23] Corbett agreed: permanent command meant that opponents could still act, but only at great risk.[24]

Some might argue that command is less about control of the sea than about relative dominance. The side with command is relatively stronger than its opponents and thus can more effectively use the seas for its own purposes. This certainly reflects the two men's definitions and how control applied historically, but it also signals a significant weakness in their vocabulary. The words "command" and "control" signal absolutes when in fact the theorists' definitions indicate something far less categorical.

There is another critical weakness in both theories. Corbett wrote for the established sea power and Mahan for a rising sea power. Neither man pondered the utility of a vastly inferior navy. Neither developed serious arguments for states with more limited maritime ambitions that in peacetime included maritime policing and enforcing good order at sea. Neither focused significant attention on what weak naval powers could accomplish in wartime through strategies aimed at making it more costly and difficult for dominant navies to command the sea.

So far, their arguments about command of the sea show little divergence. Mahan, however, took his discussion of command of the sea in a secondary direction that brought him into the realm of grand strategy, and in doing so confused and obscured his argument. Mahan called control of the sea the "predominant influence in the world; because, however great the wealth product of the land, nothing facilitates the necessary exchanges as does the sea." Elsewhere, he called control "chief among the merely material elements in the power and prosperity of nations."[25] He insisted that "national and international functions can be discharged, certainly only by command of the sea . . . the exponent of which is the navy, and in which ships and stations are interdependent factors. To place the conclusion concretely and succinctly, the question of command of the sea is one of annual increase of the navy. This question is not 'naval,' in the restricted sense of the word. It is one of national policy, national security, and national obligation."[26] This argument linked command of the sea with the idea of sea power and how it could provide a theory of security.

As is often the case when comparing their naval strategic theories, one must search for nuggets among Mahan's many writings while Corbett presented his arguments with the precision of a trained lawyer. Corbett saw command of the sea as "only a means to an end. It never has been, and never can be, the end itself." Command of the sea indicated the degree of leverage a state possessed in the naval domain. "Yet obvious as this is," Corbett chided, "it is constantly lost sight of in naval policy."[27] In this, he seemed to be criticizing his American counterpart for expressing multiple meanings of the term depending upon the level of his analysis. At the grand strategic level, Mahan pointed toward command of the sea being an objective or an end state, while his definition merged with Corbett's when he was speaking of naval strategy and operations.

OBTAINING COMMAND OF THE SEA: THE QUEST FOR BATTLE

Both theorists wrote for and about states with navies capable of fighting fleet-on-fleet engagements. Victory in battle could solidify command of the sea while defeat could bequeath that advantage to the opponent. Though battle served as one of the defining aspects of naval warfare, Corbett reminded his audience:

> We forget what really happened in the old wars; we blind ourselves by looking only on the dramatic moments of naval history; we come unconsciously to assume that the defeat of the enemy's fleets solves all problems, and that we are always free and able to apply this apparently simple solution. Thus, until quite recent years, naval thought had tended to confine itself to the perfection of the weapon and to neglect the art of using it. Or, in other words, it had come to feel its sole concern was fighting, and had forgotten the art of making war.[28]

Balancing the risk of battle with its rewards required a thorough understanding of the naval instrument and national objectives.

Of the two theorists, Mahan focused more on the advantages of battle, emphasizing offensive operations against the opposing fleet to obtain command of the sea: "The one object of a navy is to control the sea; the direct corollary from which is that its objective is the enemy's navy—his organized force afloat." Other missions were secondary. He argued emphatically, "'Kill the ships' is the first demand of naval warfare."[29] His emphasis on battle derived from his reading of Jomini.[30] Mahan never changed this view. He stated it in *The Influence of Sea Power upon History* in 1890, and reiterated it more than twenty years later in his last major work.[31] His insistence reflected theories of continental warfare that extolled the primacy of the offense and the necessity of bringing overwhelming force to bear on the opponent's armed forces with the object of annihilation.[32]

Though Mahan was adamant regarding the importance of naval battle, he was not extremely clear as to how it yielded the desired strategic effects. A casual reading of his works reveals statements such as "control of the sea must be established by a battle, more or less decisive" and "to destroy the French fleet was the one thing for which the British fleet was there, and the one thing by doing which it could decisively affect the war."[33] He indicated that battles are "decisive," but what did that word mean for Mahan? As previously noted, the word "decisive" is a charged term more often used than clearly defined. While some argue that "decisive" events lead directly to a war's end, Mahan argued that "decisive" events ensure the outcome.

Like many of his concepts, his views on battle are more nuanced than a cursory perusal of his writings suggests. Mahan did not condone fighting battles on all occasions, admonishing his readers to avoid "the sterile glory of fighting battles merely to win them."[34] "Unless the position won is strategically decisive, by its correspondence to the conditions of the war or of the nation, the battle might as well, or better, never have been fought."[35] Moreover, he added that if "control of the sea . . . can be attained equally well by other means, the battle fleet should be preserved as both a political and military factor of the first importance."[36] One should risk the fleet only to obtain political objectives.

"The disabling or destruction of battleships, one or many, . . . is itself only a means, not an end, and the two cannot be confounded," wrote Mahan.[37] "If the true end is to preponderate over the enemy's navy and so control the sea, then the enemy's ships and fleets are the true objects to be assailed on all occasions." In other words, one fights a sea battle neither to win the war nor to sink the opposing fleet, but rather to "control the sea." Battles are the most effective means of shifting the command of the sea. The object of battle "is to break up the enemy's power on the sea, cutting off his communications with the rest of his possessions, drying up the sources of his wealth in his commerce, and making possible a closure of his ports." Permanently obtaining such effects can occur only by destroying "his organized military forces afloat; in short, his navy."[38]

Corbett strongly disagreed and crafted a sarcastic response to Mahan's argument: "The only way of securing such a command [of the sea] by naval means is to obtain a decision by battle against the enemy's fleet. Sooner or later it must be done, and the sooner the better. That was the old British creed. It is still our creed, and needs no labouring."

Mocking the prevailing mindset of British naval officers, who longed to emulate Nelson in quest of a twentieth-century Trafalgar, Corbett noted: "No one will dispute it, no one will care even to discuss it, and we pass with confidence to the conclusion that the first business of our fleet is to seek out the enemy's fleet and destroy it. . . . To examine its claim to be the logical conclusion of our theory of war will even be held dangerous."[39] Corbett later summed up his objection: "By a strange misreading of history, an idea had grown up that its primary function is to seek out and destroy the enemy's main fleet."[40]

Corbett linked this battle-hungry ethos to foreign sources, Mahan chief among them.[41] He went so far as to label the quest for the decisive naval battle a "crude Mahanism" and chastised those who considered it "a panacea for all strategical difficulties." He told a confidant, "This as you know is the idea I always fight against."[42] The great Japanese naval victory over the Russian fleet at Tsushima in 1905 and Japan's subsequent victory in the Russo-Japanese War did nothing to dispel the impression that Mahan was correct.[43]

Naval battle itself was not the issue, for Corbett considered it a legitimate tool of naval strategy. He in fact labeled battle the fleet's "cardinal function" and asserted that a fleet "cannot get absolute command" without it.[44] These statements parallel Mahan's argument, showcasing an often-overlooked similarity between the two theorists. Battle was certainly an advantageous course of action for the dominant naval power. Corbett even argued, "Nine times out of ten the maxim of seeking out the enemy's fleet . . . is sound and applicable."[45] The strategist must, however, determine the exception.

One could even argue that Corbett purposely downplayed the role of battle in naval strategy as a counterargument against the prevailing mentality. His students, the British naval leadership, and what passed for defense intellectuals in England had become infatuated with battle. One 1905 report, for example, noted, "The first duty of British fleets and squadrons will be to seek out the corresponding fleets and squadrons of the enemy with a view to bringing them to action and fighting for that which is the only really decisive factor—the command of the sea." And in 1907, the commander of Britain's Channel Fleet called the quest for the decisive battle "so evident, it seems a platitude to mention it."[46] That faith in battle remained hard to shake. During World War I, one of Corbett's friends lamented that British naval leaders "by a crude reading of Mahan, have absorbed the idea that all naval war consists in a battle of Armageddon."[47]

The war did not change Corbett's mind. A review of his official history of the naval war included the following critique: "There is nowhere in Sir Julian's volume such a definite enunciation of the truth that the first aim of a fleet is to defeat and destroy the hostile fighting force."[48] Powerful voices opposed Corbett's argument: his response to the opposition overcompensated, minimizing the significance of battle more than his theory required.

Corbett warned that battle did not always occur where and when the stronger side desired it. "That largest & most efficient fleet cannot always get a decision [battle] by successful activities," he insisted. Many factors had to align to bring about a battle.[49] World War I only confirmed that conclusion. He even fell victim himself. In his official naval history, Corbett's consternation is almost palpable when he described almost perfectly executed Royal Navy deployments in December 1914 that failed to destroy a German squadron raiding the British coast.[50]

"In applying the maxim of 'seeking out the enemy's fleet' it should be borne in mind that if you seek it out with a superior force you will probably find it in a place where you cannot destroy it, except at very heavy cost. It is far better to make it come to you, and this has often been done by merely sitting on the common communications."[51] His historical studies indicated that placing a fleet at focal or terminal point along the sea lines of communication created conditions that most favored battle. "When we say that the primary object of our battle fleets must always be the destruction of the battle fleets of the enemy, what we really mean is that the primary function of our battle fleets is to seize and prevent the enemy from seizing the main lines of communication." Corbett added that the proper course of action "must always be to get our battle fleet at once into such position that it occupies the common lines of communication, and so compels the enemy either to accept the situation or to break it down by battle."[52]

During World War I, Corbett assessed the effects of Britain's naval concentration in home waters. By dominating the North Sea, Britain gained command of the sea in the world writ large. Germany was cut off from maritime trade because the German navy was too weak to break the Royal Navy's iron grip. Germans starved as a result. Geography coupled with naval dominance allowed the Royal Navy to maintain a position that placed the Germans on the horns of a dilemma. If the German people were not to starve, the outnumbered fleet had to fight to break the blockade. "There was always the hope," Corbett noted, "that the pressure so exercised would sooner or later force him to offer battle."[53] Though words signaled his wish, he admitted privately, "I have never believed the Huns would risk their hold on the Baltic by coming into the N. Sea to fight us & I still don't believe they will except in a fit of mad desperation."[54]

Mahan likewise understood the importance of the lines of communication and their strategic significance. He even wrote of "the decisive effect exercised upon any strategic position, or movement, by a valid threat against the communications."[55] The difference between the two is the context of battle. While the act of battle dominated the American's arguments, Corbett concentrated on the difficulties of obtaining an advantageous battle and trying to find other strategic choices when the opponent refused to fight.

The difference in their arguments reflects their national perspectives. Dominant naval powers like Britain traditionally face difficulties when seeking battle because weaker fleets shy away from contests: the weaker fleet does not wish to die. Mahan wrote for the United States, a rising naval power, with the understanding that an inferior fleet can take advantage of the dominant fleet's desire for battle by being selectively aggressive. Battle is thus a more likely course of action for a naval power that does not possess permanent command of the sea, while the dominant naval power must rely on deception to engage the weaker fleet.

Without careful reading, both theorists can be easily misunderstood with respect to battle. It may seem that Mahan viewed battle as the end in itself, but this is not the case. That interpretation is merely the result of his convoluted writing or a selective reading of his works. Corbett is also frequently misunderstood. He did not disparage battle: if attainable, it was the surest way to take command of the sea by permanently altering the naval balance. All other courses of action, including blockades, were temporary expedients in comparison.

NAVAL BLOCKADES

Blockade proves useful in a variety of contexts. A naval blockade is a means of restricting the movement of the opponent's warships: it aims at temporary command of the sea. A commercial blockade, which restricts merchant shipping, is possible only for a navy that possesses command of the sea. A commercial blockade does nothing to affect the naval balance; its purpose is to influence events ashore. Since both Mahan and Corbett considered naval blockade a means of commanding the sea, this section focuses on naval blockade. Given its different objective, commercial blockade will be introduced in chapter 10 to explain how it is a means of using command of the sea to affect events ashore.

Though battle provides a quicker, more permanent means of obtaining command of the sea, it may not be possible or desirable. The naval blockade provides an option in such cases, but nothing is simple when it comes to naval blockades. As Mahan explained, "'Bottling' a hostile fleet does not resemble the chance and careless shoving of cork into half-used bottle,—it is rather like the wiring down of champagne by bonds that cannot be broken and through which nothing can ooze."[56] While this quote highlights the intricacy of the subject, it fails to consider that the primary aim of a blockade might not even be the confinement of the opposing fleet. The quote by Mahan is in fact indicative of the general lack of precision in his writings on blockades. In comparison, Corbett developed the advanced course on the subject. As such, Mahan's theories will serve as a springboard into Corbett's more complex considerations.

Though Mahan published an article on blockades and discussed blockades in several of his works, he had a tendency to describe a broad range of operations under the umbrella of "blockade." Indeed, he did not always differentiate between commercial and naval blockades.[57]

Naval blockades can have two purposes: the blockader seeks either to lure the opposing fleet out to fight or to bottle it tightly in port. Regrettably, Mahan did not differentiate between the two courses of action. His explanations of Nelson's operations off Toulon (1803–5) in the Napoleonic Wars are an example. In one article, Mahan implied that Nelson's actions were a blockade, but later in the same article, he admitted, "It is well known that Nelson . . . emphatically rejected the term 'blockade' as applicable to his own operations before Toulon."[58] A decade later, he revisited the same example, noting this time that "the correct use" of the word "blockade" describes the "blocking of movement." Nelson's actions off Toulon were thus not properly a blockade, "for its object usually is not to keep the hostile fleet in, thus prolonging tension and exposure, but to tempt it out in order to bring the question to a quick decision." He concluded, "There will be, however, no great difference in method."[59] His failure to create specific terminology to differentiate the two courses of action tends to muddy his explanations of the different types of naval blockade.

The Spanish-American War (1898) provided Mahan with another example of a blockade. Early in the war, the United States deployed its fleet in blockade operations off the Cuban coast. The blockade's importance, Mahan claimed, "lay in its twofold tendency to exhaust the enemy's army in Cuba, and to force his navy to come to the relief. No effect more decisive than these two could be produced." He added, "The blockade . . . was the one decisive measure, sure though slow in its working, which could be taken the necessary effect of which was to bring the enemy's ships to this side of the ocean, unless Spain was prepared to abandon the contest."[60] This blockade created the best possible conditions for a U.S. victory. Either the Spanish would abandon Cuba, or the U.S. blockade would force the Spanish navy to steam across the Atlantic to reestablish communications—both unpalatable courses of action for Spain. Yet, was Mahan describing a commercial blockade or a naval blockade? His description seems to have elements of both, demonstrating the difficulty in categorizing blockades. A naval blockade likely has commercial objects, and commercial blockades might aim to influence the actions of the opposing fleet.

Mahan's position on blockades is problematic for his theory on several levels. As mentioned, he was not particularly careful when differentiating between naval and commercial blockades, often describing both as "blockades" and leaving it to the reader to grasp the difference. This probably reflected the significant overlap between the two types. Moreover, he tended to conflate naval blockades designed to keep the opposing fleet in port with deployments aimed at enticing the opponent to sail.

Corbett provided a more systematic approach to blockades. Britain, the dominant sea power at the turn of the twentieth century, was far more likely than a lesser naval power like the United States to conduct a blockade. It is telling that Mahan gave his most detailed description of blockades in a lecture to an audience in London.[61] Moreover, Corbett had the advantage that Britain's geographic position drove the Royal Navy to study blockade in the years before World War I. Unsurprisingly, Corbett's War College lectures often addressed blockades, and he refined his understanding of blockades under contemporary conditions by studying Japanese naval operations off Port Arthur in the Russo-Japanese War. These lectures served as a testing ground for a chapter in *Some Principles of Maritime Strategy*, in which Corbett concluded, "Under the term blockade we include operations which vary widely in character and in strategical intention." There was no such thing as just a blockade; a blockade was either naval or commercial. On the one hand, the commercial blockade was an aspect of using or exercising command of the sea. On the other hand, naval blockades, were "a method of securing command of the sea." He further broke naval blockades down into two types: "close" and "open."[62]

A close blockade attempted to hem the opposing fleet inside its anchorage using forward deployments. Both theorists used this term. Mahan argued, "The close blockade of the enemy's fleet . . . may be considered rather a defensive than an offensive operation; for though the intention certainly was to fight if opportunity offered, the chief object was to neutralize an offensive weapon in the enemy's hands; the destruction of the weapon was secondary."[63] Corbett agreed with Mahan's conclusion at the strategic level but then added a twist, claiming the tactical action was offensive: "We advance toward enemy we seize his lines at the starting point we operate in his waters."[64] Actions that demanded the tactical offense to obtain a strategically defensive object failed to align risk to the fleet with potential reward. Forward deployments increased the risks to warships, but being strategically defensive were unlikely to yield a war-winning result.

Mahan and Corbett also differed in their views of which fleet possessed the advantage: the blockaded fleet or the blockading fleet. Mahan recognized the wear and tear that the blockading squadron would sustain but thought that the longer the blockade persisted the more adverse the effects on the blockaded fleet's readiness and training would be. A blockaded fleet might look powerful, but time magnified the disparity in skill between the inactive blockaded force and the squadron doing the blockading.[65] The damage imposed on blockading ships by the sea would be more than offset by the decline in capability of those in port. Moreover, the moral advantage went to the blockader. Corbett disagreed: "As attack grows weaker as it advances so does blockade as it is prolonged owing to the moral & physical strain on personnel."[66] In all, Corbett considered "close naval blockade . . . one of the weakest and least desirable forms of war. Here again when we say 'weakest' we do not mean 'least effective,' but that it was exhausting, and that it tended to occupy a force greater than against which it was acting."[67] Close blockade had many disadvantages, but Corbett admitted that circumstances existed when it was strategically desirable to keep the opposing fleet trapped in port by close blockade.

Corbett labeled operations executed with the intent of luring the opponent outside its anchorage so as to engage in battle on the blockader's terms "open" blockade.[68] Though Mahan described this option, he was not precise with his terminology and tended to lump open blockades with close blockades in his writings. Corbett separated the two. Since an open blockade "aims at the destruction of an enemy's naval force," Corbett concluded that it had the advantage of being "a definite step towards securing permanent command." This was the strongest of combinations. Strategically, the aim was offensive—the destruction of the opposing fleet. To accomplish this object, the fleet assumed an advantageous defensive posture and forced the opponent to attack. Open blockade's primary

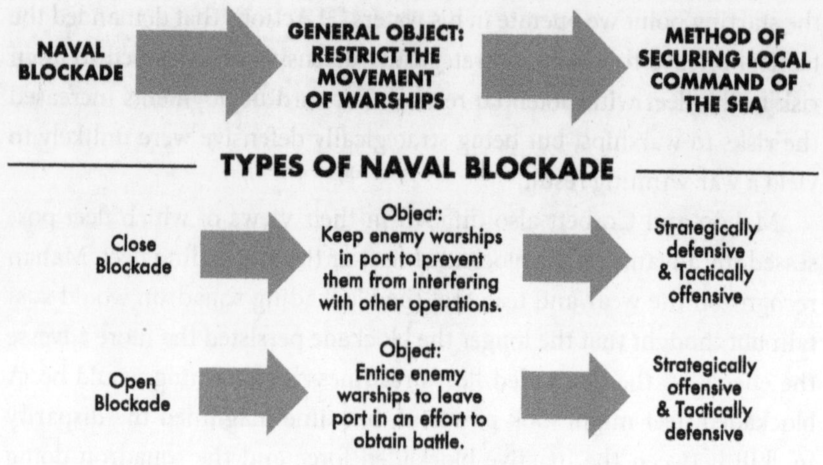

6.2. **Naval Blockades**

weakness was that it allowed the opponent the freedom to slip out single ships and small squadrons to raid commerce.[69]

Choosing between open and close blockade required answering the question "what are we trying to do?"[70] Corbett viewed a close blockade as "a method of securing local and temporary command." Confining an opposing fleet in port could facilitate other goals such as shielding a major amphibious operation or a commercial convoy. Without the rewards of such special circumstances, the extra risks incurred by a close blockade were unacceptable. Rather, Corbett argued, "It was to our interest to incline the enemy's mind towards the bolder choice. . . . The means was to tempt him with a prospect of success, either by leading him to believe the blockading force was smaller than it was, or by removing it to such a distance as would induce him to attempt to evade it, or both."[71] Corbett advised his students: "Therefore perhaps the nature of blockade should be determined by primary intention of the movement. . . . If to force enemy to action, it should be most distant possible observation compatible with ensuring contact if enemy comes out. . . . If it is mere question of communication and a decision is not sought for at the moment then it should be as close as possible."[72]

Historically, these uses of blockades might all have been correct, but questions emerged in the years before World War I about the continuing viability of blockades as new technologies like torpedoes, submarines, mines, and wireless threatened to undermine their usefulness and feasibility. In 1895 the Royal United Service Institution asked Mahan to speak on that very issue. He asserted that blockade was still a viable option: "Steam, in my opinion, has simply widened the question, not changed its nature."[73] This argument fit his broader theory that technologies change, but underlying principles remain constant.

Close blockade became increasingly dangerous as developments in torpedo technology provided the flotilla with increased battle power that magnified the risk to large surface combatants, particularly in the littorals. Minefields added to the danger. This was the beginning of what twenty-first-century practitioners would recognize as an anti-access, area denial environment.

While close blockade became riskier, the opportunities for open blockades expanded. Wireless communications made it much easier to maintain control at a distance. Scouting ships could report movements of the opposing fleet in real time, making it much more difficult for a blockaded force to escape port undetected. Corbett concluded, "As under modern developments the possibilities of open blockade have increased, so the difficulties and dangers of close blockade have certainly not decreased."[74]

The new technologies forced Corbett to revisit close and open blockades. In *Some Principles of Maritime Strategy*, he observed, "Nor must it be forgotten that for a squadron to take station off a port in the old manner is not the only means of close blockade." He explained, "Close blockade, . . . as formerly conceived, is generally regarded as no longer practicable; but the antithetical ideas, which the two forms of blockade connote, can never be eliminated from strategical consideration."[75] The principles of positioning ships to pin an opposing force in port or deploying warships to tempt the opposing fleet to escape so it can become snared in a trap remained viable options. Technology had affected the execution rather than the underlying principles.

The Russo-Japanese War provided the best contemporary examples for Corbett's analysis of the subject. It should be remembered that the volumes Corbett produced on that war were not designed for public consumption. They were staff studies utilizing restricted information, which allowed Corbett to develop a unique perspective on the effectiveness of blockades in the contemporary environment. Among other things, he concluded that mines benefited the blockading squadron. This might seem counterintuitive, but mines are tools available to both sides. The Japanese blockaders used minefields to restrict the ability of the Russian fleet to put to sea quickly. "It was a new factor in strategy of blockade which went far to obliterate any practical distinction between the close and the open form." Mines could do much of the work of a close blockade while the Japanese fleet assumed a position with the advantages of the open blockade. Steam propulsion and wireless communications gave the Japanese additional advantages. By restricting movements with mines, announcing the movements of the Russian fleet in real time with wireless, and using steam to facilitate the speed of their response, the Japanese approximated the close blockade of old. The effects of a close blockade remained possible even though it looked nothing like a close blockade from the age of sail.[76] The underlying principle remained the same even if the instrument's employment altered dramatically.

▪▪▪

Mahan's theory demanded—and Corbett's theory expected—a fleet capable of fighting a fleet-on-fleet engagement. Both believed that battle was the surest way to obtain permanent command of the sea. The two differed not on battle's strategic effects, but on the ability to obtain battle. When battle was not feasible, blockade provided opportunities for temporary or local command. But in the end, both theorists recognized that battle and blockade are merely means of obtaining command of the sea.

Even command of the sea was not the end state objective; rather it created conditions that brought a state closer to victory. Command is an intermediate object and serves as a point of departure for the remainder of this book. The next chapters will examine how offense, defense, and concentration guide the employment of force either to obtain or to contest command. Subsequent chapters on disputing and exercising command of the sea provide follow-on courses of action when one side possesses a high level of command.

CHAPTER 7

RECONCILING THE OFFENSE AND THE DEFENSE

"Every war," Mahan wrote, "has two aspects, the defensive and the offensive." Corbett agreed: "A clear apprehension of their relative possibilities is the corner stone of strategical study."[1] Mahan called offense and defense "complementary" but also "the opposing sides of war."[2] Though offense and defense work in conjunction, they express different attitudes. This subject requires a particularly careful reading of Mahan and Corbett. Their theories respecting offense and defense differ greatly from naval tactics, on one end of the spectrum, to a nation's political objectives, on the other.

In terms of political objectives, the two theorists are in lockstep agreement. Mahan provided his thoughts on policy objectives for the United States: "Politically, it has always been assumed in the United States, and very properly, that our policy should never be wantonly aggressive. . . . This it will be seen, is a political idea, one which serves for the guidance of the people, and of the statesmen of the country in determining—not *how* war is to be carried on, which is a military question, but—under what circumstances war is permissible, or unjust." Mahan elaborated: "A navy for defence only, in the *political* sense, means a navy that will only be used in case we are forced into war."[3] In reference to the political objective, Mahan emphasized defensive wars for the United States but also recognized the potential for offensive political objectives. The reason for war was a political matter decided upon by statesmen and, in democratic societies, the people.

Corbett agreed with Mahan that the decision for war was a political determination. Corbett did not develop theory to advocate for specific political objectives; that was the province of the political leadership.

Rather, Corbett recognized that political leaders might use force for political objectives that could be either offensive or defensive in nature. This was dependent on the interests of the nation.

On the other end of the spectrum, naval tactics entails the use of individual ships—or as Mahan described it, "the manner in which the battle was fought" when opposing warships are in "*contact.*"[4] The nature of the environment determines tactical possibilities. Mahan saw the sea as a wide common devoid of natural barriers. On land, rivers, hills, and swamps make movement more difficult and facilitate the tactical defense.[5] The lack of natural barriers at sea has historically pointed to the impossibility of prepared defensive positions. Unlike war on land, where one can entrench, use terrain for concealment, or profit by obstacles that slow and channel movements, naval tactics have traditionally relied on mobility and hitting first with overwhelming force. In fact, Corbett argued that tactical *defense* at sea occurs only under very narrow conditions.[6] Though Mahan generally avoided tactical discussions his general thoughts led him toward a similar conclusion. Tactically, warships in the open water had only one choice: the offense.

The previous paragraph charts the historical argument, but does that argument hold true in the twenty-first century? Striking first with overwhelming force remains critical, but concealment underwater or in terms of electromagnetic signatures as well as the employment of mines and anti-access, area-denial systems creates new possibilities for a naval defense. This is in part why Mahan was quite leery of applying principles of war to the level of tactics. Technological developments tend to upset previous tactical practice.

Moving to the realm of naval strategy, we find their theories diverge. Mahan maintained a visceral disdain for defense while Corbett was convinced of its necessity. On the surface, the two argued toward opposite poles, but in reality, they often talked past one another. Mahan's argument suffers from a lack of precision. His theories changed according to whether he was describing a naval battle, the general movement of a squadron, or the use of an entire navy, but the lack of clarity in his writing often makes it difficult to follow his thought process. He left it to the reader to piece his argument together. Corbett was more meticulous. He focused on minor strategy, which he defined as "'Naval Strategy' or better 'Fleet Strategy.' It deals with the Fleet alone, & regards the method of attaining the object of the war, rather than the object itself."[7] When Corbett ventured into more tactical issues, he was more likely than Mahan to inform his audience.

MAHAN ON OFFENSE AND DEFENSE IN NAVAL STRATEGY AND OPERATIONS

At the national level, Mahan maintained, "A blustering aggressiveness is as unbecoming in a nation as in an individual." However, his view changed "when the political movement has culminated into war, then we want a navy to be as aggressive as we can."[8] At the strategic, operational, and even tactical levels of naval war, Mahan emphasized the offense regardless of the political object. "The navy is the chief arm by which the offensive is to be carried on; for, while in the defense the navy plays a secondary role, in offensive naval war it takes a leading place."[9] Offensive action exploited the fleet's inherent mobility and paralleled prevailing military thought.

Warships at sea are much more mobile than troops on land. That mobility, Mahan wrote, is "the distinguishing feature of naval force."[10] Mobility drove navies during Mahan's lifetime toward the offense at the tactical level, and he extended this argument to the employment of fleets, insisting, "The navy, by its mobility, is preeminently fitted for offensive war."[11]

The Royal Navy's Nelsonian tradition drove Mahan even further toward theories aimed at seeking battle. Such arguments were received enthusiastically in Britain, where the offense during the century after Trafalger had attained an almost cultlike status.[12] Mahan's studies of British naval history in the age of sail enhanced his conviction of the importance of the offense.

The years before World War I also found theorists of land warfare extolling the offense. Mobilizing and acting first offered significant advantages.[13] It is not surprising that Mahan wrote the following:

- It must be added as a received military axiom that war . . . must be waged aggressively if it is to hope for success.

- Among all masters of military art—including therein naval art—it is a thoroughly accepted principle that mere defensive war means military ruin, and therefore national disaster.
- We have the highest military authority for saying that the best and only sure form of defence is to take the offensive.[14]

Mahan claimed that seeking positive gains through offensive action increased morale, but when a force assumed the defensive, "The evil spirit of backwardness finds room to enter."[15] Though difficult to quantify, he believed that "no purely defensive attitude can be successfully maintained. There must be preparation at least for offense."[16] The possibility of success multiplied when leaders had a "willingness and promptitude to assume the offensive, to take risks: a really fundamental factor alike in tactics and in strategy, permanent as the everlasting hills."[17]

Defense sacrificed the initiative while offense provided the choice of "where, when, and how to strike with . . . superior numbers."[18] Mahan explained, "The state which in war relies simply upon defending itself, instead of upon hurting the enemy, is bound to incur disaster, and for the very simple reason that the party which proposes to strike a blow has but one thing to do; whereas he who proposes only to ward off blows has a dozen things, for he cannot know upon which interest, of a dozen that he may have, the coming blow may fall."[19] Offense facilitated concentration of force at the decisive point to seek positive advantage, while defense resulted in dispersal of forces in an attempt to be strong everywhere. He entreated his students to remember that "the force that stands on the defensive plays not so much its own game as the game permitted to it by the errors of its adversary."[20] The defender lacked its own agency and relied on its opponent to make self-defeating actions.

Mahan's arguments changed the perception of naval power. One commentator at the time of Mahan's death wrote, "The significance of Mahan is chiefly that he swept away the comfortable maxim in which most of us were nursed, that a navy is only a weapon of defence. Its function in history has been, primarily, the acquisition of Empire."[21] Mahan certainly emphasized the offense, but only in terms of naval strategy and tactics. The commentator seems to believe that Mahan prejudiced the offense in political objects relating to national strategy, but this is not true. At the national level, Mahan decried "the aggressiveness which is wicked as a national policy." However, he argued that same aggressiveness "becomes a virtue, when the appeal to arms has been sounded."[22] The navy, as an instrument of national strategy, was best used offensively; failing to employ it in that way sacrificed the inherent strengths of the fleet and put the state at risk.

OFFENSE AND DEFENSE: CORBETT AND MAHAN COMPARED

While Mahan followed the prevailing contemporary narrative that emphasized the offense, Corbett explicitly countered arguments that offense was the sole means of waging naval war. He railed against the "amateurish notion that defence is always stupid or pusillanimous, leading always to defeat. . . . Nothing is further from the teaching or the practice of the best masters."[23] Elsewhere, he described the overemphasis on offense as "our crude modern dictum" and "the characteristic disease of contemporary strategy." He went on to write, "There is no clearer lesson in history how unwise and short-sighted it is to despise and ridicule a naval defensive."[24] His studies had led him to numerous historical cases when defensive naval strategies had proven effective.[25]

Corbett aimed his arguments specifically at British naval officers in the first years of the twentieth century. He had little interest making his theories applicable to an international audience. His statements on the offense and defense are particularly poignant in this regard: "The worst of all mis-readings of British naval history is that extraordinary fetish of the offensive, as if the offensive were a thing that could stand by itself. It is a fetish that kills strategy. It grew up in the days when we had that easy command after Trafalgar."[26] His writings sought to change a century of naval tradition.

Fixation on the offense, Corbett thought, had seeped dangerously into British strategic documents. These included the "1902 Memorandum on Sea Power," which declared:

> In the foregoing remarks the word *defence* does not appear. It is omitted advisedly, because the primary object of the British Navy

> is not to defend anything, but to attack the fleets of the enemy, and by defeating them to afford protection to British Dominions, shipping, and commerce. This is the ultimate aim. To use the word *defence* would be misleading. . . . The traditional role of the British Navy is not to act on the defensive, but to prepare to attack the force which threatens—in other words to assume the offensive.[27]

Corbett countered with, "How amateurish it is for British officers to think defensive is no affair of theirs." He insisted that "if an officer adopts the offensive, he does so, not because it is a British tradition, but because it is right."[28]

These arguments reflect Corbett's keen study of Clausewitz and particularly the Prussian's contention that defense is "the stronger form of war."[29] Corbett called it the "most disputed maxim of Clausewitz." How could defense be stronger when it only provided the negative object of retaining what one possessed while the offense yielded the positive object of seizing something from an opponent? Corbett interpreted Clausewitz's "stronger" as meaning that defense "entails less force to make it successful."[30]

Conversely, Mahan found Clausewitz's contention troubling: "I do not like the expression, for it seems to me misleading as to the determinative characteristics of a defensive attitude." On the one hand, Mahan understood the argument put forward by Clausewitz and Corbett: "What is meant by it is that in a particular operation, or even in general plan, the party on the defense, since he makes no forward movement for the time, can strengthen his preparations, make deliberate and permanent dispositions while the party on the offensive, being in continual movement, is more liable to mistake, of which the defense may take advantage."[31] On the other hand, Mahan saw moral characteristics in the word "stronger." For the American, offense demonstrated the stronger will and moral character.

OFFENSE-DEFENSE AND COUNTERATTACKS

When Mahan disparaged defense, he meant passive defense, which he defined as "defence pure and simple, which strengthens itself and awaits attack."[32] In this he aligned with Jomini, who explained that defense "promises many chances of success, but only when the general has the good sense not to make the defense passive: he must not remain in his positions to receive whatever blows may be given by his adversary."[33] Mahan agreed: "Mere defence is ultimate ruin."[34] When Mahan wrote "mere defense" or used the term "defense" without any qualifiers, he was describing defense in its passive form.

In contrast, Mahan extolled the possibilities of active defense using such descriptors as "offence is the best defence,"[35] or merely "offensive-defensive."[36] Even more often, Mahan tended to label both the active defense and the true offensive movement just "offense" and let the reader develop conclusions. He did not clearly explain that the correlation of forces dictates the type of offense. If one is stronger, a true offensive movement is preferable. If weaker, the best choice is an active defense. "Such continual offensive action," Mahan noted, "is of the essence of dexterous defence."[37] He cited the following statement, supposedly from Napoleon: "When you can combine defense with an offensive movement, you make the enemy run more risks than he causes to the body which he attacks."[38] He even elevated this to the level of a principle: "The principle is that every defensive disposition should look to offensive action—or at the least to offensive effect."[39]

Mahan understood the potential confusion: "Such a defence may seem to be really offensive war, but it is not; it becomes offensive only when its object of attack is changed from the enemy's fleet to the enemy's country."[40] This statement is critical to remember because it separates his theory of naval strategy from higher considerations regarding the political object of the war.

Mahan included the following example in *The Influence of Sea Power upon History*. With France entering the American Revolution in 1778 and Spain joining the war the following year, Britain, now outnumbered, had no alternative but to seek a defensive political object; however, Mahan chastised British naval leaders for assuming a passive defense with their fleet operations. "She everywhere awaited attacks which the enemies, superior in every case, could make at their own choice and their own time." This strategy passed the initiative to Britain's opponents. Offensive action was the key, he insisted, even if the ultimate objective of the war involved the negative aim of defending the British Empire. "It only remained, therefore, to use this inferior force with such science and vigor as would frustrate the designs of the enemy, by getting first to sea, taking positions skilfully, anticipating their combinations by greater quickness of movement, harassing their communications with their objectives, and meeting the principal divisions of the enemy with superior forces."[41] This quote outlines Mahan's conditions for a naval strategy utilizing active defense. Breaking the above quotation down further, he argued for the weaker fleet to conduct the following sequence of actions:

1. Get to sea first.
2. Take positions skillfully.
3. Anticipate the enemy's fleet combinations by greater quickness of movement.
4. Harass the enemy's lines of communication.
5. Meet the principal divisions of the enemy with superior forces.

For the commander of the weaker fleet, Mahan argued, "There is no salvation except by action vigorous almost to desperation."[42] He did not consider "desperation" a negative quality; it became so only when it crossed the line to "recklessness."[43] Rather than lead the weaker fleet on a mad dash for glory against impossible odds, the naval leader needed to gain or regain the initiative through an active defense resting on aggressive action guided by sound principles.[44]

Corbett found such arguments less than clear, chiding those like Mahan who used the phrase "attack is the best defence," describing it as a maxim that entailed a kernel of truth laced with misunderstanding.[45] Words convey meaning, and Corbett worried that "a somewhat loose reading of Captain Mahan's works" tended to confuse readers. They either misinterpreted his writings or believed what they had wanted to believe in the first place.[46] It concerned Corbett that most failed to understand that Mahan's diatribes against defense applied only to its passive form, and that when Mahan emphasized offense, it was often unclear whether he meant a true offensive movement or an active defense.

While Mahan looked to Jomini, Corbett drew inspiration from Clausewitz, who argued: "Usually, those defences pass for the best which make the most of active or even offensive means."[47] Corbett concurred: too often leaders "dismiss the idea that only offensive means valiant attacks, bold decisions, confusing surprises & that the defensive implies only indecision, timidity & lack of enterprise." Nothing could be further from the truth. "Defensive is despised because we exclude the idea of action from it."[48] In describing Britain's actions in the Wars of the French Revolution, Corbett noted the strategy was to "seize every half chance to strike, and if striking was not possible, to try to scratch. This, whenever he found a finger free, he was prepared to do." This course of action preserved the offensive attitude until a true offensive opportunity opened.[49]

Rather than blindly apply Clausewitz, Corbett carefully adapted the Prussian's theories to the maritime domain. He argued, "For the classification 'offensive and defensive' implies that offensive and defensive are mutually exclusive ideas, whereas . . . it is a fundamental truth of war, that they are mutually complementary." This argument reflects the nature of maritime communications. Ashore, each belligerent has distinct lines stretching from the army in the field to its depots and eventually its homeland. At sea, communications are not in the possession of a single power. The sea-lanes are common to all and are impossible to occupy. "The strategical effect is of far-reaching importance," Corbett noted, "for it means that at sea strategical offence and defence tend to merge in a way that is unknown ashore . . . we as a rule cannot attack those of the enemy without defending our own."[50]

Corbett preferred a defensive posture while preserving "the offensive spirit," utilizing selective moments of tactical offense coupled with a strategic naval defense. He urged officers to understand that "defence is a condition of restrained activity—not a mere condition of rest."[51] They should aim at making "defence as active as possible."[52] "It may be laid down as a general principle of strategy that no defensive disposition is perfect unless it threatens or conceals an attack."[53] Corbett raised this advice to the level of a principle to demonstrate its significance. In effect, he argued for "the spirit of restless and vigilant counter-attack," which he defined as "waiting deliberately for a chance to strike—not cowering in inactivity." Not surprisingly, Corbett argued that the "counter-attack is the soul of defence."[54]

Mahan and Corbett described two sides of the same coin. Both criticized any action that reeked of passive defense. While Mahan noted the importance of the "offense-defense," Corbett affirmed the significance of the "counterattack." Both mixed offensive elements into defensive schemes. The two did not, however, develop identical concepts. Mahan saw greater potential for true offensive movements, especially when a fleet possessed some sort of advantage: "If stronger, it will seek, and if possible compel battle" so as to use the navy as a true offensive instrument; but "if weaker, it will try to draw the enemy away and to divide his forces by threatening other strategic points or vital interests."[55] Only in the latter situation did active defense come into play. At the level of naval strategy Corbett advocated defense, harnessing its advantages as the stronger form of war and combining it with the offensive tactical characteristics of the fleet. He explained, "To assume the defensive does not necessarily mean that we do not feel strong enough to attack. . . . On general principles it is better strategy to induce the enemy to come to us than for us to go to him and seek a decision in his own waters."[56]

MAHAN'S DEFENSIVE ELEMENT: BASES

While Corbett described how offense and defense complemented one another in fleet operations, Mahan developed a similar interdependent relationship between the offensive fleet and its defensive base, asserting that "neither is secure without the other. . . . [A] fleet must be able to go away for a calculated time, with a reasonable prospect of finding its ports unsurprised, still its own, when it returns. The port must be able to spare the fleet for a similar period, confident that it can look out for itself till reinforced or supplied."[57] But he did not make bases and the fleet equal partners: "As a general proposition, ships and land fortifications do not contend on equal terms, either as regards their relative importance to the issues of war, or to their susceptibility to vital injury. Ships are much more useful and much more delicate than land works."[58]

Bases required fortification. A base without fixed defenses had to rely on the fleet for protection, which in turn restricted the fleet's mobility; but with a fortified base able to survive on its own for a reasonable period, the fleet could maneuver freely.[59] The bases benefited as well because the fleet could always provide succor if needed.[60]

Mahan recognized that a fleet at sea could not sustain itself indefinitely: "It needs to find on every scene of operation established bases of refit, of supply, and, in case of disaster, of security."[61] The fleet became ever more reliant on bases as the endurance of ships declined with the introduction of coal-based propulsion systems that traded range for movement in all weather conditions.[62]

Mahan divided bases into two categories: homeports and forward operating locations. Regarding the latter, he entreated leaders to develop a basing architecture in regions of national interest. Bases enhanced presence and provided a stronger means of sustaining operations. British positions such as Jamaica and Gibraltar were "no mere jewels in her crown, but foundation-stones of her sea power."[63] In both peace and war, such positions sustained long-term forward deployments by providing logistical support so the navy could "take the offensive instantly." A navy acting without bases is a prisoner. Bases "add a percentage of value to a given mobile force . . . for they by so much increase its power and its mobility."[64]

Mahan cited three factors governing the selection of bases: geographic location, resources, and survivability. Though much had changed since the age of sail, these were constants.[65] "Of the three," Mahan observed, "the first is of most consequence, because it results from the nature of things; whereas the two latter, when deficient, can be supplied artificially, in whole or in part. Fortifications remedy the weaknesses of a position, foresight accumulates beforehand the resources which nature does not yield on the spot; but it is not within the power of man to change the geographical situation of a point."[66] The critical component of geographic location was nearness to the trade routes. Naval stations had to be positioned along a country's critical sea lines of communication to serve as defensive strongpoints whence the fleet could sally for offensive operations.[67]

Too many bases, however, resulted in the dispersal of forces, weakening the state's overall strategic position.[68] Moreover, distant stations required costly fortifications and sustenance. "If you cannot hope to control the whole field," Mahan argued, "it is an advantage to hold such points as give you control of the greater part of it." The number of bases should reflect a balance among the strength of the fleet, the state's commitments, and its commercial interests. "The just balance, between too few and too many [bases], should therefore be carefully struck."[69]

Mahan criticized Britain for defending too many bases in the West Indies during the American Revolution: "The fault of the English policy was in attempting to hold so many other points of land, while neglecting, by rapidity of concentration, to fall upon any of the detachments of the allied fleets." In other words, British naval commanders attempted to be strong in too many places and suffered the characteristic weakness of the defense, and in the process, they lost sight of the essential positive offensive mission of the fleet. One or at most two strongly fortified and garrisoned bases in the West Indies would have given the fleet the ability to sustain regional operations while not being hamstrung by trying to provide relief for numerous garrisons. Limiting the number of bases would have freed the fleet for operations against opposing fleets. Rather than defend all its colonies directly with fortifications, Britain's offensive fleet operations indirectly protected the islands by preventing the French and Spanish from gaining local command of the sea.[70]

Often, Mahan intended his writing to educate the American people. What he wrote about bases is particularly revealing in this regard. The United States possessed an extensive coastline, and in the last years of the nineteenth century, its overseas possessions grew dramatically. His arguments respecting bases sought to convince an often-skeptical American audience of their value and purpose. Building a fleet was not enough: it needed the supporting architecture that only bases could provide.

THE BLUE WATER SCHOOL

Mahan admitted that naval bases were "a much debated point" and recognized that "there is, unhappily, much exaggerated talk on one side and the other as to the relative advantages of navies and fortifications for purposes of defense."[71] "Much exaggerated" was an understatement. Mahan's position on the value of bases brought virulent criticism from a group in England known as the Blue Water School.

The Blue Water School included naval propagandists who favored the fleet almost to the exclusion of every other instrument of war. Vice Admiral Philip Colomb likely founded the school with the publication of *Naval Warfare*, which some authors have claimed comes close to describing naval warfare "as an end in itself and not a means to an end."[72] Mahan described their arguments as follows: "The navy defends better than any fortress can. They conclude: Therefore money spent on fortresses is wasted, and should be spent on the fleet."[73]

Members of the Blue Water School perhaps read Mahan's initial sea power volumes too hastily. They incorrectly believed that initially, he also adhered to their theory regarding the relationship between the fleet and its bases. Like so many others, they only scratched the surface of Mahan's writings. Instead of realizing—or admitting—that they had failed to appreciate the totality of his argument, they claimed that the American theorist sold them out by changing his views in subsequent writings.[74] A troubled Mahan noted, "I see that Colomb says I have gone over. . . . The truth is I have always put forward fortifications and fleets as complementary giving both sides; but what can I do if people insist on looking upon only one, or overlook the other."[75] As early as *The Influence of Sea Power upon History*, Mahan had argued for the symbiotic relationship between the fleet and its base and insisted that principal bases required sufficient fortification to allow the fleet the opportunity to operate unfettered. Yet, Mahan also admitted the divisiveness of the issue: "Coast fortification, seacoast fortresses, are on a mental border line, between the conceptions of naval and military . . . between the spheres respectively of fleets and armies. It is therefore not extraordinary that debate should arise on this debatable ground."[76]

When the Blue Water School accused Mahan of changing his mind, he reinvestigated both sides of the argument and confirmed his original belief that naval bases need fortification to free the fleet for its offensive mission.[77] "Strategically," he argued, "coast fortresses are not for defense, but for offense, by sheltering and sustaining that force which against an invader is the offensive arm; that is, the navy."[78]

CORBETT, BASES, AND THE BLUE WATER SCHOOL

While Mahan sought to convince a skeptical public that America needed bases that could support its growing overseas ambitions, Corbett developed theories for a maritime empire that already possessed an unparalleled basing architecture. He never had to make arguments about whether Britain should possess bases: these were the debates of prior generations.

Moreover, bases, as Mahan learned, were divisive. We can speculate that Corbett did not value this argument enough to add additional controversy to his theories. One must, as a result, deeply engage his writings to determine his views on bases, or what he labeled "naval positions."[79]

Corbett's thoughts on bases generally appeared in restricted documents, including his lecture notes and his study of the Russo-Japanese War. Given the nonpublic nature of his work, Corbett did not provoke the ire of the Blue Water School in that regard, although they made their displeasure clear for other aspects of his theory.

The balance of power at sea, Corbett wrote, is "not only a question of navies, but also of naval positions."[80] Referring to the eighteenth century, he noted, "It is clear that the result of our long war experience had been rather to enhance than diminish the strategic importance of such naval positions. The men who knew what naval war was were dominated by the idea that though battles might place in our hands the command of the sea, the exercise of that command was impossible, without advanced bases rightly distributed."[81] This is critical. Winning was possible without bases, but sustaining a long-term presence in a region required facilities where the fleet could receive supplies and maintenance. Conversely, if one side sought command of the sea, the other side could undermine that objective merely by possessing a base in the contested area. Eliminating enemy bases was one way to transform temporary command of the sea to permanent command.[82]

Corbett followed Mahan by outlining the complementary relationship of the fleet and its bases. When Russia used bases for passive defense at Sebastopol in the Crimean War (1853–56) and at Port Arthur in the Russo-Japanese War (1904–5), the results were less than desired because "passive defense as usual gave way before patient and persistent attack." Corbett argued, "The whole object, it must be remembered, of a belligerent's keeping a naval base in being is to enable his fleet to act from it so as to prevent the enemy's fleet accomplishing something in the area of that base; and all experience shows that with anything like equal force the best way of thwarting the enemy's fleet is to attack it."[83] This reads more like Mahan than Corbett. On one level, the quote demonstrates that Corbett and Mahan held similar beliefs regarding bases. On a broader level regarding offense and defense, the quote signals Corbett's belief in active defense and the significant effects attainable from seeking battle.

Mahan placed great emphasis on bases; Corbett in comparison paid them scant attention because Britain already possessed bases for its far-flung navy. What Corbett did have to say about bases linked closely to his arguments about the sea lines of communication and specifically about how naval positions affect the ability to command the sea. Whereas Mahan would not have taken issue with Corbett's arguments, the American placed greater emphasis on how bases served as an element of the offensive-defensive combination.

PREFERRED COURSES OF ACTION

When *Some Principles of Maritime Strategy* was published in 1911, Britain's most likely naval opponent was Germany, and Corbett focused on that threat in the book's latter chapters. In a war with Germany, Britain possessed great geographical advantages. The British Isles served as a barrier to prevent the escape of the German fleet beyond the North Sea. A fleet deployed in the North Sea both protected Britain's seaborne empire and prevented Germany from using the resources of the globe.

The weaker German fleet would be forced to break down Britain's geostrategic position through offensive movements into the North Sea. Knowing where the opponent would attack conferred a significant advantage on Britain. Corbett advocated a strategic defense relying on counterattacks with the intent of wearing down German naval forces, explaining, "You really seize the initiative by forcing a certain movement on the enemy."[84] "By hook or by crook you must snatch from him the advantage of the defence."[85] Corbett's "ideal situation" forced the opponent to assume the offense: "Force your enemy against his will to assume the weaker form (offensive)."[86] Corbett explained, "It is usually said that it is best to take the offensive whenever and wherever you are strong enough, but there is a better thing than this. Better than taking the offensive yourself, is to force the offensive upon an enemy who is too weak for it."[87] He emphasized that "the primary and all-absorbing object of a superior naval power is not merely to take the offensive, but to force the enemy to expose himself to a decision as quickly as possible."[88] Corbett advocated an active defense that took advantage of the peculiarities of the maritime environment to attain command of the sea by a series of crippling counterattacks against an opposing fleet that was forced onto the offensive, thus making "his every attempt an opportunity for a counterstroke."[89]

Across the Atlantic, Mahan advocated for a U.S. Navy strong enough to confront national threats. He argued, "It is vain to maintain a military or naval force whose power is not equal to assuming the offensive soon or late; which cannot, first or last, go out, assail the enemy, and hurt him in his vital interests."[90] This was a critical difference between Britain and the United States. At the dawn of the twentieth century, no one doubted that Britain's leaders would continue to fund a massive fleet, but there were certainly questions about whether the United States could—and would—build and maintain a fleet large enough to keep itself and its new colonies secure. Moreover, no matter the preparation, the U.S. Navy would not be as large as every conceivable opponent it might face. The fleet thus had to be prepared to strike first.

Mahan's preferred course of action was a true offensive movement: "The one decisive objective of the offensive is the enemy's organized force, his battle-fleet."[91] Many who read Mahan understood his argument to this point but then missed the significance of what came next. He did not advocate offense as an end unto itself; rather, he considered the offensive action necessary to enable a longer campaign of economic exhaustion. In writing about the American Revolution, he claimed, "The ultimate crushing of the Americans, too, not by direct military effort but by exhaustion, was probable, if England were left unmolested to strangle their commerce and industries with her overwhelming naval strength. This strength she could put forth against them, if relieved from the pressure of the allied navies; and relief would be obtained if she could gain over them a decided preponderance. . . . Such preponderance, however, could only be had by fighting."[92]

A larger purpose thus grounded Mahan's advocacy of the offense. Seeking battle through offensive action was a necessary prerequisite for controlling the seas and achieving the leverage necessary to strangle the opponent's maritime economic activity. Mahan sought to "keep open communications by acting, or threatening to act, upon the offensive. This can only be done through its power of movement on the open sea, and by assuming an initiative suited to its strength whenever opportunity offers for the initiative is the privilege of the offense." This required either an offensive movement or an active defense to contest and eventually win control of the sea.[93]

His lack of precision sometimes makes Mahan's arguments on the offense and defense difficult to follow. When he mentioned "defense," he implied "passive defense" not "active defense." A similar lack of precision plagues the term "offense." It can mean either a true offensive movement or an active defense. The differences are significant. Corbett used terminology with greater precision. He too disparaged the passive defense and advocated more active uses of the fleet; however, he saw fewer possibilities for true offensive movements given the geographic position of Britain's likely opponents and the relative strength of the British fleet as compared to those opponents. As a result, he advocated strongly for an active defense grounded in the counterattack.

CHAPTER 8

CONCENTRATION

THE PRIMARY FORCE AND THE ULTERIOR EFFORT

Both Mahan and Corbett identified concentration among the principles of war.[1] Concentration supported Mahan's emphasis on offense, for one needed to be strongest at the critical point for offensive action to offer the greatest potential for success. Carefully balanced concentration of force and effort also proved necessary for Corbett's emphasis on counterattacks and forcing the weaker opponent onto the offensive. Though concentration appears a straightforward concept, its application in naval warfare is anything but simple.

MAHAN AND CONCENTRATION OF FORCE

"The military necessity of sustained concentration," Mahan explained, "is as absolutely certain as anything human can be."[2] In numerous writings, he extolled its centrality. Concentration was, he said,

- a word which may be said to include the whole of military art as far as a single word can
- the essential maxim of all intelligent warfare
- the watchword of military action
- the single eye that gives light in warfare
- the essence of warfare
- the secret of success in war.[3]

Concentration served an essential purpose even before the outbreak of hostilities: "It is . . . a distinct gain for a man to realize that the military principle of concentration applies to the designing of a ship, to the composition of a fleet, or to the peace distribution of a navy, as effectively as it does to the planning of a campaign." Fleet deployments in peacetime "should conform to the most probable needs, if war should arise."[4] But above all, the fleet needed to remain united. Especially true for his country with its widely separated coasts, Mahan maintained that "concentration of the battle-fleet of the United States is a matter of much more consequence than its precise position."[5]

Once war occurred, Mahan stressed concentration of force to gain numerical preponderance at the most advantageous place and time to provide the best guarantee of victory in battle. This would have follow-on effects resulting in general numerical superiority. It would steel the morale of the victor and sap the will of the defeated.[6]

Mahan borrowed from others to develop his theories of concentration. Using interior lines, seeking the decisive point, and then massing overwhelming force were hallmarks of Jomini's theory that Mahan adopted. In describing land warfare, Jomini warned, "You must guard against yielding to attractions of multiplied detachments."[7] Mahan agreed: "To have the greater force and then to divide it, so that the enemy can attack either or both fractions with decisively superior numbers, is the acme of military stupidity; nor is it the less stupid because in practice it has been frequently done."[8] Furthermore, Mahan noted, "There is . . . in the human mind an inveterate tendency to dispersion of effort, due apparently to the wish to do at once as many things as may be." He entreated leaders to avoid the temptation of secondary operations, because these tended to disperse force.[9] Mahan argued even more strongly than land power theorists about maximizing numbers and efficiency at the decisive point.[10] On the nautical plain, concentration provided a pivotal advantage.

Dennis Hart Mahan might also have played a critical role in influencing his son's thoughts on concentration. The operative word is "might" because the younger Mahan never explicitly cited his father's influence.[11] The elder Mahan also borrowed heavily from Jomini and then placed his own emphasis on rapidity: "No great success can be hoped for in war in which rapid movements do not enter as an element."[12] Alfred Thayer Mahan agreed. "The ocean, the scene of naval warfare, from the vastness of its extent, and the consequent great distance to be covered, makes a special demand upon mobility, the getting there first; but also it is upon the sustained power of the individual ship arriving with the 'most' men—the most ships—also depends."[13] A combination of offense, speed, and concentration provided distinct advantages.

Mahan also emphasized concentration off the enemy's principal naval bases. This would not stop every movement, but if properly conducted it would thwart larger operations. The fleet would be positioned at the point where the opponent's movement originated. If battle did not occur when the opposing fleet proceeded to sea from its base, it could be pursued to distant theaters. In the American Revolution, Mahan argued, "England stood on the defensive; but . . . she gave up the first line of the defence, off the hostile ports, and tried to protect all parts of her scattered empire by dividing the fleet among them." He saw this as a significant factor in Britain's defeat: "The key of the situation was upon the ocean; a great victory there would have solved all the other points in dispute. But it was not possible to win a great victory while trying to maintain a show of force everywhere."[14] Dividing the fleet on distant stations was akin to conducting a series of secondary operations.

Mahan assumed that the larger fleet would likely be dispersed on various missions and would have to concentrate before it could assume the offensive. This left an opening for the weaker fleet to

> procure a decisive momentary preponderance in some quarter, the due use of which, by the injury done the enemy, shall establish a permanent and decisive superiority. This is the one object of war scientifically—or better, artistically—considered. . . . The movements necessary to accomplish this are the opportunity of the offensive, to strike the converging divisions before their junction gives the desired local superiority. Herein is the skill; herein also the chance, the unexpected, the risk, which the best authorities tell us are inseparable from war, and constitute as much of its opportunity as of its danger.[15]

A naval officer needed to act quickly, operate in mass, and engage early. Striking an unprepared opponent entailed less risk than a protracted campaign. This course of action held particular relevance for the United States at the turn of the twentieth century. Britain was America's most dangerous potential naval opponent. In the unlikely event of war, Mahan advocated offensive operations off British naval bases in North America or in the Caribbean to level the field early in the contest. This was critical given the size of the British navy. Moreover, the Royal Navy had to disperse its forces to protect Britain's empire: acting quickly could allow the smaller U.S. fleet to defeat a stronger navy in detail.

CONCENTRATION IN EVOLUTION: MAHAN AND ELASTICITY

"Before quitting this part of our subject, it seems expedient to guard myself from the appearance of mere dogmatic insistence upon the close concentration of direct contact."[16] Mahan wrote this in 1911, toward the end of his literary career. He would not have included such a statement twenty-one years earlier in *The Influence of Sea Power upon History*, but during the early to mid-1890s Mahan seems to have reassessed his views on concentration. He explained, "You will understand that by that expression I don't mean packed like herrings, but so disposed that all parts were in mutual supporting distance, ready to move where needed."[17] The power of the fleet did not reside in single units or in keeping all the ships together, but in its mobility. He attributed this change of heart to his study of Napoleonic warfare.[18] It also parallels certain concepts presented by Jomini and Dennis Hart Mahan.[19]

The fleet's mobility gave it elasticity in concentration. Like a rubber band, a fleet could stretch its deployments to cover large expanses of ocean but contract when facing a threat. Mahan also compared fleets to "a fan that opens and shuts, vessels thus organically bound possess the power of wide sweep, which insures exertion over a great field of ocean, and at the same time that of mutual support. . . . Such is concentration, reasonably understood; not huddled together like a drove of cattle, but distributed with regard to a common purpose, and linked together by the effectual energy of a single will."[20] Naval forces needed to patrol the largest expanse possible but should never disperse to the point where ships could become isolated and individually overwhelmed.

Finally, Mahan observed, "Like every sound principle, concentration must be held and applied in the spirit, not in the letter only exercised with understanding, not merely literally." Principles, that is, are more like guides than absolutes. Thus, "a very considerable separation in space may be consistent with such mutual support."[21] In one of his last writings, Mahan confirmed his idea: "Concentration, of which we hear so much, and so justly, means simply communications so preserved as to enable the whole to live and the parts to unite betimes."[22]

Though Mahan emphasized ever-greater elasticity to stretch deployments over ever-larger expanses of water, he never forgot that there were limits beyond which fleets should not go.[23] Concentration entailed a keen understanding of how far warships could disperse to patrol the largest possible expanse of water before exposing themselves to defeat in detail. Tension existed between the need for mass at the decisive point and the need to disperse so as to control the largest area possible. Mahan advocated massed forward deployments off enemy bases, but he came to understand that this was insufficient. "Concentration means the maximum of affect exerted on the point chosen for attack: it by no means necessarily means the greatest amount of effort compressed in the smallest amount of space."[24]

CORBETT: ELASTIC CONCENTRATION REDEFINED

Regarding concentration, Corbett noted, "The term, which is one of the most common and most necessary in strategical discussion, has never acquired a very precise meaning, and this lack of precision is one of the commonest causes of conflicting opinion and questionable judgments." He elaborated, "No strategical term indeed calls more urgently for a clear determination of the ideas for which it stands."[25] In making this determination, Corbett developed a theoretical model unique to naval warfare.

Theories of concentration had become perverted in the century following the Napoleonic Wars: "The effect of prolonged peace has been to make 'concentration' a kind of shibboleth, so that division of a fleet tends almost to be regarded as a sure mark of bad leadership."[26] This statement recalls Mahan's original definition, but Corbett's obvious sarcasm implies that he considered something missing from this simplistic view of concentration.

The peculiarities of the maritime environment required a more sophisticated theory. Events of World War I only confirmed Corbett's opinion. He questioned "whether the principle of extreme concentration [of the fleet in home waters] . . . was not the child of pure theory rather than of sound doctrine founded on the practical experience of past naval warfare." Corbett quoted Sir Arthur Wilson, a former First Sea Lord and strategic wartime adviser: "The dream of most naval officers seems to be a great sea fight in which . . . we are to be enabled to collect all our forces together and crush the Germans at one blow. This, however, is only a dream."[27]

Reality came closer to approximating Mahan's elastic concentration; Corbett even quoted Mahan's views in *Some Principles of Maritime Strategy*. This should not be surprising. The American theorist wrote first in a rapidly evolving field. Corbett could avoid the same developmental process by utilizing Mahan's theory regarding elastic concentration. Concentration according to Corbett allowed the fleet to balance the need to act as one while simultaneously dispersing it to command as much of the ocean as possible. This required both effective communication and clear direction: "Concentration, in fact, implies a continual conflict between cohesion and reach, and for practical purposes it is the right adjustment of those two tensions—ever shifting in force—which constitute the greater part of practical strategy." This required a leader who could balance the conflicting demands of concentration and dispersion so as to deploy the fleet to cover the widest expanse of sea possible while not allowing elements of the fleet to be overwhelmed by a superior force.[28]

Corbett was not content merely to parrot Mahan's arguments. Elasticity worked "if enemy plays your game but what if he doesn't?"[29] Deployment within supporting distance might protect against surprise and allow command of significant areas of water, but it had little prospect of defeating an opponent. The problem is one of interaction: a thinking adversary has a vote on how the campaign will develop. Corbett noted the puzzle when he wrote, "The maxim, indeed, has become current that concentration begets concentration, but it is not too much to say that it is a maxim which history flatly contradicts."[30] If both sides executed an elastic concentration, deadlock would result: elasticity always allowed the weaker fleet to escape danger.[31] In such instances, both fleets would begin by dispersing to patrol the largest possible expanse of ocean. When they came into contact, both would attempt to mass. The side that concentrated more quickly would attempt to obtain battle, but the slower or weaker side would use elasticity to seek further concentration or merely avoid battle because it did not wish to lose. Elasticity might ensure the survival of the fleet, but it did not yield battle.

Moreover, a strategist also had to ponder the outcome if the weaker party dispersed its naval force. This, Corbett thought, also generally resulted in stalemate because the stronger fleet would be unable to obtain battle. The weaker fleet could protract the war by preventing a major engagement. This delayed the outcome and gave the weaker fleet the time to redress the naval balance.[32] For the stronger fleet, Corbett argued that elastic concentration—keeping warships within supporting distance and coalescing at the proper moment—was unlikely to defeat a dispersed opponent.

To gain victory, Corbett recommended concentration of *effort* rather than *force*. Concentrating force "tends to simplify problems for [the] enemy," who has only a single target to confront and can mass against it or avoid it. But "concentration of effort without actual concentration of force tends to confuse him [because it] does not reveal your intentions."[33] Though Mahan approached this formula when developing his elasticity arguments, he never developed concentration of effort in depth. It was Corbett who pushed past Mahan by entreating leaders to concentrate effort while dispersing force. Not an easy concept to master, it required a nuanced understanding of elastic concentration. Rather than elasticity allowing the force to combine at the moment of battle, the effort needed to coalesce on a single object.[34] This required deception, diversion, and misdirection. "The ideal concentration," to Corbett, was "an appearance of weakness that covers a reality of strength."[35] If properly executed, such a concentration would "tempt

Alfred Thayer Mahan.
NH 64579-KN, Naval History & Heritage Command

Denis Hart Mahan.
Alfred Thayer Mahan's father. He possibly influenced his son's naval theories.
Stockbridge Collection, USMA Archives

Stephen B. Luce. Founder of the United States Naval War College and the person responsible for bringing Mahan onto its teaching faculty. *NH 2323, Naval History & Heritage Command*

The United States Naval War College, circa 1895. *Naval War College Museum*

Antoine-Henri Jomini. A military officer in the Napoleonic Wars. Best known for his extensive writings about the Napoleonic way of war. Widely read and studied in the nineteenth century, his works had a minor influence on Corbett and a major influence on Mahan.
Painting by Marc-Charles-Gabriel Gleyre

Alfred Thayer Mahan. From a sketch made on board U.S. cruiser *Chicago* at Gravesend. *U.S. Naval Institute photo archive*

THE INFLUENCE

OF

SEA POWER UPON HISTORY

1660–1783

BY

CAPTAIN A. T. MAHAN

UNITED STATES NAVY

LONDON

SAMPSON LOW, MARSTON, SEARLE, & RIVINGTON

(LIMITED)

The Influence of Sea Power upon History 1660–1783.
Title page for the first British edition. *Naval War College Archive*

Alfred T. Mahan. *Naval War College Museum*

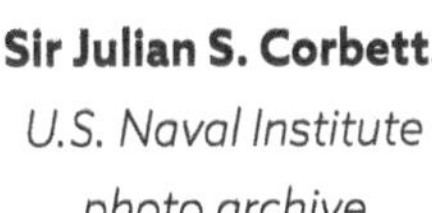

Sir Julian S. Corbett. *U.S. Naval Institute photo archive*

Carl von Clausewitz. A Prussian military officer who served in the Napoleonic Wars. He thought deeply about war and strategy. Corbett was deeply influenced by Clausewitz's writings. *Clausewitz.com*

SOME PRINCIPLES OF

MARITIME STRATEGY

BY

JULIAN S. CORBETT, LL.M.

LONGMANS, GREEN AND CO.
39 PATERNOSTER ROW, LONDON
NEW YORK, BOMBAY, AND CALCUTTA
1911

Some Principles of Maritime Strategy. Title page for the first edition. *Naval War College Archive*

[the] enemy to try something for which he is not strong enough."[36] This in turn required the proper alignment of what the two theorists labeled the "ulterior" and "primary" objects.

ULTERIOR OBJECTS AND PRIMARY OBJECTS

Both men considered the opposing fleet the primary object.[37] The ulterior object is more complex. Corbett called it "the objective of the campaign."[38] Mahan was less precise, calling it "the mission in hand."[39] Though they did not use identical terminology, there is enough congruence in their definitions to signal that the ulterior object concerns the objective for which force is used, or the strategic objective of a campaign, or even a war.

It is quite unlikely that the primary and ulterior objects will both be the opposing fleet. Corbett was particularly adamant on this point. He saw only one possible exception: conflicts over purely maritime issues such as the seventeenth-century Anglo-Dutch Wars.[40] Corbett reasoned that people live on land, so wars are usually fought over some ulterior territorial object.[41] Defeating the opposing fleet, though important, will not by itself result in a successful campaign or a victorious war. Something beyond defeating the opposing fleet must occur, because the object of the campaign generally requires seizing a geographic position: the opposing fleet merely stands in the way of this occurring. Mahan wrote less on the point, but his description of ulterior and primary objects leads toward a similar conclusion.

Understanding the primary and ulterior objects aligns the fleet's purpose with the overall objective of the campaign and allows a clear distinction between the theorists. Concentration of effort led Corbett to emphasize the ulterior object, while concentration of force caused Mahan to accentuate the primary object.

Considering that the word "ulterior" means "beyond the obvious" or "beyond what is currently present," it makes sense that one should obtain the primary object and then proceed to the ulterior one. The meanings of the terms indicate a sequence: the primary object should be obtained first. Mahan concurred: there was a progression to events in naval warfare beginning with the attainment of the primary object. Since the primary object was the opposing fleet, his preferred course of action entailed defeating the opposing fleet in battle. Mahan cited "Jomini's dictum, that the organized forces of the enemy are ever the chief objective."[42] This required a navy capable of winning a naval battle.

According to Mahan, during the age of sail English and French naval officers employed their fleets differently, with the French shunning battle to focus on the ulterior object while the British followed a sequence of first defeating the opposing fleet and then securing the ulterior object. Mahan even chastised one English admiral because "he was governed in his action by the French rather than the English naval policy, of subordinating the attack of the enemy's fleet to the particular mission in hand." Mahan concluded that the French generally "subordinated the control of the sea by the destruction of the enemy's fleets, of his organized naval forces, to the success of particular operations, the retention of particular points, the carrying out of particular ulterior strategic ends." Mahan considered this an inferior strategic choice and instead prioritized defeating the opposing fleet (the primary object). With no fleet to protect it, the ulterior object became untenable. The result was a sequence: obtain success over the organized forces of the enemy fleet before seeking the object of the campaign.[43] Rather than become sidetracked by ulterior objects, Mahan determined "the true way to secure ulterior objects is to defeat the force which threatens them."[44] Defeating the opposing fleet created freedom of maneuver so the navy could pursue the ulterior object.[45]

Corbett disagreed entirely. He thought Mahan's formula would work only in a world devoid of thinking opponents: "In naval warfare, however great may be our desire to concentrate our effort on the enemy's main forces, the ulterior object will always obtrude itself." Corbett maintained that ulterior objects were not present in the same degree ashore, and that allowed the commander of a land force to keep "a single eye on the force you wish to overthrow without regard to ulterior objects."[46] The maritime environment was far more complex than the terrestrial realm of military strategy.

At sea, it was not always possible for a leader to obtain the desired objectives. Seeking battle with unerring tenacity tended to leave commerce

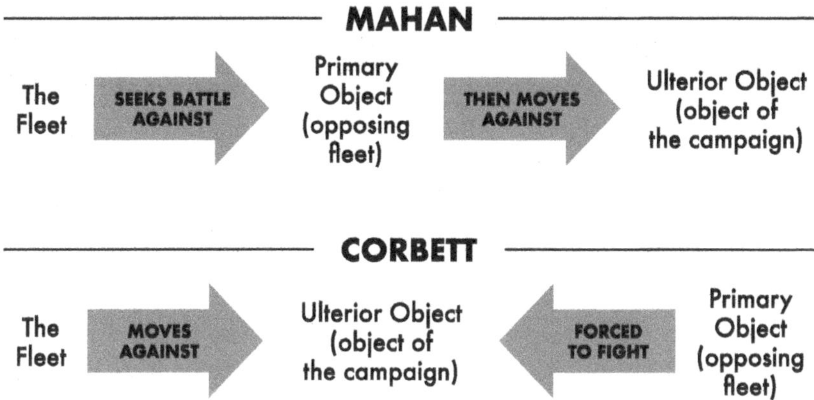

8.1. **The Ulterior and Primary Objects**

unprotected. That was unacceptable for a state heavily dependent on maritime trade for its survival. "Experience tells us that for economic reasons alone, apart from the pressure of public opinion, no one has ever found it possible to ignore the deflection entirely," Corbett explained. ". . . Nor is it more profitable to declare the only sound way to protect your commerce is to destroy the enemy's fleet. . . . As a canon of practical strategy, it is untrue. . . . What are you to do if the enemy refuses to permit you to destroy his fleets? You cannot leave your trade exposed to squadronal or cruiser raids while you await your opportunity."[47]

Commerce provides but one example of how the ulterior object prevents a fleet from obtaining the primary object of defeating the opposing fleet. Other examples include territorial objectives and diplomatic interests. A similar argument applies to each: what happens when the opposing fleet refuses to consent to battle? Rather than admit a stalemate or await a naval engagement that may never occur, Corbett advocated concentration of effort against the ulterior object, which is the object of the campaign or even the war.

THE ULTERIOR OBJECT, CONCENTRATION, AND BATTLE

One way to approach the ulterior and primary objects is through the lens of concentration and its relationship to naval battle. Many officers at the turn of the twentieth century were captivated by the idea of seeking battle with the opposing fleet. Even Corbett considered battle the most "economical" and "effective" way to obtain command of the sea, and eventually the ulterior object. Thus, he was more than willing to have the Royal Navy go toe-to-toe against a concentrated naval foe. "Indeed we have no reason for preventing the enemy's concentration," maintained Corbett. "It was our best chance of solving effectually the situation we have to confront."[48]

In the abstract, both theorists proclaimed the effectiveness of battle between two concentrated fleets, yet Corbett thought that real-world conditions made battle elusive. "Winning great actions [are] the most important," he admitted, but they are also the "rarest features in war."[49] Mahan agreed with him that "the battles of naval warfare are few compared to those of land."[50] Desiring battle and obtaining it are quite different things.

Writing for a navy that was the largest in the world in the early twentieth century, Corbett focused on how a stronger fleet could compel a weaker one to fight. To that end, he asserted, "To secure a decision, especially against a weaker enemy, is the main preoccupation and the greatest difficulty of naval strategy."[51] The weaker side does not want to die. "If circumstances are advantageous to us, we are not always able to effect a decision; and if they are disadvantageous, we are not always obliged to fight. Enough has now been said to show that 'seeking out the enemy's fleet' is not in itself sufficient to secure such a decision."[52]

Corbett spent considerable intellectual capital on the problem of obtaining battle against a weaker opponent. His solution entailed putting the ulterior object at risk. This object was often "a position which controls communications vital to his [the opponent's] plan of campaign."[53] Threatening this position forced the opponent to make an unpalatable choice: either accept battle even though loss was almost certain or accept the loss of the ulterior object. Thus, moving against the ulterior object led to a win-win proposition: the weaker opponent either fought at a disadvantage to protect the ulterior object or sacrificed the ulterior object.[54] This strategy was a "special characteristic of naval warfare which always permits action against the ulterior object when the enemy denies you any chance of acting against his armed force."[55]

Mahan's theory was more linear than Corbett's: build the fleet, prepare the fleet, concentrate the fleet, bring the opponent to battle through proper concentration of force, and only then secure the ulterior object. He concluded that success generally came to the side that sought out the primary object (the opposing fleet). Pursuing the ulterior object led to stalemate or defeat.

Corbett did not believe such a linear course of action would work in real-world situations, because "you are not always free to adopt the plan which is best calculated to bring your enemy to a decision."[56] Corbett's nonlinear approach to create a dilemma for the opponent required concentrated effort on an ulterior object that the opponent valued more than the survival of its fleet. Not a simple proposition, it led Corbett to conclude, "In naval warfare there is nothing more difficult than a correct adjustment of action between the ever-competing claims of the ulterior and primary object—between striking directly to secure the object of the campaign, and using the indirect but more drastic method of a concentrated stroke at the enemy's fleet."[57]

How they handled the ulterior object aligned with how the theorists conceived concentration in the maritime domain. Corbett's preference for the ulterior object (the object of the campaign) aligned with theories aimed at concentration of effort. Rather than concentrate the naval force to seek battle, the state's instruments of power, including the fleet, would focus their efforts on obtaining the object of the campaign. This had the greatest possibility of bringing the opponent's fleet to battle as it attempted to defend the object of the campaign. Conversely, concentration of force led Mahan to emphasize the primary object—the opposing fleet. Mahan's theory emphasized the fleet by giving it the mission of seeking out the opposing fleet and defeating it with overwhelming force. Eliminating the primary object through concentration of force removed it as a factor in the campaign and exposed the ulterior object.

Their views on ulterior and primary objects aligned with their agendas and their views on concentration. Writing for the dominant naval power, Corbett wanted to exploit naval dominance while breaking the weaker opponent's naval power. He understood weaker opponents would not voluntarily consent to fight against overwhelming odds. His emphasis on concentration of effort sought to compel the weaker side into self-defeating actions. Focusing on the ulterior object provided such a pathway. Mahan wanted to develop a theory for a rising sea power to help it grow to dominance in peace and war. He assumed the dominant naval power would be spoiling for a fight: concentration of force allowed the weaker naval power to take advantage of the stronger power's desire for battle.

CHAPTER 9

SEA DENIAL

DISPUTING COMMAND OF THE SEA AND SECONDARY OPERATIONS

What are the possible strategies for navies when their object is something less than obtaining command of the sea? One alternative considers strategies available to weak navies confronting much stronger opponents; another entails options for the dominant navy that must accept temporary inferiority in specific theaters so it can mass its fleet at a more decisive point. In modern parlance, much of this chapter addresses "sea denial": what are the options when attempting to limit or deny another, generally stronger, naval power from using the sea?

Corbett labeled the concept "disputing command of the sea." Under this umbrella are the options he considered for fleets not powerful enough to engage in a traditional fleet-on-fleet battle or mount an effective naval blockade. Disputing command of the sea entails options that "endeavour by active defensive operations to prevent the enemy either securing or exercising control for the objects he has in view." Corbett included two methods under disputing command: "a fleet in being" and "minor counterattacks."[1]

Corbett employed two similar phrases to mean very different things: "disputing command of the sea" and "command in dispute." "Command in dispute" describes the overall naval balance when no side possesses command of the sea. It can mean that the various sides are more or less equally matched, or it can mean that one side is stronger but not quite strong enough to obtain general command of the sea. In contrast, "disputing command of the sea" entails methods used by powers not currently capable of securing command of the sea "to defer a decision until military or political developments so far redress the balance of strength that we are able to pass to the offensive."[2] Disputing command occurs in two situations: first, to buy time to redress a temporary imbalance in naval force; and second, to undertake a protracted campaign of attrition when facing permanent naval inferiority.

Even though Mahan did not specifically use the term "disputing command of the sea," he engaged the concept and added a term of his own by describing certain operations as "secondary." Under this heading he notably included commerce raiding—diffuse action against maritime commerce by single ships and small squadrons. Mahan viewed commerce raiding as a strategy secondary to the primary object of securing command of the sea through battle and blockade.[3]

CONFRONTING TEMPORARY INFERIORITY: A FLEET IN BEING

The idea of "a fleet in being" spurred lively debate among naval commentators at the turn of the twentieth century. Both Mahan and Corbett joined the discussion. The origin of "a fleet in being" is generally ascribed to Admiral Arthur Herbert, 1st Earl of Torrington, who used the phrase in reference to operations against a more powerful French fleet in 1690.[4] Overall, Mahan thought there were better courses of action than a fleet in being, while Corbett championed its possibilities.

A fleet in being is a strategy of a fleet that must accept temporary inferiority in one or more regions. It is not a strategy for a fleet that is hopelessly outmatched. According to Mahan, it serves as a "a paralysing factor."[5] It "is a perpetual menace to the various more or less exposed interests of the enemy, who cannot tell when a blow may fall, and who is therefore compelled to restrict his operations, otherwise possible, until that fleet can be destroyed or neutralized."[6] Corbett added a qualification: he considered a fleet in being effective only when a stronger opponent required command of the sea to attain its objectives.[7]

Corbett thought it an effective stratagem that used the methods of the active defense to postpone a decision until a more favorable situation developed. Historically, the Royal Navy had used it in the following manner: "The idea was to dispute the control by harassing operations, to exercise control at any place or at any moment as we saw a chance, and to prevent the enemy exercising control in spite of his superiority by continually occupying his attention. . . . Everything was counterattack, whether upon the enemy's force or his maritime communications. . . . For a maritime Power, then, a naval defensive means nothing but keeping the fleet actively in being—not merely in existence, but in active and vigorous life."[8]

It troubled Corbett that many commentators had restricted "a fleet in being" to narrow conditions when in fact it could be applied to any form of active defense and particularly to those leveraging counterattacks. Even though Britain was the dominant naval power, its global commitments prevented it from being superior in every region simultaneously. Rather than a global strategy for the dominant navy, a fleet in being only applied to theaters where the fleet had to accept temporary inferiority. Corbett used the concept to explain to British naval officers how massing at the decisive point might entail accepting inferiority elsewhere. A fleet in being provided a possible strategy that allowed Britain to minimize risk and maximize reward when relying on inferior forces in specific theaters. Corbett explained that a fleet in being "goes no further than this, that where the enemy regards the general command of a sea area as necessary to his offensive purposes, you may be able to prevent his gaining such command by using your fleet defensively, refusing what Nelson called a regular battle, and seizing every opportunity for a counterstroke."[9] Corbett's interpretation of a fleet in being required a fleet trained to the level that few navies could attain because it required the weaker fleet to execute a campaign at sea against a stronger opponent.

In *The Influence of Sea Power upon History*, Mahan analyzed Torrington's 1690 naval campaign, where the concept of a fleet in being originated, but he did not use the actual term.[10] Several years later Mahan admitted, "My treatment of Torrington excited more adverse comment than any point in my first book, which certainly did not do him justice."[11] Of Torrington, who commanded the British fleet, Mahan said, "I think upon the whole he managed well, and certainly was perfectly right not to risk battle which could have availed only to destroy his force." He refused, however, to automatically endorse a fleet in being: "I have never subscribed . . . in thinking that his fleet in being *should* have prevented the descent of the French . . . the operation could have gone on." Mahan's implication was clear—a more audacious French admiral might very well have succeeded against Torrington's fleet in being.[12] This view aligned with Corbett's description. Neither theorist considered a fleet in being a panacea for every situation of weakness. It was an option, but like all courses of action chosen out of inferiority, it entailed high levels of risk.

Both Mahan and Corbett drew their examples from the age of sail, yet much had changed by the time they wrote. Mahan thought technological advances added additional risk to a fleet in being. Specifically, coal limited the endurance of the force employing the strategy, and the need to refuel created special vulnerabilities.[13] Corbett disagreed: with ships no longer tied to the wind for maneuver, a fleet in being could more easily escape trouble. Moreover, he believed submarines might significantly enhance the effectiveness of a fleet in being.[14]

While Corbett recognized that a fleet in being could be a useful strategy in some instances, Mahan had reservations. The effectiveness of a fleet in being "has always to me appeared exaggerated," he noted, even claiming that "the danger incurred by failure exceeds the advantage to be gained by success."[15] The fleet in being's primary defect concerned its reliance on "discouragement, perplexity, and consequent frustration of the adversary's purposes." He thought such effects difficult to manage. "Is such effect always legitimate, inherent in the existence of the fleet itself, or does it not depend often upon the characteristics of the man affected?" Too much could go wrong, resulting in the loss of ships, or worse, the entire fleet. "The probable value of a 'fleet in being' has, in the opinion of the writer, been much overstated; for, even at the best, the game of evasion, which this is, if persisted in, can have but one issue. The superior force will in the end run the inferior to earth."[16]

Mahan found it galling that some, particularly in England, "by overlooking the necessary qualification . . . are erecting it into a dogma—a fetish—which involves the danger of becoming 'doctrinaire.' Now of all dangerous conditions a military doctrinaire is one of the worst."[17] It remains unclear whether Mahan specifically placed Corbett among this group. If he did, he was wrong. Corbett admitted that a fleet in being "was stretched to occasions it would not fit."[18] It provided only a defensive option: it could not gain command of the sea. This argument actually differs little from Mahan's: neither theorist considered a fleet in being a war-winning strategy. Corbett merely thought a fleet in being possessed greater potential for a temporary advantage than Mahan did. It is important to provide one qualification. Corbett thought that a fleet in being was not just a fleet tucked away in the safety of a port. This has been a source of confusion since Torrington used the phrase in 1690.[19]

In contrast, Mahan's thoughts on the subject evolved. In 1898 he wrote, "The safest, though not the most effective, disposition of an inferior 'fleet in being' is to lock it up in an impregnable port or ports, imposing upon the enemy the intense and continuous strain of watchfulness against escape."[20] Here he indicated that placing a fleet inside a protected anchorage is a type of strategy employing a fleet in being. He reaffirmed this in his early writings on the Russo-Japanese War to describe the possibilities for the Russian warships at Port Arthur.[21] As those operations played out, it became obvious to Mahan that the squadron in that port would not contribute actively to the campaign, so he started referring to it as a "fortress fleet"—a fleet tied to the area around the port it was tasked to defend. By 1911 he even claimed, "The phrases, 'Fortress Fleet' and 'Fleet in Being,' are the antipodes of each other."[22]

By 1911, neither Mahan nor Corbett saw much value in sequestering a fleet in the safety of a port, because it denied the fleet its mobility. Mahan labeled it a passive defense to imply its wrongheadedness.[23] Corbett maintained that defended anchorages should be utilized only when everything else failed, and even then should be employed as the most temporary of expedients. The prime fallacy of placing a fleet in a fortress is that it cedes command of the sea. Even a weaker naval force should actively seek to disrupt the sea lines of communication.[24]

CONFRONTING PERMANENT INFERIORITY

A fleet in being requires a large, balanced fleet compelled by temporary inferiority to dispute command. Corbett argued that a fleet in being was best employed as an economy-of-force mission where a fleet accepted inferiority in one location to gain superiority elsewhere. But what are the possibilities for a permanently inferior navy? One can analyze this from two perspectives. First, how can a somewhat inferior balanced fleet slowly redress the naval balance? And second, what possibilities exist for a vastly inferior naval force?

THE WEAKER BALANCED FLEET

Barring a catastrophe, Britain during Corbett's lifetime would never possess a permanently inferior balanced fleet, but this was a problem for Mahan's country. The United States was a rising power with a credible and growing, but not dominant, naval force. In war, the U.S. Navy would likely face situations when it was the inferior force, especially against its most dangerous naval foe—Britain. For Mahan,

> Correct military principle . . . imperatively dictates that the belligerent so situated must at once assume an active offensive. By rapid and energetic movement, while the opponent's forces are still separated, every advantage must be seized to destroy hostile detachments within reach, and; to establish one's own front as far in advance of the great national interests, as it can be reasonably hoped to maintain it with communications unbroken. . . . [O]nly by causing such diminution, greater relatively than his own, can the weaker hope eventually to reverse the odds and win the game.[25]

Though Mahan was describing land operations, he used land warfare as a conscious point of departure for his theories of naval war.[26] Specifically, the quote describes the best course of action for the Boers of South Africa in their war against Britain (Boer War, 1899–1902). As the weaker belligerent, the Boers faced a situation roughly analogous to what the U.S. Navy would face against the Royal Navy. Mahan applied these concepts to naval warfare to create the following courses of action for an inferior fleet:

- Remain at sea to maintain an active existence.
- Concentrate the fleet's main strike force (in Mahan's day the battleships).
- Utilize the inherent mobility of the warships.
- Operate as far forward as the lines of communication allow.

- Compel the opponent to disperse warships on other missions.
- Engage the opponent before it can concentrate.
- Defeat detachments of the opposing fleet or the main body if severely reduced.[27]

Whether on land or sea, Mahan advocated aggressive action to defeat the stronger opponent in detail. Only then could a weaker force emerge victorious.

The method Mahan called for aligns with "a fleet in being," but the object differs. Whereas a fleet in being awaited the return of elements dispatched on other missions, in this method Mahan emphasized incremental victories whose cumulative effect would allow a fleet to transition to missions designed to obtain command of the sea.

The dominant navy did not, in Mahan's opinion, possess absolute advantages: "To compare the force of the two may be a matter of curious interest; but for the purpose of making comparisons . . . is a mere waste of ink, important only to those who conceive the chief end of war to be fighting, and not victory."[28] One could not total existing naval platforms to determine the victorious side. One must assess circumstances more broadly, from preparation and training to commitments and deployments. Mahan did not consider it a death sentence to fight with a somewhat inferior fleet: "In a conflict of smaller numbers against much larger, nowhere does organization and development count as much as in navies."[29] Skilled leaders could succeed with a smaller fleet as long as it was well trained and possessed the most advanced technologies. Moreover, "the biggest navy that ever existed cannot all be sent on one mission, in any probable state of the political world." Mahan believed that a smaller fleet could obtain disproportionate effects against the larger opponent, but only if the smaller navy maintained concentration, avoided overextension, and remained cognizant of its comparative weakness so that it could obtain the numerical advantage at the decisive point.[30]

THE VASTLY INFERIOR NAVAL FORCE

Corbett placed options for the vastly inferior fleet under the umbrella of "minor counterattack." He explained, "Where a Power was so inferior in naval force that it could scarcely count even on disputing command by fleet operations, there remained a hope of reducing the relative inferiority by putting part of the enemy's force out of action." He offered little hope for such a force: historically, Corbett could find no "case where the ultimate question of command was seriously affected by a minor counterattack."[31] In the age of sail, warship design and armament meant that small craft had almost no possibility of rendering large surface combatants like ships of the line ineffective.[32]

Mahan concurred in describing an event from the American Revolution: "The experience illustrates again the unlikelihood that great results can be obtained by petty means, or that massed force, force concentrated, can be effectually counteracted either by cheap and ingenious expedients, or by the cooperative exertions of many small independent units."[33] In a 1897 lecture he provided his reasoning: "It is more difficult at sea than on shore to escape the results of inferiority of numbers . . . there are no accidents of the ground, which can be utilized to impede the movements of the enemy—to lessen his mobility—[and this] places the inferior at sea in a condition of disadvantage, whose hopelessness is not to be compensated for as it may be on shore. Strong battalions tell more certainly afloat than they do on the land."[34]

Though such reasoning was hard to refute using examples from the age of sail or even from the 1890s, the velocity of technological change in the years leading up to World War I presented new possibilities for what Corbett labeled the "minor counterattack" utilizing the "flotilla." Corbett identified the flotilla as constituting one of the three main types of fighting ships found in period navies (he identified the other main types as battleships and cruisers). The flotilla included small vessels, often designed for missions in the littorals. By the early twentieth century the flotilla had undergone progressive development that first married the torpedo with the small surface warship, resulting in the development of torpedo boats and destroyers. By World War I, the flotilla also included submarines. Armed with torpedoes, inexpensive warships of the flotilla were now capable of sinking even the largest battleship. Corbett explained, "The acquisition by the flotilla of battle power . . . is a feature of naval warfare that is entirely new."[35]

"The degree of that importance is at present beyond calculation," Corbett asserted in 1911. Yet he temporized in the very next sentence when expressing the minor counterattack's significance: "There is at least no evidence that it would be very high in normal conditions and between ordinarily efficient fleets." Without historical evidence, Corbett refused to speculate further about how new technologies increased the effectiveness of the minor counterattack. For example, he explained, "The unproved value of submarines only deepens the mist which overhangs the next naval war. From a strategical point of view we can say no more than that we have to count with a new factor, which gives a new possibility to minor counterattack." Although he admitted that new technologies would alter naval warfare, Corbett's understanding of historical trends indicated that the psychological effect of the new technologies would diminish over time, counters would be developed, and the new technologies would not be as deadly as some believed.[36]

Mahan, like Corbett, recognized the promise of torpedo-armed warships. He thought they would prove most effective in the littorals where they could sortie from ports, often under the cover of darkness, to attack unsuspecting foes. Success rested with a carefully executed active defense in which torpedo-armed warships would be most effective when achieving surprise.[37]

Though both Mahan and Corbett admitted the possible effectiveness of new technologies, neither thought they would utterly revolutionize naval warfare. The dominant fleet could reduce their effectiveness through training and vigilance, while the weaker side needed very high levels of training and morale to execute attacks.[38] Prior to World War I, Corbett concluded, "In the absence of a sufficient volume of experience it would be idle to go further."[39] Mahan concurred.[40]

COMMERCE RAIDING AS A SECONDARY OPERATION

War on commerce follows one of two basic models. First, a dominant navy can function as a single organism to lock down the sea lines of communication; or second, the war on commerce can entail diffuse action by single ships and small squadrons, generally conducted by the weaker naval power.[41] These two methods are quite distinct. The first is the province of the dominant navy and becomes possible only by commanding the sea, and the second is the resort of an inferior navy. Described by the

French as guerre de course and the English as commerce raiding, it is the topic of the following sections.

Mahan's views on commerce raiding changed while he was writing *The Influence of Sea Power upon History.* Prior to the mid-1880s, Mahan held a belief then widespread among American naval officers "that commerce destroying was the great efficient weapon of naval warfare. Everybody—the navy as well—believed we had beaten Great Britain in 1812, brought her to her knees, by the destruction of her commerce."[42] In 1885 Mahan explained, "The surest deterrent will be a fleet of swift cruisers to prey on the enemy's commerce. . . . This threat will deter a possible enemy, particularly if coupled with adequate defense of our principal ports." Although Mahan emphasized a commerce-raiding strategy, he admitted, "My theory however is based on the supposition that we don't have interests out of our own borders. If we are going in for an Isthmian policy we must have nothing short of a numerous and thoroughly first class iron clad navy—equal to either England or France."[43]

While writing *The Influence of Sea Power upon History*, Mahan came to believe that the United States had interests even more extensive than building and protecting a canal connecting the Atlantic and the Pacific. A fleet of commerce raiders would not suffice to project America's power and influence. "The small results from the general war, dominated as it was by the idea of commerce-destroying, show strongly the secondary and indecisive effect of such a policy upon the great issues of war." Statements in *The Influence of Sea Power upon History* demonstrate a change from his earlier belief. That book emphasizes concentration of the battle fleet to bring overwhelming force to bear at the decisive point to gain control of the sea, while commerce raiding required the opposite.[44]

Over time, Mahan's views on commerce raiding moderated, and he became more apt to describe it as a viable "secondary operation," indicating that it had a supporting function but could not provide significant results on its own. Though this message appears late in *The Influence of Sea Power upon History*, it reached its fullest formulation in 1905 with the publication of *Sea Power in Its Relation to the War of 1812*, where Mahan reaffirmed the "secondary" status of commerce raiding as "a minor offensive operation." He continued, "The depredations of scattered cruisers may inflict immense vexation, and even embarrassment; but they neither kill nor mortally wound, they merely harass. Co-operating with other influences, they may induce yielding in a maritime enemy; but singly they never have done so, and probably never can."[45] Mahan did not make a blanket denunciation of commerce raiding, he merely noted that it should be employed as a secondary operation supporting a larger, multifaceted strategy.

Corbett's conclusions on commerce raiding demonstrated no such evolution of thought. His first serious historical work, *Drake and the Tudor Navy*, written even before he joined the War Course, explained, "Here we have the idea, since so often proved fatal and so often re-born as a new strategical discovery, that a naval war may be conducted on economical principles, and a great Power be brought to its knees by preying on its commerce without first getting command of the sea." He described it as "mere commerce-destroying," and "the lessons to be learnt . . . are amongst the sharpest and most valuable which it has for the modern student."[46] Thirteen years later, in *Some Principles of Maritime Strategy*, he presented a similar argument: "A plan of war which has the destruction of trade for its primary object implies in the party using it an inferiority at sea. Had he superiority, his object would be to convert that superiority to a working command by battle or blockade."[47] Battle and even blockade, that is, brought more significant results than commerce raiding.

Corbett did not include commerce raiding under the umbrella of operations for disputing command of the sea in *Some Principles of Maritime Strategy*, but he did include it in his official history of World War I written a decade later.[48] While he never believed that commerce raiding could achieve victory on its own, the experience of war led him to refine his theories under modern conditions.

THE LEGACY OF THE NAPOLEONIC WARS AND THE JEUNE ÉCOLE

By the time Corbett and Mahan started writing, some three-quarters of a century had elapsed since the dominant naval power had faced a serious threat to its commerce. Much had changed in the intervening years. The Industrial Revolution had yielded myriad technological advances, including the transition from sail to steam as well as new weapons and communications systems. Merchant shipping tonnage had grown tremendously, and the nature of maritime cargoes had grown from luxury items to include the resources and foodstuffs necessary for modern states to survive. Moreover, significant alterations in international law had occurred.

By the eighteenth century, European states had refined the rules and legal frameworks relating to the capture of merchant shipping to include admiralty courts and regulations covering the seizure of merchant vessels belonging to the enemy or neutral ships carrying cargo considered contraband. The result was a regularized, formulaic process applied to all captures. Theoretically, the same rules applied whether the merchant vessel was captured by a warship, seized in port, or taken by a privateer.[49]

Privateers—ships of war fitted out by private individuals as business ventures with the object of financial gain—complicated the situation. Since privateers operated for profit, it was not uncommon for one to turn a blind eye to legal procedure; some were nearly pirates. The 1856 Paris Declaration respecting Maritime Law sought to abolish privateering. Though the United States declined to sign the Paris Declaration, Britain and many other nations did.[50] This was a significant event in the history of commerce raiding. Theorists at the turn of the twentieth century grappled with the future of commerce raiding in the absence of privateers, which had historically been one of its most effective instruments. Corbett speculated, "It is, of course, uncertain how far the Declaration of Paris will hold good in practice. . . . Any attempt to revive in this way the old *picaresque* [privateering] methods could only amount to a virtual repudiation of statutory international law, which would bring its own retribution."[51]

The years before World War I were a period of uncertainty in commerce warfare. Developments in international law seemed to limit the potential effectiveness of commerce raiding, while other issues, like the changing nature of cargoes to include the food a population required to survive, appeared to increase its importance. The effects of new technology were as yet unclear.

Both theorists recognized the need to balance numerous considerations in formulating their theories regarding war on commerce. Mahan in 1890 noted, "The attack and defence of commerce is still a living question."[52] If anything, the problem had become more acute by 1911 when Corbett wrote, "Modern developments and changes in shipping and naval material have indeed so profoundly modified the whole conditions of commerce protection, that there is no part of strategy where historical deduction is more difficult or more liable to error."[53] Both theorists worried that historical cases would not provide an adequate basis for their commerce warfare theories, but neither developed an alternative method for evaluating the subject. Neither could think outside the bounds of historical experience.

The Jeune École, a group of French naval thinkers during the late nineteenth century, contributed to the uncertainty of commerce warfare. The group's adherents recognized that the French navy would always be second in funding and importance to the army. As a result, France would never have a true battle fleet that could symmetrically challenge Britain for global naval dominance. This, however, did not temper their aspirations to defeat Britain in a maritime struggle. Given the history of the long wars between England and France during the eighteenth century and the expansion of the French colonial empire in the nineteenth, questions about French global security and the nature of the British threat remained very real grand strategic concerns. The Jeune École provided an economical answer using technologies like the fast torpedo boat and its weapon, the torpedo, to make France capable of inflicting disproportionate damage on the British battle fleet. The proponents of the Jeune École determined that the risk of losing expensive battleships would restrict British naval operations, creating a stalemate. With the fleets in deadlock, "the only real activity would be commercial warfare," which, followers of the Jeune École claimed, "would be absolutely merciless."[54] Merchant ships would be torpedoed without warning and their crews left to drown. The result would send cataclysmic shocks through world commodity and insurance markets that Britain could not survive.

Though followers of the Jeune École made some of their most cogent arguments in the 1880s, the viability of their theory remained questionable. In 1890 Mahan jested, "Human movement is not always advance; and there are traces of a somewhat similar ideal in the naval periodical literature of our own day."[55] There was a right way and a wrong way of conducting naval warfare, and Mahan believed that the Jeune École and its heirs belonged in the latter category.

In America, the 1880s witnessed an increased emphasis on American naval power, but questions lingered as to purpose of the U.S. Navy. America built several cruisers during the decade and advanced a doctrine of commerce raiding. Questions however lingered: was this the future or was the commerce raiding force merely a temporary development as the U.S. Navy burgeoned into a hemispheric or even global force, as Mahan hoped it would.[56] *The Influence of Sea Power upon History* was an argument for a global fleet and against a navy designed for commerce raiding. This type of warfare "is doubtless a most important secondary operation of naval war," Mahan explained, ". . . but regarded as a primary and fundamental measure, sufficient in itself to crush an enemy, it is probably a delusion, and a most dangerous delusion, when presented in the fascinating garb of cheapness to the representatives of a people."[57] Cost effectiveness could make a commerce-raiding fleet seem enticing for a democratic state where taxpayers elected the politicians.

The concepts espoused by the Jeune École faded but refused to die, and Mahan feared that these ideas coupled with new technologies would upend his vision of sea power. In 1904 Mahan noted, "Naval History bears witness to two continuous streams of belief; one in the superior efficacy of big ships, the other in the possibility of reaching some cheap means of offence, which will supersede the necessity of large vessels." Specifically, he addressed this in terms of the

> hope of bringing an enemy to terms by commerce destruction alone, to be effected by a number of small cruisers instead of obtaining control of the sea by preponderance of great fleets, supposed to be more expensive. No disappointment kills this expectation; experience is powerless against it, and is equally powerless to repress the theory, continually recurring, that some class of small vessel, with peculiarly redoubtable qualities will be found to combine resistlessness with cheapness, and so put an end to the supremacy, never heretofore shaken, of the great ship or the order of battle . . . the control of the sea will pass to the destroyer.[58]

Corbett developed a different set of arguments against the Jeune École. He did not worry that the Royal Navy would build the type of fleet the Jeune École advocated. Britain was an established naval power with a global empire, and commerce raiders were inadequate for its needs. Instead, Corbett downplayed the potential effectiveness of the Jeune École. Addressing the attack and defense of trade, he claimed, "The old strategical conditions, so far as can be seen, are unaltered except so far as the reactions of modern material make them tell in favour of defence rather than of attack."[59] This was a plea to harken back to historical precedent along with wishful thinking that technology benefited those tasked with commerce defense more than it helped those who wanted to attack commerce.

Their varying agendas led Mahan, Corbett, and even advocates of the Jeune École to ground commerce warfare within the question of its decisiveness: could commerce raiding by itself end a conflict? Members of the Jeune École thought so and sought to convince skeptics and receive funding to implement the strategy. Both Mahan and Corbett presented arguments to counter them. Adopting such a strategy could derail the rise of American naval power and create unacceptable perceptions of vulnerability for Britain's global maritime empire. Neither Mahan nor Corbett ever truly escaped the initial question of decisiveness.[60] Both developed narrow theories on commerce raiding based on its decisiveness rather than its lesser strategic effects. They espoused what they hoped would occur rather than analyzing all of the factors that might affect the ability of contemporary commerce raiding to influence and enable outcomes. Both remained focused on whether its effect was sufficient by itself to defeat a maritime state.

THEORY CONFRONTS PRACTICE

People write what they know: Mahan and Corbett knew the history of the age of sail and used that understanding to ground their respective theories. Yet both wrote in an era of rapid change. By 1914 a century had passed since the last great power naval war. Corbett bemoaned "the never ceasing change in the power, range and character of naval material [that] . . . left no stable factors on which a solid scheme could be built up."[61]

Without significant examples of how technology was affecting contemporary warfare, Mahan preferred to avoid conjecture. Writing of the Russo-Japanese War (1904–5) he noted: "It would be advisable . . . to caution persons not to jump too hastily to conclusions from the incidents that may present themselves. Such incidents will be facts; and a fact is a fact; but few facts are unconditioned, unrelated to other facts, without due consideration of which they cease to be facts and become pure fancies."[62] Both men became uneasy when speculating.

The submarine became a particular bugbear. In a 1907 article Mahan concluded, "The submarine possesses in high degree armored protection, invisibility, and the power to strike a blow deadly as the rattlesnake or cobra, and of as little warning in practise, if performance rise to the level of promise, her deeds may resemble the freaks of those personages of fairy tales, who possess an invisible cloak and deal bullets alike unexpected and unaccountable." The problem again dealt with the utter lack of proven capability. In the near term, Mahan thought submarines would be most effective contesting blockades. He admitted that "larger boats, of wider action and doubtless of intended greater speed, are being built; but it is neither requisite nor safe to speculate upon them, until tested." Mahan also realized that submarines might be only a temporary benefit to the side disputing command; more robust naval powers would find ways to counteract them.[63] The possibility for error was immense if Mahan let his speculations run wild; there were too many variables to provide a more detailed assessment.

Mahan remains difficult to pin down on the subject of new technology. He did not shun it, though one could cite his adage that "the old foundations of strategy so far remain, as though laid upon a rock" to make that claim. A stronger case can be made with his statement: "From time to time the superstructure of tactics has to be altered or wholly torn down."[64] Tactics changed, but strategy remained constant. Technological developments of the early twentieth century had modified the old tactical structures, and he found their effects difficult to assess. Thus, Mahan wrote at the outbreak of World War I, "I was non-committal on submarines and aero-planes, not because I have not opinions, but because after all only the test of war, which is now on, can give any reliable bases for estimate."[65] Mahan wanted evidence before delivering his verdict.

World War I provided such an opportunity. As the war began, he, like Corbett, thought the minor counterattack would prove most beneficial for the weaker fleet—in this case Germany.[66] He also thought that the Germans would attempt to reduce their level of inferiority "by attacks of torpedo boats, of submarines, and very probably by air-craft." Unlike the Russo-Japanese War, Mahan thought World War I would provide greater insight for theorists given the comparative skills of the adversaries. Several months later, in mid-October 1914, Mahan assessed the employment of new technologies: "I have been accordingly surprised that no more has been attempted."[67] He admitted that most such operations would be conducted in secrecy, however, and "if a full return of all submarine prowlings were obtainable, we should find many failures against each success." Given these thoughts, Mahan took a middling approach: "This question of the use of the increased efficiency of the submarine is assuredly one of the most important to be tested in actual warfare." He did not think that the submarine would be so effective as to result in "the complete effacement of the battleship."[68] But he also had "not ventured so positive an adverse opinion as sometimes I see attributed to me."[69] Mahan's full thoughts will never be known: he died on 1 December 1914.

Corbett lived another eight years. During that time he bore witness to British decision-making in World War I and wrote the first three volumes of the official naval history of that conflict. The third volume took the history of the war to the conclusion of the Battle of Jutland (1916).[70] Writing the official history finally allowed him to test his theories against actual events. The contrast between his prewar and postwar writings is significant. Prior to the war, Corbett's theory reflected the Victorian sensibilities of a soon to be bygone era, including his faith in international law. Addressing commerce raiding, Corbett thought it would be fought with the decorum and legalism that had appeared to govern much of its conduct in the Napoleonic period. Three years before the war, he went so far as to write, "No power will incur the odium of sinking a prize [merchant vessel] with all hands."[71] In retrospect, these words appear naïve.

In terms of minor counterattacks, he compared World War I with the age of sail in an attempt to distinguish the constants from the factors that changed. At the most basic level, Corbett believed Germany faced a strategic challenge similar to the one France often encountered in the eighteenth century: how to dispute Britain's command of the sea. Whereas the French lacked the means to do any more than threaten British trade, technological advances provided the Germans with new options. "By the enormously increased power of minor attack Germany could at least hope to reduce our margin of superiority so low as eventually to warrant her taking the offensive," Corbett posited. "Her policy had, therefore, even greater justification and greater promise than that which the French had been wont to adopt in analogous circumstances." He continued, "It appeared, indeed, we were faced with a new problem in naval warfare for which our old experience would not serve."[72]

Germany's "guerrilla warfare," as Corbett called it, did much "to shake the national faith in our old power of commanding the sea." Minor counterattacks changed how navies fought. The tools of the minor counterattack such as the mine, the submarine, and the torpedo eviscerated the old rules and decorum of European naval warfare. In the face of "Germany's flagrant contempt for the time-honoured customs of the sea," Corbett said, ". . . it was now clear that the niceties of the old naval code must be abandoned."[73] Warfare was suddenly more deadly.

Submarines posed a particular riddle. "Never before, perhaps, had a military operation been so deeply affected by means so small," Corbett said of one German submarine attack. But in another instance he judged the submarine no more than an "annoying irritation." Technology promised much and sometimes delivered, particularly when disputing command of the sea, but the record was mixed. The British adopted countermeasures and refined tactics to minimize risk while the Germans groped in the dark as they learned to utilize new technologies for disputing command of the sea. Still, Corbett considered the minor counterattack Germany's best option and questioned why the Germans failed to press counterattacks to the fullest useful extent and instead "turned its promising method of offence against a commercial objective instead of persevering against the naval one."[74]

Germany's employment of submarines as commerce raiders stunned Corbett. Though he admitted, "Naval authorities of the highest distinction had foretold before the war that the Germans would not scruple to use the new weapon against merchant ships both belligerent and neutral," Corbett had thought the Germans "were too sound strategists to risk raising fresh enemies against them by so flagrant a violation of the ancient customs of the sea." Several factors played into Corbett's assessment. First, "the almost incredible capacity which the Germans displayed for misunderstanding the psychology of their opponents during the war was one of its surprises." Second, Corbett sought examples from history, particularly the War of 1812 between Britain and the United States, to demonstrate how failure to respect neutral shipping had "always tended to raise up fresh enemies for the offending belligerent."[75]

When assessing the contemporary events of World War I, Corbett admitted, "The submarine as a commerce destroyer was threatening to become one of the most formidable factors in the war at sea." Even so, he saw the submarine's limitations:

> Owing to its essential vulnerability it could not operate in a true offensive spirit. Immunity from attack was the first consideration, and it therefore had to act by stealth and evasion. Consequently its only chance of avoiding destruction was too often to sink at sight with the inevitable risk of inflicting on powerful neutrals an unpardonable affront. The Germans thus found their new method of disputing the command of the sea was involving them in an insoluble dilemma. The more vigorous, extended and ruthless their submarine campaign against commerce became, the more likely it was to increase the strength opposed to them by sooner or later forcing neutrals into the ranks of their enemies.[76]

Having studied the dominant naval power for decades, Corbett had difficulty viewing the world from the weaker power's perspective. Facing British naval superiority and an ever-tightening blockade, Germany's leaders decided that the old rules did not apply. Corbett's consternation is palpable. This is most apparent when he was discussing a weaker naval power's attempts to dispute command of the sea. On the one hand,

Corbett's arguments are rational and clearly reflect Germany's limitations. Corbett shows how the submarine campaign against commerce inexorably drew the neutral United States into the war. On the other hand, Corbett failed to understand how British naval dominance made neutrality seem illusory, or how human suffering in Germany compelled dire strategic choices. In the end, Corbett never fully understood the near apocalyptic nature of naval warfare made possible by twentieth-century industrialization.

CHAPTER 10

OBTAINING STRATEGIC EFFECTS THROUGH THE CONTROL OF MARITIME COMMERCE

"Popular historians confine themselves to the great battles—St. Vincent, the Nile, Trafalgar—the single supreme days, the lofty mountain peaks in the landscape of time." Written as part of a review of Corbett's naval history of World War I, this quotation illuminates a conundrum in naval historical writing: "The battles, taken by themselves, distort the perspective; they are the merest pinpricks on the chart of history."[1] Battles tend to dominate naval historical literature even though naval warfare neither starts nor ends with battle; it is an inflection point within a broader story. To put it another way, battle is an intermediate object on the way to something more important: victory. Neither Mahan nor Corbett considered battle the aim of naval war; rather, weakening the opposing fleet through battle allowed the victor to more effectively exploit command of the sea.

Specifically, Mahan insisted that naval warfare did not end when one side could "preponderate over the enemy's navy." Instead, operations assumed a new character as the dominant navy utilized control of the sea to bring the full weight of sea power to bear against its opponent. He developed this argument in *The Influence of Sea Power upon the French Revolution and Empire* to describe how Britain after Trafalgar exerted economic pressure on Napoleon's empire.[2] A similar prospect developed in World War I. Writing in August 1914, Mahan described the possible effects of British sea power: "It is the unremitting daily silent pressure of naval force, when it has attained control of the sea against an opponent,—the sustained blocking of communication,—which has made sea power so decisive an element in the history of the world." Mahan speculated that Britain's naval dominance could exploit Germany's vulnerabilities. Its own geography restricted Germany's access to the global maritime commons. The British fleet positioned in the North Sea could take advantage of Germany's geographic predicament by sealing off Germany from world commercial markets. Without seaborne trade, its industries would wither and its people starve.[3] Mahan believed that British sea power would eventually break both the German economy and the will of its people. Though some might claim that this ran counter to Mahan's position on the pivotal nature of naval battles, one must consider the role of battle within his theory. Successful battle brought control of the sea, but it did not end a war. A sea power that had control of the sea did not need to fight a battle because it already possessed the ability to leverage control of the sea to wear down the enemy's economy.

Corbett agreed in principle: "For it is not successful battles that bring peace, but the fear or experience of what these battles give the victor power to do. On land it is clearly understood that military successes of the victor give him the power to choke the national life of his adversary so that there is nothing left but to submit or perish. With the less familiar contests on the sea, this has never been so self-evident."[4] He attempted to clarify this argument by developing a more precise vocabulary than Mahan's to explain the objects and phases of naval warfare.

"In the conduct of naval war all operations will be found to relate to two broad classes of object," he explained. "The one is to obtain or dispute command of the sea, and the other to exercise such control of communications." Obtaining or disputing command of the sea comprises operations that pit one naval force against the other. It is in this phase that great naval battles are fought: it is part of a contest to neutralize the opposing fleet with the object of commanding the sea. Once one side attains command, it can then exploit its advantages to bring its full weight against the opponent. This appears to parrot Mahan's argument; however, Corbett provided a caveat: the phases overlap. Many of the missions that fall under exercising command like commerce protection and prevention begin before neutralizing the opposing fleet and continue long after obtaining command.[5]

To a friend, Corbett explained, "I must confess that I have always thought one of my best bits of work was to formulate the distinction between holding the command & exercising it. It seems to me to go to the root of the whole thing, but few except yourself have caught on to it."[6] This is a bit disingenuous. Certainly Corbett coined the terms and considered the distinction more systematically, but Mahan had previously described the idea and noted the need to conduct the missions Corbett placed under its umbrella.

Since Corbett coined the terminology, we should define it within his intended context: "We engage in exercising command whenever we conduct operations which are directed not against the enemy's battle-fleet, but to using sea communications for our own purposes, or to interfering with the enemy's use of them. Such operations, though logically of secondary importance, have always occupied the larger part of naval warfare. Naval warfare does not begin and end with the destruction of the enemy's battle-fleet, nor even with breaking his cruiser power." Exercising command includes operations aimed at the protection or destruction of trade as well as the projection of military forces over the water.[7]

Exercising command is monotonous—Corbett called it "donkey work"—and for this reason far less has been written about it than the more dramatic battles fought to gain or dispute command. "Besides being dull," Corbett noted, exercising command "is of exceptional difficulty—can't be done so cleanly as of old."[8] Just months into World War I he lamented the tediousness of writing about it: "To begin with there is no sign at present that our naval war will make nearly so deep a mark from the point of view of development [of naval strategy] as did the Russo-Japanese War. The sides are too unequal. So far as we can see there will be no question of a struggle for command of the sea—it will only be a question of exercising command. So strongly do I feel this that I do not look forward to writing the history with any pleasure."[9] Even so, Corbett admitted, "Such colourless periods have occupied the greater part of naval wars and upon their right treatment most wars have turned."[10]

Though it was tedious, both Corbett and Mahan asserted that exercising command of the sea gave a naval power its most important leverage.

THE PROTECTION OF SHIPPING

An essential element in exercising command entails the ability to use the sea with limited risk for the transport of cargo, people, and military force. Corbett addressed using the sea as a highway from the perspective of the dominant naval power with the world's largest merchant fleet. Mahan's focus aligned with his own national perspective. The War of 1812 had left a strong impression on Americans. Approaching the war's centennial, Mahan thought, "Everybody—the navy as well—believed we had beaten Great Britain in 1812, brought her to her knees, by the destruction of her commerce."[11] He wrote his most scholarly work, *Sea Power in Its Relation to the War of 1812*, to refute the point. This forced him to consider commerce warfare in a level of detail that Corbett never did, but it kept Mahan's focus more fully historical.

Both theorists concluded that commerce could not be made invulnerable to attack. Even victory in great battles like Trafalgar and Tsushima could not guarantee security for commerce. Shipping losses should be anticipated so as not to upset the larger questions of strategy; or as Mahan put it, "One does not go to war expecting never to get a shin barked or a limb broken."[12] He explained, "Entire immunity for commerce must not be anticipated, nor should an occasional severe blow be allowed to force from panic concessions which calm reason rejects. Inconvenience and injury are to be expected."[13] Corbett agreed: "By no conceivable means is it possible to give trade absolute protection. . . . We cannot make war without losing ships. To aim at a standard of naval strength or a strategical distribution which would make our trade absolutely invulnerable is to march to economic ruin."[14]

World War I tested their views to the limit. The Germans took advantage of new technologies like the submarine and mine to make an unprecedented attack on commerce. This led Corbett to wander if

> the command could no longer be measured by the old standards. If command of the sea meant the power to move fleets, troops

> and trade freely where we would, then our command was not undisputed, and indeed it seemed to be growing gradually more precarious, as the mining activities of the enemy extended to our western coasts and their submarines with increasing power and range spread further and further afield. By the time we had freed the ocean highways there was scarcely an area in the Narrow Seas where movement could be considered safe. We found ourselves, in fact, faced with a new struggle of which we had no experience.[15]

Corbett wondered if the losses inflicted by the Germans rested on the precipice of becoming too extreme. Submarines certainly made the old principles on which command of the sea rested less secure, but one must ask whether command of the sea tends to appear more precarious during hostilities than in hindsight. Possessing command does not give complete exemption from loss, merely the expectation of executing critical operations at reasonable cost. But what amount of loss is reasonable? Experiencing the losses firsthand is very different from assessing their impact afterward. It might also be that Corbett's terminology, derived from the age of sail, did not accurately reflect conditions at the turn of the twentieth century given society's increased reliance on maritime food imports.

Though shipping losses reached unprecedented levels in World War I, the very fact that the Germans attacked merchant shipping was in no way unusual. Navies had from time immemorial linked their existence to commerce. Mahan explained, "The necessity of a navy, in the restricted sense of the word, springs, therefore, from the existence of a peaceful shipping, and disappears with it."[16] Corbett concurred: "We forget that so soon as the mercantile marine became a recognised burden on the navy, the main lines of commerce became also the main lines of naval strategy."[17]

Commerce protection can be characterized in two ways. First, the mere existence of a fleet protected commerce. The level of security was reflected in the overall naval balance. When a fleet could command the sea, commerce became even more secure. The stronger a navy was relative to its rivals, the greater the level of commercial security. Second, navies took specific actions to protect commerce. Mahan and Corbett identified four such courses of action: (1) convoys, (2) patrols, (3) doing nothing in hope that commerce raiders prove incapable of inflicting significant destruction, and (4) destroying commerce raiders' bases. Mahan and Corbett differed in the relative weight they assigned to each of these.

During the Anglo-French Wars of the eighteenth century, British leaders established an increasingly effective convoy system. Both Mahan and Corbett were quite aware of it from their historical studies. Convoys had drawbacks, however. Mahan noted several: "It is scarcely necessary to remark that much time was lost in collecting such huge bodies, and that the common rate of sailing was far below the powers of many of their members; while the simultaneous arrival of great quantities of the same goods tended to lower prices."[18] Moreover, the valuable convoys attracted attackers. The only counter entailed a powerful escort that could fend off the threats.[19]

Even with their financial disadvantages and their vulnerability to attack, Mahan preferred convoys as a means of commerce protection: "In the defence and attack of commerce, as in other operations of war, concentration of effort will as a rule be found a sounder policy than dissemination."[20] Convoys provided an obvious form of concentration. Moreover, Mahan thought the vulnerability of convoys much exaggerated: "A convoy is doubtless a much larger object than a single ship; but vessels thus concentrated in place and in time are more apt to pass wholly unseen than the same number sailing independently, and so scattered over wide expanses of sea."[21] A convoy could disappear into the vastness of the ocean by proceeding off the established trade routes. It was more likely that the convoy would pass unnoticed while commerce raiders would intercept several of the same ships sailing alone.

Corbett believed that convoying actually enhanced the risk to ships. Convoys moved only as fast as the slowest vessel and often added a leg or two to an oceanic passage because the merchant ships needed to proceed from their ports of embarkation to the convoy's assembly point, and the convoy's destination might not be a merchant vessel's terminus. Corbett speculated that the inefficiency of the convoy system would cause a greater loss in productivity than the losses that commerce raiders could actually inflict on individual ships. Further, the need to protect convoys modified the risk calculus for the entire fleet. Fear of losing a convoy caused naval leaders to alter deployments, creating vulnerabilities elsewhere.[22]

Instead of convoys for defending shipping, Corbett emphasized patrols focused on areas near arrival and departure ports—he called them "terminal" and "focal" points—where the sea-lanes converged: "Where the carcase is, there will the eagles be gathered together." Historically, "The most fertile areas always attracted the strongest attack." Britain's terminal points were near its naval bases and fleet concentration areas; they were of limited geographic expanse; and they did not change. These factors facilitated their defense and complicated attacks on shipping. Areas beyond terminal and focal points were rather infertile with regard to shipping given the ratio between the ocean's size and the number of merchant vessels.[23]

Mahan did not disagree with Corbett's assessment, specifically noting the vulnerability of terminal points.[24] "The commerce that congregates at the great centres scatters from them, far and wide, like the spokes of a wheel, end in fractions of varying size."[25] Moreover, he recognized the importance of sending warships on patrols.[26] In the end, he thought it "probable that both modes will be used; the convoy system being the dependence for the main supply, supplemented by the occasional single vessels. . . . Single ships must depend upon their speed, upon choosing routes with view to avoiding danger, and upon the general police of the seas by ships of the cruiser class."[27]

Mahan's emphasis on convoys and Corbett's on patrols at terminal and focal points reflected their geographic considerations. Britain's position on the map gave it a strategic advantage against a German, a Dutch, and to a lesser degree, a French threat. The British Isles provided a bulwark cordoning off many of the fertile areas where commerce raiders could effectively feast, and patrols could look after the remaining terminal points. The United States, with its Atlantic, Pacific, and Gulf frontiers, was less well positioned for defense of shipping. The geographic expanse required that patrols be stretched more broadly across the sea lines of communication. This would dilute their effectiveness, especially in comparison with the more concentrated area the British would have to patrol. It is hardly surprising that Mahan recognized the significance of patrols but did not focus on them as Corbett did.

A third means of protecting commerce entailed doing nothing. According to this argument, the cost of patrols and convoys exceeded the value of the losses that commerce raiders could inflict. The cost–benefit calculus accepted a small percentage of merchant ship losses as the price of maintaining maritime commercial links. Both theorists considered this possibility. Mahan's analogy to commerce being like "the spokes of a wheel [that] end in fractions of varying size" is indicative of this idea. Where there is little commerce, toward the end of each spoke, Mahan accepted doing nothing because the risk was not that great.[28]

Corbett considered the idea more fully in *Some Principles of Maritime Strategy*. While he never suggested leaving shipping unprotected at the terminal or focal points, doing nothing held greater potential in the intervening seas. Specifically, there were many areas of the world where there was a very low density of merchant commerce. These comparatively "infertile areas" spread commerce widely across the vastness of the ocean and made their defense impracticable.[29] This was especially true of Britain with its global empire. Big as it was, the Royal Navy lacked the numbers to be everywhere, and Corbett speculated that certain areas with very little merchant commerce did not need patrols. He accepted risk in these areas to be able to concentrate naval forces elsewhere.

Fourth, Mahan noted the importance of eliminating the commerce raiders' bases. As long as the raider hoped to bring its capture to port rather than sinking it, the base needed to be close to the hunting ground. Limits on endurance posed by coal capacity further added to the base's significance. Mahan recognized the importance of eliminating bases as early as *The Influence of Sea Power upon History*.[30] This should not be surprising given his broader arguments respecting bases. Corbett put less emphasis on bases and thus this course of action.

Mahan and Corbett used historical trends from the Anglo-French Wars of the eighteenth century to support their positions on commerce protection. In the intervening years, significant technological advances and alterations in the international environment had occurred. Mahan recognized the need to reassess: "The control of sea-borne commerce is a factor in the policy of naval states which is receiving little attention, and what is given is marred by prepossession and imperfect consideration."[31] Multiple writings contain snippets discussing the ways that modern conditions affected commerce protection; however, he did not address the concept as systematically as Corbett did in *Some Principles of Maritime Strategy*, where he wrote, "Modern developments and changes in shipping and naval material have indeed so profoundly modified the whole conditions of commerce protection, that there is no part of strategy where historical deduction is more difficult or more liable to error."[32]

The Paris Declaration Respecting Maritime Law (1856) had resulted in many states renouncing the use of privateers. Without privately owned commerce raiders to do the job for them, governments took full responsibility for the war on merchant shipping. Corbett imagined that naval vessels functioning as commerce raiders would follow the rather civilized, legalistic formulas refined during the eighteenth century. "The probability, then," Corbett considered, "is that in the future the whole problem will be found to be simplified, . . . with the result that the change should be found to tell substantially in favour of defence and against attack."[33] Corbett thought the threat of commerce raiders would become more manageable in the absence of privateers.

Corbett also considered the magnitude of commerce in his theory. Compared with the age of sail, there was substantially more commercial shipping tonnage by the turn of the twentieth century. "It is far more a matter of life and death to the nation than in the days when food and raw material did not constitute the bulk of our imports," he concluded.[34] Though some believed that a greater percentage of the navy should be devoted to trade defense as a result, Corbett came to the opposite conclusion: "The greater the bulk of commerce, the more difficult does it become to make any serious impression upon it."[35] In fact, he speculated that "the effective vulnerability of sea-borne trade is not in direct but in inverse proportion to its volume." Commerce raiders would make numerous captures, he thought, but losses would never amount to anything more than an annoyance for Britain.[36]

Technology also affected commerce protection. The most important factor entailed coal-powered propulsion systems. While wind-powered warships had virtually unlimited endurance but required wind for mobility, coal-powered ships could move under any conditions but were tied to coaling depots.[37] Mahan concurred, "The principal trammel which now rests upon the movements of vessels destined to cripple an enemy's commerce—the necessity to renew the motive power, coal, at frequent brief intervals—did not then exist."[38]

While both men addressed technology, Corbett's analysis generally went deeper, as in the case of wireless communications. He speculated that equipping merchant ships with wireless would result in immediate reports of attacks. Other merchantmen could then steer clear of trouble because "speed of conveying naval intelligence has increased in a far higher ratio than the speed of sea transit."[39]

After completing *Some Principles of Maritime Strategy*, Corbett wrote a detailed study of the Russo-Japanese War. His research provided data he needed to assess contemporary warfare. Corbett affirmed, "It was in fact being demonstrated that the changed conditions of naval warfare had not affected the fundamental principle on which our traditional system of commerce defence was based."[40] The old rules still applied. In this he agreed with Mahan, who noted: "Changes in weapons affect practice, but not principles."[41]

In hindsight, the two men's theories on commerce protection seem quaint and perhaps naïve given the level of brutality and destruction that occurred in both world wars. But Corbett's views aligned with prevailing thought within British naval circles during the decade before World War I.[42] Then, the first year of the war seemed to vindicate both theorists. Describing 1914 operations, Corbett wrote, "The vast extent of the Seven Seas was occupied in the traditional manner, not by patrolling the trade routes, but by guarding in such force as our resources permitted the main focal areas where they converged, and where the enemy's commerce destroyers were most likely to be attracted and had the only chance of making a serious impression upon the huge volume of our trade."[43]

This was exactly the argument he had put forward three years earlier in *Some Principles of Maritime Strategy.* Germany's surface warships were swept up in the war's opening months, and the losses they inflicted were quite manageable. Only with the introduction of the submarine and the erosion of ethical norms are the theories of Mahan and Corbett called into question. Mahan had died by that time, and Corbett never provided a full explanation of submarines' effect on warfare. His history of the naval war ended in 1916 with Jutland: he took his full thoughts on the submarine menace to his grave.

THE FLEET AND COMMERCE PREVENTION

Neither Mahan nor Corbett considered commerce raiding decisive for ending a war. Their more extensive views on individual commerce raiders as a means of disputing command of the sea appear in Chapter 9 in this volume. This section addresses the issue on a larger scale by considering how a fleet combines with various financial and governmental instruments of power to form a single commerce-eliminating organism. To describe this concept, both Mahan and Corbett used the terms "commerce destruction" and "commerce prevention."[44] They considered it among the most decisive possible tools of naval warfare.

Mahan argued, "Control of the highways of the ocean by great fleets destroys an enemy's commerce, root and branch."[45] Or, more famously, "It is the possession of that overbearing power on the sea which drives the enemy's flag from it; or allows it to appear only as a fugitive; and which, by controlling the great common, closes the highways by which commerce moves to and from the enemy's shores. This overbearing power can only be exercised by great navies."[46]

To understand the implications of the previous statements, we should return to Corbett's definition of command of the sea: "establishing ourselves in such a position that we can control the maritime communications of all parties concerned."[47] The more complete the command of the sea, the greater the ability to control the movement not just of hostile shipping but that of friends and even neutrals as well, thus resulting in the ability to regulate a regional or even the global maritime economy.

Mahan offered a similar argument: "For what purposes, primarily, do navies exist? Surely not merely to fight one another—to gain what Jomini calls 'the sterile glory' of fighting battles in order to win them." Though it is often lost in Mahan's writings, he clearly argued that one does not fight battles for the sake of fighting. Battles are fought for the purpose of controlling the sea lines of communication so the victorious naval power can control the movements of all parties. The victor can prevent commerce from supporting its opponent and regulate what it allows. Mahan explained, "Great Britain's navy, in the French Wars, not only protected her own commerce, but also annihilated that of the enemy; and both conditions—not one alone—were essential to her triumph."[48] The commonality of the sea lines of communication meant that a warship tasked with hunting enemy commerce simultaneously protected and regulated friends and neutrals as well.

Mahan continued, "If navies as all agree, exist for the protection of commerce, it inevitably follows that in war they must aim at depriving their enemy of that great resource; nor is it easy to conceive what broad military use they can subserve that at all compares with the protection and destruction of trade." Mahan noted that too many failed to comprehend "the difference between the guerre-de-course, which is inconclusive, and commerce-destroying (or commerce prevention) through strategic control of the sea by powerful navies." The latter was more effective because "blows at commerce are blows at the communications of the state; they intercept its nourishment, they starve its life, they cut the roots of its power, the sinews of its war . . . in very truth blows against it [commerce] are the most deadly that can be struck."[49]

Whereas Mahan noted the importance of preventing commerce by using the fleet's concentrated power, Corbett added arguments about the economic effects of doing so: "It is commerce and finance which now more than ever control or check the foreign policy of nations." Corbett placed more explicit emphasis than Mahan on finance: "Anything, therefore, which we are able to achieve towards crippling our enemy's finance is a direct step to his overthrow, and the most effective means we can employ to this end against a maritime State is to deny him the resources of seaborne trade."[50] Commerce raiding, Corbett admitted, can "produce inconvenience, but cannot paralyse finance." Instead, he claimed, "To injure credit to such an extent as to amount to a real consideration of war, operations against trade must be systematically carried on by land and sea till its main sources and the possibility of transit are practically destroyed."[51]

Though the fleet is the essential component of a successful commerce prevention campaign, it is insufficient alone. Land forces, the treasury, diplomats, the judicial system, and the government bureaucracy assist. Land forces eliminate hostile trading centers; the treasury monitors the flow of money; diplomats soothe neutrals whose interests are damaged by a commerce prevention campaign; admiralty courts adjudicate captures and legal disputes arising from actions against commerce; and the bureaucracy sets and enforces regulations. Only a sea power has such broad infrastructure as well as a fleet for enforcement.

COMMERCIAL BLOCKADE

Commercial blockade is a subset of commerce prevention. As Corbett explained, a commercial blockade's "immediate object is to stop the flow of the enemy's sea-borne trade, whether carried in his own or neutral bottoms, by denying him the use of trade communications."[52] Mahan made an important distinction in his description: "It is necessary to keep in mind the distinction between a blockade, in the loose use of the term, which closes a port only to the ships of the hostile nation, and the commercial blockade which forbids neutrals as well."[53] Moreover, Mahan claimed, "It is directed against merchant vessels, and is not a military operation in the narrowest sense, in that it does not necessarily involve fighting, nor propose the capture of the blockaded harbor. . . . Its object, . . . is the destruction of commerce by closing the ports of egress and ingress."[54]

Commercial blockades are possible only for fleets capable of exercising command of the sea. For a commercial blockade to be legal, public pronouncements must not only announce it but also specifically define the geographic parameters of the blockaded area, and then warships must maintain a permanent presence off the stated region.[55] These factors create a degree of predictability that can make the blockading fleet vulnerable to attack, so command of the sea is necessary to minimize risk.

Mahan and Corbett agreed broadly in matters of commercial blockade because both grounded their theories within established international law, which provided clear parameters in that regard. Commercial blockade held particular significance for Mahan because he had witnessed its effects as a young officer during the U.S. Civil War. In *Gulf and Inland Waters*, published before *The Influence of Sea Power upon History*, he explained, "The blockade was not defensive, but offensive; its purpose was to close every inlet by which the products of the South could find their way to the markets of the world, and to shut out the material, not only of war, but essential to the peaceful life of a people, which the Southern States were ill-qualified by their previous pursuits to produce."[56] Revisiting the topic in one of his last writings, he declared, "The four years' struggle of the Confederate States might not have ended in exhaustion, had it not been for the blockade, which shut in their cotton and shut out their supplies."[57]

Mahan considered commercial blockade "the most systematic, regularized, and extensive form of commerce-destruction known to war."[58] Corbett agreed: "By closing his commercial ports we exercise the highest power of injuring him which the command of the sea can give us. . . . He must, therefore, either tamely submit to the worst which a naval defeat can inflict upon him, or he must fight to release himself. He may see fit to choose the one course or the other, but in any case we can do no more by naval means alone to force our will upon him."[59] The last statement is critical. Though exercising command of the sea gives a naval power its greatest leverage, navies have limited ability to influence the outcome of a war. Whereas armies can occupy territory, navies do not possess this option. Navies rely on indirect attack. Preventing maritime commerce does not directly affect an adversary; rather, it relies on second- and third-order effects to convince an enemy population or government that resistance is futile. It aims to weaken an opponent and is often part of a multifaceted strategy that can include land operations. The latter is what Mahan witnessed in the Civil War.

Though both naval theorists came to similar conclusions regarding commercial blockade, their national perspectives resulted in different concerns. Mahan, writing for the United States as a developing sea power, considered how a state with a powerful navy might "interpret the phrase 'effective blockade' in the manner that best suits its interests at the time." He pondered whether the rights of neutrals, such as those advanced at the 1856 Paris Declaration Respecting Maritime Law, including definitions of neutral cargoes and commercial shipping, would affect a state's ability to enforce a blockade or limit captures at sea. He concluded, "The determination of such a question will depend, not upon the weaker belligerent, but upon neutral powers; it will raise the issue between belligerent and neutral rights; and if the belligerent have a vastly overpowering navy may carry his point."[60] This was a thinly veiled reference to Britain, which had the power to dictate the rules of commerce warfare. Corbett sought to manipulate this advantage by marrying aspects of commercial blockade with naval supremacy and global presence.

THE STRATEGIC BLOCKADE OF TRADE ROUTES

In 1911, Corbett advocated "an organised system of operations to secure a real strategical control of the enemy's maritime communications." This required a broad understanding of naval power. As he explained, "A riper and sounder view of war revealed that what may be called tactical commercial blockade—that is, the blockade of ports—could be extended to and supplemented by a strategical blockade of the great trade routes. In moral principle there is no difference between the two. . . . Except in their effect upon neutrals, there is no juridical difference between the two."[61] By equating the commercial blockade to a "tactical" action, Corbett sought to demonstrate how the ideas behind it could be applied to a strategy of global economic warfare, and he went on to claim that international law did not stand in the way. Corbett understood that Britain had the power to define the norms of international law and then execute a strategic blockade of the trade routes.

Accomplishing Corbett's strategic mission involved many layers beyond a commercial blockade. Together, Mahan and Corbett provided a menu of options grounded in geography. Britain's location vis-à-vis

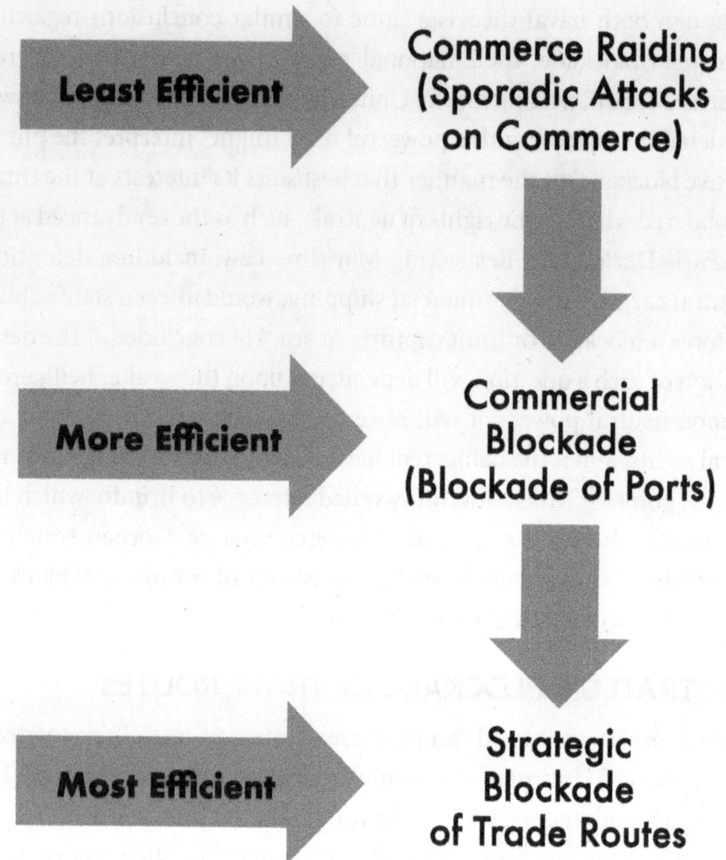

10.1. **Mahan and Corbett on Commerce Warfare**

Germany, France, and Holland provided tremendous advantages. Corbett acknowledged this, and Mahan agreed, noting Britain's "throttling geographical position towards German trade seems to me a factor of decisive importance in any conclusions reached."[62] Britain's geographic position combined with its global basing architecture allowed it to control movements on a global scale.

The strategic blockade of trade routes also depended on the relative positions of the fleets. Corbett noted, "It is well worth study even to-day, if only to note how entirely the arrangements took their shape from the presence or absence of an enemy's battle fleet."[63] The presence of an opposing battle fleet might make it impossible to exercise command of the sea and make the strategic blockade of the trade routes too risky. As long as the Royal Navy confined the German High Seas Fleet in the North Sea during World War I, however, Britain was able to execute a strategic blockade of the trade routes that approached a global scale.

Another factor entailed the location of the sea lines of communication. Mahan explained that "national maritime commerce does not consist in a number of ships sprinkled, as by a pepper-pot, over the surface of the ocean. Rightly viewed, it constitutes a great system, with the strength and weakness of such." He went on to identify where the weakness lay: "The weaknesses of commerce—the fatally vulnerable parts of its system—are the commercial routes over which ships pass. They are the bones, the skeleton, the framework of the organism. Hold them, break them, and commerce falls with a crash, even though no ship is taken, but all locked up in safe ports." Attacking maritime commerce thus should not be "the work of dispersed cruisers picking up ships here and there, as birds pick up crumbs, but of vessels massed into powerful fleets, holding the sea, or at least making the highways too dangerous for use."[64]

Corbett noted more clearly how to obtain this objective by dividing the maritime commons into fertile and unfertile regions. The best opportunities for attacking shipping were in the fertile regions (the terminal points), but those areas are often near naval bases and fleet concentrations. Given these factors, Corbett concluded, "These considerations lead us directly to the paradox which underlies the unbroken failure of our enemies to exercise decisive pressure upon us by operations against our trade." As long as Britain possessed the dominant navy or at least a navy capable of challenging command of the sea, Britain's opponents could not break its control of the terminal points, and thus could not put decisive pressure on the system.[65] The ability to defend one's own commerce was one side of the coin; the other side concerned the vulnerability of other states to this kind of attack: specifically were their terminal and focal points vulnerable? If so, naval power provided powerful leverage. This was particularly true of Germany. The geography of the North Sea placed Britain astride Germany's critical focal points, and Corbett sought to exploit this advantageous position for the Royal Navy.

Both theorists agreed that surgical strikes were not the most effective means of commerce prevention; a sea power had to use its raw strength to impose its will on enemy, neutral, and even friendly shipping. Government regulation was just as necessary to that as naval presence. Policing shipping demanded naval patrols and declarations of commercial blockade to limit the movement of belligerent shipping and restrict neutrals. Finally, commerce prevention required the strength to reinterpret international maritime law. Though Mahan and Corbett highlighted different aspects of commerce prevention, neither argued for a strategy of finesse; instead, they called for a strategic blockade maximizing the sea power's broad capabilities to impose its will forcefully on the maritime commons.

CHAPTER 11

JOINT, EXPEDITIONARY WARFARE

A navy that exercises command of the sea can regulate the commerce of friends, foes, and neutrals. Though this ability creates significant leverage, it may not be enough to obtain a state's objectives. Thus, it is not surprising that Corbett wrote of the "limitation of maritime power" in 1900.[1] A decade and half later, at the height of World War I, he asserted, "By naval means alone you can never end a war against a military Power."[2] Corbett understood the limits to what the naval instrument used in isolation could accomplish: he claimed that navies attained their most significant effects when working in combination with the army. Even the great naval victory at Trafalgar had no direct effect on the outcome of the Napoleonic Wars. "Its real importance," Corbett wrote, "was what it afterwards enabled Wellington to do [in the Iberian Peninsula]." More pithily, Corbett related, "We speak glibly of 'sea-power,' and forget that its true value lies in its influence on the operations of armies."[3]

Corbett divided operations into three broad categories: land, naval, and those that combined the two.[4] On the rare occasions when he wrote of strictly land operations he described them as the "continental" method of war. He believed Britain was not configured to wage this kind of conflict.[5] While the previous chapters have explored the naval category, this chapter focuses on operations in which the army and the navy worked in combination to provide what Corbett called "the characteristic expression of the British method of making war."[6]

The navy, by obtaining command of the sea, provides the necessary foundation for successful expeditionary warfare. As Corbett explained, "It was on the command of the sea that everything turned . . . without command . . . the war might be prolonged, [but] it could never be brought to a successful issue."[7] With command of the sea, various options of exercising command of the sea emerge. Whereas the previous chapter addressed the commercial and economic options possible for a navy exercising command of the sea, this chapter addresses how land operations become possible when a navy exercises command.

Corbett considered the navy an enabler in the pursuit of the state's political objectives, but this did not sit well with British naval leaders. Naval officers, Corbett thought, tended to emphasize the means of obtaining command of the sea rather than understanding how naval power brought the state closer to its political objectives: "To the sailor the aim of naval strategy must always seem to be the command of the sea." Obtaining command of the sea prioritized the naval instrument, but, Corbett, warned, "a bigoted adherence to it may become pedantry and ruin the higher strategy of the campaign." A focus on battles and the use of pure naval power resulted in a narrow, even counterproductive, view of strategy. While the navy provided a means of approaching the political objective, the actual object generally resided ashore.[8]

Maritime states achieved their greatest success when their leaders sought joint solutions in which the navy enabled more decisive land operations. Corbett claimed, "The interaction of naval and military policy and naval and military operations in our own case has always been so strong and close that neither can be rightly understood without the other."[9] "All our mistakes are due to neglecting to treat Naval and Military Strategy as one."[10] Much of his argument in *Some Principles of Maritime Strategy* was a warning: "We are accustomed, partly for convenience and partly from lack of a scientific habit of thought, to speak of naval strategy and military strategy as though they were distinct branches of knowledge which had no common ground. It is the theory of war which brings out their intimate relation. It reveals that embracing them both is a larger strategy which regards the fleet and army as one weapon."[11]

The complexities of expeditionary warfare are immense. There is no simple formula, for "in wars of this nature neither service can ever be entirely free to work for its own special ends."[12] Cooperation is essential. Each service must understand not only itself but also the other instruments of power to mitigate their respective weaknesses and maximize their particular strengths. Though Corbett called expeditionary warfare "that most difficult and least appreciated form of operation," he also believed that it leveraged Britain's greatest advantages.[13]

Though some have argued that Corbett's focus on joint warfare placed him virtually alone among his contemporaries, nothing could be further from the truth.[14] Edward Bruce Hamley in his 1866 study *The Operations of War* wrote about cooperation between the services.[15] Likewise, Philip Colomb in 1896 argued, "The work of building up the Empire has been done by the Army and Navy in conjunction, and it is absolutely necessary."[16] C. E. Callwell, in his 1899 book *Small Wars*, wrote, "The influence which sea power, judiciously employed, exerts upon land operations has attracted marked attention of late years. Its great importance is acknowledged, and its meaning is understood."[17] Three years later, G. F. R. Henderson, a noted commentator on land warfare, claimed a navy "without the help of an army ... can hardly force a hostile Power to ask for terms. Exhaustion is the object of its warfare; but exhaustion, unless accelerated by crushing blows, is an exceedingly slow process." Corbett even cited Henderson's influence on his own studies.[18] Edmond Slade, Corbett's closest naval colleague, wrote in 1907: "We ought now to have a very good chance of shewing that the Army & Navy are not two separate forces, but—only divisions of our force which should never be thought of as apart from each other." Corbett should very well have cited this passage, given its close parallel to a statement in *Some Principles of Maritime Strategy*.[19] Likewise, the final chapter of Corbett's book drew extensively from George Aston's recently published *Letters on Amphibious Warfare*.[20] Leading British defense intellectuals understood the importance of joint warfighting, but it was Corbett who brought their disparate voices together. As one of his contemporaries noted, "I don't think that anyone can do it so well as you."[21] In Corbett's final years, he was called "an apostle of the creed of 'amphibious warfare.'"[22]

CORBETT, EXPEDITIONS, AND THE DISPOSAL FORCE

In 1905, Colonel Sir Henry Rawlinson, commandant of the British Army Staff College at Camberley, asked Corbett to deliver a lecture he descriptively titled "The Functions of the Army in Relation to Gaining Command of the Sea, and in Bringing War with a Continental Power to a

Successful Conclusion." Rawlinson explained the lecture's intent: "So far as the British Empire is concerned in European war, where Naval objectives in the first instance must be paramount, and it seems almost probable that it may be necessary to call on the Army to co-operate in order to completely attain these objectives."[23] Though Corbett used Rawlinson's title, for the lecture he asserted the "army should never be employed for purely naval purpose." Unless fighting for purely naval objectives, a purely naval purpose would not suffice; instead, Corbett reaffirmed one of his prime analytical approaches: he asked his audience to determine the war's political object.[24] A clear answer to that question avoided the pitfall of assuming a one-size-fits-all approach to war. Only then could Britain employ its dominant navy and small army to maximum effect.

Corbett labeled the actual expeditionary army—the part of the land force not tied to imperial or home defense—"a disposal force." "Its operative power," he argued, "in fact, appears to bear some direct relation to the intimacy with which naval and military action can be combined to give . . . a weight and mobility that are beyond its intrinsic power."[25] When the fleet and army were not used in conjunction, "it was as if a man chose to fight with one hand at a time instead of fighting with both. Our Army certainly is weak, but when used with the Navy . . . it acquires certain peculiar powers out of all proportion to its numerical strength."[26]

After exploring numerous uses of the disposal force, Corbett concluded that it tended to be most effective when employed in theaters susceptible to isolation and where surprise was possible. Corbett admitted that surprise and isolation were often conflicting objectives because the act of isolating the theater tended to telegraph intentions: "A nice adjustment between the two opposing aims was always a cardinal point in settling the plan of operations."[27]

Corbett identified several means of isolating a theater. In overseas operations, a fleet possessing command of the sea could physically bar the movement of the opponent's forces into the theater of operations.[28] Geography could also create isolation: examples included Iberia in the Napoleonic Wars (1807–14), the Siege of Sebastopol in the Crimean War (1854–55), and Manchuria/Korea in the Russo-Japanese War (1904–5). In each of these wars, primitive road or rail networks made resupply overland difficult, in essence isolating the theater.[29] Corbett concluded, "Thus it is that in these cases we find the most conspicuous exhibitions of sea power; i.e. the preponderant sea power is able to confine the war to areas where it is comparatively strong enough to take the offensive."[30]

Corbett named flexibility the expeditionary land force's "most formidable characteristic."[31] The mobility the fleet provided such a force created an advantage equivalent to interior lines in land warfare.[32] Corbett thought that an amphibious force able to strike anywhere tended to "bewilder" and "baffle" opponents, who were forced "to split up their force into impotency."[33]

In the months before World War I, Corbett worried that British army leaders would sacrifice surprise by announcing the commitment of the expeditionary force to France. "That is the last thing we ought to do with it. As soon as its line is known, half its power is gone. At least that is what the old masters of amphibious war thought, but they don't seem to study them much now-a-days. They prefer German strategists. I don't."[34]

By 1914 a deep rift had developed between Corbett's theory and British practice. Corbett visualized disposal force operations in the context of the eighteenth century. His models included the Seven Years' War, in which Britain secured Canada from France and demonstrated the power of diversions on the French coast. In addition, he pointed to the Peninsular War in Iberia where the Duke of Wellington used favorable geography to extend disposal force operations into a long-term campaign against continental France.

Corbett also advocated keeping the expeditionary force in close communication with the fleet. If the army advanced too deep into the opponent's territory, it lost the advantages it possessed by operating with the fleet. Its operations then began to resemble the continental form of war.[35] Wellington faced setbacks when he made this mistake in Iberia, and Corbett believed British leaders were making an even greater mistake in World War I.[36]

MAIN LINES OF EFFORT, DIVERSIONS, AND ECCENTRIC ATTACKS

Keeping the purpose of an expedition in focus was, in Corbett's opinion, "one of the most vexed & difficult questions in strategy."[37] To simplify the topic he divided expeditions into three categories: invasions, small-scale diversions, and eccentric attacks. These, he thought, "mark actual vital changes in the essential character of the operation."[38] Corbett explained, "Only by keeping the classification in view, [do] we have a better chance of concentrating the discussion & arriving at an agreement between the services."[39]

Joint forces such as those Corbett envisioned could be employed as the main line of effort. Such invasions require a large force and significant preparation; thus, achieving surprise is difficult. The size of the invasion force makes this type of operation quite complex in execution and sustainment. Though operationally invasions stand among the most complicated forms of expeditionary warfare, they are strategically quite simple. They seek conquest "aimed as definite thrusts at the decisive points of a world-wide war." Corbett identified specific examples such as Quebec (1759) and Havana (1762) in the Seven Years' War, Walcheren (1809) in the Napoleonic Wars, and what the Japanese operations in Korea and Manchuria sought during the Russo-Japanese War (1904–5).[40]

In contrast to invasions, small-scale diversions aim at confusing the opponent's strategy.[41] Corbett identified diversions as "essentially a defensive operation, and if used otherwise or with higher intention is false strategy." Diversions employed small raiding forces that relied on surprise.[42] There was no thought of holding the objective; the diversion was a temporary expedient to draw forces from other theaters and disrupt the opponent's war plan: it was strategically defensive. At the tactical level, however, the diversion had many offensive characteristics because it required striking the opponent to put something the opponent valued at risk. It functioned as a type of counterattack possessing the hallmarks of active defense.[43]

While a single diversion might achieve the desired effect, multiple diversions historically had proved anathema. Corbett explained, "In the first place a diversion, if made at all, should be in such strength as to force the enemy to attend to it; and in the second all possible means should be taken to conceal the fact that it is only a diversion." Trying to execute simultaneous diversions would counter both points: "for by dividing his diversionary force he rendered each section too weak to do serious harm, and told his enemy plainly that he had nothing but a diversion in his mind."[44] Diversions must appear credible by being "directed against something which the enemy cannot afford to lose, otherwise he may ignore them and they will fail as diversions."[45]

Corbett's treatment of diversions required an evolution in his strategic thought. *England and the Mediterranean*, published in 1904, treated diversions in a less than positive light, describing them as "raids upon the coasts, which had no higher object than that of crippling the action of privateers and confusing the strategy of the French armies."[46] Over the next few years, Corbett's studies led him to reassess. He admitted, "Most of the operations are regarded as useless pin-pricks."[47] However, diversions can serve an important strategic purpose if they are intended to disturb the equilibrium and deflect the opponent's strategy. The objective is secondary to the intended effect, because the strategic effect rests in the opponent's reaction to the diversion.[48]

Clausewitz believed that diversions weakened the ability of the main force to mass at the decisive point; as a result, he advocated diversions only in rare and narrowly defined conditions. In Book VII, Chapter 20, Clausewitz actually provided examples of maritime expeditions from the Wars of the French Revolution and Napoleon, specifically the 1799 landing of an Anglo-Russian army in northern Holland and the 1809 British landings at Walcheren Island at the mouth of the Scheldt Estuary. Both expeditions sought to eliminate opposing naval forces and support coalition partners fighting elsewhere in Europe. Describing these, Clausewitz claimed,

> Regarded as diversions, [they] are only to be justified in so far that there was no other way of employing the English troops; but there is no doubt that the sum total of the means of resistance of the French was thereby increased. . . . To threaten the French coast certainly offers great advantages, because by that means an important body of troops becomes neutralised in watching the coast, but a landing with a large force can never be justifiable unless we can count on the assistance of a province in opposition to the Government.[49]

Corbett contended that Clausewitz's continental mindset blinded him to the strategic purpose of these operations. Specifically, there was a class of operations that differed from either a true diversion or an invasion bent on conquest. He labeled this third category the "eccentric attack," which he defined as a "complex or 'continual' diversion."[50] Corbett developed his understanding of the eccentric attack by studying Pitt's decision-making in the Seven Years' War. A series of operations in that war did not fit the parameters of either a diversionary raid or a main line of effort. "Such well-adjusted combinations of land and sea force present probably the most difficult and confusing of all strategical problems. Their power was Pitt's great discovery, the method of employing them his strategical legacy—and it is in the skilful and instructed use of them that lies the greatest power of a maritime state to this day."[51] Even though an eccentric attack might be one of few options for a maritime power fighting a continental state, Corbett did not consider the eccentric attack a weak method of war. Rather, it used the comparative advantages of the maritime state in the most effective way.[52]

In the proper conditions, a maritime state could employ an eccentric attack to great effect. It worked most effectively when that power had a

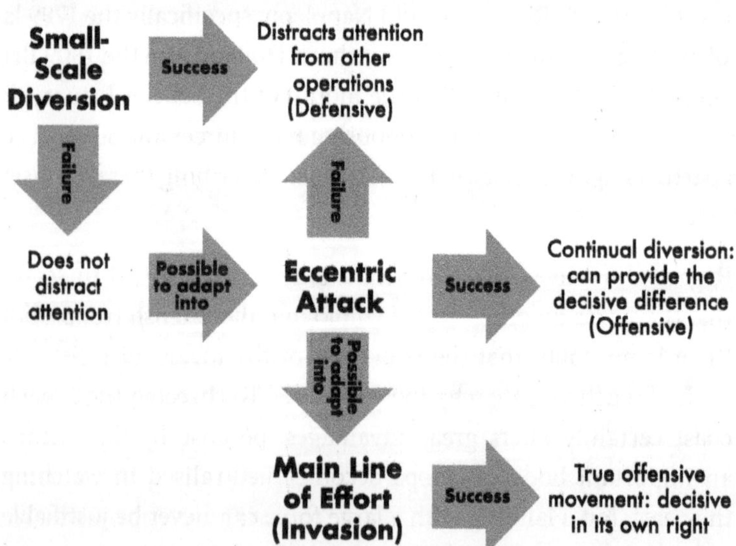

11.1. **Corbett's Types of Expeditions: Diversions, Eccentric Attacks, and Invasions**

continental ally that could go toe-to-toe with the mass of the opponent's army, creating a stalemate on the main front while the maritime state struck amphibiously with its disposal force at the point that could provide the decisive difference.[53] This was neither a transitory raid aimed at distracting an opponent nor an invasion designed to win the campaign on its own.

An eccentric attack aimed at taking an object and holding it, and thus was "primarily offensive in its action." Such attacks suffered from several inherent limitations. "The reason for this appears to be that . . . as such an expedition rises in strength so it loses the advantages of rapidity, secrecy, and surprise; the objectives at which it is likely to aim become fewer and consequently more easily determined." Given these weaknesses, Corbett advised against eccentric attack "unless we seek to acquire some definite point from the enemy and to hold it, in order to set up a permanent diversion."[54]

It should be noted that a diversion might develop into an eccentric attack and an eccentric attack into an invasion; an eccentric attack might even be relegated to the lesser status of a diversion. The mobility of the fleet gave the maritime state significant flexibility to reassess when it proved necessary. For example, the object of a diversion must be something of importance; otherwise, an opponent will not divert forces to defend it. But what occurs if the opponent fails to react? Chances are that the expeditionary force will seize the object. It failed as a diversion because the opponent did not shift forces from other efforts, but by seizing the object, the expeditionary force gained a position of importance. Rather than abandon the venture altogether, Corbett recommended turning the diversion into an eccentric attack where the maritime state holds the object to gain greater strategic effects over the long term. Likewise, if the expedition aims at seizing the object but the opponent unexpectedly diverts enough forces to prevent this from occurring, leaders should reassess the purpose of the expedition because it now functioned as a diversion.[55] The distinction between a diversion, an eccentric attack, and an invasion rests to a great extent on the opponent's reaction.

Though leaders needed the agility to reassess, this must always occur while keeping the object, intention, and possibilities of the expeditionary operation clearly in focus. Particularly troublesome was the tendency of what today would be termed "mission creep," in which an operation that began as a diversion developed into an eccentric attack or even began to be treated as a true invasion even though the object or the intent of the operation within the original war plan had not changed.[56] Corbett witnessed this problem firsthand in the Dardanelles (1915–16), where he watched as a diversion "was pushed too far," morphed into an eccentric attack and ended in failure.[57]

RELEVANCE

In the decade before World War I, Corbett searched for a historical answer to the real-world strategic problem regarding Britain's best course of action should war with Germany break out. He worried that the British army would be drawn into a continental war in France instead of taking advantage of Britain's joint capabilities. Corbett looked to the eccentric attack as a solution. He modeled his ideas on Pitt's actions from the Seven Years' War coupled with an even more effective operation in the Iberian Peninsula during the Napoleonic Wars and attempted to apply these forms of joint warfare to a potential showdown with Germany. Questions, however, existed about the effectiveness of eccentric attacks given modern technologies, including more lethal flotilla craft that could contest amphibious landings, and improved communications and transportation technologies that quickened the continental states' response to amphibious operations. Corbett even hinted at this, noting a "wide difference of military opinion as to whether such operations are possible now." However, Corbett's choices were limited. The geography and the nature of the German opponent restricted options, as did the means at Britain's disposal.[58]

It concerned Corbett that expeditionary operations were never popular with either the army or the navy.[59] Moreover, he worried that British leaders misunderstood the effects such operations could provide. A miscalculation could prove disastrous if an eccentric attack mushroomed into a main line of attack beyond Britain's means. The eccentric attack might also expand the war geographically and steel the resolve of the enemy.[60]

Try as he might, Corbett found his theories of expeditionary warfare ever more out of step with Britain's strategy. Sending the whole expeditionary force to France in 1914 created the conditions for Corbett's nightmare scenario, or what he later called "a costly method of war, beating the Germans at their own game."[61] He believed that British leaders had forsaken the joint advantage, to Britain's great detriment. Describing British strategy in the middle of World War I, Corbett lamented, "Now there was to be a complete divorce, and each service was to play a lone hand."[62] He wrote to Jacky Fisher in June 1918, "I wept when our whole Expeditionary Force was going to France, and felt what it would mean, and how Pitt would turn in his grave." He went on to explain the result. "When the time came to strike amphibiously for a decision, we had nothing to strike with. . . . It is a lamentable tale for me to tell. . . . It is the most bigoted 'soldier's' war we have ever fought, and this at the end of all our experience." In disgust, he asked, "Why didn't I devote my life to writing comic opera, or collecting beetles? I might just as well."[63]

MAHAN AND EXPEDITIONARY WARFARE

A casual understanding of Mahan would indicate that his theory has little applicability to joint approaches, but he actually paid them more attention than is often credited. Failure to understand this has led to inaccurate comparisons with Corbett.[64] Theories about joint warfare were not uncommon in period military writings, and both Mahan and Corbett based their respective arguments on a similar theoretical foundation. Thus, we should not be surprised that the American wrote for all intents and purposes about the same disposal force concept as Corbett, noting Britain's "small disposable force which she maintains in excess of the constant requirements of her colonial interests."[65] In other writings Mahan described the mobility conferred on the amphibious force by its close cooperation with the navy.[66] Mahan did not, however, develop joint concepts in Corbett's level of detail, and regrettably, his thought process was not as clear.

Mahan's first foray into historical writing, *Gulf and Inland Waters*, told the history of joint expeditions in the U.S. Civil War, and he reprised this narrative in his biography of David Farragut. His study of the Spanish-American War also pointed in this direction, for he concluded, "It has

. . . the special value of illustrating the reciprocal needs and offices of the army and the navy, than which no lesson is more valuable to a nation situated as ours is."[67]

As early as the *Influence of Sea Power upon History*, Mahan wrote, "In it we have seen and followed England, with an army small as compared with other States, as is still her case to-day, first successfully defending her own shores, then carrying her arms in every direction, spreading her rule and influence over remote regions."[68] At its heart, this is an argument quite similar to Corbett's, noting Britain's small army functioning most effectively in coordination with the Royal Navy. Mahan added to this argument in *The Influence of Sea Power upon the French Revolution and Empire*, noting that the Iberian Peninsula was "where the British sea power had at last found the place to set its fangs in his [Napoleon's] side and gnaw unceasingly." Mahan described the favorable geographic position of the peninsula, which was "for the French a salient thrust far out into the enemy's domain on the sea." Geography created ideal conditions for Britain to use a combination of naval and land power.[69] Just as they served Corbett's theory, Wellington's operations in Iberia provided a powerful example for Mahan to illustrate the effectiveness of a small army operating in a favorable geographic location.

Mahan's argument differed from Corbett's in explicitly asserting that the navy was the decisive factor: "the scales rose and fell according as the one navy or the other appeared on the scene." The navy provided the expeditionary force with protection, sustainment, and escape. While Corbett emphasized the coordination of the naval and land elements, Mahan placed greater emphasis on the navy's role. Addressing the Yorktown campaign of 1781, Mahan asked, "What was the determining factor in this strife? Surely the navy, the organized military force afloat." Moreover, "the conclusion continually recurs, whatever may be the determining factors in strifes between neighboring continental States, when a question arises of control over distant regions, politically weak . . . it must ultimately be decided by naval power, by the organized military force afloat, which represents the communications that form so prominent a feature in all strategy."[70] For Mahan, control of the lines of communications was the deciding factor in joint campaigns. While describing operations against Quebec in the Seven Years' War, for example, Mahan noted that British operations "depended wholly upon the control of the water by the navy." He felt the significance of controlling maritime communications was often overlooked. In the case of Quebec, it "was so quietly exerted as to draw no attention from the general eye."[71] This is a critical issue: sea power works quietly to isolate the opponent and creates conditions in which the land element can act most effectively. Mahan was not anti-army; he was pro-navy.

GREAT EXPEDITIONS AND DIVERSIONS

Mahan remained more circumspect about joint operations than his British counterpart. He described British joint operations on the eastern seaboard of the United States in the War of 1812, for example, as "in spirit and in execution essentially desultory and wasting."[72] Mahan believed that such operations had little influence on the outcome of the war, or at least no influence commensurate with the cost. It is important to dissect Mahan's thoughts on the types, effectiveness, and limitations of joint actions. He divided them into two kinds: great expeditions and diversions.[73] Though he wrote about eccentric movements, he did not follow Corbett's contention that it was a special type of joint action.

For "invasions in force," Mahan emphasized the advantage of rapid movement but was willing to sacrifice a certain amount of speed for better preparation, greater numbers, and what he termed "a graduated advance." Large expeditions were too costly and significant to be risked lightly, so they required an adequate fleet to cover, protect, and sustain them. An invasion in force aimed at "a permanent sustained action" entailing conquest through offensive movements at the critical point, or "keystone," of the campaign or war.[74]

Mahan based his arguments on the practices of land warfare. To him, the components of a joint campaign differed little from those of a land campaign. Both required "the choice of a base, an objective, and of a line of operations."[75] This is part of a larger argument he crafted in his Naval War College lectures and developed further in his last major work: *Naval Strategy Compared and Contrasted with the Principles and Practice of Military Operations on Land* (1911). As the title suggests, Mahan attempted to apply theories of land warfare to naval campaigns. He found large expeditions a point of significant overlap. In this, he contrasted sharply with Corbett, who railed against "the fallacy—against which I am always preaching—of arguing directly from military to naval conditions."[76]

Though Mahan found significant resemblances between land and naval operations, his comparisons generally provided only a point of departure. This was also very much in keeping with his attempts to find similarities while remaining cognizant of differences. With expeditions, he concluded that the more geographically distant the object the more a joint expedition differed from its counterpart on land, for the feasibility of water transport allowed for greater mobility. However, distant overseas expeditions lacked the decisiveness of their counterparts on land "because the blow is delivered upon the extremities and not at the heart. They are also harder to sustain than to make."[77]

Whereas great overseas expeditions are offensive movements, diversions are defensive in character. In this, Mahan and Corbett agreed. "Diversions, in truth," Mahan argued, "are feints, in which the utmost smoke with the least fire is the object. Carried farther, they entail disaster; for they rest on no solid basis of adequate force, but upon successful deception."[78] Elsewhere he noted, "Strategically, the success of a diversion, although it may be eminently contributable to the success of war, is not vital to it."[79] He defined the concept more specifically: "Pressure is possible, more or less, in all conditions of life, where interests are extensive, various, or scattered. It is notably so in international life, where action in one quarter is continually hindered by the consciousness of weakness elsewhere. Brought into action for military ends, this means of constraint is known technically as 'diversion.'"[80] Thus, a diversion supported operations on the main front but was not a war-ending strategy, and leaders who sought decisive results through diversionary action should expect failure. Diversions are based on deception and the threat of action, and they take advantage of the close joint coordination of naval and land forces. So far, Mahan's conclusions closely align with Corbett's.

Unlike invasions, which require a powerful navy to project and sustain them, "promising diversions are permissible even with an inferior navy, . . . [t]he deciding consideration being whether the prospect of gain reasonably overbalances the probable losses from a failure." Diversions "may naturally accept risks greater, proportionately to their size, than would be proper in the graver undertakings; because the total hazard is not so great, nor will failure be so disastrous. Chances may be taken with a boat which would be unjustifiable with a ship, and with a ship that would be indiscreet with a fleet."[81]

Mahan, however, held diversions in less esteem than did Corbett, as evidenced by his opinion of expeditionary operations on the French coast in the Seven Years' War: "It is more than doubtful whether this direction of British power, in partial, eccentric efforts, produced results adequate to the means employed."[82] Diversions were antithetical to Mahan's emphasis on concentration. "All which goes to show that upon the whole it is better to rely upon superior numbers to overcome your enemy than upon powerful diversions to mislead him."[83]

His views on concentration also led Mahan to use the word "eccentric" differently than Corbett, even though he was aware of Corbett's argument linking it to a specific type of expedition.[84] Mahan used "eccentric" to indicate how peripheral the expedition was to the main line of effort or to describe any action that took forces "away from the centre." He considered eccentric movements "inconsistent with [the] well-founded and generally accepted principle of war."[85] Eccentric action diluted force

MAHAN AND CORBETT LARGELY AGREE ABOUT DIVERSIONS

They are defensive, designed to support operations elsewhere: they do not provide war winning effects.

ONLY CORBETT ADDRESSED THE ECCENTRIC ATTACKS

They provide "continual diversion" aimed at seizing a position that provides the maritime power leverage: they aim at making the decisive difference in a larger war.

MAHAN AND CORBETT LARGELY AGREE ABOUT INVASIONS

They are offensive movements with the object of conquest.

11.2. **Types of Expeditionary Operations**

and scattered effort; as a result, "the reasons for such action should be most closely scrutinized."[86] Mahan concluded that "such a movement is perfectly proper and wise, *upon the condition* that you not embark in it so many men as to weaken your main effort, and yet do send so many as to alarm the enemy seriously."[87]

THE RELATIONSHIP BETWEEN THE LAND AND NAVAL INSTRUMENTS

Mahan advised those responsible for expeditions to develop a broad-ranging net assessment that dealt first with the naval balance; second, delineated the roles of naval and land forces; third, assessed risk carefully; fourth, addressed the distance that the force needed to be projected; and, finally, examined the physical geography of the theater of operations.

Determining the naval balance between the opponents is the critical first question before mounting an expedition. If the two navies were equally matched, Mahan recommended dispensing with the expeditionary force and instead seeking the opposing fleet. As long as the enemy fleet survived, one should not dilute naval power for joint expeditions. Seeking and defeating the opposing fleet created freedom of maneuver on a grand scale. However, if the navy possessed a preponderant advantage in size, it should support amphibious operations to seize objectives ashore that enhanced command of the sea, including the capture of the bases of commerce raiders.[88]

The second question concerned the respective roles of the naval and land instruments. "When war exists between two nations separated by the sea, it is evident that the instrument of offense is the arm which carries on the invasion, that is, the army." The army served as the offensive factor while "the navy preserves, and assures, the communications of the army. That the navy alone makes invasion possible, does not make it the invading force. That it alone makes the offensive possible, does not make it the offensive arm. That its own mode of action is offensive does not necessarily constitute it the offensive factor in combined operation. In the joint action it takes the defensive."[89] This is significant. From the joint perspective, the army assumed the offensive while the navy provided the defensive support.

This might appear antithetical to Mahan's overall theory, but the defensive naval function was not to be of the passive variety. Instead, the navy was to undertake an active defense: "That, in pursuit of this defensive rôle, it takes continual offensive action whenever opportunity offers to destroy an enemy's ships, does not alter the essential character of its operations."[90] By seeking out and destroying opposing ships that could interfere with the expedition, the navy defended the expeditionary force, controlled the sea, and allowed the land force to secure its objective. This is quite consistent with Mahan's views on the active defense.

Expeditionary warfare entails significant risk: Mahan's third point of assessment asks leaders responsible for the expedition to determine the acceptable level of risk. This was particularly true for the decidedly weaker naval power. If the value of the object was high, the only course entailed rapid movement, with the object of seizing the critical objective ashore. Though outnumbered, the weaker power had the chance to succeed. "The question then would arise whether the superior naval state would be willing to endure the protracted contest necessary to expel the intruder."[91]

The distance the expeditionary force needs to be projected is the fourth point of assessment. Mahan recognized that soldiers move more quickly by sea than by land. This conferred enhanced mobility on an amphibious expeditionary force, but the price for mobility was mass. Limits to shipping tonnage restricted the size of the expeditionary force. The further the force must be projected, the weaker it became as supply considerations removed shipping devoted to amphibious lift.[92]

Finally, geography is the critical determinant. The Iberian theater of the Napoleonic Wars serves as the classic example. Surrounded on four of five sides by water, it was the ideal environment for the sea power. But, this was not enough: the sea power needed harbors, like Lisbon, and access to the interior through river systems.[93] When discussing the viability of expeditionary operations, Mahan reprised the geographic attributes from his six elements of sea power. The actual location in respect to the home country and friendly bases proved critical. Geographic location also foretold whether the theater could be isolated. Geography allowed for access that enhanced the effectiveness of joint expeditions. Moreover, the size of the land theater could work against the sea power. Britain encountered this very issue in the American Revolution.

■ ■ ■

Mahan presented his most cogent arguments on expeditionary warfare in chapter 9 of *Naval Strategy Compared and Contrasted.* Elsewhere, hints and quips are the rule. Although he recognized their usefulness in certain situations, he spent comparatively little time on expeditions, primarily because he was propagandizing sea power. The more he engaged expeditionary warfare, the more he removed "the sea" from his overall argument. Diminishing the significance of diversions and even great expeditions aimed at eccentric targets further supported his emphasis on concentration. Still, Mahan could not escape expeditionary warfare. Projecting forces overseas is an essential course of action. His early experiences in the U.S. Civil War attested to this, his studies of England noted it, and witnessing the Spanish-American War confirmed it.

Germany's emergence as Britain's chief competitor and potential opponent in the early years of the twentieth century forced Corbett to engage expeditionary warfare far more systematically than did Mahan. Real-world debates in Britain about the use of force to confront Germany led some to extoll continental operations in France, while Corbett—and his employer, the British navy—sought to highlight joint approaches. Corbett emphasized the relevance of the navy in the contemporary debate. He used his deep historical understanding of British grand strategy to describe how an enabling navy multiplied the strength of its smaller but effective army for decisive political effects.

CHAPTER 12

MAHAN'S WAY OF WAR

Rather than presenting a disjointed smattering of principles, concepts, and observations, both Mahan and Corbett linked ends, ways, and means as they attempted to develop a comprehensive explanation of how states with powerful navies could operate most effectively in the international environment. This included the sequencing of objectives and the reliance on different instruments of national power for attaining them. Neither Mahan nor Corbett described every instrument of power or every contingency in the same detail. Where they focused their attention often illuminates what each writer considered most significant for his country. While the previous chapters have addressed specific aspects of their theories, this chapter and the one that follows draw their concepts together to present the distinct "way of war" each man advocated.

Naval powers, according to both Mahan and Corbett, can wage war more efficiently than continental land powers by taking advantage of what Corbett labeled "free strategical design."[1] States with powerful navies can more effectively adapt to circumstances, define areas of operation, modulate the intensity of the action, and dictate the type of war on which they embark. Naval power, however, was no silver bullet for either Mahan or Corbett; both noted its significant limitations. They explicitly detailed some of these weaknesses in their writings; others are implicit within their arguments.

Many who have commented on Mahan's theories—among both his contemporaries and subsequent generations—have fixated on his treatment of battle and gaining command of the sea. Mahan is at least partially to blame for an incomplete comprehension of his theory: he wrote a tremendous amount on varied subjects, but his writings are not particularly systematic. He never laid out his theory of war in a single document. He had the opportunity in his 1911 book, *Naval Strategy Compared and Contrasted*, but chose not to do so. Indeed, Mahan described the book as "the most perfunctory job I have ever done in book writing." One reviewer noted that it did not have the same clarity as Corbett's concurrent volume, *Some Principles of Maritime Strategy*.[2]

SEA POWER, SECURITY, AND DETERRENCE IN PEACETIME

One major difference between Corbett and Mahan lies in the breadth of their respective theories. Corbett focused on what occurred during hostilities. British leaders already understood how to use the navy in peacetime to support diplomatic objectives and protect the British Empire. A more significant strategic problem in the years before World War I concerned the effective use of naval power in wartime. Mahan confronted a different worldview that necessitated a much broader theory. He needed to explain to Americans the importance of sea power in both peace and war. To do so, he created a narrative starting with how various elements could coalesce in peacetime to develop the economic and naval elements of sea power, then he developed an argument to chart the employment and utility of sea power across the peace–war continuum.

Mahan first asked leaders to assess their state's peacetime strengths and weaknesses. Not every state was destined to become a sea power: many factors had to align to make that happen. Some of those, including geographical factors, were beyond the scope of possible change; a state's position on the map could by itself kill the sea power dream. In addition to a favorable geography, the state's population needed to encourage overseas ambitions. Only with a supportive population and advantageous geography could a government effectively nurture sea power. Mahan developed the six elements of sea power as a metric to determine if its pursuit would benefit the state.

Sea power had naval and commercial elements. Naval power alone or economic power in isolation did not constitute sea power. The union of the two elements created the wealth and strength necessary for sea power. During Mahan's lifetime, the global sea power was Great Britain, and he used that country as his model. Before addressing sea power in war, Mahan insisted, "We have first to consider the influence of the maritime power in itself, and the functions discharged by Great Britain simply in consequence of possessing this great and unique resource."[3] The economic side of sea power created wealth. Commerce brought riches to the people and investments in industry and markets. Wealth also generated tax revenue that funded a stronger navy. In effect, the government and people formed a pair of intertwined virtuous circles, one of power and the other of wealth, that allowed the sea power to prosper in peacetime and grow in wartime.

Mahan believed that "the most beneficial use of a military force is not to *wage* war, however successfully, but to *prevent* war."[4] He was not a warmonger, regardless of what some contemporaries claimed; rather, his perspective was that of a Social Darwinist who believed that only the fittest society would survive. In a highly competitive international environment, Mahan wanted the navy prepared to meet contingencies. Only then could the navy assist the state in attaining national policy objectives while averting hostilities.

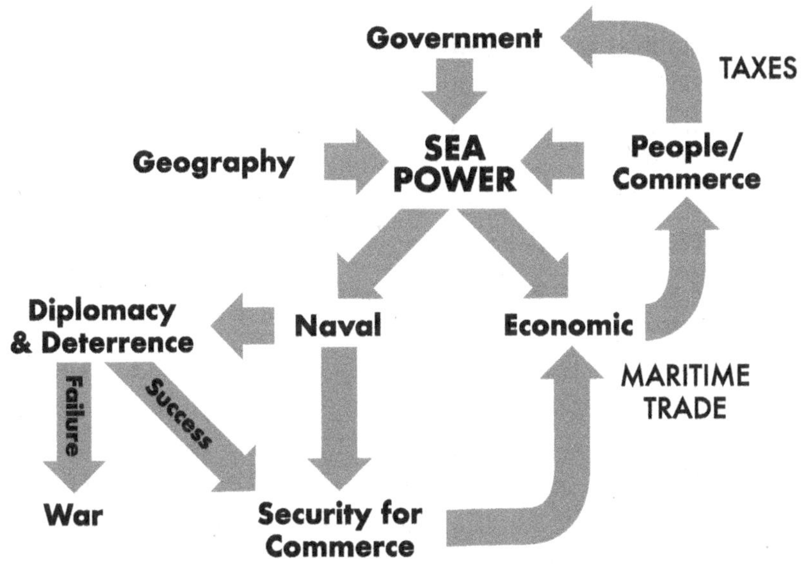

12.1. **Mahan's Theory of Sea Power in Peacetime**

Of the armed services, Mahan emphasized the navy, which he considered less threatening domestically and more effective internationally than the army: "A navy . . . can very rarely be used to oppress the people of its country in their domestic conditions, as armies often have been. While thus more strictly international, the scope of navies is also far wider."[5] But this occurred only if the navy could sustain forward deployments. A coastal defense force was inadequate to provide leverage in international disputes.[6] Navies capable of projecting force supported diplomacy through the perception of power and the threat of force. Mahan called this "war without bloodshed" in that a well-prepared military organization could secure political objects without recourse to violence.[7]

"One price . . . alone has ever insured peace," he asserted, and that was "readiness for war."[8] In 1912, on the eve of World War I, he noted, "The last decade has seen a half-dozen bloodless wars, and decisive victories, effected by adequate armament." Further, he said, "The armaments of other States have a definite object, which object is not war, but the enforcement of National purpose in moments of international crisis by being ready for war if the worst come. Statesmen are arming, not because they want fighting, but because they consider that conditions of which they have familiar knowledge render armament necessary."[9] Thus, "the organization of force tends to diminish *violence*, which is the characteristic that distinguishes force in exercise from force in effect—War from Diplomacy."[10] Though preparation certainly created a powerful deterrent, Mahan did not comprehend the effects of preparation when deterrence failed. By that point, nations had become armed camps: preparation for war contributed to the slaughter that occurred in World War I. In conclusion, Mahan preferred diplomatic responses to crises instead of war but demanded preparedness to ensure that diplomatic options stood the greatest chance of success.

His arguments emphasizing preparedness were especially relevant for Mahan's own country. "It is in preparation beforehand, chiefly if not uniformly," he asserted, "that the United States has failed."[11] A significant example was his understanding of the War of 1812 between the United States and Britain. In his final years, he found striking parallels between that period and his own.[12] In both eras, the United States was a neutral party in European disputes. Before 1812, the United States prepared poorly. The army and navy were too small to defend the nation, much less obtain objectives that U.S. leaders sought at the start of the war. The nation's economy collapsed during the War of 1812, and Mahan thought the United States was fortunate to emerge from it as well as it did. Mahan asked Americans to learn from this experience. "The neutral which fails to do so, which leaves its ports defenceless and its navy stunted until the emergency comes, will then find, as the United States found in the early years of this century, an admirable opportunity to write State Papers."[13] Without effective military force, the government found diplomatic statements to be its only recourse.

The War of 1812 example haunted Mahan: "One does not need to be a soldier or a seaman to comprehend the difficulty of making ends meet when there is not enough to go round."[14] To avoid a similar situation in the early twentieth century, he advocated a fleet "of power great enough—not to overcome any naval force that might conceivably be brought against us, for that would be beyond our means, but—to make it evidently inexpedient, politically, for the greatest navy to contest our predominance in the Caribbean."[15] The U.S. Navy did not need a force as large as the entire Royal Navy to challenge Britain in the Caribbean; it only needed to be large enough to challenge the portion of the fleet that Britain could send there. Though preparation reduced the possibility of conflict, the United States must first field a naval force large enough to confront possible threats.

THE DECISION FOR WAR

Sometimes preparation and deterrence did not suffice. Mahan believed there were occasions when nations must go to war: "If war is always avoidable, consistently with due resistance to evil, then war is always unjustifiable; but if it is possible that two nations, or two political entities, like the North and South in the American Civil War, find the question between them one which neither can yield without sacrificing conscientious conviction, or national welfare, or the interests of posterity, of which each generation in its day is the trustee, then war is not justifiable only; it is imperative." States fought wars over interests of principle. This was not something open to negotiation, for "the nation or man is disgraced who shirks an obligation to defend right."[16]

Once the decision for war was made, "It should ever be the aim of commander-in-chief to reach his result without wastefulness, with a minimum expenditure of men and material." However, he did not argue for the avoidance of casualties at all costs: loss was unavoidable in war, and Mahan castigated leaders who refused to accept that. He explained, "If the object is not worth the expenditure, spend nothing. If it is worth while, and yet can be equally attained by less expenditure, economize; but do not economize any amount, however great and desirable, necessary to put the attainment of the object beyond all possibility of failure, or even of completest success."[17] War is serious business. States should fight only when the value of the object is sufficiently high, and in those cases, they should do everything possible to obtain the political object.

Mahan advocated bringing the fight to the opponent with the object of winning as quickly as possible: "For success of war, offence is better than defense; and in contemplating this or any other military measure, let there be dismissed at once, as preposterous, the hope that war can be carried on without someone or something being hurt. . . . [W]hatever tends to make war more effective tends to shorten it and to prevent it."[18] Blows that inflict the greatest damage might be bloodier in the short term and seem riskier, but in the long term, paying a higher initial cost shortened the conflict and reduced bloodshed.

Mere offensive action was, however, not enough: "Hard blows are useless if not struck on the right spot." Wars were not decided "by rambling operations, or naval duels, . . . but by force massed, and handled in skilful combination."[19] Leaders who conducted purposeless campaigns or fought naval battles for mere glory were wasting precious resources. These operations brought sea powers no closer to peace: they only risked defeat, barren results, and unnecessary cost. One instead had to employ an effective strategy that entailed a fine understanding of the workings of sea power.

THE WORKINGS OF SEA POWER IN WAR

Defeating the opposing fleet through battle, blockade, or any operation that removed it as a threat was Mahan's first critical step in naval war. Commentators have tended to fixate on this aspect of Mahan's strategy to overstate the role of battle, even though this is but a single component of his overall theory.

Mahan contended that the destruction of the opponent's fleet served one of two broader strategic purposes. It could break the will of the opponent, or it could set conditions for a strategy of exhaustion. "First, the whole decision of the contest will rest upon actual conflict; and second failing decisive results in battle, the war will be prolonged."[20]

Much depended on the nature of the war. A country might not be willing to endure great hardship if the value of the object was low, and a single battle or campaign might in that case prove decisive, as was the case with the Spanish-American War. In wars fought for higher stakes, such as the Napoleonic Wars, Mahan explained, "A really great military power under an incomparable general . . . is not to be brought to terms by ordinary military successes." Instead, he claimed, "The question thus resolved itself, as has before been perhaps too often said, into a conflict of endurance,—which nation could live the longest in this deadly grapple." Endurance entailed both physical and moral elements; one did not merely destroy material and wreck the opponent's economy; one had to make the opponent understand the hopelessness of its position.[21]

Failure to achieve decisive results through a battle or a campaign would protract the conflict. Economic exhaustion then became the sea power's means of compelling its opponent using a combination of naval force, geographic position, and economic power. Through control of the sea, a sea power exerted relentless pressure on the opponent's economy and simultaneously insulated the sea power from similar effects.[22] The sea power could then protract the war while using slow, grinding economic pressure to exhaust its opponent.

Mahan could point to several historical examples. He found the Napoleonic Wars particularly instructive. His most cogent arguments describing how sea powers win wars by exhaustion are in the final chapters of *The Influence of Sea Power upon the French Revolution and*

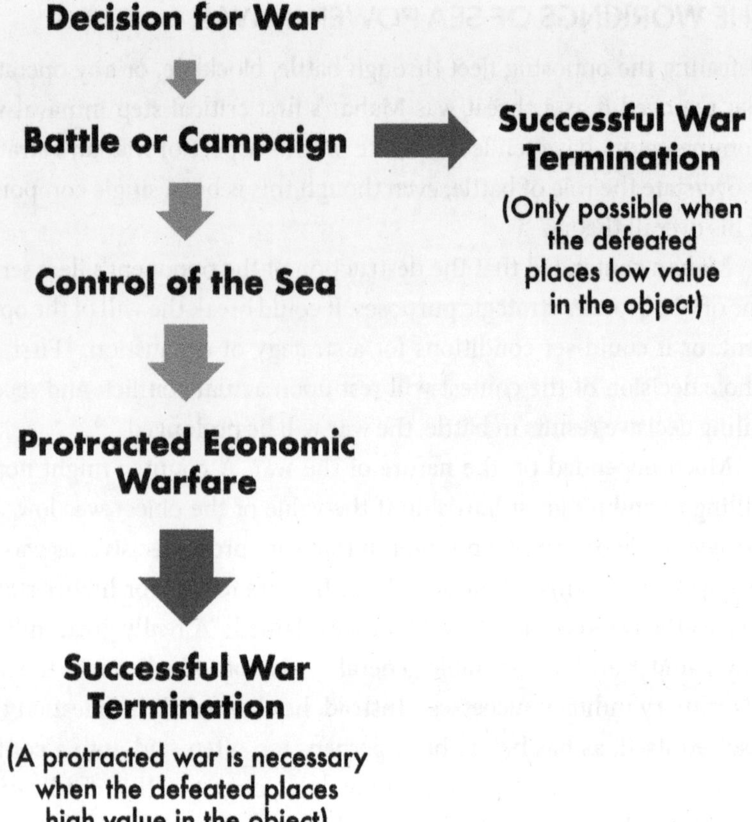

12.2. **War Termination in Mahan's Sea Power Theory**

Empire. In those wars, Britain's geography provided a protective moat in the form of the sea. While continental armies marched to and fro across the increasingly ravaged landscape, Britain became the manufacturing center, the warehouse, and the untouchable base whence supplies and subsidies flowed. Though Napoleon's armies might dominate continental Europe, they could not defeat Britain. Throughout the wars, resources and capital flowed across the sea-lanes and into Britain. Wealth allowed Britain to not only survive but to provide subsidies to its continental allies. Only Britain, the sea power, possessed this capability.[23] Sea power "sustained the material forces of the state and the spirit of the people." Simultaneously, it strangled Napoleon, "curtailing the resources and sapping the strength . . . and . . . compelling him to efforts at once inevitable, exhausting, and fruitless." This "process of constriction" cut Napoleon off from the resources of the world. Simultaneously, sea power shielded Britain, fostered its industry, and built wealth "upon the ruin of all other commerce, her power upon the ruin of all other navies."[24]

Mahan witnessed a similar process in the U.S. Civil War: the Union naval blockade maintained "a steady and strangling pressure upon the enemy's lines of communication, with the result of producing exhaustion through the failure of necessary resources."[25] He added, "More than any other one means, blockade crushed the South in our War of Secession." Though others could certainly disagree, Mahan emphasized the decisiveness of economic strangulation, especially when coupled with the Union's continued access to global commerce. As he neared the end of his life, he saw a similar process beginning to take shape in World War I: "If the German rush proves indecisive or prolonged the financial pressure thus in the power of Great Britain may determine the issue."[26] He believed that sea power "will vindicate itself again, and exhaustion effect that . . . [which] Entente armies cannot."[27]

Stepping beyond World War I, Mahan made a general comparison of sea power and land power. He saw both "expending their capital, and drawing freely drafts upon the future, the one in money, the other in men, to sustain their present strength."[28] By using money to wage war, the sea power could protect its people, who continued to create wealth to sustain its war effort.

Mahan believed that commerce was in this sense "the decisive element."[29] Through its commerce the sea power could "bring the pressure of war to bear upon the whole population, and not merely upon the armies in the field." This, he thought, was "the very spirit of modern warfare."[30] Preventing commerce indirectly weakened the opponent's resistance by disorganizing its financial system.[31] Mahan considered this a more humane way of war, for "it has been the glory of sea-power that its ends are attained by draining men of their dollars instead of their blood."[32] This form of pressure reduced the tax in human capital that the sea power had to pay, but Mahan failed to consider the effects of this type of warfare on the sea power's opponents: their populations starved and their economies ceased to function effectively.

A sea power did not rely on finesse or surgical strikes; it employed overwhelming force in the maritime domain. Britain used sea power to deny opponents access to the sea and control the movement of merchant commerce. Mahan concluded, "The results were due, not to the skill with which the force was used or distributed, but to sheer preponderance of existing brute strength. . . . By the destruction of the enemies' own shipping and by denying neutrals the right to carry to them many articles of the first importance, Great Britain placed the hostile countries in a state of comparative isolation."[33] The action that most contributed to victory entailed the sea power exerting overbearing economic pressure to control the lines of communication with the object of regulating the global economy. A sea power did not rely on negotiation, discussion, or cooperation to achieve victory; it used its weight and power to strangle opponents, manipulate the commercial transactions of neutrals, and sustain its own access to global markets. These in combination allowed the sea power to prosper while its opponents faltered.

SEA POWER AND COALITIONS

Mahan preferred sea powers to go it alone without the aid of international partners. This gave the sea power the advantage of "unity of aim imparted by belonging to one nation" as opposed to "the feebleness of alliances, or rather of co-operation, when compared with force concentrated in a single hand."[34] He maintained, "The proverbial weakness of alliances is due to inferior power of concentration." He went on, "Granting the same aggregate of force, it is never as great in two hands as in one, because it is not perfectly concentrated. Each party to an alliance usually has its particular aim, which divides action."[35] Describing a campaign between a single state, on the one hand, and a coalition, on the other, Mahan concluded, "As a rule . . . a single state against a coalition holds the interior position, the concentrated force."[36] Unity of purpose eroded with the addition of each coalition partner.

Coalitions among naval powers not only had to reconcile aims and objectives, they also had to integrate capability, reconcile administrative processes, and build infrastructure, all while operating in an unforgiving environment.[37] This made Mahan particularly skeptical of naval powers working together.

Needless to day, Mahan did not believe that coalitions provided an easy path to success, but under specific conditions he found them absolutely necessary: "Each man and each state is independent just so far as there is strength to go alone, and no farther. When this limit is reached, if farther steps must be made, co-operation must be accepted."[38] This became especially true if the sea power lacked the ability to obtain the desired object on its own.

Mahan found coalitions most effective when each member contributed a unique capability. He preferred a coalition between a sea power and a land power because each could operate in its specific environment while focusing on a common object. Mahan considered this significant. During the Seven Years' War, for example, Britain supported Prussia with subsidies. The wealth of Britain's sea power allied with the manpower of Prussia created an effective partnership. Even when navies could not directly influence events on land, they could still support allies by maintaining "that flow of subsidies upon which the land war depended."[39]

Geographic position also influenced a sea power's use of coalitions. An insular state like Britain could dictate its level of engagement. It could always withdraw from the continent, refuse to provide subsidies, and rely on its moat for protection. Isolated from continental threats, it could protract the war, knowing that its opponent could not invade and content in the knowledge that its wealth would continue to grow. This was not a war-winning strategy; it merely bought time for conditions to change. When an opening emerged, the sea power had the wealth to subsidize new coalition partners.

In sum, Mahan preferred to avoid coalitions because they upset concentration, were difficult to manage, and required significant effort to maintain; sometimes, however, circumstances made them necessary. At the strategic level, coalitions provided a means of burden sharing. A coalition added capability, often in the form of land power, and that was particularly important when a sea power was confronting a large continental state. Yet, he also recognized that each coalition partner has its own

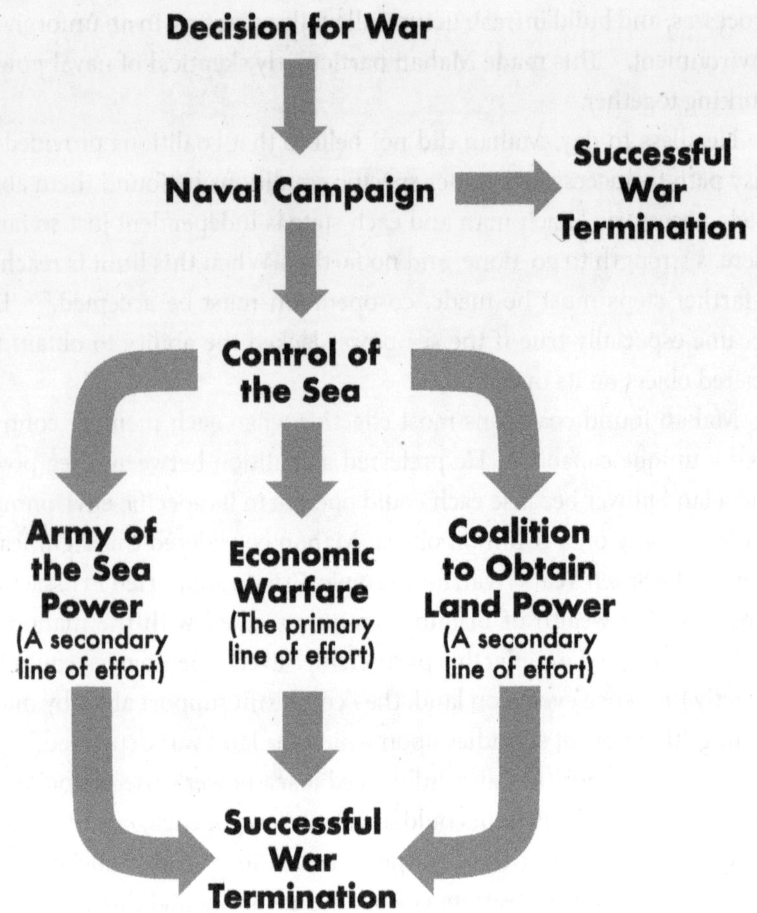

12.3. **Mahan's Theory of Sea Power in War**

agenda, and thus considered it dangerous to rely too much on allies. He did not believe in integration of forces; rather, he sought divided responsibility and the independent use of national forces for shared objectives.

THE SECONDARY STATUS OF EXPEDITIONARY OPERATIONS

While coalitions provided one source of land power, Mahan recognized that the sea power needed its own capability to project force ashore and sustain influence in distant regions. In the relationship between land

and naval forces, Mahan warned of "the natural tendency of each to exaggerate its own importance to the common end."[40] We should ponder whether Mahan's theories exhibited this very tendency.

Mahan did not assign equal importance to the land and naval components of a sea power; the navy dominated the relationship. One of Mahan's contemporaries explained, "He proved that, while many wars have culminated with the victory of some army, the victory of some navy had been the previous essential. He proved that the immediate cause of success had often resulted inevitably from another cause, less apparent because more profound; that the operations of the navy had previously brought affairs up to the 'mate in four moves,' and that the final victory of the army was the resulting 'checkmate.'"[41] Regarding Yorktown in the American War for Independence, Mahan admitted that French and American soldiers made the result possible, but without the French navy in the Chesapeake "the soldiers would have found nobody to fight."[42] Given Mahan's agenda, it is unsurprising that he designated the naval instrument to set the conditions for victory.

Using British expeditionary operations in the Napoleonic Wars as an example, Mahan wrote, "They were mixed military and naval expeditions, based upon the fleet and upon the control of the sea, scattered in all quarters of the world, employing bodies of troops small when compared to the size of continental armies, and therefore for the most part bearing individually, the character of secondary operations, however much they may have conduced to a great common end."[43] He argued that the fleet exerted the principal influence and ascribed secondary status to joint operations. "Secondary" to Mahan meant something less than decisive: supporting and assisting but incapable of bringing war to a conclusion. He applied the same secondary status to commerce raiding.

Mahan presented the Iberian campaign in the Napoleonic Wars (1807–14) in a similar manner. It was an excellent example of an operation "based absolutely on control of the sea." "Spain [was] saved at a most critical moment, by the petty army which had come from the sea, and which had only dared to make this move—well nigh desperate at best—because it knew that, in the inevitable retreat, it would find in the sea no impassible barrier, but a hospitable host." The critical factor was the

British navy.[44] Although it was an especially effective example of expeditionary warfare, Iberia was a secondary operation. It supported broader objectives of the sea power and relied on the navy for its very survival.

WAR TERMINATION

Mahan insisted that "no extreme short of absolute incapacity to resist justifies surrender." But he added a caveat: "unless it is evident that no other interest is compromised; and that practically is never the case."[45] Successful war termination takes advantage of other interests to avoid having to fight to the bitter end. This is particularly true when the overthrow of the opponent's government is not the objective. The Spanish-American War (1898) is an example. Instead of fighting Spain to its "absolute incapacity" and overthrowing the government in Madrid, the United States isolated Cuba, seized it, and sought a negotiated settlement to end the war. Spain's position had been compromised by the loss of its navy, and this gave the United States leverage in the peace negotiation. Mahan recommended using this leverage as an ultimatum to the effect that without a navy Spain stood no chance.[46] Mahan was no diplomat; he epitomized the naval officer who understood the use of force and applied it to war termination. Without a fleet Spain could not wage war in a meaningful manner. Destroy the opponent's power to resist and then dictate terms: this is how Mahan believed the United States had obtained the decisive advantage against Spain.

In high-stakes wars such as the Napoleonic Wars, the loss of a fleet or the capture of a colony was not enough to force the opponent to yield. In such cases, the sea power needed to use its control of the sea to gain leverage. This might take several forms. The navy could provide the springboard for amphibious operations conducted by the sea power's small but effective army. The sea power could also assist allies with subsidies, which was particularly important when the sea power was allied with a continental state possessing significant manpower reserves. Gaining land forces through coalitions or using the sea power's army were not in Mahan's opinion necessarily enough to gain decisive effects.

The sea power's most potent weapon was its ability to leverage the world economy and deny trade to its adversary. It slowly suffocated its opponent by denying it the resources it needed to survive. In the Napoleonic Wars, Mahan argued, France was strangled, "clutched by the throat in the iron grip of the British sea power."[47] Mahan charted how this occurred: "Great Britain, by the strategic direction she gave to her efforts in this war, forced the French spirit of aggression into a line of action which could not but result fatally." Britain's policies led Napoleon to enact the Continental System, which sealed his ruin. In a vain attempt to enforce his trading policies, Napoleon became involved in costly military campaigns and occupations from Spain to Russia that bled his empire of money and soldiers. The result divided his attention, scattered his forces, and wrecked his concentration.[48] Britain had forced Napoleon into catastrophic, self-defeating behavior. The victory of sea power was all but assured.

Mahan equated war to business: a state sought the greatest success for the least cost. Given his sea power thesis, this made perfect sense. Sea powers had the ability to wage war for financial gain while expending little human capital. The population, thus preserved, could expand the economy and participate in commercial exchange. The sea power grew wealthy by war. "People forget," reminded Mahan, "that war is largely economic."[49] Mahan's clearest expression of how sea powers win multi-theater great power wars appears in *The Influence of Sea Power upon the French Revolution and Empire*, which ends in 1812, just as Napoleon's army marched into Russia. Three years before the armies met at Waterloo, Mahan believed the war had for all intents and purposes been decided in Britain's favor given the triumph of finance bolstered by Britain's commercial and economic advantages.

CHAPTER 13

CORBETT'S WAY OF WAR

Corbett grounded his theoretical arguments in both knowledge and worldview. He saw the world through a distinctly British lens, amassed a deep understanding of British history, and aimed his writings specifically at British leaders. He believed that his own country possessed unique strengths and weaknesses that in combination facilitated a specific way of war. It concerned him that others did not support his belief.

That the German, or continental, method of war seemed to be gaining popularity among leaders in Britain troubled Corbett. He worried that "an unintelligent and slavish appeal to German practice should ever be allowed to influence our own system, because our national habits of thought and work, our British characteristics, and the problems we have to deal with are so different from theirs." The German continental method differed fundamentally from the British maritime approach. Each had a specific strategic focus, and each addressed a distinct worldview. Corbett asserted that the Germans saw war in specifically narrow terms of land warfare while the British followed a more flexible joint approach: "The German habit is to think out the most perfect system he can and stick to it as closely as possible in every detail. The British is rather to encourage every man to use, within certain wide lens, the originality and initiative that is in him."[1]

In the years before World War I, Corbett developed extensive arguments in favor of a flexible approach involving multiple instruments of national power aimed at common objectives. Although it would be a stretch to call it a modern "whole of government approach," Corbett's "major" strategy employed naval, land, diplomatic, and economic elements in a complex and interlocking manner.

Major strategy is the realm of the statesman. For that reason Corbett's arguments emphasized political leaders like Pitt the Elder while Mahan focused on naval officers such as Nelson and Farragut. Their differing focal points had ripple effects through both theories. Mahan focused on what the naval element could accomplish, while Corbett explained how the naval element integrated with other instruments of power to form a national strategy. As a result, Corbett's way of war is more complex than Mahan's.

THE NAVAL INSTRUMENT

Corbett's entire way of war revolved around the Royal Navy and the advantages it provided. This should not be surprising. He was a naval historian before he developed strategic theory; he worked for the Royal Navy; and the navy was Britain's most powerful, unique, and flexible instrument of war.

Surprising similarities dominate when Corbett's naval strategy is compared with Mahan's. Though the two often took very different routes to their determinations, their theories are not polar opposites; rather, they differ by degree. A case in point concerns their respective points of departure. Mahan used theories of land warfare to inform his thoughts on naval strategy, while Corbett found this quite dangerous given the differences between the land and the maritime environments. Moreover, Corbett needed to assert the distinctiveness of naval strategy in order to contrast the continental with the British maritime ways of war. Yet Mahan and Corbett developed similar conclusions about the roles of the offense and defense in naval strategy. Their definitions of "command of the sea" (often "control of the sea" in Mahan's writings) are nearly identical, as is its role within naval strategy. Confusion often results from their different vocabularies, imprecise explanations, and the distribution of their theoretical concepts across multiple writings.

Corbett argued that "the object of naval warfare is to control maritime communications."[2] The metric to express how well a navy regulates communications is "command of the sea." Command can rest with one side, the other side, or be in dispute. Corbett considered obtaining command of the sea a critical objective, but not the end point. Rather, it set conditions for naval power to provide its greatest influence. Corbett and Mahan largely agreed on the above points. Moreover, both agreed that battle was the most effective way of attaining command of the sea. If battle proved impossible, however, Corbett was more willing than Mahan to consider other ways of obtaining command.

The critical aim of naval war was not command of the sea but using the advantages accrued from having obtained command to exert pressure on opponents. This could occur in three ways, which Corbett labeled "the function of the fleet in war." First, possessing command could create conditions that enabled the targeting of commerce; second, it could affect diplomatic action; and third, it could facilitate land operations. These three ways allowed naval action to be translated into political effects.[3] People live on land, and warships operate at sea: in most cases navies do not exert direct pressure on terrestrial affairs. Rather, pressure results from second- and third-order effects that are often difficult to control and translate into predictable outcomes. How, for example, could the regulation of commerce through protecting friendly merchant shipping, denying trade to opponents, and regulating what neutrals could and could not do impact an opponent' s society?

Corbett, like Mahan, argued that naval power acting alone found its most important strategic effect in the control of commerce through the domination of the sea lines of communication. "The influence of Naval Power in the world is measured by the extent to which it can exercise

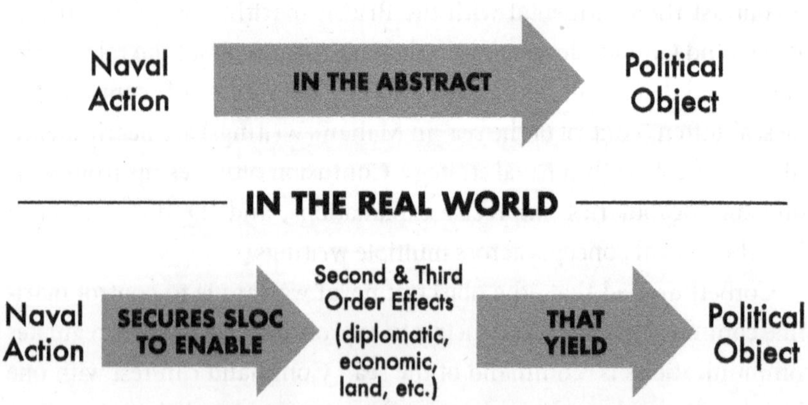

13.1. **How Naval Operations Yield Political Results**

13.2. **Corbett's Naval and Economic Strategies**

command of the sea, every restriction in this direction," he explained, "tends to diminish the influence of the Naval Powers."[4] Britain's naval strategy against Germany during World War I, Corbett explained, was intended "to paralyse the economic life of the nation . . . with perfect justice."[5] To attain this goal, the battle fleet worked to gain and then maintain command of the sea.

If the opposing fleet could be destroyed or contained, the dominant naval power could then exercise command of the sea by acting as a single organism to "choke the enemy's national life at sea." Corbett maintained, "It is only by the prevention of [the] enemy's commerce that fleets can exercise the pressure which armies seek." Naval power thus aimed at stifling commercial exchange, or what some labeled "private property."

Responding to contemporary efforts to restrict belligerents rights to capture commercial shipping, Corbett worried, "Without the right to capture private property, naval battles become meaningless as a method of forcing the enemy to submit. . . . It comes, then, to this—that the total prohibition of capturing private property at sea would amount in practice to a prohibition of effective naval warfare altogether."[6]

Corbett's views on commercial warfare paralleled Mahan's. Both argued that the only effective way for navies to exert direct influence on a war was through preventing maritime commerce. Where they differed was in its decisiveness. Mahan argued that economic pressure was the critical factor that made sea powers such fearsome opponents. Corbett noted the importance of economic warfare but considered it slow and often insufficient. Rather, the fleet often obtained its greatest effects by supporting diplomatic efforts and expeditionary land forces.

LIMITED WAR

While Mahan developed a theory of war that rested on obtaining control of the sea followed by applying economic pressure, Corbett followed a different route. Though he never claimed economic pressure an insignificant factor, he considered it insufficient by itself. A combination of instruments of national power was necessary for obtaining political objectives. Moreover, Mahan's theory tended to result in protracted conflicts because economic coercion ground down the means of resistance little by little. Mahan's theory not only protracted hostilities, it also tended toward escalation. Attempts to control international trade would damage economies beyond the intended target. In response, other states would tend to enter the conflict so as to prevent further economic damage. In contrast, Corbett attempted to restrict escalation while seeking a quicker victory using theories of limited war.

To frame his limited war argument, Corbett found Clausewitz's description of two types of war valuable: "The two kinds of war are, first, those in which the object is the *overthrow of the enemy*, whether it be that we aim at his destruction, politically, or merely at disarming him and forcing him to conclude peace on our terms; and next, those in which our object is *merely to make some conquests on the frontiers of his country*, either for the purpose of retaining them permanently, or of turning them to account as matter of exchange in the settlement of a peace."[7] Corbett labeled these two classifications of war "unlimited" and "limited" respectively.[8] He thought Clausewitz's definition went "to the root of all war policy and plans of operation."[9] Moreover, "The distinction between the two kinds of war may appear academical, but it will be found, nevertheless, of the greatest assistance in arriving rapidly at a just appreciation of the situation and in detaching at once the main lines on which our war must be planned."[10]

Corbett agreed with Clausewitz that the distinction between limited war and unlimited war tended to blur in wars between states with contiguous borders such as France and Germany. In such continental wars, geography allowed and perhaps promoted escalation to the unlimited form. First, if the side with the limited objective attained success, it might become greedy and exceed the bounds of limited war. Second, the country pursuing a limited object might encounter an opponent pursuing an unlimited one. Third, the losing side might escalate to unlimited war in a bid to stave off defeat. Lacking a geographical barrier, the continental state pursuing a limited objective had to create an artificial one by incurring the cost of defending its entire border. Too much could go wrong in that situation, which led Clausewitz to consider the unlimited object the more cost-effective option. The outcome was potentially quicker, more decisive, and did not require extensive defensive measures. Militaries at the turn of the twentieth century tended to focus on Clausewitz's unlimited form with the "principle of the enemy's military force being the chief objective."[11] Destroying the opponent's army shattered its means of resistance, and the victor could dictate the outcome.

Though this strategy might prove effective in wars among continental states, Corbett found, "Where a maritime empire is concerned caution is required in applying the simple formulae of continental strategists. Oceanic and continental war differ widely in some of their cardinal conditions. It is not enough to apply the maxims of the one raw to the intricacies of the other."[12] Corbett contrasted the British way of maritime war with the continental school's strategy:

> Our own idea had long been to attack the enemy at the weakest point which could give substantial results, and to assume the defensive where he was strongest. The continental method was to strike where the enemy's military concentration was highest and where a decisive victory would end the war by destroying his armed forces. By general agreement this method, being the quicker and more drastic of the two, was the better, provided there was sufficient preponderance of force to ensure a decision, and the reason why in past great wars we had never adopted it, when the initiative lay in our hands, was that we never had military force enough to enjoy that preponderance.[13]

Corbett's theory was intended to mitigate Britain's comparative weakness in land power by modifying Clausewitz's "limited" type of war. "It is clear that Clausewitz himself never apprehended the full significance of his brilliant theory," Corbett observed. "His outlook was still purely continental, and the limitations of continental warfare tend to veil the fuller meaning of the principle he had framed."[14] Corbett was not contending that Clausewitz was wrong, just that the two were writing for different types of states. Clausewitz had the situation of a continental power clearly in view, while Corbett sought to reengineer the concept to apply it to a maritime state.

Corbett labeled his modification of Clausewitz's limited type "war limited by its political object."[15] His theory entailed several key points. First, "limited object" had nothing to do with the means employed: "You may, and usually must, employ your whole force."[16] Rather, the word "limited" reflected the desired political object. Second, in addition to a limited political object, the object needed to be restricted geographically so as to be susceptible to isolation.[17] Corbett asserted, "It would seem he [Clausewitz] was unaware that he had found an explanation of one of the most inscrutable problems in history—the expansion of England—at least so far as it has been due to successful war."[18] Corbett's adaptation

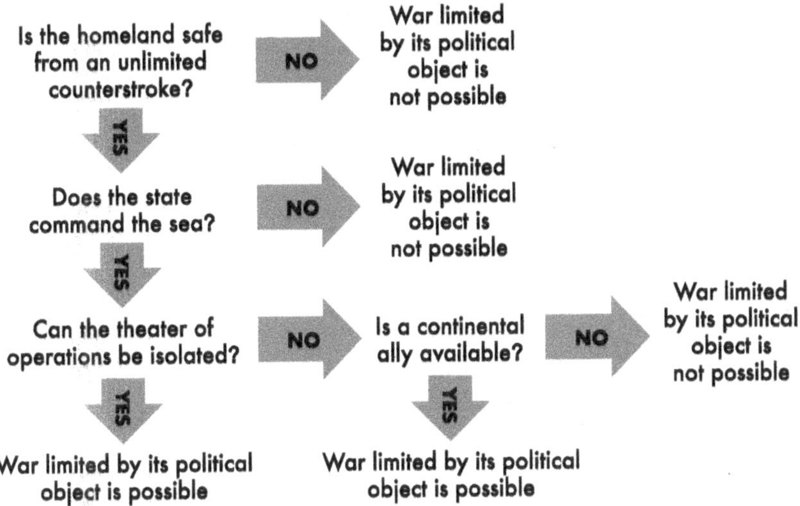

13.3. **Testing for Corbett's War Limited by Its Political Object**

of Clausewitz's limited war theory is among the most important of his theoretical legacies.

Maritime states had a distinctive ability to isolate objectives through command of the sea.[19] Isolation greatly diminished the importance of size among the respective land forces; by isolating the object, the maritime state fought only the portion of the opponent's land force in the actual theater of operations. "Success will depend not on relative armed strength," Corbett explained, "but on proportion of it which each side can develop against the object."[20]

While isolation was necessary, it was insufficient to achieve victory. When one side begins to win a limited war, Corbett maintained, "the other party . . . will seek to redress the balance by striking him at the centre of his power. In other words, the losing party will seek to destroy or cripple his enemy's resources for war at their base and to inflict upon his home population suffering more intense than the attainment of the special object is worth. A war conducted on these lines is unlimited in character."[21] Corbett labeled this "the unlimited counterstroke."[22] Since the armies of maritime states were insufficient either to stop the unlimited counterstroke or to execute one of their own, these states required some form of geographical separation that created a buffer.

The effectiveness of the buffer increased if it included a moat that forced the opponent to face the maritime state's powerful navy.[23] Corbett concluded, "We come, then, to this final proposition—that limited war is only permanently possible to island Powers or between Powers which are separated by sea, and then only when the Power desiring limited war is able to command the sea to such a degree as to be able not only to isolate the distant object, but also to render impossible the invasion of his home territory."[24]

Isolating the area of operations required a high level of naval dominance. In Corbett's terms, this necessitated "command of the sea," which he defined as "establishing ourselves in such a position that we can control the maritime communications of all parties concerned."[25] This resulted in the following paradox: a maritime state fighting for limited objects on land could do so only with a navy dominant at sea. Corbett explained that pure land wars tended to escalate toward the unlimited object because of the state's ability to mount an unlimited counterstroke; similarly, purely naval wars also tended to escalate toward an unlimited object. The possibility for limited war increased when the conflict was neither entirely naval nor military. In such wars, the maritime power could regulate escalation through command of the sea. Though the defeated side might wish to escalate the conflict and even mount an unlimited counterstroke, command of the sea made escalation all but impossible. Moreover, the maritime power generally lacked sufficient land power to seek unlimited objects of its own.[26] As long as the maritime power limited its own objects, limited war became possible through joint action. The expeditionary land forces pursued limited political objectives protected by a navy that isolated the theater of operations and protected the homeland from invasion.

DIPLOMATIC FACTORS

Corbett's limited war theory places great value on diplomatic engagement. Limited war is possible only when the maritime power can manipulate the number of belligerents involved in a conflict. By preventing third-party intervention, a maritime state can further the opponent's isolation and reduce its endurance, while attaining international support transforms these factors into advantages. Perhaps even more important, limited wars must end in a diplomatically negotiated settlement. The victor in limited war cannot compel its opponent to seek terms: the opponent still possesses the ability to resist. The end of the war becomes a bargain in which the victor must sacrifice some of its spoils to sate a partially defeated opponent. If the defeated power is diplomatically isolated and the maritime state has partners, conditions are more propitious for a favorable settlement.

Thus, "to decide a question of grand strategy without consideration of its diplomatic aspect, is to decide on half the factors only," Corbett insisted.[27] He reasoned, "It is evident that we require for the guidance of our naval policy and naval action something of wider vision than the current conception of naval strategy, something that will keep before our eyes not merely the enemy's fleets or the great routes of commerce, or the command of the sea, but also the relations of naval policy and action to the whole area of diplomatic and military effort."[28] Such statements, however, do little but scratch the surface. Though Corbett outlined the importance of diplomacy, he did not explain how it functioned from a theoretical standpoint. Rather than develop his own theories regarding diplomacy and international relations, he generally explained diplomatic activity in terms of historical context. Corbett worked for the Royal Navy, not the Foreign Office, and he was educating naval leaders, not diplomats. Rather than trespass on international relations theory, Corbett attempted to explain to his diplomatic counterparts the most effective way that Britain could pursue maritime-focused strategies.

As a result, his views on strategy often narrowed to describe how Britain should manage international relations to obtain the greatest effect when employing its land and sea forces. Using the British army as a mere auxiliary to support allies, in Corbett's opinion, led to disastrous consequences.[29] Instead, British land forces needed to maintain their independence, with the army operating from the sea in conjunction with the British navy. Implicit in his arguments was the assumption that the allies needed to work for Britain's diplomatic objects rather than Britain working for the interests of its allies. It was best if Britain's interests coincided with those of its allies, but when objectives did not align, British leaders should use their allies to achieve Britain's objectives and hope the coalition held together long enough to win.

It seems peculiar that Corbett wrote so little about diplomacy given Britain's eighteenth-century record: the only major war Britain lost during that century—the American War for Independence—was also the only one Britain fought diplomatically isolated. Contemporary resonance adds to the puzzle. On the eve of World War I, Britain sought to solidify its international position through an entente with France and Russia, but to what end? *Some Principles of Maritime Strategy* treats these diplomatic arrangements implicitly at best, even though they provide essential foundations to the context of Britain's security environment, and their existence influences his argument. Moreover, Corbett's preference for limited war required escalation management: diplomacy is a significant factor in making this occur, but Corbett had little to say on the subject.

Additional factors complicate diplomacy. Each state has unique objectives that often work at cross-purposes with those of its allies. For Britain to be an effective coalition partner, Corbett admitted, "we have always had to spoil our hand . . . to keep allies in a good temper." Yet he failed to specify how this occurred or how it could be mitigated. This is even more glaring given Corbett's description of one World War I naval leader: "He has been so much in touch with diplomatic people that he has a much greater chance of seeing things whole than the ordinary N.O. [naval officer]."[30] Even though Corbett thought the average naval officer a diplomatic neophyte, he did little more than acknowledge the importance of diplomacy and provide a cursory explanation of its workings.

THE PHASES OF LIMITED WAR

Since most wars were decided on land, Corbett believed that maritime powers, with their small armies, had little capability to directly influence the decisive land theater. Corbett's theory of "war limited by its political object" sought to overcome this significant weakness. The Russo-Japanese War (1904–5) provided a potent example. "Strictly speaking," Corbett said of Japan, "her armies had not occupied an inch of Russian territory, and her navy, though completely victorious at sea, could not use its control so as to have any appreciable effect on Russian finance or subsistence. She was far from having crushed her enemy's armed forces or his power of resistance; his real national life was practically unaffected."[31] Even so, Japan achieved victory through carefully executed operations that kept the limited political object clearly in view.

Corbett deduced that war limited by its political object had the greatest possibility of success when the maritime states executed operations through a series of distinct phases. Over time, his views on the number and nature of the phases evolved.

He seems to have broached the concept of phases while writing *England and the Seven Years' War*, where he maintained, "It is recognised as fundamental principle that lies at the root of the higher strategy that wars tend to exhibit two successive phases—phases not always distinct, yet always existing, and so important in their differences that unless they be kept firmly grasped the conduct of any great war is sure to go astray." In the first phase, the aim must be the destruction of the opponent's armed forces. In the second phase, "we seek to assert our ascendency over him by . . . general pressure in order to force him to accept our terms."[32] Corbett used this two-phase approach to explain war in general but soon applied the concept to war limited by its political object. This required some modification to the phases. Instead of aiming at the opposing army in the first phase, he focused on the objective. In limited war, the aim is not the destruction of the opponent's army but seizing something from the opponent. The second phase of war limited by its political object did not require modification, for the winning side still needed to compel the opponent to accept the gains of the first phase.[33]

His analysis of the Russo-Japanese War led Corbett to expand his theory from two to three phases. The first phase still involved taking the territorial objective; the second now entailed solidifying control of that objective; and the third necessitated some form of general pressure to compel the opponent to accept the territorial loss.[34]

The first phase required seizing the objective by employing a combination of local naval superiority and the disposal force (the expeditionary land force). The navy had a subordinate role in this phase. Rather than destroy the opposing fleet, the navy secured the line of communication

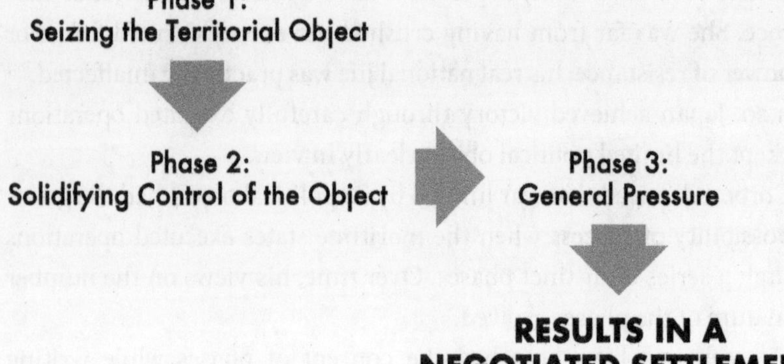

13.4. Three Phases of War Limited by Its Political Object for Maritime States

with the theater of operations. Done correctly, operations in this phase allowed the disposal force to seize the object while at the same time guarding against the unlimited counterstroke.[35]

Japan's decision in the Russo-Japanese War to project its land force into the theater of operations before possessing complete command of the sea allowed Corbett to confront those in Britain who believed "we cannot move a man till we have absolute command of the sea." This was a maxim of the same Blue Water School that had given Mahan such trouble regarding bases.[36] Even during World War I the concept remained contentious. Corbett wrote, "The question whether such an operation was a legitimate risk of war before a decided command of home waters had been established had long been in debate."[37] To send an expedition overseas, he claimed, "absolute command [is] unnecessary—we never waited for that—you can never do much in war if you wait to make everything absolutely safe—[it is] always a question of risk."[38] Rather, Corbett entreated naval leaders to secure the line of passage through naval deployments, utilizing speed, favorable geographic position, and a willingness to withdraw if the risk became too high.[39]

Corbett asserted that Japanese forces intended to seize Korea and Port Arthur in the first phase of the Russo-Japanese War. Though they succeeded with the former, they failed with the latter. Corbett criticized "the slowness with which their war plan was developed" and their excessive caution over their lines of communication. The first phase of Corbett's limited war theory required the maritime state to accept risk commensurate with the value of the object, for "as great as would have been the risk, success would have brought a gain far greater."[40]

The mobility of naval forces allowed the maritime state to seize the objective. "This done, we have the initiative, and the enemy being unable . . . to attack us at home, must conform to our opening by endeavouring to turn us out." But "we are in a position to meet his attack on ground of our own choice and to avail ourselves of such opportunities of counter-attack as his distant and therefore exhausting movements are likely to offer."[41]

During the second phase, the maritime power solidified its hold on the territorial object. On land, this entailed an active defense including counterattacks to maintain the initiative. The Japanese did not possess the capability to defeat the entire Russian army, so they sought to inflict casualties sufficient to break Russia's will while making Japan's hold on the territorial object "practically impregnable."[42]

At sea during the second phase, Japan sought to turn its local superiority into general command of the sea. This required the destruction of both the Russian Pacific Squadron and the Russian Baltic Fleet, which

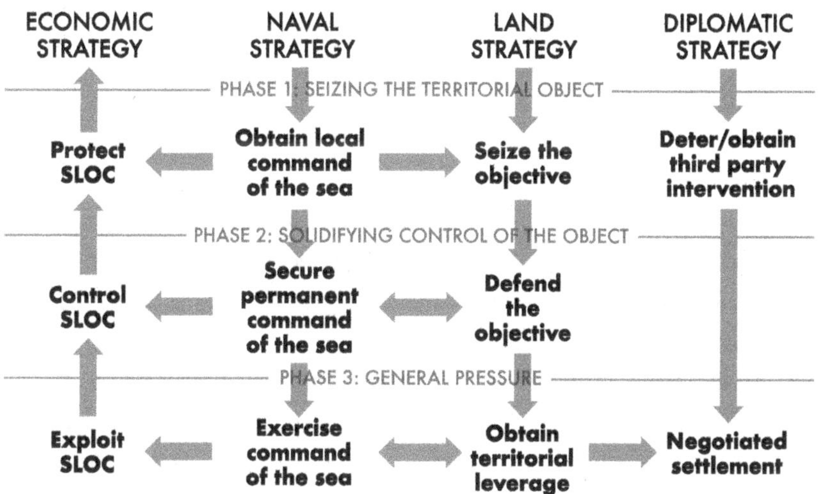

13.5. **Three Phases of Maritime Limited War: Major and Minor Strategies**

was then steaming around the globe to restore the naval balance. "The second phase, well established as it was from the military point of view, could not be regarded as complete in its combined aspect until the Baltic Fleet had been met and fought. Without definite command of the sea, the Japanese could not regard the territorial hold as absolute."[43]

The third and final phase involved Japan's return to the offensive to "demonstrate that her enemy stood to lose more than he could gain by continuing the war."[44] Japan occupied the Russian territory of Sakhalin Island, being careful to avoid overextension. The third phase poses significant risk for the maritime power. The general pressure resulting from the return to the offensive could escalate the war to the unlimited political object either because the maritime power lost sight of its limited goals or because the offensive action steeled the resolve of the losing side.[45] The critical component entailed finding something important enough to use as a bargaining chip at the peace conference but not so important as to result in escalation.

The way that Corbett analyzed the Russo-Japanese War made it seem almost the perfect example of war limited by its political object. It could be argued that he made the example too perfect, and thus not applicable to other limited wars. In *Some Principles of Maritime Strategy*, Corbett even questioned himself: "It must not of course be asked that these phases shall be always clearly defined. Strategical analysis can never give exact results. It aims only at approximations, at groupings which will serve to guide but will always leave much to the judgment. The three phases in the Russo-Japanese War, though unusually well defined, continually overlapped. It must be so; for in war the effect of an operation is never confined to the limits of its immediate or primary intention."[46]

Corbett's arguments were provocative because he altered the traditional relationship between the offense and the defense. His three phases gave the maritime state the advantages of the defense while it acted offensively to seize the state's objectives. This entailed using speed and surprise to attain the object against an unprepared opponent and then forcing that opponent to use offensive operations to regain the object. Concurrently, the three phases created the conditions necessary to avoid the usual problems associated with defense in continental wars. "These drawbacks," Corbett explained, "are chiefly that it tends to surrender the initiative to the enemy and that it deprives us the moral exhilaration of the offensive." Moreover, it created what Corbett considered the ideal situation: the strategic offensive aimed at obtaining a positive object while employing a tactical defense.[47] The opponent had to waste itself in offensive movements to regain the positions it had once possessed.

APPLYING LIMITED WAR THEORY TO UNLIMITED WARS

Corbett thought Britain possessed a comparative advantage when fighting for limited political objects, but limited war could not encompass every contingency requiring the use of force. What possibilities existed if political conditions compelled Britain to undertake unlimited war? Or if geographic conditions were not conducive to war limited by its political object? To meet such scenarios, Corbett developed what he called "war limited by contingent." Corbett's use of the word "limited" to describe two related phenomena—"war limited by contingent" and "war limited by its political object"—requires further explanation.

"War limited by its political object," more simply termed "limited war," seeks limited political objects. The term concerns only the desired end state. "War limited by contingent," however, ". . . is not a *form* of war, but a *method*." It could be applied to any kind of conflict ranging from those limited by their political object to those seeking unlimited

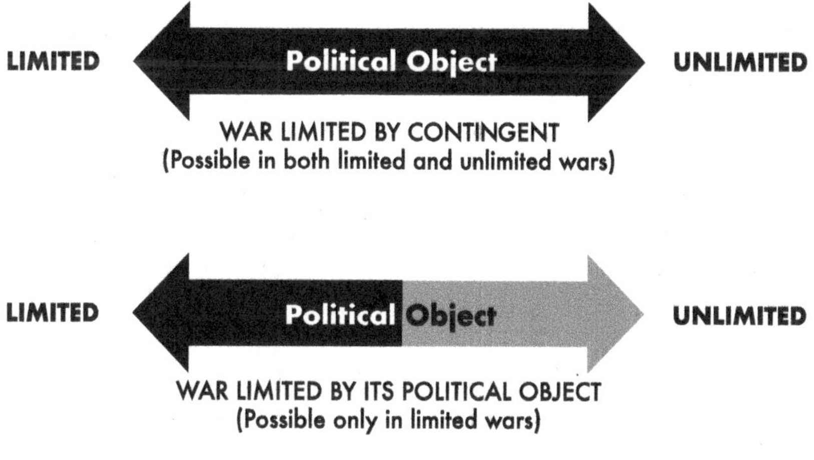

13.6. **Nature of the Political Object**

political objects. Corbett considered war limited by contingent particularly applicable to Britain because it provided a means for Britain to use its powerful navy to protect the homeland and still to project small expeditionary land forces (or contingents) into theaters where the army could inflict disproportionate damage. This allowed Britain to intervene in wars seemingly beyond the capability of its military establishment.

Since war limited by contingent could be applied to any war, we will first discuss it in terms of war limited by its political object. In such cases, the army (the limited contingent) seizes the objective and the dominant navy isolates it. Britain had followed this course of action against French, Spanish, and Dutch colonies in its eighteenth-century wars. The United States isolated Cuba in the Spanish-American War (1898), and geographic distance created something akin to isolation for Japan in its war with Russia (1904–5). Corbett considered this the most effective method of employing war limited by contingent.[48] In such cases, Corbett's two concepts of limited war overlap: war limited by contingent serves as a method of executing war limited by its political object.

When applied to large continental wars of a more unlimited type, Corbett expressed reservations about utilizing war limited by contingent: "More failures appear to have been the rule and prospects in future most unpromising."[49] Thus, war limited by contingent was not a panacea: Britain's options were few and its means scant when waging unlimited war. Even so, Corbett considered war limited by contingent the best option as long as the maritime state could make war "sufficiently maritime in character for the sea to become an essential factor."[50] Wellington's campaign in the Iberian Peninsula provided a potent example of "a theatre for war limited by contingent in which all the conditions that make for success were present." Specifically, "Our object was unlimited. It was nothing less than the overthrow of Napoleon. Complete success at sea had failed to do it, but that success had given us the power of applying the limited form, which was the most decisive form of offence within our means."[51]

War limited by contingent allowed a maritime state to "wrest the initiative from the land Powers . . . by giving the Continental war a new direction." This entailed using command of the sea, "freely combining naval and military force against the point where [the opponent] . . . was

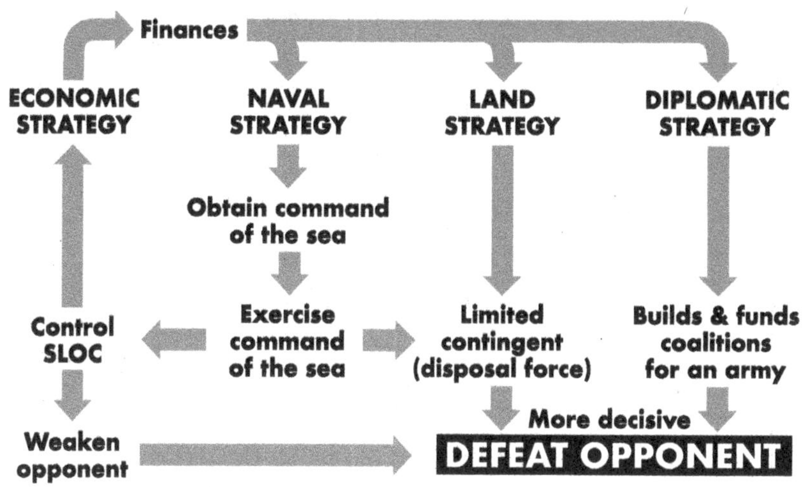

13.7. **War Limited by Contingent**

weakest, while standing securely on the defensive in the main theatre, where its [the continental state's] strength was greatest."[52]

Should Britain have to fight an unlimited war, Corbett could not envision a situation where it would fight without allies. He expected that "vast armies of continental states balance one another approximately & as of old [our] small army acting from the sea may still turn the scale."[53] Britain and its allies would not enjoy working together, but a coalition provided significant advantages to all parties. Corbett asserted, "The fact remains that all the great continental masters of war have feared or valued British intervention of this character even in the most unfavourable conditions."[54]

Geography once again proved essential to Corbett's theory: "The real secret of Wellington's success—apart from his own genius—was that in perfect conditions he was applying the limited form to an unlimited war."[55] War limited by contingent required geographic conditions similar to war limited by its political object. The maritime state needed to find a theater susceptible to at least partial isolation, and the theater's geography also had to allow for close cooperation between the army and the navy.

An effective joint approach increased the possibility of success. The navy's role was to ensure the entry, sustainment, and exit of the land force. Thus, Britain required command of the sea if not in absolute terms, at least in the region where the operation occurred. Command of the sea allowed Britain to use its small army surgically where its continental opponent did not expect it or was unable to counter it.

The conditions outlined in the above paragraphs significantly restrict situations where war limited by contingent could succeed. Corbett admitted as much and asked, "What if the conditions of the struggle in which we wish to intervene are such that no truly limited theatre is available?" Corbett provided three solutions: (1) be audacious enough to take the risk; (2) creatively identify possible options; and (3) wait until the proper conditions develop.[56] Even Corbett's most potent example—Wellington's Iberian campaign—occurred several years after the reopening of hostilities in 1803 and was not designed to be decisive. Rather it developed by fits and starts before evolving into a potentially war-winning campaign.

Corbett attempted to provide more specific guidance by noting two conditions in which Britain's small land force could effectively intervene in an unlimited war. "Firstly, there is the intrusion into a war plan which our enemy has designed without allowing for our intervention." To meet this criterion, the continental power needed to do something self-defeating: namely, fail to account for Britain's intervention. "Secondly, there is intervention to deprive the enemy of the fruits of victory." Corbett understood that the continental state had to do more than merely destroy the opposing army: "There usually remains the difficult work of conquering the people afterwards with an exhausted army."[57] These two circumstances gave Britain's small army the best opportunity to intervene with decisive effect.

CRITIQUES OF LIMITED OPTIONS

The concept of war limited by contingent allowed Corbett to apply the advantages Britain possessed in wars limited by their political object to unlimited war.[58] This was not an easy process, and the chapter on the topic in *Some Principles of Maritime Strategy* ("Wars of Intervention—Limited Interference in Unlimited War") requires some mental gymnastics to understand. This lack of clarity is particularly disappointing given the charged environment in the years preceding World War I. War limited by contingent provided a potential maritime solution to Britain's most pressing strategic quandary: how to fight Germany. Needless to say, Britain did not follow Corbett's course of action when war came in 1914; instead, the army became drawn into an ever-larger continental commitment in France.

Corbett's concepts of limited war stirred up criticism among his contemporaries. Just two years before the outbreak of World War I, a prominent commentator noted indignantly that Corbett "infers that in future Great Britain may be engaged in a limited war. . . . Nothing could be further from the truth."[59] Corbett nevertheless failed to develop alternatives. He refused to abandon his concepts of limited war, and they remained central to his theory, with four of thirteen chapters in *Some Principles of Maritime Strategy* having "Limited War" in their titles. This may have been part of the problem. Corbett was not succinct in his description of limited war: he developed enough variations and nuances to make it anything but an easy concept to digest.

"It may well be questioned," another contemporary noted, "whether under modern conditions of trade and international credit, a limited war of this description could result even in the very slow wearing down of the enemy. . . . Political considerations, moreover, may make limited war impossible."[60] This commentator seems to have missed the nuance of Corbett's argument by failing to separate "war limited by its political object" from "war limited by contingent."

He was not alone in missing the subtlety. One British admiral after studying Corbett's concept claimed that limited war was a secondary consideration, insisting that "the first essential in any sort of war is to do the enemy all the harm possible," which "can only be done by keeping on pulverising him till he sues for peace."[61] Rather than being a carefully calibrated tool, the admiral saw the navy as a blunt instrument to be used to inflict maximum damage. Corbett's message was lost on this officer and others who failed to understand the relationship among means, ways, and ends.

Another contemporary reviewer questioned the continued applicability of limited war: "Mr. Corbett has shown us that the limited objective had a place in the armoury of British war in the past; but the fact remains limited war can only be used in very special circumstances." Britain's most likely opponent when *Some Principles* was published in 1911 was Germany, but many questioned whether Germany was susceptible to limited war.[62] Corbett wondered that himself, admitting it in a lecture when he asked students to ponder "whether the same methods are still possible—that is, how far changed conditions have affected their feasibility." Railroads and communications technologies had greatly enhanced the mobility of continental armies. Moreover, continental armies were larger, allowing states to maintain a military presence in more locations. These factors had to be balanced against the "size and mobility of our 'striking force.' "[63]

Part of the answer resides in Britain's official history of naval operations in World War I. Writing the first three volumes gave Corbett the opportunity to confront his critics. Even after writing these volumes, he remained wedded to war limited by contingent. Though he did not use the term in the official history, the idea echoes through his assessment of conditions in May 1915: "So long at least as there was any hope of a decision coming from the Russian side, the correct course and the one most in accordance with our traditions was to assume an alert but general defensive in France and throw everything that was not required for that defensive into an alternative theatre where decisive success was attainable, and where consequently we could hope to influence definitely the course of the war."[64] The attempt occurred at the Dardanelles and the following Gallipoli operation, which Corbett called a "venture so rightly aimed—but aimed without the energy of true faith."

He thought the failed strategies in the eastern Mediterranean determined the course of the war: "The bold plan for striking Turkey out of the German combination by a *coup de main* had finally broken down, and with it went all reasonable hope of bringing the war to a speedy termination. That hope depended on the power of the Allies to deliver a concentric attack upon the Central Powers in overwhelming force—and Turkey was the sole obstacle that stood in the way of its development." Had the allies been able to knock the Turks out of the war, Corbett asserted, "The bulk of our troops in India and Egypt would be free, the vital communications with Russia would be open, and the attitude of the Balkan States would no longer be doubtful. Then, except for the little sustenance that could reach the enemy across the Baltic, the investment of the Central Powers would be complete, and the mass of force that could be launched against them would be as irresistible as the tide."[65]

Instead, the continental method took ever stronger hold among British leaders: "It would seem to them as though a conviction was growing in military circles that the sole way to win the war was by 'killing Germans,' a method which could only be effective in the main theatre." Corbett seemed close to despair when he wrote, "To men whose outlook had been so long fixed on the promise of a great strategical stroke in the Near East, such a view of the war meant mere bankruptcy of leadership. It meant, moreover, entirely ignoring the fleet and its oft-proved capacity for substantially increasing the power of the army. It was impossible not to protest."[66]

Years later, in the aftermath of World War I, one of Corbett's war course students recounted, "In his lectures on Combined Operations he was full of interest, and brought much to light." However, the former student thought his teacher had failed to provide concepts that were repeatable in contemporary conditions. In the Dardanelles, for example, the student thought that Britain's actions demonstrated "ill digested" attempts to mimic what Corbett had written about the Seven Years' War.[67] What worked in the eighteenth century, he thought, could not achieve similar effects in the twentieth.

This was not a completely groundless claim. In 1907, Richard Haldane, then secretary of state for war, noted that Corbett's study of the Seven Years' War "contains an impressive lesson; the more we consider naval and military operations in combination the more lessons there are for today. One of the drawbacks of our time is that we have, so far as we ourselves are concerned, had but little opportunity of realizing either what a Navy can be to an Army, or what an Army can be to a Navy." Haldane concluded, "It has especial bearing on the problems with which . . . we are engaged in the Defence Committee at the present moment."[68] Corbett's work had contemporary resonance. This did not occur by happenstance: he wrote with an agenda that entailed an ever more forceful plea toward joint and limited approaches to war. The effect was significant. Years later, one commentator posited an explanation for the problems Britain faced in the war: "Maybe it was because he did write so well that other folk did not take enough trouble to think for themselves."[69]

Even so, Corbett's concepts of limited war are among his most original theoretical contributions.[70] He wrote about a maritime way of war and applied it to Britain systematically through a succession of historical studies that analyzed strategy over a period of centuries.[71] He argued for his theory being Britain's national way of war. Identifying a way of war forces one to assess warfare over a long period and generalize. Exceptions will exist as well as counterarguments by those who wish to highlight different agendas.[72]

■ ■ ■

Though not applicable in all circumstances, and arguably not as applicable as he thought it should be, Corbett's way of war based on limited options provides a compelling strategic narrative for a maritime state. If he had avoided using the word "limited" in both "war limited by its political object" and "war limited by contingent" and had written about the concepts more succinctly, his legacy would likely be more powerful. Even so, the ideas he presented concerning war limited by its political object and war limited by contingent remain the basic model of maritime strategy today. Not easy, it requires joint approaches to war that link not only diplomacy with land, naval, and economic strategies, but also the myriad other instruments of power available to decision makers today.

CONCLUSION

"I wish sometimes I could live a century hence & write the story of it all." Corbett penned these words while reflecting on British policy and strategy decisions in 1909.[1] He returned to this theme at the height of World War I, adding, "I envy the man who is free to tell the tale 100 years hence."[2] These wistful thoughts were certainly laments, but his relationship with the government prevented him from fully expressing his opinions. Wanting to study contemporary events from a hundred years in the future signaled Corbett's deep respect for history and a keen desire to provide the most accurate possible account. When approaching contemporary issues Corbett was fettered in ways he found deeply discouraging, yet this did not deter him. He thought his country required his expert opinion, and that was more important than his personal desire to provide the most accurate account. Even so, the uncertainty of the contemporary environment led to wistful thoughts of knowing more, being unbound by government restrictions, and being dispassionate enough to provide more balanced assessments.

Details never concerned Mahan as much: what mattered to him were the big ideas like sea power. They drove his popularity and defined much of his writing. Mahan worried more about remaining relevant to his readers than about getting the small points accurate. Just after publishing *The Problem of Asia* in 1900, he admitted, "It ought to be, & I intend it shall be, my swan's song on contemporary politics. . . . I become continually more and more convinced that the average man can't tell—as years advance—when he has really got out of touch with his times, & becomes a mere 'wind jammer'—to use a naval expression for useless talk."[3] Needless to say, the book was not his swan song. The allure of remaining a relevant voice led him to continue writing on contemporary subjects.

While Mahan more pointedly emphasized building and maintaining his stature in the field, Corbett believed respect and influence would follow on the heels of sound research and careful assessments. This difference lies at the heart of their methods, theories, arguments, and even their legacies.

That we study their writings today would certainly flatter Mahan more than Corbett. Following the publication of *The Influence of Sea Power upon History*, Mahan received continual praise. Writing for financial fulfillment, he crafted a carefully constructed reputation to support book sales and increase his article fees. Many of his writings aimed at contemporary policy debates. These included histories, designed to project contemporary lessons and relevance; arguments about America's place in the world; writings about new naval developments; and professional writings about the U.S. Navy. He understood that his early books made his reputation, so he would not be surprised to learn that the early pages of *The Influence of Sea Power upon History* remain his most identifiable work.

Corbett would likely find his contemporary prominence disconcerting and the theories we choose to emphasize confounding. Though he certainly addressed joint approaches, today that part of his argument is exaggerated both by commentators on his writings and in relation to his contemporaries. Moreover, it would likely astound him that he is still considered a leading authority on naval strategy. That the field has not advanced further would be unfathomable to him given its rapid development during his own lifetime. This says nothing of changes in technology and the operating environment. Specifically, Corbett would likely find it shocking that *Some Principles of Maritime Strategy* has become a foundational work of strategic thought given the criticism it received upon publication. Developments in the field should have led his successors to construct powerful strategic arguments to supplant what many in his day considered Corbett's flawed reasoning.

How does one account for the lasting significance of Mahan and Corbett? What makes certain strategic writings transcend time to speak to new generations even more clearly than they spoke to their original audience? This certainly does not stem from the clarity of their prose, for the difficulties of reading Clausewitz, Thucydides, and particularly Mahan do not detract from their significance. More important is the value of the message. But even this is not enough.

All of those men were the first, or among the first, to write on the subject after profound changes in the international environment; it is key to enter at the ground floor with new ideas and fresh perspectives. A writer who comes early to the discussion frames arguments, defines questions, and sets boundaries. Subsequent generations can find this simultaneously empowering and imprisoning. Readers of Mahan and Corbett still look at issues through the lens of the early twentieth century and from the perspective of the type of navy each advocated. Perhaps unconsciously, this perspective has led subsequent generations to fixate on concepts such as Mahan's six elements of sea power. While that concept might work more to empower thinking, his arguments detailing the decisiveness of naval power might have imprisoned his readership, especially in Imperial Japan during World War II.

Understanding the actual worth of Mahan and Corbett requires a comprehensive assessment of their writings. Placing their specific theories within their ways of war minimizes distortion. This begins with the navy's role in national strategy, which reaches far beyond the employment of warships. Naval strategic thought begins with a state's theory of security, and for this we can thank Mahan for framing the subject with his theory of sea power. Understanding the navy's role in national strategy also requires an understanding of grand strategy to explain how the navy functions with and among the other instruments of national power. Corbett's "major strategy" provides such an approach.

The relevance of Corbett's admonition that wars are fought for objects on land not only holds true today but also can be extended to broader national policies. Rarely are policy issues entirely naval in character. Considering the naval instrument in isolation is at best myopic, akin to staring down a stovepipe. Today, we highlight the joint and interagency environments: government documents discuss it, agencies strive for it, and students often wish to see it developed more fully in discussions of strategy. Working among the services or with different agencies is however difficult because they use different languages and have parochial agendas. In effect, these tensions of today are relatable to the maritime theorists. Corbett's lofty aspirations of cooperation among the instruments of national power can be juxtaposed against Mahan's more parochial naval propaganda.

Mahan's agenda asked Americans to look seaward for their security; in doing so, he channeled their strategic, cultural, and economic behavior. His admonition demanded an expansive view of grand strategy. He used Britain as his model and France as the cautionary tale, particularly in *The Influence of Sea Power upon History*. Over time, Mahan increasingly focused on the British model. Corbett had a different agenda: he wrote to influence his country's elites. He never attempted to popularize his writings to the same degree that Mahan did. British leaders at the turn of the twentieth century already understood their dependence on the sea: it was embedded in Britain's survival as an independent nation. How best to use the navy as a tool of wartime policy was not so clear to them, so Corbett focused on the relationship between the navy and the other instruments of power.

Even so, both theorists leave the reader wanting to know more about the mission of the navy within national strategy. Corbett explained it more effectively than Mahan did, but he often merely recognized the importance of various instruments of power instead of analyzing each in detail or the interactions among them.

As war or the threat of war approaches, their theories of grand strategy become inadequate. Both understood that the use of force provided a means of attaining policy objectives. Whereas Corbett safely followed the theories of Clausewitz that war is a "continuation of policy by other means," Mahan noted a similar relationship between war and political objectives but then went on to equate war with business. Since his concept of sea power brought together the naval and economic instruments, his development of a business analogy made sense. In business, one uses the available tools to turn a profit. Mahan's available tool was the navy, and he thought the proper application of naval power in war created economically beneficial results: he sought the greatest results at the least possible cost.

Though nesting naval strategy within national policy helped Mahan and Corbett to develop their arguments, this again proved insufficient.

Both men needed additional analytical frameworks. Worried that contemporary issues would distort their theory, both used history as their foundation. The past provided numerous data points to confirm their theoretical approaches. Historical examples allowed both to minimize the possibility that their arguments would turn out to be based on outliers.

While both men developed theoretical frameworks grounded in historical data, these theoretical constructs were not entirely their own. Land power theorists such as Clausewitz and Jomini dominated Western strategic thought, and Mahan and Corbett applied their frameworks to naval warfare. This included an attempt to establish principles for naval warfare. Given the rapid changes in technology at the turn of the twentieth century, principles inherent to all wars provided stability in an otherwise chaotic environment where new weapons could blind strategic thinking with the wonders of innovation. Principles along with their evil cousins—maxims and dogmas—were not passing fancies; rather, Corbett and Mahan returned to them in numerous writings, and their views eventually converged.

In terms of naval strategy, Mahan and Corbett are not as different as they might seem at first glance. Much of the perceived difference arises from their unique vocabularies, evolving arguments, imprecise writing, and the failure of subsequent generations to digest their expansive and highly scattered output.

Of all responsibilities entrusted to a navy, Mahan and Corbett were in lockstep agreement that the most important mission was control of the sea lines of communication. When facing a powerful naval rival, this necessitated the rival's diminution, preferably through battle. Though Mahan is often labeled the exponent of decisive naval battle, he wrote less about battle than most credit him, and he did not consider that naval battles alone could win wars. He made it clear, for example, that Trafalgar was not the decisive event in Napoleon's defeat. The battle was pivotal, however, because it allowed Britain to control the sea lines of communication more effectively, which in turn set the conditions for economic warfare, "the most decisive, field of work open to the British navy."[4] Controlling sea-lanes provided the means of building one's own economy while constricting the opponent's wealth and spawning self-defeating actions.

Corbett believed in battle as much Mahan. The difference between the two is one of perspective. Writing for the world's dominant naval power, Corbett understood that weaker fleets would not accept battle if it were suicide. Thus, he sought conditions that compelled the weaker naval power to consent to battle and then explained how the dominant power could exploit command of the sea, or, in his terminology, "exercise command of the sea."

Both Mahan and Corbett became quite detailed in explaining the workings of large naval forces; unfortunately, neither described the subject clearly or succinctly. Corbett comes close in the Green Pamphlet, "Some Principles of Naval Warfare," and finally *Some Principles of Maritime Strategy*, while Mahan scattered his thoughts across innumerable writings. Moreover, Mahan's book on naval strategy is less coherent than Corbett's similar volume.[5] It is here most of all that their different vocabularies cause confusion. Mahan, on close reading, is not so offensive-minded as he is often said to be, largely because many of his statements relating to offense actually apply to an active defense. Corbett seems much more amenable to the defense at the operational and strategic levels, but his emphasis on counterattacks is actually similar to Mahan's active defense. They entirely agree that passive defense has no place in war at sea. This spills into their thoughts on concentration, the utility of bases, and even the use of stratagems like "a fleet in being." This is not to suggest that their naval theories are identical. Rather, the differences come by degree, the result of unique vocabularies, points of emphases, and national perspectives.

Corbett often seems more nuanced, but we should remember that he wrote later than Mahan in a rapidly evolving field. He could build on the ideas of others, including Mahan's. Moreover, Corbett, in the first decade of the twentieth century, had much closer engagement with the naval community in the form of lecturing, discussions with leading officers, and assisting with policy projects. Mahan retired in 1896. His association with the U.S. Navy then became episodic. He wrote more, and when he did interact with the U.S. Navy, it was with a smaller officer corps operating for a country with less expansive global interests.

Mahan and Corbett had distinct agendas. This should not be surprising. Theorists develop arguments to address specific problems.

Mahan wrote for a rising naval power aspiring to command the sea, and Corbett for the dominant navy that did command the sea. Neither aimed their arguments at a power with less expansive maritime objectives such as a desire only to dispute command of the sea. A weak navy would not serve Britain, and Mahan did not want it to serve the United States.

Arguments extolling the viability of lesser options certainly existed at the time that both wrote, most notably from the Jeune École and its heirs. Whereas adherents of the Jeune École argued for obtaining decisive outcomes by *disputing* command of the sea, Mahan and Corbett attempted to explain how naval powers could obtain the greatest results only through command of the sea. Understanding lesser effects such as how navies could execute cost-incurring strategies or how naval power could exert secondary influences that contributed to securing peace did not interest either, leaving a large gap in their respective theories.

An understanding of their relative perspectives is crucial to understanding how Mahan and Corbett placed the navy within broader theories of national strategy. As contemporaries, they focused on a similar set of instruments of national power, leading both to consider diplomatic, land, and economic factors. Yet, they weighted these factors differently, often in striking and perhaps counterintuitive ways.

Mahan developed sea power by emphasizing the link between naval power and economic power. In fact, he considered economic might decisive in providing a sea power with its resiliency. He explained this most clearly in the final chapter of *The Influence of Sea Power upon the French Revolution and Empire*. It is not that he disparaged the land capabilities of the sea power or the diplomatic factors a sea power could exploit; rather, he emphasized the symbiotic relationship of the navy and commerce and their mutual exploitation of the sea lines of communication. This made his argument credible. Land and diplomatic strategies are secondary to sea power's naval and economic union. A sea power engaged in a large, multi-theater great power war can prevail only by exhausting the opponent through grinding economic attrition. This is how Mahan believed Britain defeated Napoleon and how he thought Britain would triumph over Germany in World War I.

Corbett was less enthralled with the prospect of a long, protracted campaign of exhaustion. Too much can go wrong while a sea power slowly grinds away at the economic might of a powerful rival. Instead, he tried to find ways to accelerate the sea power's victory. The result was a theory of maritime strategy linking naval power with the land instrument in a joint environment. He was a believer in power projection—not the projection of massive armies but, rather, smaller contingents he called disposal forces. Expeditionary in nature, disposal forces are capable of obtaining limited political objectives through targeting secondary theaters. Instead of going toe-to-toe with the opponent's concentrated strength, disposal forces make indirect strikes at weak points. They rely on the navy for their movement; likewise the navy's presence isolates the joint theater and limits the opponent's ability to project its own counterforce. In larger, more unlimited wars, Corbett's theory assumed a large continental ally to do the majority of the ground fighting.

Economic and diplomatic strategies are other tools in Corbett's theory. The economic instrument is difficult to control because its use tends to offend neutrals and expand the number of belligerents. If economic warfare does provide war-winning results, it is possible only after a protracted campaign. This aligns with Mahan's argument, but Corbett was less willing to accept risk of escalation in protracted campaigns of economic exhaustion.

Corbett's theory is weakest on diplomacy. This is odd given the developing British entente with France and Russia in the years before World War I. A close student of Britain's eighteenth-century wars, Corbett understood that Britain's greatest defeat in that century, the American Revolution, was the only war it fought diplomatically isolated. Though Corbett wrote about diplomatic engagement and recognized its importance, it does not appear as prominently as one might expect.

Mahan's agenda led him to downplay land military and diplomatic options. The result is a level of diplomatic engagement that largely parallels Corbett's, but Mahan had far less to say in terms of land strategy. This should not be surprising given Mahan's ultimate aim to make the United States a sea power.

Corbett's wistful "envy [of] the man who is free to tell the tale 100 years hence" is in effect this volume's reality.[6] Time has bestowed the perspective denied to him. It should, however, be recognized that navies today are not driven by theoretical models any more than navies were at the dawn of the twentieth century. Navies do not develop strategies or execute operations to support either Mahan or Corbett. The chain of causality flows in reverse. The works of thinkers like Mahan and Corbett broaden the mental aperture of those who focus on naval issues. The effect is not easy to assess. Even Corbett had difficulty doing that. Writing to Captain Herbert Richmond in in December 1917, at the height of World War I, Corbett grappled with the limits of his own contribution: "Your belief that the Service might have learnt a little more from my books is a comfort to me. I seem to have written so entirely in vain & seldom see any effect except where someone has mistaken or misapplied the teachings & consequently gone wrong."[7]

As a civilian close to the actual events, Corbett missed the inherent limitation of his own writing. This is something Richmond, a serving British naval officer, seems to have implicitly understood. Theory provides a springboard to approach events. Mahan described it as "the indirect influence of spreading sound ideas."[8] It also reflects his admonition to understand what is the same but never forget to identify the differences.[9]

Both Mahan and Corbett wrote in a world that had not seen a great-power naval war for nearly a century. In the intervening years, technological change had transformed navies. This led Mahan to posit in 1897, "All ideas about naval warfare at present are—more or less—imaginative. I say designedly, more or less; for some are much more, and some a little less than imaginative. With wild speculation, there has unquestionably signaled a considerable amount of grave, well-considered thought."[10] Given today's international and naval environments, we have again arrived at such a moment.

NOTES

ABBREVIATIONS

ADM	Admiralty Papers
BL	British Library, London
CBT	Corbett Papers, National Maritime Museum, Greenwich, U.K.
"Considerations"	Mahan, "Considerations Governing the Disposition of Navies"
FISR	Fisher Papers, Churchill Archives Centre, Churchill College, Cambridge
French Revolution	Mahan, *The Influence of Sea Power upon the French Revolution and Empire, 1793–1812*, 2 vols.
Green Pamphlet	"Strategical Terms and Definitions used in Lectures on Naval History," NMM, CBT 6/15, and "Notes on Strategy," 1909, CBT 6/16
Influence	Mahan, *The Influence of Sea Power upon History, 1660–1783*
Laughton	*Letters and Papers of Professor Sir John Knox Laughton, 1830–1915*, ed. Andrew Lambert
LC	Library of Congress, Washington, DC
Lessons	Mahan, *Lessons of the War with Spain and Other Articles*
Letters	*Letters and Papers of Alfred Thayer Mahan*, 3 vols., ed. Robert Seager II and Doris D. Maguire
LHC	Liddell Hart Centre, King's College, London
Naval Operations	Corbett, *History of the Great War: Naval Operations*, 3 vols.
Nelson	Mahan, *The Life of Nelson: The Embodiment of the Sea Power of Great Britain*, 2nd rev. ed.
NMM	National Maritime Museum, Greenwich, U.K.
NWC	Naval War College Archive, Newport, RI
NYT	*New York Times*
"Possibilities"	Mahan, "Possibilities of an Anglo-American Reunion"
RG	Record Group

RJW	Corbett, *Maritime Operations in the Russo-Japanese War, 1904–1905*, 2 vols.
Seven Years' War	Corbett, *England and the Seven Years' War: A Study in Combined Strategy*, 2 vols.
South Africa	Mahan, *The Story of the War in South Africa 1899–1900*, 3rd ed.
SPMS	Corbett, *Some Principles of Maritime Strategy*
Times	*The Times* (London)
TNA	The National Archives, Kew, U.K.
Trafalgar	Corbett, *The Campaign of Trafalgar*
War of 1812	Mahan, *Sea Power in Its Relations to the War of 1812*, 2 vols.

INTRODUCTION

1. Obituary, "Admiral Mahan, Naval Critic, Dies," *NYT*, 2 Dec 1914.
2. Obituaries: *Daily Telegraph* and *Morning Post*, 22 Sep 1922.
3. "Julian Corbett: An Appreciation," *Morning Post*, 25 Sep 1922.
4. *Times*, 11 May 1894.
5. Roosevelt, Review of *Influence of Sea Power upon History* and *Influence of Sea Power upon the French Revolution and Empire*, *Political Science Quarterly* 9 (March 1894): 171.
6. "Captain Mahan's New Work," review of *The Influence of Sea Power upon the French Revolution and Empire*, *Times*, 1 Apr 1893.
7. "Defeat of the Spanish Armada," review of Naval Record Society Publication, vol. 1: *Papers Relating to the Defeat of the Spanish Armada*, ed. J. K. Laughton, *Times*, 1 Oct 1894; "Captain Mahan's New Work," review of *The Influence of Sea Power upon the French Revolution and Empire*, *Times*, 1 Apr 1893.
8. Sumida, *Inventing Grand Strategy*, xi.
9. Gray, *Leverage of Sea Power*, 4.
10. Kennedy, *Rise and Fall of British Naval Mastery*, 9.
11. Rosinski, "Mahan and World War II," 21; Moll, "A. T. Mahan: American Historian," 131.
12. Black, *Naval Power*, 139.
13. Stanford to Hughes, 18 Feb 1945, CBT 7/19.
14. Press notices for *History of the Great War: Naval Operations*, vol. 2, citing a review for the *Daily Telegraph*, CBT 28/3.
15. Widen, *Theorist of Maritime Strategy*, 159.
16. Rodger, "Significance of Trafalgar," 79. A similar statement can be found in N. Lambert, "Admiral Sir John Fisher and the Concept of Flotilla Defence," 649n.
17. Heuser, "Regina Maris and the Command of the Sea," 226.

18. Gough, "Maritime Strategy," 57–58.
19. Churchill, *World Crisis*, 93.
20. Mahan to Merrell, 20 Dec 1908, Mahan to Rodgers, 16 Apr 1910, *Letters*, 3:273, 3:338.
21. Mahan to Corbett, 12 Aug 1907, CBT 2/4/6. The article is Corbett, "The Capture of Private Property at Sea."
22. Mahan to Merrell, 20 Dec 1908, *Letters*, 3:273.
23. Mahan, *Naval Strategy*, 15, 116. This quote demonstrates that Mahan disagreed with at least one assessment Corbett put forward in *The Campaign of Trafalgar*.
24. Conclusions based on extensive notes found in a notebook written in Mahan's hand titled "Notes Naval Strategy Lectures," NWC, MS 17, Box 3.
25. Corbett, Review of Mahan's *Types of Naval Officers*, in *American Historical Review* 7 (April 1902): 559; Corbett, *SPMS*, 131.
26. Corbett, "Capture of Private Property," 139.
27. Corbett, Lecture Notes: "Sea Common Wealth," LHC, Corbett Papers, Box 2.
28. Corbett's 1908 diary, memoranda from 1907, CBT 43/9; marginal notes in "Great Britain, Germany and Limited War," review comparing Corbett's *SPMS* and Mahan's *Naval Strategy*, *Edinburgh Review* (April 1912): 505, found in CBT 5/3.
29. Corbett to Callender, 19 Jul 1914, NMM, LES 4/1.
30. Gat, *Development of Military Thought*, 218n.
31. Corbett, "Teaching Naval and Military History," 16.
32. Corbett, "The Revival of Naval History," 2, in CBT 4/5.
33. Corbett is compared with Mahan in the following book reviews: "Great Britain, Germany and Limited War," *Edinburgh Review* (April 1912): 485–514; *New York Evening Post*, 10 May 1912; review of *History of the Great War: Naval Operations*, vol. 2, in *South Africa*, 21 Oct 1921, CBT 24/8; press notices for *History of the Great War: Naval Operations*, vol. 2, citing a review for *Literature*, CBT 28/3. Obituaries in the *Times* and *Morning Post*, both of 22 Sep 1922, compare the two men.
34. "Books of the Week," review of *Drake and the Tudor Navy*, *Times*, 4 Mar 1898.
35. "Reviews of Books: Recent Naval Literature," review of Corbett's *Successors of Drake*, *Times*, 12 Mar 1901.
36. "Great Britain, Germany and Limited War," *Edinburgh Review* (Apr 1912): 490.
37. *Athenaeum*, 10 Feb 1912.
38. Obituary for Julian S. Corbett, *Times*, 22 Sep 1922.
39. *Athenaeum*, 10 Feb 1912.
40. St. John, "European Naval Expansion and Mahan," 76; Field, "Origins of Maritime Strategy," 82; Fiske, *Navy as a Fighting Machine*, 46.
41. Angell, *World's Highway*, 159.
42. Draft obituary for Mahan, *Laughton*, No. 273, 259–61; see also Graham, *Politics of Naval Supremacy*, 5.

43. Schurman, *Education of a Navy*, 150.
44. Corbett, *Naval Operations*, 3, insert.
45. Hunt, "Strategic Thought of Corbett," 113.
46. Remarks delivered by Admiral Mike Mullen, Current Strategy Forum, Newport, RI, 14 Jun 2006.
47. Admiral John Richardson, *A Design for Maintaining Maritime Superiority*, ver. 1.0, pp. 2, 4.
48. Kaplan, "America's Elegant Decline," *Atlantic*, Nov 2007.
49. Reitzel, "Mahan on the Use of the Sea," 95.
50. A contention made by John Hattendorf. See "The Anglo-French Naval Wars," 51.
51. Sumida, *Inventing Grand Strategy*, 2, 5.
52. Quester, "Mahan and American Naval Thought since 1914," 177.
53. One only has to cite Schurman to highlight the difficulty in labeling Mahan. In 1984 he noted that "Mahan was above all a great historian" (see *Education of a Navy*, 62); but in 1989 he revisited Mahan and stated, "Perhaps the best judgment of Mahan was that he was a political scientist, who 'guessed right about the future'" (see "Mahan Revisited," 96).
54. Mahan, *The Harvest Within*.
55. N. Lambert, "False Prophet?" 1066.

CHAPTER 1. THE GRAND STRATEGIC FOUNDATIONS

1. Brands, *Promise and Pitfalls*, 1.
2. Strachan, *Direction of War*, 151.
3. Kennedy, ed., *Grand Strategies*, 5.
4. Posen, *Sources of Military Doctrine*, 13.
5. Brands, *Promise and Pitfalls*, 4–6. Brands identified six aspects of grand strategy. Mahan's sea power thesis at least partially echoes four of Brands' points.
6. Milevski, *Evolution of Modern Grand Strategic Thought*, 6.
7. Mahan to Luce, 4 Sep 1884, *Letters*, 1:577–78.
8. Report of the Board on a Post-Graduate Course, by Luce, W. T. Sampson, and C. T. Goodrich, 13 Jun 1884, U.S. Senate, *Executive Documents of the Senate*, 48th Cong., 2nd Sess., Ex. Doc. 68, p. 3.
9. Mahan to Luce, 4 Sep 1884, *Letters*, 1:577–78.
10. Mahan, "Naval Education"; Seager, *Alfred Thayer Mahan*, 120.
11. Ferreiro, "Mahan and the 'English Club.'"
12. Mahan to Marston, 19 Feb 1897, *Letters*, 2:493–94; Mahan, *From Sail to Steam*, 277.
13. Mahan, *From Sail to Steam*, 277.
14. Mahan to Luce, 16 May 1885, *Letters*, 1:606–7.
15. Mahan to Luce, 2 Sep, 16 Oct 1885; Mahan to Ashe, 13 Jan 1886, *Letters*, 1:613–14, 620–21.

16. Mahan, Strategy Lecture 1: Introductory, NWC, MS 17, Box 6.
17. Mahan, *From Sail to Steam*, 281.
18. See the bibliography for a list of Mahan's works cited in this study.
19. This description of sea power aligns with what Brands argues in *Promise and Pitfalls*, 4–6.
20. Mahan, *Influence*, 539.
21. Mahan, "Effect of Asiatic Conditions," 163–64.
22. Mahan, *Interest of America in International Conditions*, 87.
23. Sumida, *Inventing Grand Strategy*, 35; Rubel, *Navies and Economic Prosperity*, 2–3.
24. See Vesey Hamilton comment in J. Colomb, "British Defence," 233–34; Laughton, "Scientific Study of Naval History," 510; Hamley, *National Defence Articles and Speeches*, 147.
25. David, "Our Merchant Marine," 155–56; Seager, *Alfred Thayer Mahan*, 200–201.
26. Fiske, introduction to Fiennes, *Sea Power and Freedom*, vi.
27. Fiske, *Navy as a Fighting Machine*, 45–46.
28. Bridge, *Sea-Power*, 4. For a similar statement, see Clarke and Thursfield, *The Navy and the Nation*, 189.
29. Holmes and Yoshihara, "Influence of Mahan upon China's Maritime Strategy," 25.
30. Mahan, *Problem of Asia*, 126.
31. Mahan, "Effect of Asiatic Conditions," 158.
32. Mahan, *Influence*, 1.
33. Mahan, "Future in Relation to American Naval Power," 138–39.
34. Mahan, *Influence*, 1.
35. Mahan, *French Revolution*, 2:184; Mahan, *Influence*, 275, 278.
36. Dull, "Mahan, Sea Power," 59–60.
37. Mahan, *Types of Naval Officers*, 102.
38. Mahan, *Interest of America in International Conditions*, 83.
39. Mahan, *Influence*, 225.
40. Draft obituary for Mahan, *Laughton*, No. 273, pp. 259–61.
41. Laughton, "Captain Mahan on Maritime Power" (1890), 420.
42. Discussion by Thomas Maguire in Laughton, "Study of Naval History," 814.
43. Mahan obituary in "Personal Notes," *American Historical Review* 20 (Jan 1915): 445–46.
44. Mahan to Benjamin F. Tracy, 7 Dec 1892, *Letters*, 2:89.
45. Laughton, "Study of Naval History," 797.
46. Laughton, "Captain Mahan on Maritime Power" (1890), 453.
47. Mahan, *Influence*, 198–99.
48. Mahan, *Influence*, 209.
49. Laughton, "Captain Mahan on Maritime Power" (1890), 453; see also, Fiennes, *Sea Power and Freedom*, 255.

50. Mahan, *Influence*, 57, 91, 226.
51. Mahan, *Influence*, 326.
52. Mahan to Ellen Evans Mahan, 13 Jul 1893, entry for 14 Jul, *Letters*, 2:121–22.
53. "Third Annual Message to Congress," 9 Dec 1891, in Harrison, *Public Papers and Addresses*, 114.
54. Mahan, "Navy as a Career," 283.
55. Mahan, *Naval Strategy*, 446.
56. Examples by Mahan include "Hague Conference," 168; *Influence*, 67; "Navies as International Factors," 60–62; and *Interest of America in International Conditions*, 111–14.
57. Britain had "been induced to concede to neutrals the principle that the flag covers the goods. It is a concession wrung from relative weakness—or possibly from a mistaken humanitarianism." See Mahan, "Possibilities," 562.
58. Mahan, "Effect of Asiatic Conditions," 179.
59. Additional sources where Mahan considered Anglo-American cooperation include: "Place of Force in International Relations"; "Hawaii and Our Future Sea Power," 55; "Effect of Asiatic Conditions," 195; "Twentieth Century Outlook," 259. Jon Sumida demonstrates the pervasiveness of this subject within Mahan's writings in *Inventing Grand Strategy*, 83–84, 89–90.
60. Mahan, "Possibilities," 555.
61. Mahan, "United States Looking Outward," 31.
62. Mahan, "Persian Gulf," 249; and "Effect of Asiatic Conditions," 186.
63. Mahan, "Panama Canal and Sea Power," 180.
64. Mahan, *Influence*, 28–29.
65. Sumida, "Alfred Thayer Mahan, Geopolitician," 46 (the quote); Seager, *Alfred Thayer Mahan*, 205–6; Varacalli, "National Interest and Moral Responsibility," 109; Kennedy, "Influence and Limitations of Sea Power," 3.
66. David, "Our Merchant Marine," 152, 155–56. Sumida ("Mahan, Geopolitican," 46) and Seager (*Alfred Thayer Mahan*, 200–201) have both noted David's influence on Mahan.
67. Mahan to Luce, 22 Jan 1886, *Letters*, 1:622–24.
68. Mahan, *Influence*, 29.
69. Mahan, "Persian Gulf," 247.
70. Mahan, *Interest of America in International Conditions*, 27; and "Possibilities," 552.
71. Mahan, *Influence*, 29–32.
72. Mahan, "Considerations," 169.
73. Mahan, *Influence*, 170.
74. Mahan, "Persian Gulf," 247.
75. Mahan, *Influence*, 35.
76. Mahan, *Influence*, 43–44.
77. Mahan, "Panama Canal and Sea Power," 178.

78. Mahan, *Influence*, 45.
79. Mahan, *Types of Naval Officers*, 447.
80. Mahan, *War of 1812*, 1:38.
81. Mahan, *Influence*, 46, 48.
82. Mahan, "Preparedness for Naval War," 586.
83. Mahan, *Influence*, 53, 56; Mahan, *French Revolution*, 2:373–74.
84. Mahan, *Influence*, 28.
85. Mahan, *Influence*, 67.
86. Corbett, *Successors of Drake*, 410.
87. Corbett, *Seven Years' War*, 1:v, 5.
88. Green Pamphlet, p. 8, CBT 6/15.
89. Corbett, *Successors of Drake*, vii.
90. Corbett, *SPMS*, 8, 10.
91. Corbett to Colles, his agent, 1 Jan 1901, NMM, MS 67/030.
92. May to Corbett, 19 Aug 1902, CBT 13/3.
93. Document titled "War Course" attached to Slade to Corbett, 20 May 1906, CBT 13/2; "The Naval War Course" by Corbett, *Times*, 5 Jun 1906; *Western Mercury* (Plymouth), 3 Jul 1906.
94. Corbett to his wife, 12 Aug 1903, CBT 10/1/10.
95. Corbett to his wife, 20 Oct 1909, CBT 10/8/3.
96. Corbett to Fisher, 25 Jan 1910, FISR 1/9.
97. Corbett to his wife, 9 Feb 1909, CBT 10/7/9.
98. Corbett's 1908 diary, memoranda from 1907, CBT 43/9; Rawlinson to Corbett, 25 Aug 1905, LHC, Corbett Papers, Box 2; Corbett's note to document, Fisher to Corbett, 24 May 1905, FISR 1/4.
99. Fisher to Corbett, 17 Mar 1907, FISR 1/5.
100. Fisher to Corbett, 9 Mar 1907, FISR/1/5; War Plans, Part I: "Some Principles of Naval Warfare," TNA, ADM/116/1043B: pt. 1.
101. Fisher to Sir Edward Grey, 23 Jan 1908, FISR 1/6.
102. Preface to 1907 War Plans, ADM/116/1043B: pt. 1.
103. Response to Part I of the War Plan, by Charles Beresford, 8 May 1907, ADM/116/1037.
104. Corbett to Sydenham, 30 Nov 1916, CBT 7/12; Green Pamphlet, CBT 6/15.
105. It went through at least three editions. The first edition listed only Corbett as the author (see CBT 6/15). A slightly modified second edition titled "Notes on Strategy" dated War College, Portsmouth, No. 1, Sep 1906 listed both Slade and Corbett as the authors (see "Notes on Strategy," BL, Add MS 82,516 D). A third, or "Bayly" edition, named after then president of the War College, Rear Admiral Lewis Bayly, dates from Jan 1909 (see CBT 6/16, NMM, NAI 2/30 and RIC 2/2).
106. Schurman, "Julian Corbett's Influence," 59–60; Gooch, "Maritime Command," 38; A. Lambert, "Corbett and the Naval War Course," 41.

107. Martin, "1907 War Plans," 841.
108. Corbett to Colles, no date, NMM, MS 67/030.
109. A. Lambert, "Sir Julian Corbett," 192.
110. A. Lambert, ed., *21st Century Corbett*, 10.
111. Haldane to Corbett, 6 Dec 1907, CBT 14/3.
112. Corbett, *Seven Years' War*, 1:vi.
113. Heuser, *Evolution of Strategy*, 176–77.
114. Corbett to Admiral Sir W. H. Fawkes, 27 Nov 1911, NMM, AGC 2/27.
115. Richmond, "The Late Sir Julian Corbett," 18; Corbett's diary, 10 Oct 1910, CBT 43/11.
116. A. Lambert, "Sir Julian Corbett," p. 194, contends this is the message found in Corbett's diary, 27 Oct 1909, CBT 43/10. The still blank journal can be found at NMM, TUN 226.
117. Ottley to Fisher, 12 Jan 1910, FISR 1/9.
118. Corbett's diary, 25 Jun 1910, CBT 43/11.
119. Corbett's diary, 25 Jun 1910, CBT 43/11.
120. Corbett to Newbolt, 12 Oct 1911, CBT 3/7/75. Andrew Lambert contends that Corbett's description of *Some Principles of Maritime Strategy* as "tasteless" was sarcasm rather than his actual belief ("Sir Julian Corbett," 197). However, a different interpretation supported by his statement about becoming an armchair strategist reflects the risks he took writing this book.
121. Corbett's diary, 31 Dec 1910, CBT 43/11, 15 Feb 1911, CBT 43/12.
122. Corbett's diary, 26 Jan 1911, CBT 43/12; Troubridge to Corbett, 10 Jul 1911, Wilson to Corbett, 11 Jul 1911, CBT 13/3.
123. Corbett to his wife, 6 Dec 1911, CBT 11/2/30. The article in reference is "Mr. Churchill and the Navy: The Changes in the Board," *Times*, 4 Dec 1911.
124. "'Super-Mahan': The Uncertainties of Naval War," *Standard*, 2 Dec 1911, CBT 5/3.
125. "Maritime Strategy: Mr. Julian Corbett's Theories Criticized," *Naval and Military Record*, [most likely 10 Jan 1912], p. 821, CBT 5/3.
126. Corbett to his wife, 28 May 1912, CBT 11/3/45.
127. Stanford, "Work of Sir Julian Corbett," 67.
128. Schurman, *Education of a Navy*, 174.
129. A. Lambert, *Foundations of Naval History*, 233.
130. A. Lambert, "Sir Julian Corbett," 196; Ranft's foreword to *Some Principles of Maritime Strategy* (1972 ed.), x.
131. Corbett, *SPMS*, 16.
132. Corbett, *SPMS*, 274.
133. Corbett, Lecture: "Strategical Use of Combined Expeditions," given at Aldershot to the 2nd Division, 7 Jan 1907, LHC, Corbett Papers, Box 2.
134. Corbett, "Staff Histories," 33.
135. Corbett, *SPMS*, 15.

136. Corbett, *SPMS*, 15–16.
137. Corbett, *Seven Years' War*, 1:5.
138. Corbett, "United Service," 204.
139. "Naval War Course" by Corbett, *Times*, 5 Jun 1906.
140. Corbett used "grand," "major," and "higher" strategy in *England and the Seven Years' War*; see 1:2, 77, 273. In *Some Principles of Maritime Strategy*, he confined himself to the term "major" strategy.
141. Corbett, Lectures on Naval Strategy, Lecture 1, p. 2, CBT 31.
142. Green Pamphlet, CBT 6/15; see also Corbett, "Reorganisation of the War Office," 32, in CBT 3/10.
143. Corbett, *Naval Operations*, 3:45.
144. Corbett, Lectures on Naval Strategy, Lecture 1, p. 1, CBT 31.
145. Corbett, Lecture: "Naval Strategy as Modified by Political Considerations," Feb 1904, LHC, Corbett Papers, Box 1.
146. Clausewitz, *On War*, trans. Graham, 1:85.
147. Andrew Lambert disagrees and argues that Corbett "condemned [or dismissed] naval strategy as a 'minor' or operational issue." See *21st Century Corbett*, 9; and "Sir Julian Corbett," 191.
148. Corbett, Lectures on Naval Strategy, Lecture 1, p. 3, CBT 31
149. Corbett, Lectures on Naval Strategy, Lecture 1, p. 2, CBT 31.
150. Lukas Milevski provides a different interpretation indicating that Corbett eventually concluded that ends and means are aspects of major strategy and ways are part of minor strategy. See *Modern Grand Strategic Thought*, 39.
151. Strachan, "Lost Meaning of Strategy," 38.
152. Milevski, *Modern Grand Strategic Thought*, 5.
153. Mahan, Lowell Institute Lecture: "Naval Warfare," circa 1897, p. 1, Papers of Mahan, LC, Container 5, Reel 3.
154. English original, p. 2 of "Le Canal de Panama au point vue militaire," *Revue* Économique *Internationale*, Jan 1913, Papers of Mahan, LC, Container 6, Reel 4.
155. Mahan to Roosevelt, 13 Jan 1909, *Letters*, 3:276.
156. Mahan, Notes Naval Strategy Lectures, p. 7, NWC, MS 17, Box 3.
157. Mahan, *Influence*, 98, 523.
158. Corbett to Callender, 19 Jul 1914, NMM, LES 4/1.
159. Aron, "Evolution of Modern Strategic Thought," 7.
160. A. Lambert, "Sir Julian Corbett," 192–96.
161. Mahan, *Influence*, 425, 541. The quote ends: "concerning which nothing conclusive had been established by the war," referring to failures in the American Revolution. This only strengthens his argument.
162. Corbett, *SPMS*, 12, 16.
163. Mahan to Marston, 19 Feb 1897, *Letters*, 2:493–94; see also Mahan, "Word Coinage," *NYT*, 25 Aug 1901.

CHAPTER 2. THE USE OF HISTORY AND THE DEVELOPMENT OF THEORY

1. Mahan to Laughton, 8 Aug 1902, *Laughton*, No. 224, pp. 216–18.
2. Mahan, *Influence*, 21.
3. Corbett, "The Revival of Naval History," 6, in CBT 4/5.
4. Laughton, "Vice Admiral Baron von Tegetthoff," 671–72.
5. Mahan, Introduction to *Ironclads in Action*, xi.
6. Corbett, *England and the Mediterranean*, 1:v.
7. Mahan, "Subordination of Historical Treatment," 253–54.
8. Mahan to Marston, 19 Feb 1897, *Letters*, 2:493–94.
9. Mahan, "Subordination of Historical Treatment," 261.
10. H. H., "Naval History: Mahan and His Successors," 9.
11. "Admiral Mahan's Warning," *Fortnightly Review* (August 1910), 233.
12. Reitzel, "Mahan on the Use of the Sea," 74; see also Seager, "Alfred Thayer Mahan: Christian Expansionist, Navalist, and Historian," 35.
13. Mahan to Marston, 19 Feb 1897, *Letters*, 2:493–94.
14. Mahan, *From Sail to Steam*, 284.
15. Mahan to Laughton, 21 Mar 1893, 20 Jul 1906, *Laughton*, Nos. 78, 243, pp. 85–87, 236–37.
16. Mahan, "Principles Involved in the War between Japan and Russia," 89–90; see also Mahan, *Naval Administration and Warfare*, v.
17. Sumida, *Inventing Grand Strategy*, 33.
18. Mahan to Brown, 1 Jan 1907, *Letters*, 3:199–200.
19. Corbett, *England and the Mediterranean*, 1:319–20.
20. Corbett, "The Revival of Naval History," 3, in CBT 4/5.
21. Corbett to Jellicoe, 18 Jul 1922, Jellicoe Papers, BL Add. MS 49,037, 181, 84.
22. Corbett, *Drake and the Tudor Navy*, 1:v.
23. Books of the Week [review of *Drake and the Tudor Navy*], *Times*, 4 Mar 1898; Schurman, *Education of a Navy*, 155–56; Stanford, "Work of Sir Julian Corbett," 63.
24. Laughton, *Review of Drake and the Tudor Navy*, 2.
25. Schurman, *Education of a Navy*, 149.
26. Sumida, "Historian as Contemporary Analyst," 139–40.
27. Corbett to Richmond, 12 Jan 1917, NMM, RIC 9, pt. 1; Corbett, Review of Mahan, *Types of Naval Officers*, *American Historical Review* 7 (Apr 1902): 556–59.
28. Corbett, *Naval Operations*, 1:vii.
29. Corbett, "Methods and Discussion," 322, 324.
30. Corbett, "Staff Histories," 24.
31. Mahan, *Lessons*, 7.
32. Dewar to Corbett, 15 Oct 1911, CBT 6/13/9.

33. Corbett, "Recent Attacks on the Admiralty," 203.
34. Mahan, *Problem of Asia*, vi–vii.
35. Fuller, "What Is a Military Lesson," 38–41.
36. Corbett, Lecture on Naval History, no date, LHC, Corbett Papers, Box 1.
37. Corbett to his wife, 16 Dec 1909, CBT 10/8/21.
38. Mahan used the words quoted here in "The Naval War College," 201.
39. Mahan, Notes Naval Strategy Lectures, passim, Strategy Lecture 2: "Montenotti," p. 40, NWC, MS 17, Boxes 3, 6; Mahan, *Naval Strategy*, 13, 15–17, 20, 83–84, 107, 236.
40. Inventory of Corbett's Library, TNA, ADM 1/8650/244. The naval sources include Bridge, *Sea-Power and Other Studies* (1910) and *The Art of Naval Warfare* (1907); Castex, *Les Ideés Militaires de la Marine du XVIIIe siècle* (1911); Clarke and Thursfield, *The Navy and the Nation* (1897); Colomb, *Naval Warfare* (1895); Custance, *The Ship of the Line in Battle* (1912); Darrieus, *La Guerre sur Mer* (1907); Daveluy, *La Lutte pour l'Empire de la Mer* (1906), *L'Esprit de la Guerre Navale* (3 vols.) (1909–10); Mahan, *The Influence of Sea Power on the French Revolution and Empire* (2 vols.), *Naval Strategy*, *The Life of Nelson* (2 vols.), *Types of Naval Officers*, *Sea Power in Its Relation to the War of 1812* (2 vols.), *The Influence of Sea Power upon History*, and *Lessons of the War with Spain*; Thursfield, *Naval Warfare* (1913), *Nelson and Other Naval Studies* (1909).
41. Mahan to Luce, 16 May 1885, 22 Jan 1886, *Letters*, 1:606–7, 622–24.
42. Luce, "Intellectual Focus," 55.
43. Corbett, *SPMS*, 28, 46–47.
44. Strachan, *Clausewitz*, 88–93; Stoker, *Clausewitz*, 72.
45. Corbett, Lectures on Naval Strategy, p. 1, CBT 31, also in CBT 15/6/6.
46. A. Lambert, "Development of Education," 52; Bassford, *Clausewitz in English*, 73.
47. Corbett, *England and the Mediterranean*, 2:229, 236, 253. Note: Corbett did not mention Clausewitz by name in *England and the Mediterranean*. Several authors make different claims about Corbett's introduction to Clausewitz. These include Gat (*Development of Military Thought*, 216) and A. Lambert, who definitively states, "Corbett read Clausewitz in 1906" (*Foundations of Naval History*, 224).
48. Mahan to Luce, 3 Nov 1885, *Letters*, 1:616–17.
49. Mahan, Address delivered at the Naval War College, Sep 1892, *Letters*, 3:580.
50. Hattendorf, "Alfred Thayer Mahan and His Strategic Thought," 84.
51. Mahan, Strategy Lectures 2, 3, 5, and 6, NWC, MS 17, Box 6.
52. Sumida, *Inventing Grand Strategy*, 23–24.
53. Mahan, *From Sail to Steam*, 278.
54. Mahan to Luce, 30 Sep 1897, *Letters*, 2:526; Mahan, *From Sail to Steam*, 278.
55. Sumida, *Inventing Grand Strategy*, 112–14.

56. Puleston, *Mahan*, 280; Bassford, *Clausewitz in English*, 83.
57. Mahan, *Naval Strategy*, 279.
58. Mahan, *From Sail to Steam*, 273; Seager, *Alfred Thayer Mahan*, 4; Sumida, *Inventing Grand Strategy*, 23–24.
59. Clausewitz, *On War*, trans. Graham, 1:80; Jomini, *Art of War*, trans. Mendell and Craighill, 169; Mahan, Strategy Lecture 1: Introductory, pp. 1–2, NWC, MS 17, Box 6; Corbett to Callendar, 2 Dec 1914, NMM, LES 4/1.
60. Laughton, "Study of Naval History," 795. For an extended discussion, see Reynolds, *Command of the Sea*, 10–11.
61. Mahan to Lodge, 19 May 1890, Mahan to Chambers, 27 Jul 1892, *Letters*, 2:11, 2:75–77.
62. Mahan, *Admiral Farragut*, 314.
63. Mahan to Luce, 9 Apr 1890, *Letters*, 2:2–3.
64. Corbett, "The Naval War Course," *Times*, 5 Jun 1906.
65. Luce, "Intellectual Focus," 53.
66. Mahan, Strategy Lecture 1: Introductory, pp. 1–2, NWC, MS 17, Box 6.
67. Fiske, *From Midshipman to Rear-Admiral*, 107.
68. *United States Army and Navy Journal and Gazette*, 17 Sep 1892, 58.
69. Mahan, Introduction to *Ironclads in Action*, xiii–xiv.
70. Only Mahan published on the Sino-Japanese War: "Lessons from the Yalu Fight." For the Russo-Japanese War, see Mahan, "Principles Involved in the War between Japan and Russia," "Retrospect upon the War between Japan and Russia," and numerous articles in *Collier's Weekly* and *The Times* (London); Corbett, *RJW*. For the Spanish American War, see Mahan, *Lessons*; Corbett, *SPMS*, 56–57, 167–70.
71. Mahan, "Torpedo Craft vs. Battleships," 16.
72. Corbett, *SPMS*, 18–19.
73. Corbett, *SPMS*, 3, 18–19.
74. Corbett, Lectures on Naval Strategy, p. 1, CBT 31, also in CBT 15/6/6.
75. Corbett, *SPMS*, 3–4.
76. Clausewitz, *On War*, trans. Graham, 1:55. Corbett made extensive use of *On War*, including many quotes, especially in *Some Principles of Maritime Strategy*. The most modern English translation of *On War*, edited and translated by Michael Howard and Peter Paret, was not available to Corbett, and that translation is generally not used in the following text. The volume Corbett likely consulted was the 1873 translation by J. J. Graham. At the time of Corbett's death, his library included the Graham translation; it did not include Clausewitz in its original German. See Inventory of Corbett's Library, TNA, ADM 1/8650/244; Book Inventory, CBT 16/3. Both of the above inventories include the 1873 translation of *On War*. The book inventory in CBT 16/3 indicates it was in one volume. This corresponds to the edition used in the following pages of

this book. That version of *On War* put the three volumes of Graham's translation into a single binding. It should also be noted that Corbett did not quote the Graham translation exactly, although the quotes are undeniably similar to Graham's words. It seems that Corbett took some license, perhaps because he was working off a translation. The differences allowed Corbett to fit Clausewitz into his own vocabulary and his own text. The Graham translation is the version of Clausewitz generally quoted throughout the following pages. The use of this translation becomes especially important when determining how Clausewitz influenced Corbett's overall theory.

77. Corbett, Lectures on Naval Strategy, p. 24, CBT 31, also in CBT 15/6/6.
78. Clausewitz, *On War*, trans. Graham, 1:48.
79. Corbett to Sydenham, 30 Nov 1916, CBT 7/12.
80. Slade to Corbett, 2 Dec 1906, CBT 13/2/6. Nicholas Lambert supports this argument, specifying "that this document was framed for immediate pedagogical reasons, not as an abstract exposition of theoretical principles" ("False Prophet?" 1067). The "immediate pedagogical reasons" was aimed at providing foundational terms and concepts for students in the War Course.
81. Corbett, *SPMS*, 7–8.
82. Corbett, *SPMS*, 4–6.
83. Clausewitz, *On War*, trans. Graham, 1:ix.
84. Mahan, Strategy Lecture 1: Introductory, p. 1, NWC, MS 17, Box 6.
85. Mahan to Ashe, 2 Feb 1886, *Letters*, 1:624–25.
86. Mahan to Henderson, 5 May 1890, *Letters*, 2:9.
87. Mahan to Luce, 22 Jan, 24 Apr 1886, *Letters*, 1:622–24, 1:628–30.
88. Mahan to Luce, 24 Apr 1886, *Letters*, 1:628–30.
89. Mahan, *Naval Administration and Warfare*, x.
90. Mahan, "Principles Involved in the War between Japan and Russia," 94–95; Mahan, introduction to *Ironclads in Action*, vii; Mahan, Lowell Institute Lecture: "Naval Warfare," circa 1897, p. 4, Papers of Mahan, LC, Container 5, Reel 3.
91. J. Colomb, *Protection of Our Commerce*, 1; Schurman, *Education of a Navy*, 27.
92. Laughton, "Scientific Study of Naval History," 523; Luce, "Intellectual Focus," 60; see also Luce, "Tactics and History," 76.
93. Jomini, *Art of War*, trans. Mendell and Craighill, 48, 71.
94. Mahan, *Influence*, 8.
95. Mahan, "Naval War College," 206.
96. Jomini, *Art of War*, trans. Winship and McLean, 48, 283–84.
97. D. H. Mahan, *Advanced-Guard, Outpost*, 169–70.
98. Mahan, *Influence*, 88–89; see also Mahan, Lowell Institute Lecture: "Naval Warfare," circa 1897, p. 23, Papers of Mahan, LC, Container 5, Reel 3.
99. Gat, *Development of Military Thought*, 199; Karsten, *Naval Aristocracy*, 344.

100. Sprout and Sprout, *Rise of American Naval Power*, unpaginated introduction.
101. Mahan, *Nelson*, 200.
102. Mahan, *Influence*, 88–89.
103. Mahan, *Naval Strategy*, 299.
104. Mahan, *From Sail to Steam*, 282; Mahan, "Objects of the United States Naval War College," 191.
105. Mahan, Strategy Lecture 4: "Bussano," p. 79, NWC, MS 17, Box 6.
106. Mahan, *Naval Strategy*, 28.
107. Mahan, "Blockade," 852.
108. Mahan, Review of "*The War in South Africa*: First of Six Volumes Just Published by the London Times," *NYT*, 30 May 1902.
109. Mahan, *Influence*, 2–3, 5.
110. Corbett, *Seven Years' War*, 1:1.
111. Corbett, *SPMS*, 9.
112. Clausewitz, *On War*, trans. Graham, 1:67–68, 72. The most recent English translation of Clausewitz by Howard and Paret describes this as "critical analysis" (p. 156); however, in Corbett's time, the available translation described this concept as "critical examination."
113. Corbett, *Trafalgar*, 236.
114. Corbett, *SPMS*, 6.
115. Corbett, *SPMS*, 8–10.
116. Corbett, ed., *Fighting Instructions*, 135.
117. Corbett, *SPMS*, 281.
118. "'Super-Mahan': The Uncertainties of Naval Warfare," *Standard*, 2 Dec 1911, in CBT 5/3.
119. "Under the White Ensign," by Fred T. Jane, *Evening Standard*, 15 Jan 1912, CBT 5/3.
120. Corbett, "Napoleon and the British Navy," 240.
121. "'Super-Mahan': The Uncertainties of Naval Warfare," *Standard*, 2 Dec 1911, in CBT 5/3.
122. Clausewitz, *On War*, trans. Graham, 1:63; Jomini, *Art of War*, trans. Mendell and Craighill, 84; Jomini, *Art of War*, trans. Winship and McLean, 95.
123. Corbett, *SPMS*, 103.
124. Corbett, "Recent Attacks on the Admiralty," 199.
125. Corbett, *RJW*, 2:174.
126. Corbett, *SPMS*, 167.
127. Mahan to Clarke, 30 Sep 1894, *Letters*, 2:336–38.
128. Mahan, Notes Naval Strategy Lectures, p. 32, Strategy Lecture 3: "Mondovi, Lodi, Lanato and Castiglione," p. 52, NWC, MS 17, Boxes 3, 6.
129. Mahan, *Naval Strategy*, 300.

CHAPTER 3. WAR, POLICY, AND CIVIL-MILITARY RELATIONS

1. Note of 10 Jul 1827, Clausewitz, *On War*, trans. Graham, 1:vii (italics in the original) and supported by information on 1:12.
2. Corbett, *SPMS*, 17.
3. Mahan, "Preparedness for Naval War," 579; see also Strategy Lecture 1: Introductory, p. 11, NWC, MS 17, Box 6; Lowell Institute Lecture: "Naval Warfare," circa 1897, p. 4, Papers of Mahan, LC, Container 5, Reel 3.
4. Mahan, "Navies as International Factors," 64–65, and *Lessons*, 203; see also Mahan, *From Sail to Steam*, 283.
5. Mahan to Roosevelt, 13 Jan 1909, *Letters*, 3:275–77.
6. Corbett, *Seven Years' War*, 1:23–24.
7. Clausewitz, *On War*, trans. Graham, 1:85.
8. Corbett, "United Service," 205.
9. Green Pamphlet, p. 1, CBT 6/16.
10. Corbett, Staff College Lecture: "Function of the Army in Relation to Gaining Command of the Sea . . . ," 21 Nov 1905, LHC, Corbett Papers, Box 2.
11. Jomini, *Art of War*, trans. Mendell and Craighill, 69, 178; Freedman, *Strategy*, 84.
12. Mahan, "Practical Words: An Address to the Naval War College," Sep 1892, *Letters*, 3:580; Milevski, *Modern Grand Strategic Thought*, 30–31.
13. Mahan, *Lessons*, 163; Corbett, Staff College Lecture: "Function of the Army in Relation to Gaining Command of the Sea . . . ," 21 Nov 1905, LHC, Corbett Papers, Box 2.
14. Mahan, *Types of Naval Officers*, 269–70; see also Mahan, "Naval War College," 214.
15. Mahan, "Subordination of Historical Treatment," 264.
16. Corbett, *RJW*, 1:266.
17. Corbett, *SPMS*, 27; see also Clausewitz, *On War*, trans. Graham, 1:11–12.
18. Corbett, *SPMS*, 226.
19. Mahan, *War of 1812*, 1:293, 2:78; see also Mahan, Strategy Lecture 2: "Montenotti," p. 37, NWC, MS 17, Box 6; Mahan, *Major Operations War of American Independence*, 193.
20. Mahan to the editor of the *New York Times*, 22 May 1912, *Letters*, 3:459. See also "Principles of Naval Administration," 7. In this case, Mahan diverged from the previous assessment by indicating the navy is "the instrument . . . [and] the means are the various activities which we group under the head of administration." However, "the end necessarily conditions the others."
21. Mahan, "Preparedness for Naval War," 580.
22. Mahan, *South Africa*, 184.
23. Mahan, *Naval Strategy*, 107.

24. Mahan, *From Sail to Steam*, 283.
25. Jomini, *Art of War*, trans. Mendell and Craighill, 15–16, 91; Sumida, *Decoding Clausewitz*, 14–15; Handel, *Masters of War*, 73–74.
26. Mahan, *French Revolution*, 2:391–92.
27. Mahan, *Influence*, 108.
28. Mahan, *French Revolution*, 2:392.
29. Mahan, "Principles of Naval Administration," 6–7.
30. Mahan, "Panama Canal and the Distribution of the Fleet," 412; see also Mahan, *Naval Strategy*, 375.
31. Mahan, *Naval Strategy*, 21.
32. Mahan, *Naval Strategy*, 21.
33. Mahan, "Panama Canal and the Distribution of the Fleet," 412.
34. Mahan, *French Revolution*, 2:385–86.
35. Mahan, *Influence*, 475n.
36. Mahan, Review of "*The War in South Africa*: First of Six Volumes Just Published by the London Times," *NYT*, 30 May 1902.
37. Mahan, "Considerations," 142–43.
38. May to Corbett, 22 Aug 1902, CBT 13/3.
39. Corbett, "Teaching Naval and Military History," 17–18.
40. Corbett, Naval Strategy Lecture 2: "System of Clausewitz," pp. 3–4, CBT 15/6/6.
41. Corbett, *Seven Years' War*, 1:16.
42. Corbett, *SPMS*, 17.
43. War Plans, 1907: Part I, "Some Principles of Naval Warfare," TNA, ADM/116/1043B.
44. Clausewitz, *On War*, trans. Graham 1:6.
45. Corbett, *Naval Operations*, 1:290, 3:165.
46. Mahan, "Current Fallacies upon Naval Subjects," 286.
47. Mahan, "Lessons from the Yalu Fight," 629 (italics in the original).
48. Mahan, *Major Operations War of American Independence*, 31.
49. Corbett, Lectures on Naval Strategy, p. 4, CBT 31.
50. Corbett, "The Naval War Course," *Times*, 5 Jun 1906.
51. Corbett, *Seven Years' War*, 1:58–59, 2:178.
52. Corbett, *SPMS*, 5–6; see also his *Naval Operations*, 2:177–78.
53. Corbett, *SPMS*, 7–8.
54. Corbett, *Naval Operations*, 2:106.
55. Corbett, *Seven Years' War*, 2:15–16.
56. Mahan, *War of 1812*, 2:78; War Plans, 1907: Part I, "Some Principles of Naval Warfare," p. 2, TNA, ADM/116/1043B. Corbett cited Turpin de Crisse, a commentator on the works of Montecuculi.
57. Corbett, *Seven Years' War*, 1:61.

CHAPTER 4. INTRODUCTION TO NAVAL STRATEGY

1. Corbett, *Naval Operations*, 1:305.
2. Mahan, *Naval Strategy*, 5; Corbett, Lectures on Naval Strategy, p. 1, CBT 31.
3. Clausewitz, *On War*, trans. Graham, 1:85.
4. Mahan, *Influence*, 22–23.
5. This topic is developed in far greater detail in chapter 1.
6. Corbett, *Seven Years' War*, 1:273.
7. Corbett to Richmond, 13 Aug 1912, NMM, RIC 9, pt. 1.
8. Corbett, *SPMS*, 93, 155–56; Corbett, *Trafalgar*, 251.
9. Lowell Institute Lecture: "Naval Warfare," circa 1897, p. 1, Papers of Mahan, LC, Container 5, Reel 3.
10. "Sea Power in the Present European War," *Leslie's Illustrated Weekly*, 20 Aug 1914, reprinted in *Letters*, 3:706–10.
11. Luce to Mahan, 15 Jul 1907, NWC, RG1, Box 3, Folder 14. For his 1886 writing, see "Intellectual Focus."
12. Mahan, *Naval Strategy*, 121; see also Lowell Institute Lecture: "Naval Warfare," circa 1897, p. 35, Papers of Mahan, LC, Container 5, Reel 3.
13. Mahan, Strategy Lecture 5: "Arcola," p. 85, NWC, MS 17, Box 6.
14. Corbett, *SPMS*, 20–21; Heuser, *Evolution of Strategy*, 176.
15. Corbett, *SPMS*, 155.
16. Abstract of Lectures on Strategy by Mahan, 1899, NWC, RG15, Box 1; Lectures 1–6, NWC, MS 17, Box 6.
17. Lowell Institute Lecture: "Naval Warfare," circa 1897, p. 36, Papers of Mahan, LC, Container 5, Reel 3; Mahan, *Influence*, 329, 338–39, 374.
18. Corbett, *SPMS*, 93, 155–56. The bulleted points are direct quotations.
19. Mahan, Strategy Lecture 6: "Rivoli," circa 1896, NWC, MS 17, Box 6.
20. Corbett, *Seven Years' War*, 1:1. For Mahan, see *Influence*, 8, and *Naval Strategy*, 243–44, 433. For a comparative context, see Mahan's Notes for Naval Strategy Lectures, p. 7, NWC, MS 17, Box 3.
21. Mahan, *Influence*, 23.
22. Mahan, Lowell Institute Lecture: "Naval Warfare," circa 1897, p. 30, Papers of Mahan, LC, Container 5, Reel 3.
23. Mahan, *Major Operations War of American Independence*, 4.
24. "De Grasse," no date, p. 3, Papers of Mahan, LC, Container 6, Reel 4.
25. Corbett, *SPMS*, 15.
26. Corbett, Lecture on Blockade, Portsmouth, 24 Oct 1907, CBT 15/6/4.
27. Corbett to Clarke [draft letter] 30 Nov 1916, TNA, CAB/45/265.
28. War Plans, Part I: "Some Principles of Naval Warfare," p. 24, TNA, ADM/116/1043B.
29. Corbett, *Seven Years' War*, 1:6.
30. Corbett, "Strategical Value of Speed in Battle-Ships," 826–27.

31. This held true during World War I, and Corbett noted its effects in *Naval Operations*, 1:2–3.

CHAPTER 5. COMMERCE, THE SEA LINES OF COMMUNICATION, AND NAVAL POWER

1. Mahan, "Conditions Determining the Naval Expansion of the U.S.," 50; see also Sumida, "New Insights from Old Books," 105.
2. Mahan, "Possibilities," 561.
3. Mahan, "Considerations," 144; see also Lowell Institute Lecture: "Naval Warfare," circa 1897, p. 6, Papers of Mahan, LC, Container 5, Reel 3.
4. Mahan to Thursfield, 12 Jan 1906, *Letters*, 3:153–54 (italics in original).
5. Mahan, "Considerations," 145.
6. A. Lambert, ed., *21st Century Corbett*, 8.
7. Corbett, *SPMS*, 99, 102.
8. Mahan, *War of 1812*, 1:285, 296; see also Mahan, *Types of Naval Officers*, 219.
9. Mahan, "Considerations," 171.
10. Mahan, *War of 1812*, 1:284–85.
11. Corbett, "Teaching Naval and Military History," 18.
12. Mahan, *French Revolution*, 2:351.
13. Mahan, *From Sail to Steam*, 305.
14. Mahan, *French Revolution*, 2:397.
15. Mahan, "Hague Conference," 168.
16. Mahan, *French Revolution*, 2:339.
17. Mahan, *French Revolution*, 1:1.
18. Corbett, *Seven Years' War*, 1:5–6.
19. Corbett, "Napoleon and the British Navy after Trafalgar," 238, 243.
20. Corbett, *Trafalgar*, 3.
21. Mahan, *French Revolution*, 2:386.
22. Corbett, *SPMS*, 102.
23. Mahan to Root, 20 Apr 1906, *Letters*, 3:157–58 (emphasis in original).
24. Semmel, *Liberalism and Naval Strategy*, 96–119.
25. Mahan to Laughton, 21 Feb 1908, *Laughton*, No. 249, pp. 241–42; A. Lambert, *21st Century Corbett*, 67–68.
26. Corbett, "Capture of Private Property"; Mahan, "Hague Conference."
27. Corbett, "Capture of Private Property," 139.
28. Mahan, "Commerce and War," *NYT*, 17 Nov 1898. For similar arguments, see Mahan to Roosevelt, 27 Dec 1904, Mahan to Root, 20 Apr 1906, Comments on the Seizure of Private Property at Sea, Feb–Mar 1906, *Letters*, 3:112–14, 157–58, 623–26; Mahan to Laughton, 31 Jan 1906, *Laughton*, No. 241, pp. 234–35; Mahan, *War of 1812*, 1:145; Mahan, *Problem of Asia*, 53–54.
29. Mahan to Laughton, 31 Jan 1906, *Laughton*, No. 241, pp. 234–35.

30. Mahan, "Hague Conference," 183.
31. Mahan, *Problem of Asia*, 126–27.
32. Mahan, *War of 1812*, 1:144; see also Mahan, "Hague Conference," 190.
33. Mahan, "Commerce and War," *NYT*, 17 Nov 1898.
34. Corbett, *SPMS*, 97.
35. War Plans, Part I: "Some Principles of Naval Warfare," TNA, ADM/116/1043B, pt. 1, p. 4.
36. Corbett, *SPMS*, 99.
37. A. Lambert, ed., *21st Century Corbett*, 70.
38. Corbett, *SPMS*, 99.
39. Mahan, "Hague Conference," 173.
40. Mahan to Roosevelt, 27 Dec 1904, *Letters*, 3:112–14.
41. Mahan, Comments on the Seizure of Private Property at Sea, Feb–Mar 1906, *Letters*, 3:624.
42. Corbett, *SPMS*, 99.
43. Corbett, "Capture of Private Property," 153.
44. Mahan, *French Revolution*, 2:262.
45. Corbett, *Seven Years' War*, 2:5.
46. Mahan, *Problem of Asia*, 54–55; see also Mahan, "Commerce and War," *NYT*, 17 Nov 1898; Lowell Institute Lecture: "Naval Warfare," circa 1897, p. 89, Papers of Mahan, LC, Container 5, Reel 3.
47. Corbett, *SPMS*, 95–96.
48. Notes on attached "War Plans," TNA, 116/1043B, pt. 1; "The Defence of Commerce, with Proposals for Its Organisation in Peace Time," 16 Sep 1908, TNA, ADM/116/1065B. Both documents contain pencil markings indicating they came from the director of naval intelligence. See also Offer, *The First World War*, 1; Cox, *War, Blockades, and Hunger*, 1–2.
49. Mahan, Strategy Lecture 3: "Mondovi, Lodi, Lanato and Castiglione," p. 50, NWC, MS 17, Box 6.
50. Mahan, *Naval Strategy*, 303; see also Mahan, Lecture: "Discourse on the Strategic Value of a Point," 1896, NWC, RG15, Box 1.
51. Mahan, Lowell Institute Lecture: "Naval Warfare," circa 1897, pt. 3, Papers of Mahan, LC, Container 5, Reel 4; Mahan, *Influence*, 25; Mahan, *Problem of Asia*, 52. These are direct quotes.
52. Corbett, *Seven Years' War*, 1:308; War Plans, Part I: "Some Principles of Naval Warfare," TNA, ADM/116/1043B pt. 1, p. 4.
53. War Plans, Part I: "Some Principles of Naval Warfare," TNA, ADM/116/1043B pt. 1, p. 4.
54. Corbett, "Capture of Private Property," 134.
55. War Plans, Part I: "Some Principles of Naval Warfare," TNA, ADM/116/1043B pt. 1, pp. 4–5.

56. Mahan, "Sea Power in the Present European War," *Leslie's Illustrated Weekly*, 20 Aug 1914, reprinted in *Letters*, 3:706–10; see also Mahan, Lowell Institute Lecture: "Naval Warfare," circa 1897, p. 29, Papers of Mahan, LC, Container 5, Reel 3.
57. Mahan, *Influence*, 529; *Naval Strategy*, 255.
58. Mahan, *Problem of Asia*, 125; see also Mahan, "Panama Canal and the Distribution of the Fleet," 417, and "Considerations," 149. Moreover, Mahan maintained in numerous writings that "communications dominate war": *Naval Strategy*, 166, 255; "Why Fortify the Panama Canal," 185; "Influence of the South African War," 62; *Problem of Asia*, 125; "Appreciation of Conditions in the Russo-Japanese Conflict," pt. 1, p. 7.
59. Corbett, *SPMS*, 158–59; Mahan, *Naval Strategy*, 136.
60. Jomini, *Art of War*, trans. Winship and McLean, 263; Mahan, *Influence*, 8.
61. Mahan, Strategy Lecture 3: "Mondovi, Lodi, Lanato and Castiglione," p. 50, NWC, MS 17, Box 6.
62. Mahan, *Influence*, 329.
63. Corbett, *SPMS*, 100; Mahan, "Considerations," 157.
64. Corbett, *Seven Years' War*, 1:308–9.
65. "Notes on Strategy," p. 11, BL Add. MS 82,516 D; Corbett, Lecture 10: "Means of Controlling Enemy's Strategy Operating against His Communications," CBT 31.
66. Papers of Mahan, LC, Container 7, Reel 5.
67. Mahan, "Hawaii and Our Future Sea Power," 51; see also Mahan, "Persian Gulf," 218.
68. Corbett to Richmond, 11 Dec 1916, NMM, RIC 9, pt. 1.
69. W. T. Stead, "What Is the Truth about the Navy," *Pall Mall Gazette*, 15 Sep 1884; J. Colomb, *Protection of Our Commerce*.
70. "The Defence of Commerce, with Proposals for Its Organisation in Peace Time," 16 Sep 1908, memorandum on: (1) Limitation of Naval Armaments; (2) Limitation of Size of Battleships, p. 5, TNA, ADM/116/1065B, ADM/116/866B.
71. Corbett, *SPMS*, 100; War Plans, Part I: "Some Principles of Naval Warfare," TNA, ADM/116/1043B pt. 1, pp. 4–5.

CHAPTER 6. COMMAND OF THE SEA

1. Bridge, *Sea-Power*, 73.
2. "The Command of the Sea: What It Is and What It Is Not," *Times*, 4 Jan 1912. Corbett seemed to agree, calling it a "loose expression" open to interpretation (*RJW*, 2:383).
3. *Landmark Thucydides*, 81, 508; Bacon, "Of the True Greatness of Kingdoms and Estates," 186; Heuser, *Strategy before Clausewitz*, 117.
4. Heuser emphasizes the role of Philip Colomb. Though Philip Colomb's use of the term is the most refined, John Colomb developed a similar concept describing "command of the Channel," and Theodore Roosevelt in his study of the War

of 1812 discussed "command of the lakes." In all cases, the idea is the same. See Heuser, "Regina Maris and the Command of the Sea," 255; Schurman, *Education of a Navy*, 177; J. Colomb, *Protection of Our Commerce*, 6, 24; Roosevelt, *Naval War of 1812*, 140.

5. Hattendorf, *Mahan on Naval Strategy*, x–xi.
6. P. Colomb, *Naval Warfare*, 1:47.
7. Schurman, *Education of a Navy*, 56.
8. Corbett, "Capture of Private Property," 130–31.
9. Grotius, *Law of War and Peace*, 190; Heuser, *Strategy before Clausewitz*, 117, 127.
10. Corbett, *Seven Years' War*, 1:308.
11. Green Pamphlet, p. 7, CBT 6/16; Corbett, Lecture: "Blockade," Portsmouth, 24 Oct 1907, CBT 15/6/4; *Seven Years' War*, 1:308; Corbett, "Capture of Private Property," 131.
12. Corbett, *SPMS*, 91.
13. Corbett, *SPMS*, 94–95.
14. Mahan, Lowell Institute Lecture: "Naval Warfare," circa 1897, p. 29, Papers of Mahan, LC, Container 5, Reel 3.
15. Mahan used both terms to mean the same thing in a single sentence in *War of 1812*, 1:86.
16. "Command of the sea" appears on pp. 248, 341, 461, and 539 of Mahan, *The Influence of Sea Power upon History*.
17. Mahan, "Principles Involved in the War between Japan and Russia," 120; Mahan, "Retrospect upon the War between Japan and Russia," 165; Mahan, "Torpedo Craft vs. Battleships," 16.
18. Mahan, Lowell Institute Lecture: "Naval Warfare," circa 1897, pp. 31–32, Papers of Mahan, LC, Container 5, Reel 3.
19. Mahan, "Appreciation of Conditions in the Russo-Japanese Conflict," pt. 1, p. 8.
20. Corbett, *SPMS*, 104.
21. Mahan, "Torpedo Craft vs. Battleships," 16; Mahan, *Naval Strategy*, 256.
22. Mahan, *Naval Strategy*, 344.
23. Mahan, "Torpedo Craft vs. Battleships," 16; see also Mahan, *Influence*, 14.
24. Corbett, *SPMS*, 104–5; see also Corbett, Lecture: "Blockade," Portsmouth, 24 Oct 1907, CBT 15/6/4.
25. Mahan, "Possibilities," 559; Mahan, "Hawaii and Our Future Sea Power," 52.
26. Mahan, "Importance of Command of the Sea," 413.
27. Corbett, *Seven Years' War*, 1:6.
28. Corbett, *Seven Years' War*, 1:5–7.
29. Mahan, *Naval Strategy*, 422; Mahan, "Torpedo Craft vs. Battleships," 17.
30. Mahan, *From Sail to Steam*, 282–83.
31. Mahan outlined his thoughts on battle in *Influence*, 287–88, 478, 514; *Lessons*, 139; *War of 1812*, 2:51, 2:132–33; and *Naval Strategy*, 254, 422–23.

32. Craig, "Delbrück," 341; Freedman, *Strategy*, 108–20; Heuser, *Evolution of Strategy*, 145–52. For annihilation, see Mahan, *Nelson*, 286–87, 721–22.
33. Mahan, *Nelson*, 137, 145–46.
34. Mahan, *From Sail to Steam*, 283; "The Future in Relation to American Naval Power," 149; "Possibilities," 561; *Nelson*, 680; and Lowell Institute Lecture: "Naval Warfare," circa 1897, p. 5, Papers of Mahan, LC, Container 5, Reel 3.
35. Mahan, "Retrospect upon the War between Japan and Russia," 136.
36. Mahan, "Principles Involved in the War between Japan and Russia," 120.
37. Mahan to the editor of the *New York Sun*, 9 May 1904, *Letters*, 3:91.
38. Mahan, *Influence*, 288.
39. Corbett, *SPMS*, 167.
40. Corbett, *Naval Operations*, 1:2.
41. Corbett, *SPMS*, 103, 156; also, memorandum on invasion, 1907, CBT 6/12.
42. Corbett to Richmond, 14 Sep 1909, NMM, RIC 9, pt. 1.
43. Heuser, *Evolution of Strategy*, 224; Schurman, *Julian S. Corbett*, 57.
44. Corbett, *Naval Operations*, 3:259; Corbett, Lecture 10: "Means of Controlling Enemy's Strategy: Operating against His Communications," p. 8, CBT 31.
45. Corbett, Green Pamphlet, p. 11, CBT 6/15.
46. "Protection of Trade in Wartime," 1905, p. 38, comments by Beresford in response to the 1907 War Plan, 8 May 1907, TNA, ADM/116/866B, ADM/116/1037.
47. Richmond to Dewar, 3 May 1917, NMM, DEW 34.
48. Review of *Naval Operations*, vol. 2, *Saturday Review*, 29 Oct 1921, CBT 28/3.
49. Corbett, Lecture 10: "Means of Controlling Enemy's Strategy: Operating against His Communications," p. 8, CBT 31.
50. Corbett, *Naval Operations*, 2:43.
51. Corbett, "Notes on Strategy," p. 11, BL Add. MS 82,516 D.
52. Corbett, *Seven Years' War*, 1:308–9.
53. Corbett, *Naval Operations*, 1:3, 161.
54. Corbett to Richmond, 26 Mar 1916, NMM, RIC 9, pt. 1.
55. Mahan, *Nelson*, 166.
56. Mahan, *Lessons*, 33.
57. Mahan, "Submarine and Its Enemies," 30.
58. Mahan, "Blockade," 856.
59. Mahan, "Submarine and Its Enemies," 30.
60. Mahan, *Lessons*, 104–5, 107.
61. Mahan, "Blockade," 851, lecture given at the Royal United Service Institution.
62. Corbett, *SPMS*, 183–85.
63. Mahan, *Influence*, 296–97.
64. Corbett, Lecture: "Blockade," Portsmouth, 24 Oct 1907, CBT 15/6/4.
65. Mahan, "Blockade," 858; Mahan, *Influence*, 297.

66. Corbett, Naval Strategy Lecture 3: "The Essentials of True Naval Defensive," p. 13, CBT 15/6/6; Lecture: "Blockade," Portsmouth, 24 Oct 1907, CBT 15/6/4.
67. Corbett, *SPMS*, 188.
68. Corbett, *RJW*, 1:240; Lecture: "Blockade," Portsmouth, 24 Oct 1907, CBT 15/6/4.
69. Corbett, *SPMS*, 186, 206–7.
70. Corbett, Lecture: "Blockade," Portsmouth, 24 Oct 1907, CBT 15/6/4.
71. Corbett, *SPMS*, 186.
72. Corbett, Lecture 10: "Means of Controlling Enemy's Strategy: Operating against His Communications," p. 5, CBT 31; see also *SPMS*, 200.
73. Mahan, "Blockade," 856, 866.
74. Corbett, *SPMS*, 201–2.
75. Corbett, *SPMS*, 184, 205.
76. Corbett, *RJW*, 1:124, 241.

CHAPTER 7. RECONCILING THE OFFENSE AND THE DEFENSE

1. Mahan, "Considerations," 151; Corbett, *SPMS*, 34.
2. Mahan, "Considerations," 153; Mahan, "Subordination of Historical Treatment," 269.
3. Mahan, "Current Fallacies," 282–83, 286; see also his Strategy Lecture 2: "Montenotti," p. 27, NWC, MS 17, Box 6.
4. Mahan, "Lessons from the Yalu Fight," 630; *Influence*, 8; and Lowell Institute Lecture: "Naval Warfare," circa 1897, p. 23, Papers of Mahan, LC, Container 5, Reel 3.
5. Mahan, *Naval Strategy*, 139.
6. Corbett, *SPMS*, 37.
7. Corbett, Naval Strategy, Lecture 1, p. 2, CBT 15/6/6, also in CBT 31.
8. Mahan, Strategy Lecture 2: "Montenotti," p. 27, NWC, MS 17, Box 6.
9. Mahan, *Naval Strategy*, 204; see also his "Effect of Asiatic Conditions," 181; and "Lessons from the Yalu Fight," 629.
10. Mahan, *Naval Strategy*, 152.
11. Mahan, "Objects of the U.S. Naval War College," 194; see also "Conditions Determining the Naval Expansion of the United States," 39–40.
12. Schurman, *Julian S. Corbett*, 57; Heuser, *Evolution of Strategy*, 223–24.
13. Shy, "Jomini," 180; Heuser, *Evolution of Strategy*, 146–52.
14. Mahan, "Future in Relation to American Naval Power," 157; "Current Fallacies," 286; and "Conditions Determining the Naval Expansion of the United States," 39–40.
15. Mahan, *South Africa*, 44–45.
16. Mahan, *Interest of America in International Conditions*, 46.
17. Mahan, Review of "*The War in South Africa*: First of Six Volumes Just Published by the *London Times*," *NYT*, 30 May 1902.

18. Mahan, *Influence*, 535; see also *Types of Naval Officers*, 271–72.
19. Mahan, "Current Fallacies," 299; see also Strategy Lecture 2: "Montenotti," p. 28, NWC, MS 17, Box 6.
20. Mahan, Strategy Lecture 3: "Mondovi, Lodi, Lanato and Castiglione," pp. 57–58, NWC, MS 17, Box 6.
21. Quoted material originally published in the *London Nation*; cited in Angell, *World's Highway*, 160–61.
22. Mahan, Strategy Lecture 2: "Montenotti," p. 28, NWC, MS 17, Box 6.
23. Corbett, *SPMS*, 36.
24. Corbett, *Seven Years' War*, 2:373, 384; "Strategical Value of Speed in Battle-Ships," 831.
25. Corbett, *SPMS*, 34–35.
26. Corbett, "Strategical Value of Speed in Battle-Ships," 832.
27. Colonial Conference, 1902, "Memorandum on Sea Power and the Principles Involved in It," Great Britain, *Accounts and Papers: Colonies and British Possessions*, 9:5.
28. Corbett, Lecture: "Concentration," CBT 15/6/4; Naval Strategy Lecture 3: "The Essentials of the True Naval Defensive," p. 24, CBT 31.
29. Clausewitz, *On War*, trans. Graham, 2:68–69, 78, 87.
30. Corbett, Naval Strategy Lecture 2: "The System of Clausewitz," p. 6, CBT 15/6/6 also CBT 31.
31. Mahan, *Naval Strategy*, 277.
32. Mahan, *Influence*, 87n.
33. Jomini, *Art of War*, trans. Mendell and Craighill, 74.
34. Mahan, *South Africa*, 186.
35. For active defense, see Mahan, Strategy Lecture 3: "Mondovi, Lodi, Lanato and Castiglione," p. 57, NWC, MS 17, Box 6. "Offensive-defensive" appears in *War of 1812*, 1:321; "Engineer in Naval Warfare," 650; and *Naval Strategy*, 205.
36. Mahan, *Naval Strategy*, 142; *Lessons*, 64.
37. Mahan, *South Africa*, 142; see also Lowell Institute Lecture: "Naval Warfare," circa 1897, p. 19, Papers of Mahan, LC, Container 5, Reel 3.
38. Mahan, Strategy Lecture 2: "Montenotti," p. 29, NWC, MS 17, Box 6. Mahan claimed this quote derived from a directive provided by Napoleon. See also Mahan, "Appreciation of Conditions in the Russo-Japanese Conflict," pt. 1, *Times*, 29 Apr 1904.
39. Mahan, *South Africa*, 186; see also "Considerations," 168.
40. Mahan, *Influence*, 87n.
41. Mahan, *Influence*, 393, 524.
42. Mahan, *Influence*, 396.
43. Mahan, *Admiral Farragut*, 310.

44. Mahan ascribes this to quote to Jomini. See Strategy Lecture 2: "Montenotti," p. 36, NWC, MS 17, Box 6.
45. Corbett, *SPMS*, 36, 103.
46. Corbett, "Strategical Value of Speed in Battle-Ships," 833.
47. Clausewitz, *On War*, trans. Graham, 2:199.
48. Corbett, Naval Strategy Lecture 3: "The Essentials of True Naval Defensive," p. 17, CBT 15/6/6.
49. Corbett, ed., *Private Papers of Spencer*, 2:224–25; see also *Seven Years' War*, 1:25, 2:373.
50. Corbett, *SPMS*, 33, 100. Mahan makes a similar explanation of the concept in "Considerations," 157.
51. Corbett, *SPMS*, 36, 211–12.
52. Corbett, *RJW*, 2:387.
53. Corbett, *Seven Years' War*, 1:188; see also Naval Strategy Lecture: "The Spanish American War," p. 42, CBT 15/6/6.
54. Corbett, *SPMS*, 32, 36, 227; see also Corbett, "Notes on Strategy," p. 5, BL Add. MS 82,516 D.
55. Mahan, *Naval Strategy*, 243–44.
56. Corbett, "Notes on Strategy," p. 5, BL Add. MS 82,516 D.
57. Mahan, "Panama Canal and Sea Power in the Pacific," 156–57. See also, Mahan, *Lessons*, 58, 63; *Problem of Asia*, 70; "Panama Canal and the Distribution of the Fleet," 417.
58. Mahan, "Appreciation of Conditions in the Russo-Japanese Conflict," pt. 1, p. 8.
59. Mahan, *Naval Strategy*, 152.
60. Mahan to George Sydenham Clarke, 5 Nov 1892, *Letters*, 2:83–85; and "Panama Canal and Sea Power in the Pacific," 156.
61. Mahan, "Persian Gulf," 226, 237; see also *Naval Strategy*, 144, 149, 289.
62. Mahan, *Influence*, 31.
63. Mahan, *Influence*, 345, 514.
64. Mahan, "Conditions Determining the Naval Expansion of the U.S.," 42.
65. Mahan, "Considerations," 140; see also *Naval Strategy*, 93, 134; Lecture: "Discourse on the Strategic Value of a Point," 1896, p. 1, NWC, RG 15; and Lowell Institute Lecture: "Naval Warfare," circa 1897, p. 42, Papers of Mahan, LC, Container 5, Reel 3.
66. Mahan, "Hawaii and Our Future Sea Power," 40.
67. Mahan, *Naval Strategy*, 134; "Strategic Features of the Gulf of Mexico," 293.
68. Mahan, *Naval Strategy*, 127, 192.
69. Mahan to J. D. Long, [15–20 Aug] 1898, *Letters*, 2:589; *Naval Strategy*, 127.
70. Mahan, *Influence*, 373, 414.
71. Mahan, *Influence*, 430n; "Panama Canal and Sea Power in the Pacific," 156.

72. Schurman, *Julian S. Corbett*, 22, and *Education of a Navy*, 55–56; Grimes, *Strategy and War Planning*, 18; Semmel, *Liberalism and Naval Strategy*, 88–89.
73. Mahan, *Naval Strategy*, 435.
74. For Colomb's critique of Mahan, see his editorial titled "Captain Mahan on Coast Defence," *Times*, 5 Jan 1899. For Mahan's response, see *Lessons*, xi–xii.
75. Mahan to Laughton, 9 Jan 1899, *Laughton*, No. 185, 176–78.
76. Mahan, *Naval Strategy*, 432.
77. Mahan, "Why Fortify the Panama Canal," 182–83; Mahan, "Panama Canal and Sea Power in the Pacific," 157.
78. Mahan, *Naval Strategy*, 435.
79. Corbett, *SPMS*, 105–6.
80. Corbett, Lecture 10: "Means of Controlling Enemy Strategy," pp. 16–17, CBT 15/6/4.
81. Corbett, ed., *Private Papers of Spencer*, 2:367.
82. Corbett, *RJW*, 2:149.
83. Corbett, *RJW*, 2:135–36.
84. Corbett, Naval Strategy Lecture 3: "The Essentials of True Naval Defensive," p. 18, CBT 15/6/6.
85. Corbett, *Seven Years' War*, 1:423–24.
86. Corbett, Naval Strategy Lecture 4: "The Essentials of a Defensive Attitude," p. 25, CBT 15/6/6.
87. Corbett, *Seven Years' War*, 1:93.
88. Corbett, *Seven Years'* War, 2:373–74.
89. Corbett, *SPMS*, 151.
90. Mahan, "Current Fallacies," 286.
91. Mahan, "Considerations," 168; see also *Influence*, 514, 466.
92. Mahan, *Influence*, 524.
93. Mahan, *Naval Strategy*, 235, 248.

CHAPTER 8. CONCENTRATION: THE PRIMARY FORCE AND THE ULTERIOR EFFORT

1. Mahan, *Naval Strategy*, 62; Corbett, *SPMS*, 293.
2. Mahan to Perkins, 11 Jan 1911, *Letters*, 3:371–72.
3. Mahan, "Panama Canal and the Distribution of the Fleet," 406; *Types of Naval Officers*, 15–16; "Subordination of Historical Treatment," 265; *Lessons*, 70; Lowell Institute Lecture: "Naval Warfare," circa 1897, p. 123, Papers of Mahan, LC, Container 5, Reel 3; and *South Africa*, 204.
4. Mahan, *Naval Strategy*, 62, 394.
5. Mahan, "Panama Canal and the Distribution of the Fleet," 410.
6. Mahan, *Types of Naval Officers*, 16; see also Mahan, "Strategic Features of the Gulf of Mexico," 308.
7. Jomini, *Art of War*, trans. Winship and McLean, 125, 179.

8. Mahan, *Lessons*, 43; see also Strategy Lecture 3: "Mondovi, Lodi, Lanato and Castiglione," p. 57, NWC, MS 17, Box 6; and Lowell Institute Lecture: "Naval Warfare," circa 1897, p. 15, Papers of Mahan, LC, Container 5, Reel 3.
9. Mahan, *War of 1812*, 1:316, 2:293; see also "Panama Canal and the Distribution of the Fleet," 415.
10. Mahan, Lowell Institute Lecture: "Naval Warfare," circa 1897, p. 36, Papers of Mahan, LC, Container 5, Reel 3.
11. Seager, *Alfred Thayer Mahan*, 4; Sumida, *Inventing Grand Strategy*, 13–14.
12. D. H. Mahan, *Advanced-Guard, Outpost*, 200.
13. Mahan to the editor of the *New York Sun*, 9 May 1904, *Letters*, 3:91.
14. Mahan, *Influence*, 414, 532, 534.
15. Mahan, "Considerations," 192–93. This course of action worked on land as well. See Mahan, *South Africa*, 116–17.
16. Mahan, *Naval Strategy*, 74.
17. Mahan, Strategy Lecture 2: "Montenotti," p. 47, NWC, MS 17, Box 6.
18. Mahan, *Types of Naval Officers*, 19; and "Military Rule of Obedience," 280–81.
19. Jomini, *Art of War*, trans. Mendell and Craighill, 98–99; D. H. Mahan, *Advanced-Guard, Outpost*, 178.
20. Mahan, *War of 1812*, 1:316.
21. Mahan, *Naval Strategy*, 74–75.
22. Mahan, "Why Fortify the Panama Canal," 185.
23. Mahan, *War of 1812*, 1:316.
24. Mahan, Lowell Institute Lecture: "Naval Warfare," circa 1897, p. 123, Papers of Mahan, LC, Container 5, Reel 3.
25. Corbett, *SPMS*, 129.
26. Corbett, *SPMS*, 134.
27. Corbett, *Naval Operations*, 2:4. Corbett included the quote from Wilson in this passage.
28. Corbett, *SPMS*, 131, 132, 134; see also Corbett, *Trafalgar*, 249.
29. Corbett, Lecture: "Concentration," no date, CBT 15/6/4.
30. Corbett, *SPMS*, 138.
31. Corbett, Lecture: "Concentration," no date, CBT 15/6/4.
32. Corbett, *SPMS*, 137.
33. Corbett, Lecture: "Concentration," no date, CBT 15/6/4.
34. "Mr. Churchill and the Navy: Changes in the Board," *Times*, 4 Dec 1911. This article discusses *SPMS*, emphasizing Corbett's theories of concentration.
35. Corbett, *SPMS*, 152.
36. Corbett, Lecture: "Concentration," no date, CBT 15/6/4.
37. Corbett, *Trafalgar*, 205; Mahan, *Influence*, 287–88; Mahan, *Naval Strategy*, 254–55; Mahan, *Types of Naval Officers*, 225. Corbett used "immediate" object in the Green Pamphlet, p. 3, CBT 6/15.

38. Corbett, *Trafalgar,* 108.
39. Mahan, *Influence,* 442.
40. Green Pamphlet, p. 8, CBT 6/15.
41. Green Pamphlet, p. 7, CBT 6/16.
42. Mahan, *From Sail to Steam,* 283.
43. Mahan, *Influence,* 338–39, 442.
44. Mahan, *Influence,* 496; see also Mahan, *Nelson,* 115–16.
45. Mahan, *Naval Strategy,* 254.
46. Corbett, *SPMS,* 155–56, 160, 207.
47. Corbett, *SPMS,* 160.
48. Corbett, *SPMS,* 119, 143.
49. Corbett, Lecture outline: "Combined Operations: No. 1," Portsmouth, spring 1910, CBT 31.
50. Mahan, "Sea Power in the Present European War," *Leslie's Illustrated Weekly,* 20 Aug 1914, reprinted in *Letters,* 3:706.
51. Part I, "Some Principles of Naval Warfare," p. 7, ADM/116/1043B.
52. Corbett, *SPMS,* 164, 180.
53. Green Pamphlet, p. 11, CBT 6/15.
54. Corbett, Staff College Lecture: "Function of the Army in Relation to Gaining Command of the Sea & in Bringing War with a Continental Power to a Successful Issue," 21 Nov 1905, Russo-Japanese War Lecture, [Nov 1910], LHC, Corbett Papers, Box 2.
55. Corbett, *SPMS,* 216.
56. Corbett, *SPMS,* 160.
57. Corbett, *Trafalgar,* 108.

CHAPTER 9. SEA DENIAL: DISPUTING COMMAND OF THE SEA AND SECONDARY OPERATIONS

1. Corbett, *SPMS,* 165–66.
2. Corbett, *SPMS,* 105, 211.
3. Mahan, *War of 1812,* 1:288; *Influence,* 539.
4. Hattendorf, "Idea of a 'Fleet in Being,'" 43–44; Rodger, *Command of the Ocean,* 144–47. Corbett described this in *SPMS,* 212–16.
5. Mahan, *Major Operations War of American Independence,* 174.
6. Mahan, *Lessons,* 76.
7. Corbett, *SPMS,* 224.
8. Corbett, *SPMS,* 211–12.
9. Corbett, *SPMS,* 212, 221, 224–25.
10. Mahan, *Influence,* 180–87.
11. Mahan to Laughton, 1 Dec 1893, *Laughton,* No. 92, pp. 95–97.
12. Mahan to Clarke, 30 Sep 1894, *Letters,* 2:336–38; see also Mahan, *Naval Strategy,* 398–99.

13. Mahan, *Lessons*, 80–81.
14. Corbett, *SPMS*, 227, 231.
15. Mahan, "Retrospect upon the War between Japan and Russia," 149, 151.
16. Mahan, *Lessons*, 78, 89; *Nelson*, 169; and *Major Operations War of American Independence*, 73.
17. Mahan to Clarke, 30 Sep 1894, *Letters*, 2:336–38.
18. Corbett, *SPMS*, 226.
19. Corbett, *SPMS*, 216.
20. Mahan, *Lessons*, 84.
21. Mahan, "Appreciation of Conditions in the Russo-Japanese Conflict," pt. 1, p. 8.
22. Mahan, "Retrospect upon the War between Japan and Russia," 155–56; Mahan, *Naval Strategy*, 384–85.
23. Mahan, *Naval Strategy*, 397–98.
24. Corbett, *SPMS*, 211–12; Corbett, *Seven Years' War*, 1:329, 332–33; Corbett, *RJW*, 1:267; Corbett, Naval Strategy Lecture 3: "The Essentials of True Naval Defensive," CBT 15/6/6.
25. Mahan, *South Africa*, 26.
26. Luce to Mahan, 15 Jul 1907, NWC, RG 1, Box 3, Folder 14.
27. List derived from Mahan, *Naval Strategy*, 236.
28. Mahan, *War of 1812*, 1:378.
29. English original, p. 14 of "Le Canal de Panama au point vue militaire," *Revue Économique Internationale*, Jan 1913, Papers of Mahan, LC, Container 6, Reel 4.
30. Mahan, "Current Fallacies," 305; Mahan, *War of 1812*, 1:378.
31. Corbett, *SPMS*, 227.
32. Corbett indicated that the exception was the fireship, but such warships did not provide consistent results. Moreover, the effects diminished over time. See *SPMS*, 228.
33. Mahan, *Major Operations War of American Independence*, 187.
34. Mahan, Lowell Institute Lecture: "Naval Warfare," circa 1897, p. 29, Papers of Mahan, LC, Container 5, Reel 3.
35. Corbett, *SPMS*, 121.
36. Corbett, *SPMS*, 227–32.
37. Mahan, "Principles Involved in the War between Japan and Russia," 113; *Naval Strategy*, 147–48.
38. Corbett, *SPMS*, 232; Mahan, *Naval Strategy*, 147–48.
39. Corbett, *SPMS*, 232.
40. Mahan, Naval Strategy Lecture 4: "Bussano," p. 75, NWC, MS 17, Box 6.
41. Corbett, *SPMS*, 261–62; Mahan, "Possibilities," 561, 563.
42. Mahan, *From Sail to Steam*, 269. Mahan did not specifically state that he ascribed to this school, but given the following quote it seems that he did.
43. Mahan to Ashe, 11 Mar 1885, *Letters*, 1:591–93.

44. Mahan, *Influence*, 31, 136, 400; see also Mahan to Roosevelt, 27 Dec 1904, *Letters*, 3:112–14; and *Influence*, 31, 376, 539.
45. Mahan, *Influence*, 539; *War of 1812*, 1:397–98, 2:126.
46. Corbett, *Drake and the Tudor Navy*, 2:129, 335.
47. Corbett, *SPMS*, 261.
48. Corbett, *SPMS*, 209–32, 261–62; *Naval Operations*, 3:142.
49. Hill, *Prizes of War*; Petrie, *The Prize Game*.
50. Declaration respecting Maritime Law, signed at Paris, 16 Apr 1856, in *Consolidated Treaties*, ed. Clive Parry, 115:1–3; Hamilton, "Anglo-French Seapower."
51. Corbett, *SPMS*, 267–68.
52. Mahan, *Influence*, 194.
53. Corbett, *SPMS*, 266.
54. Ropp, *Development of a Modern Navy*, 155–66; see also Roksund, *Jeune École*; Sondhaus, "The Jeune École."
55. Mahan, *Influence*, 211.
56. Weigley, *American Way of War*, 170–71; Seager, "Ten Years before Mahan."
57. Mahan, *Influence*, 539.
58. Mahan, "Torpedo Craft vs. Battleships," 16.
59. Corbett, *SPMS*, 278.
60. Schurman identifies the question of decisiveness and the problematic nature of the question that was framed. Schurman's conclusions are very different from those presented here because he largely failed to ask why Mahan used decisiveness to frame the issue. See Schurman, *Education of a Navy*, 135–36.
61. Corbett, *Naval Operations*, 1:3.
62. Mahan, "Problems Rozhdestvensky and Togo Must Solve," *Times*, 13 May 1905.
63. Mahan, "Submarine and Its Enemies," 17, 20–21.
64. Mahan, *Influence*, 88.
65. Mahan to Laughton, 24 Aug 1914, *Laughton*, No. 272, pp. 258–59.
66. Mahan to Marston, 14 Oct 1914, *Letters*, 3:550–51.
67. Mahan, "Sea Power in the Present European War," *Leslie's Illustrated Weekly*, 20 Aug 1914; Mahan to Marston, 14 Oct 1914, *Letters*, 3:550–51, 708.
68. Mahan, "Origins of the European War," interview with *New York Evening Post*, 3 Aug 1914, *Letters*, 3:698–700.
69. Mahan to Marston, 14 Oct 1914, *Letters*, 3:550–51.
70. Corbett, *Naval Operations*.
71. Corbett, *SPMS*, 269.
72. Corbett, *Naval Operations*, 1:163, 3:121.
73. Corbett, *Naval Operations*, 1:41, 164, 185, 257, 3:121, 134.
74. Corbett, *Naval Operations*, 1:216–17, 2:383, 3:31.
75. Corbett, *Naval Operations*, 2:132, 251, 3:283.
76. Corbett, *Naval Operations*, 2:258, 3:142.

CHAPTER 10. OBTAINING STRATEGIC EFFECTS THROUGH THE CONTROL OF MARITIME COMMERCE

1. W. Macneile Dixon, "The Navy in the Great War," review of Corbett's *Naval Operations*, vol. 1, *Scottish Historical Review* 17 (1920): 310, 312, in CBT 24/8.
2. Mahan, *Influence*, 288; and *French Revolution*, 2:298.
3. Mahan, "Sea Power in the Present European War," *Leslie's Illustrated Weekly*, 20 Aug 1914, reprinted in *Letters*, 3:706–7.
4. Corbett, "League of Peace and a Free Sea," p. 5, CBT 7/7.
5. Corbett, *SPMS*, 161, 234; see also Corbett, *RJW*, 2:13.
6. Corbett to Richmond, 18 Feb 1917, NMM, RIC 9, pt. 1.
7. Corbett, *SPMS*, 233.
8. Corbett, Lecture Notes: "Sea Common Wealth," LHC, Corbett Papers, Box 2.
9. Corbett to Callendar, 2 Dec 1914, NMM, LES 4/1.
10. Corbett, *RJW*, 1:310.
11. Mahan, *From Sail to Steam*, 269.
12. Mahan, "Blockade," 863.
13. Mahan, "Considerations," 172.
14. Corbett, *SPMS*, 104, 279; see also Corbett, *RJW*, 1:351.
15. Corbett, *Naval Operations*, 2:1–2.
16. Mahan, *Influence*, 26.
17. Corbett, *England and the Mediterranean*, 1:227; see also Ford Lecture 3, CBT 28/1.
18. Mahan, *French Revolution*, 2:204.
19. Mahan, *Naval Strategy*, 211.
20. Mahan, *French Revolution*, 2:205–6.
21. Mahan, *War of 1812*, 1:409.
22. Corbett, *SPMS*, 266, 70.
23. Corbett, *SPMS*, 101, 106, 120, 261–65.
24. Mahan, *War of 1812*, 2:229; see also "Considerations," 185.
25. Mahan, Lowell Institute Lecture: "Naval Warfare," circa 1897, pp. 92–93, Papers of Mahan, LC, Container 5, Reel 3.
26. Mahan, *French Revolution*, 2:204.
27. Mahan, *Naval Strategy*, 211; see also *Influence*, 514.
28. Mahan, Lowell Institute Lecture: "Naval Warfare," circa 1897, pp. 92–93, Papers of Mahan, LC, Container 5, Reel 3.
29. Corbett, *SPMS*, 261.
30. Mahan, *Influence*, 217, 314; Richmond to Dewar, 13 Sep [1917], NMM, DEW 34.
31. Mahan to Thursfield, 31 Jan 1906, *Letters*, 3:154–56.
32. Corbett, *SPMS*, 266.

33. Corbett, *SPMS*, 268.
34. Corbett, *SPMS*, 273.
35. Corbett, "Capture of Private Property," 146.
36. Corbett, *SPMS*, 275–76.
37. Corbett, *SPMS*, 275.
38. Mahan, *War of 1812*, 1:284.
39. Corbett, *SPMS*, 260.
40. Corbett, *RJW*, 2:25.
41. Mahan, *Naval Strategy*, 4. He made this argument in *Influence* in 1890 (pp. 2, 7) and reiterated it in his last major work, *Naval Strategy*, published in 1911 (pp. 4, 184).
42. "Protection of Ocean Trade in Wartime," 1905, pp. 34–36, TNA, ADM/116/866B.
43. Corbett, *Naval Operations*, 1:15.
44. Corbett, *SPMS*, 95; Mahan, "Possibilities," 561. Mahan preferred "commerce-destroying" to "commerce destruction."
45. Mahan, *War of 1812*, 2:126.
46. Mahan, *Influence*, 138.
47. Green Pamphlet, p. 8, CBT 6/15.
48. Mahan, "Possibilities," 561.
49. Mahan, "Possibilities," 561, 63.
50. Corbett, *SPMS*, 99, 102.
51. Corbett, *Seven Years' War*, 2:376.
52. Corbett, *SPMS*, 183–84.
53. Mahan, *War of 1812*, 2:14.
54. Mahan, *War of 1812*, 1:287.
55. Green Pamphlet, p. 9, CBT 6/16; Mahan, *French Revolution*, 2:284.
56. Mahan, *Gulf and Inland Waters*, 4.
57. Mahan, "Importance of Command of the Sea," 413; see also *Influence*, 43–44, 85, 87n; and "Blockade," 854.
58. Mahan, *War of 1812*, 1:286.
59. Corbett, *SPMS*, 185, 262.
60. Mahan, *Influence*, 138. Though Mahan did not mention the Paris Declaration respecting Maritime Law, it likely guided his thoughts on the subject.
61. Corbett, *SPMS*, 96–97.
62. Mahan to Henderson, 16 Feb 1909, *Letters*, 3:284–85; Corbett, *Naval Operations*, 1:3; see also Mahan to Roosevelt, 20 Jul 1906, *Letters*, 3:164–65.
63. Corbett, *Seven Years' War*, 1:357.
64. Mahan, "Current Fallacies," 300–301.
65. Corbett, *SPMS*, 261–62.

CHAPTER 11. JOINT, EXPEDITIONARY WARFARE

1. Corbett, *Successors of Drake*, vii.
2. Corbett, "Teaching Naval and Military History," 13.
3. Corbett, *Successors of Drake*, 410.
4. Corbett, *RJW*, 2:3.
5. Corbett, *SPMS*, 7–8, 41, 51.
6. Corbett, Combined Operations Lecture 1: Synopsis, Portsmouth, CBT 31; see also Corbett, *Fighting Instructions*, 35–36.
7. Corbett, *RJW*, 1:266.
8. Corbett, *England and the Mediterranean*, 2:506.
9. Corbett, "Teaching Naval and Military History," 12.
10. Corbett to Newbolt, 15 Jun 1904, CBT 3/37/29; see also Corbett, "United Service," 203.
11. Corbett, *SPMS*, 10.
12. Corbett, *RJW*, 2:42.
13. Corbett, *Naval Operations*, 3:84.
14. On the uniqueness of Corbett's joint approach, see Cleaver, "The Pen behind the Fleet," 50; Hunt, "The Strategic Thought of Corbett," 111. Schurman in "Historians and Britain's Imperial Strategic Stance" places Corbett within a broader group of those who advocated "amphibianism."
15. Hamley, *Operations of War*, 40, 49–50.
16. Colomb's discussion following Laughton, "The Study of Naval History," 817.
17. Callwell, *Small Wars*, 22. Callwell added to the argument in *Military Operations and Maritime Preponderance*, 4, 163, 169–71.
18. Henderson, *The Science of War*, 25–26. Corbett mentioned Henderson in *Trafalgar*, 4; "Teaching Naval and Military History," 12–13; and Combined Operations Lecture 1: Synopsis, LHC, Corbett Papers, Box 2.
19. Slade to Corbett, 1 Dec 1907, CBT 6/5/11; Corbett, *SPMS*, 11–12.
20. Aston, *Letters on Amphibious Wars*; Lambert, "Sir Julian Corbett," 195.
21. Brian Hamilton to Corbett, 22 Mar [no year], LHC, Corbett Papers, Box 2.
22. Press Notices for *History of the Great War: Naval Operations*, vol. 2, citing a review for *Morning Post*, CBT 28/3; see also Schurman, *Education of a Navy*, 181.
23. Rawlinson to Corbett, 25 Aug, 2 Oct 1905, LHC, Corbett Papers, Box 2.
24. Corbett, Staff College Lecture: "Function of the Army in Relation to Gaining Command of the Sea and in Bringing War with a Continental Power to a Successful Issue," 21 Nov 1905, LHC, Corbett Papers, Box 2.
25. Corbett, *SPMS*, 61–63; see also Corbett, *Seven Years' War*, 1:154; and "Napoleon and the British Navy after Trafalgar," 244.
26. Corbett's discussion following Aston's presentation of "Combined Strategy for Fleets and Armies," 1002.

27. Corbett, *RJW*, 2:367.
28. Corbett, *RJW*, 1:13.
29. Corbett, *SPMS*, 62; Combined Operations Lecture 1, LHC, Corbett Papers, Box 2.
30. Corbett, Naval Strategy Lecture 5, p. 30, CBT 15/6/6.
31. Corbett, Combined Operations Lecture 1, LHC, Corbett Papers, Box 2.
32. Corbett, Lecture 9: "Methods of Controlling or Influencing the Enemy's Strategy," CBT 31.
33. Corbett, *Seven Years' War*, 1:437, 460, 2:104, 2:133–34, 2:219; *RJW*, 1:26, 201, 205–6.
34. Corbett to Fisher, 6 Mar 1914, FISR 1/15.
35. Corbett, Combined Operations Lecture 1, LHC, Corbett Papers, Box 2.
36. Corbett to Richmond, 29 Jul 1916, NMM, RIC 9, pt. 1.
37. Corbett, Lecture 9: "Methods of Controlling or Influencing the Enemy's Strategy," CBT 31.
38. Corbett, *Seven Years' War*, 1:206–8.
39. Corbett, Lecture 9: "Methods of Controlling or Influencing the Enemy's Strategy," CBT 31.
40. Corbett, *Naval Operations*, 3:84.
41. Corbett, Lecture 9: "Methods of Controlling or Influencing the Enemy's Strategy," CBT 31.
42. Corbett, *Seven Years' War*, 1:208.
43. Corbett, Lecture 9: "Methods of Controlling or Influencing the Enemy's Strategy," CBT 31.
44. Corbett, *RJW*, 2:213.
45. Corbett, *Seven Years' War*, 1:192; see also Staff College Lecture: "Function of the Army in Relation to Gaining Command of the Sea and in Bringing War with a Continental Power to a Successful Issue," 21 Nov 1905, LHC, Corbett Papers, Box 2.
46. Corbett, *England and the Mediterranean*, 2:422.
47. Corbett, Combined Operations Lecture 1, Portsmouth, spring 1910, CBT 31.
48. Corbett, Lecture: "Strategical Use of Combined Expeditions," given at Aldershot to the 2nd Division, 7 Jan 1907, LHC, Corbett Papers, Box 2; Lecture 9: "Methods of Controlling or Influencing the Enemy's Strategy," CBT 31.
49. Clausewitz, *On War*, trans. Graham, 3:33.
50. Corbett, *Seven Years' War*, 1:206–8.
51. Corbett, *Seven Years' War*, 1:99–100, 265.
52. Corbett, Combined Operations Lecture 1, Synopsis, LHC, Corbett Papers, Box 2.
53. Corbett, Lecture 9: "Methods of Controlling or Influencing the Enemy's Strategy," CBT 31.

54. Corbett, *Seven Years' War*, 1:206–8.
55. Corbett, *Seven Years' War*, 1:91, 272.
56. Corbett, Lecture 9: "Methods of Controlling or Influencing the Enemy's Strategy"; Combined Operations Lecture 1, Portsmouth, spring 1910, CBT 31.
57. Corbett, *Naval Operations*, 2:vii; Corbett to Richmond, 28 Jan 1916, NMM, RIC 9, pt. 1.
58. Corbett, Combined Operations Lecture 1, Portsmouth, spring 1910, CBT 31.
59. Corbett, Lecture: "Strategical Use of Combined Expeditions," given at Aldershot to the 2nd Division, 7 Jan 1907, LHC, Corbett Papers, Box 2.
60. Corbett, Lecture 9: "Methods of Controlling or Influencing the Enemy's Strategy," CBT 31.
61. Corbett to Richmond, 29 July 1916, NMM, RIC 9, pt. 1.
62. Corbett, *Naval Operations*, 3:246.
63. Corbett to Fisher, 12 Jun 1918, in *Fear God*, ed. Marder, 3:538–39.
64. Sumida, "New Insights," 100–101, 103–4.
65. Mahan, "Preparedness for Naval War," 588.
66. Mahan, *Influence*, 328; *Types of Naval Officers*, 110–11.
67. Sumida notes this in *Inventing Grand Strategy*, 58; Mahan, *Lessons*, 16.
68. Mahan, *Influence*, 326.
69. Mahan, *French Revolution*, 2:318, 352.
70. Mahan, *Influence*, 373, 416, 468.
71. Mahan, *Types of Naval Officers*, 326.
72. Mahan, *War of 1812*, 2:332.
73. Mahan, *Naval Strategy*, 217.
74. Mahan, *Naval Strategy*, 205, 217.
75. Mahan, *Naval Strategy*, 205.
76. Corbett to Richmond, 13 Aug 1912, NMM, RIC 9, pt. 1.
77. Mahan, *Naval Strategy*, 189.
78. Mahan, *Types of Naval Officers*, 115–16.
79. Mahan, *Naval Strategy*, 217.
80. Mahan, *Problem of Asia*, 47–48.
81. Mahan, *Naval Strategy*, 217–18.
82. Mahan, *Types of Naval Officers*, 261.
83. Mahan, Lecture 6: "Rivoli," p. 104, NWC, MS 17, Box 6.
84. Mahan, Notes on Strategy, Papers of Mahan, LC, Container 8, Reel 5.
85. Mahan, *Lessons*, 168; see also his "Word Coinage," *NYT*, 25 Aug 1901; and *Major Operations War of American Independence*, 151.
86. Mahan, *Lessons*, 168–69.
87. Mahan, Lecture 3: "Mondovi, Lodi, Lanato and Castiglione," p. 64, NWC, MS 17, Box 6 (emphasis in original).
88. Mahan, *French Revolution*, 2:252.

89. Mahan, *Naval Strategy*, 432–33.
90. Mahan, *Naval Strategy*, 433.
91. Mahan, *Naval Strategy*, 177.
92. Mahan, *Naval Strategy*, 189–90.
93. For a general argument, see Mahan, *Problem of Asia*, 39–40.

CHAPTER 12. MAHAN'S WAY OF WAR

1. Corbett, *Naval Operations*, 3:246.
2. Mahan to Clark, 12 Mar 1912, *Letters*, 3:447–48; review comparing Mahan, *Naval Strategy*, and Corbett, *Some Principles of Maritime Strategy*, in *New York Evening Post*, 10 May 1912, in CBT 5/3.
3. Mahan, *French Revolution*, 2:374–75.
4. Mahan, "Current Fallacies," 286; see also Lowell Institute Lecture: "Naval Warfare," circa 1897, p. 3, Papers of Mahan, LC, Container 5, Reel 3.
5. Mahan, "Navies as International Factors," 66.
6. Mahan, "Current Fallacies," 287.
7. Mahan, "Armaments and Arbitration," 16.
8. Mahan, "A Twentieth Century Outlook," 266.
9. Mahan, "Time Ill Chosen for a Weak Navy," *NYT*, written 19 Aug 1912 and published 21 Aug.
10. English original, p. 5 of "Le Canal de Panama au point vue militaire," *Revue Économique Internationale*, Jan 1913, Papers of Mahan, LC, Container 6, Reel 4 (emphasis in the original); see also Mahan to Roosevelt, 6 May 1897, *Letters*, 2:507; and "Panama Unguarded Might Be Seized," *NYT*, written 25 Oct 1912 and published 27 Oct.
11. Mahan, *Major Operations War of American Independence*, 29.
12. In one editorial Mahan emphatically contended, "I know that war." See "Unguarded Frontiers," *NYT*, written 31 Aug 1914 and published 10 Sep.
13. Mahan, *French Revolution*, 2:357.
14. Mahan, *War of 1812*, 1:317.
15. Mahan, "Effect of Asiatic Conditions," 184; see also *War of 1812*, 2:208–9.
16. Mahan, *War of 1812*, 1:vii–viii.
17. Mahan, *Naval Strategy*, 415.
18. Mahan, "Hague Conference," 191; see also *War of 1812*, 2:52.
19. Mahan, *French Revolution*, 2:397; *War of 1812*, 1:v.
20. Mahan, *Lessons*, 106.
21. Mahan, *French Revolution*, 2:343, 406, 409.
22. Mahan, *Interest of America in International Conditions*, 29–30; *French Revolution*, 2:371.
23. Mahan, *French Revolution*, 2:17, 230, 254, 381, 390, 395, 403–4.
24. Mahan, *French Revolution*, 2:230, 381–82, 394.

25. Mahan, "Blockade," 854.
26. "Origins of the European War," interview with *New York Evening Post*, 3 Aug 1914; Mahan, "Sea Power in the Present European War," *Leslie's Illustrated Weekly*, 20 Aug 1914, reprinted in *Letters*, 3:698–700, 706–10.
27. Mahan to Laughton, 24 Aug 1914, *Laughton*, No. 272, pp. 258–59; see also Mahan, "Sea Power in the Present European War," *Letters*, 3:706–11.
28. Mahan, *French Revolution*, 2:199.
29. Mahan, *French Revolution*, 2:199.
30. Mahan to the editor of the *NYT*, 2 Nov 1910, *Letters*, 3:366.
31. Mahan, *War of 1812*, 1:286.
32. Mahan, *Lessons*, 106.
33. Mahan, *French Revolution*, 2:377.
34. Mahan, *Influence*, 338; *Problem of Asia*, 49.
35. Mahan, *Naval Strategy*, 43.
36. Mahan, "Considerations," 169.
37. Mahan, *Influence*, 338.
38. Mahan, "Effect of Asiatic Conditions," 177–78.
39. Mahan, *Influence*, 209.
40. Mahan, *Lessons*, 17.
41. Fiske, *Navy as a Fighting Machine*, 45.
42. "De Grasse," no date, pp. 1–2, Papers of Mahan, LC, Container 5, Reel 3.
43. Mahan, *French Revolution*, 2:387.
44. Mahan, *French Revolution*, 1:69, 2:296.
45. Mahan, *Naval Strategy*, 413; see also *French Revolution*, 2:384.
46. Mahan to Long, 7 Aug 1898, *Letters*, 2:577–78.
47. Mahan, *Nelson*, 459.
48. Mahan, *French Revolution*, 2:319, 400–401.
49. *Times* (London), 4 Dec 1914, included in Papers of Mahan, LC, Container 21, Reel 11.

CHAPTER 13. CORBETT'S WAY OF WAR

1. Corbett, "Reorganisation of the War Office," p. 33, CBT 3/10.
2. Corbett, *SPMS*, 117; similar statements appear on pp. 91, 94, 103, and 114.
3. Corbett, *Seven Years' War*, 1:1, 6; Green Pamphlet, p. 8, CBT 6/15. In an earlier work Corbett mentioned only commerce and land operations ("United Service," 205).
4. Corbett, "League of Peace and a Free Sea," p. 11, CBT 7/7.
5. Corbett, *Naval Operations*, 2:263.
6. Corbett, "League of Peace and a Free Sea," p. 5, CBT 7/7.
7. Notice, 10 Jul 1827 in Clausewitz, *On War*, trans. Graham, 1:vii (emphasis in original).

8. Corbett, *SPMS*, 41.
9. Corbett, *Seven Years' War*, 1:28.
10. War Plans, Part I: "Some Principles of Naval Warfare," p. 2, TNA, ADM/116/1043B pt. 1.
11. Corbett, Naval Strategy Lecture 3: "Essentials of True Naval Defensive," p. 20, CBT 15/6/6; Clausewitz, *On War*, trans. Graham, 3:71–72.
12. Corbett, *Trafalgar*, 4.
13. Corbett, *Naval Operations*, 3:41.
14. Corbett, *SPMS*, 52.
15. Corbett, *SPMS*, 60.
16. Corbett, "Methods and Discussion," 324.
17. Corbett, Lecture: "Russo-Japanese War," Nov 1910, LHC, Corbett Papers, Box 2; see also *SPMS*, 55.
18. Corbett, *SPMS*, 58.
19. War Plans, Part I: "Some Principles of Naval Warfare," p. 3, TNA, ADM/116/1043B, pt. 1.
20. Corbett, Lecture: "Russo-Japanese War," LHC, Corbett Papers, Box 2.
21. Corbett, *Seven Years' War*, 2:1–2.
22. Corbett, *SPMS*, 57.
23. Corbett, *Seven Years' War*, 2:15; Corbett, *RJW*, 2:392; Corbett, Naval Strategy Lecture 5, pp. 29–30, CBT 15/6/6 also in CBT 31.
24. Corbett, *SPMS*, 57.
25. Green Pamphlet, p. 7, CBT 15/6/6.
26. Corbett, Russo-Japanese War Lecture 1, Portsmouth, autumn session, 1909, CBT 22/3; Naval Strategy Lecture 5, pp. 29–30, CBT 15/6/6, also in CBT 31.
27. Green Pamphlet, p. 3, CBT 6/15.
28. Corbett, *Seven Years' War*, 1:5.
29. Corbett, *SPMS*, 65.
30. Corbett to Richmond, 22 Aug 1915, 1 Jan 1918, NMM, RIC 9, pt. 1.
31. Corbett, *RJW*, 2:381.
32. Corbett, *Seven Years' War*, 2:71. For similar comments, see *Seven Years' War*, 2:84, 2:119; and "Capture of Private Property," 133.
33. War Plans, Part I: "Some Principles of Naval Warfare," pp. 1–2, TNA, ADM/116/1043B, pt. 1; Corbett, Russo-Japanese War Lecture 1, Portsmouth, autumn, 1909, CBT 22/3.
34. Subsequent paragraphs explaining each of the three phases make use of the following Corbett sources: *RJW*, 1:65–66; *SPMS*, 80–83; Lecture: "Russo-Japanese War," Nov 1911, LHC, Corbett Papers, Box 2. Quotations as well as other more specific information are cited individually.
35. Corbett, Russo-Japanese War Lecture 2: "The First Phase," autumn 1909, CBT 31; *RJW*, 2:1.

36. Corbett, Combined Operations Lecture 2, Portsmouth, spring 1910, CBT 31; see also Jane to Corbett, 30 Nov 1911, CBT 14/4.
37. Corbett, *Naval Operations*, 1:74.
38. Corbett, Combined Operations Lecture 2, Portsmouth, Oct 1908, LHC, Corbett Papers, Box 2.
39. Corbett, *RJW*, 1:75; *SPMS*, 104; *Seven Years' War*, 1:109; and *Trafalgar*, 84–85.
40. Corbett, *RJW*, 1:468–70.
41. Corbett, *SPMS*, 73.
42. Corbett, Russo-Japanese War Lecture 3: "Transition from Phase I to Phase II," Portsmouth, autumn 1909, CBT 31.
43. Corbett, *RJW*, 2:157.
44. Corbett, *RJW*, 1:66.
45. Corbett, Naval Strategy Lecture 5, pp. 30–31, CBT 31.
46. Corbett, *SPMS*, 83–84.
47. Corbett, *SPMS*, 72–73.
48. Corbett, *SPMS*, 62.
49. Corbett, Combined Operations Lecture 1, Synopsis, p. 2, Portsmouth, CBT 31.
50. Corbett, *Naval Operations*, 2:291.
51. Corbett, *SPMS*, 65.
52. Corbett, *Naval Operations*, 2:290.
53. Corbett, Combined Operations Lecture 1, LHC, Corbett Papers, Box 2.
54. Corbett, *SPMS*, 66.
55. Corbett, *SPMS*, 65.
56. Corbett, *SPMS*, 66, 70.
57. Corbett, *SPMS*, 70.
58. Corbett, Naval Strategy Lecture, p. 72, CBT 31.
59. Spenser Wilkinson, "Naval Warfare," review, *Johannesburg Star*, 9 Mar 1912, in CBT 5/3.
60. "A Tract for the Times," review of *SPMS*, *Observer*, 10 Dec 1911, in CBT 5/3.
61. Response to Part I of the War Plan, by Charles Beresford, 8 May 1907, TNA, ADM/116/1037.
62. "Great Britain, Germany and Limited War," review comparing *SPMS* and Mahan's *Naval Strategy*, *Edinburgh Review*, April 1912, 495, in CBT 5/3.
63. Corbett, Combined Operations Lecture 1, Synopsis, LHC, Corbett Papers, Box 2.
64. Corbett, *Naval Operations*, 3:2.
65. Corbett, *Naval Operations*, 3:40.
66. Corbett, *Naval Operations*, 3:219; see also 3:257.
67. "Notes on the RN War College," *Naval Review* 19 (1931): 243.
68. Haldane to Corbett, 6 Dec 1907, 24 Feb 1908, CBT 14/3.
69. "Notes on the RN War College," *Naval Review* 19 (1931): 243.

70. Heuser, *Evolution of Strategy*, 176; Freedman, *Strategy*, 118; Handel, *Masters of War*, 294.
71. A. Lambert, "Sir Julian Corbett," 190–91; Howard, *British Way in Warfare*, 9; Schurman, *Julian S. Corbett*, 60–61.
72. One consistent critic is Colin Gray. See "History for Strategists," 23–24; and "Geography and Grand Strategy," 315. Howard also claims that Corbett overstated some of his argument (*British Way in Warfare: A Reappraisal*, 9–10).

CONCLUSION

1. Corbett to Fisher, 10 Nov 1909, FISR 1/9.
2. Corbett to Richmond, 24 Apr 1917, NMM, RIC 9, pt. 1.
3. Mahan to Roosevelt, 12 Mar 1901, *Letters*, 2:706–8.
4. Mahan, *Types of Naval Officers*, 422; see also *From Sail to Steam*, 308–9; and *French Revolution*, vol. 2.
5. Mahan, *Naval Strategy*.
6. Corbett to Richmond, 24 Apr 1917, NMM, RIC 9, pt. 1.
7. Corbett to Richmond, 23 Dec 1917, NMM, RIC 9, pt. 1.
8. Mahan to Chambers, 27 Jul 1892, *Letters*, 2:76.
9. Mahan, *Influence*, 5.
10. Mahan, Lowell Institute Lecture: "Naval Warfare," circa 1897, p. 97, Papers of Mahan, LC, Container 5, Reel 3.

BIBLIOGRAPHY

ARCHIVES

BRITISH LIBRARY, LONDON

Jellicoe, John, 1st Earl Jellicoe. Correspondence and Papers, BL Add. MS 49,037.

Keyes, Roger, 1st Baron Keyes. Papers and Correspondence, BL Add. MS 82,516 D: Notes on Strategy, War College, Portsmouth, No. 1, Sep 1906.

CHURCHILL ARCHIVES CENTRE, CHURCHILL COLLEGE, CAMBRIDGE, U.K.

Fisher, John, 1st Baron Fisher. Papers of 1st Lord Fisher of Kilverstone: FISR 1/4, 1/5, 1/6, 1/9, 1/15.

LIBRARY OF CONGRESS, WASHINGTON, DC

Mahan, Alfred Thayer. Papers.

LIDDELL HART CENTRE FOR MILITARY ARCHIVES, KING'S COLLEGE, LONDON

Corbett, Sir Julian S. Corbett Papers, Boxes 1–2.

NATIONAL ARCHIVES, KEW, U.K.

ADM 1/8650/244: Inventory of Corbett's Library.

ADM/116/866B: Various documents:

Memoranda on: (1) Limitation of Naval Armaments; (2) Limitation of Size of Battleships; Protection of Ocean Trade in War Time, 1905.

ADM/116/1037: Beresford's Response to the War Plan.

ADM/116/1043B: Part I: "Some Principles of Naval Warfare."

ADM/116/1065B: The Defence of Commerce, with Proposals for Its Organisation in Peace Time, 1908.

CAB/45/265: Controversy relating to the "Notes on Strategy."

NATIONAL MARITIME MUSEUM, GREENWICH, U.K.

Corbett, Sir Julian S. Papers.

CBT 2/4: Correspondence related to "The Capture of Private Property at Sea."

CBT 3/7: Correspondence with Henry Newbolt.

CBT 3/10: Corbett. "The Reorganisation of the War Office." *Monthly Review* (Mar 1904): 26–36.

CBT 4/5: Corbett. "The Revival of Naval History: Being the Laughton Memorial Lecture."

CBT 5/3: Reviews of *Some Principles of Maritime Strategy.*

CBT 6/5: Correspondence with Edmond Slade.

CBT 6/12: Memorandum on Invasion.

CBT 6/13: Press Cuttings and Documents relating to Kenneth Dewar.

CBT 6/15: Strategical Terms and Definitions used in Lectures on Naval History.

CBT 6/16: War Course, "Notes on Strategy," January 1909 ed.

CBT 7/7: Corbett, "League of Peace and a Free Sea." New York: George H. Doran, 1917.

CBT 7/12: Correspondence with Various Correspondents.

CBT 7/19: Sanford-Tunstall Correspondence relating to Corbett.

CBT 10/1, 7, 8: Correspondence with Edith Rosa Corbett (Wife), 1902–3, 1909.

CBT 11/2–3: Correspondence with Edith Rosa Corbett (Wife), 1911–12.

CBT 13/2: Correspondence with Edmond Slade.

CBT 13/3: Correspondence with Naval Officers.

CBT 14/3: Letters, Miscellaneous Correspondents, F–H.

CBT 14/4: Letters, Miscellaneous Correspondents, J–M.

CBT 15/6: Miscellaneous Lecture Notes.

CBT 16/3: Book Inventory.

CBT 22/3: Lecture Notes on the Russo-Japanese War.

CBT 24/8: Reviews of *Naval Operations*, vol. 1.

CBT 28/1: Notes for the Ford Lectures.

CBT 28/3: Reviews of *Naval Operations*, vol. 2.

CBT 31: Lecture Notes on Naval Strategy.

CBT 43/9–12: Diary, 1908–11.

Dewar, Kenneth. Correspondence and Papers.

DEW 34: Letters between Richmond and Dewar.

Lewis, Michael Arthur. Papers.

LES 4/1: Letters from Corbett to George Cookson and Sir Geoffrey Callender.

Miscellaneous Collections

AGC 2/27: W. H. Fawkes to Corbett, 27 Nov 1911.

MS 67/030: Letters from Corbett to Morris Colles (literary agent).

Naish, George Prideaux-Brabant. Papers.

NAI 2/30: Includes a copy of "Notes on Strategy."

Richmond, Herbert William. Papers.

RIC 2/2: Commonplace Book.

RIC 9, Part 1: Papers and Correspondence with Corbett.

Tunstall, Brian. Papers.

TUN 226: Blank Notebook Presented by Fisher to Corbett.

NAVAL WAR COLLEGE ARCHIVE, HATTENDORF CENTER FOR MARITIME HISTORICAL RESEARCH, NEWPORT, RI

Mahan, Alfred Thayer. Papers. MS 17, Boxes 3 and 6.

Early Records of the Naval War College, 1883–1919, RG 1, Box 3.

Naval War College Lectures, 1894–1903, RG 15, Box 1.

BOOKS AND ARTICLES

Angell, Norman. *The World's Highway.* New York: George H. Doran, 1915.

Aron, Raymond. "The Evolution of Modern Strategic Thought." In *Problems of Modern Strategy: Part One*, ed. Alastair Buchan. Adelphi Paper 54. London: Institute for Strategic Studies, 1969.

Aston, George G. "Combined Strategy for Fleets and Armies; or 'Amphibious Strategy.'" *Journal of the Royal United Service Institution* 51 (1907): 984–1004.

———. *Letters on Amphibious Wars.* London: John Murray, 1911.

Bacon, Francis. "Of the True Greatness of Kingdoms and Estates." Part of *Essays of Counsels Civil and Moral*, pp. 176–88. In *The Works of Francis Bacon.* New York: Hurd and Houghton, 1878.

Bassford, Christopher. *Clausewitz in English: The Reception of Clausewitz in Britain and America 1815–1945.* New York: Oxford University Press, 1994.

Black, Jeremy. *Naval Power: A History of Warfare and the Sea from 1500.* New York: Palgrave Macmillan, 2009.

Brands, Hal. *The Promise and Pitfalls of Grand Strategy.* Carlisle, PA: Strategic Studies Institute, 2012.

Bridge, Cyprian. *Sea-Power and Other Studies.* London: Smith, Elder, 1910.

Callwell, C. E. *Military Operations and Maritime Preponderance: Their Relations and Interdependence.* Edinburgh: W. Blackwood and Sons, 1905.

———. *Small Wars: Their Principles and Practice.* Rev. ed. London: His Majesty's Stationary Office, 1903.

Churchill, Winston S. *The World Crisis.* Vol. 1. Toronto: Macmillan of Canada, 1923.

Clarke, George, Lord Sydenham of Combe. "Sea Heresies." *Naval Review* 19 (1931): 222–36.

Clarke, George S., and James R. Thursfield. *The Navy and the Nation* or *Naval Warfare and Imperial Defence.* London: John Murray, 1897.

Clausewitz, Carl von. *On War*. Trans. J. J. Graham. 3 vols. in 1. London: N. Trüber, 1873.

———. *On War*. Ed. and trans. Michael Howard and Peter Paret. Princeton: Princeton University Press, 1976.

Cleaver, Liam J. "The Pen behind the Fleet: The Influence of Sir Julian Stafford Corbett on British Naval Development, 1898–1918." *Comparative Strategy* 14 (1995): 45–57.

Colomb, John. "British Defence, 1800–1900." *Proceedings of the Royal Colonial Institute* 31 (1899–1900): 208–45.

———. *The Protection of Our Commerce and Distribution of Our Naval Forces Considered*. London: Harrison, 1867.

Colomb, Philip H. *Naval Warfare: Its Ruling Principles and Practice Historically Treated*. Intro. Barry M. Gough. 2 vols. Reprint. Annapolis: Naval Institute, 1990.

Corbett, Julian S. *The Campaign of Trafalgar*. London: Longmans, Green, 1910.

———. "The Capture of Private Property at Sea." In *Some Neglected Aspects of War*, pp. 117–53. London: Sampson Low, Marston, 1907.

———. *Drake and the Tudor Navy with a History of the Rise of England and Maritime Power*. 2 vols. London: Longmans, Green, 1898.

———. *England and the Mediterranean: A Study of the Rise and Influence of British Power within the Straits, 1603–1713*. 2 vols. London: Longmans, Green, 1904.

———. *England and the Seven Years' War: A Study in Combined Strategy*. 2 vols. London: Longmans, Green, 1907.

———, ed. *Fighting Instructions, 1530–1816*. London: Navy Records Society, 1905.

———. *History of the Great War: Naval Operations*. Vols. 1–3. London: Longmans, Green, 1920–23.

———. *Maritime Operations in the Russo-Japanese War, 1904–1905*. 2 vols. 1914–15. Reprint with intro. by John B. Hattendorf and Donald Schurman. 2 vols. Annapolis: Naval Institute Press, 2015.

———. "Methods of Discussion." *Naval Review* (1920): 322–24.

———. *Monk*. London: Macmillan, 1889.

———. "Napoleon and the British Navy after Trafalgar." *Quarterly Review* 237 (1922): 238–55.

———, ed. *Private Papers of George, Second Earl Spencer: First Lord of the Admiralty, 1794–1801*. Vols. 1 and 2. London: Navy Records Society, 1913–14.

———. "Recent Attacks on the Admiralty." *Nineteenth Century and After* 61 (1907): 195–208.

———, ed. *Signals and Instructions, 1776–1794*. London: Navy Records Society, 1908.

———. *Sir Francis Drake*. London: Macmillan, 1890.

———. *Some Principles of Maritime Strategy*. London: Longmans, Green, 1911. Reprint. Annapolis: Naval Institute Press, 1988.

———. "Staff Histories." In *Naval and Military Essays: Being Papers Read at the Naval and Military Section of the International Congress of Historical Studies*, ed. Julian

S. Corbett and H. J. Edwards, pp. 23–38. Cambridge: University of Cambridge Press, 1914.

———. "The Strategical Value of Speed in Battle-Ships." *Journal of the Royal United Service Institution* 51 (1907): 824–39.

———. *The Successors of Drake.* London: Longmans, Green, 1900.

———. "Teaching Naval and Military History." *History* 1 (1916): 12–19.

———. "The United Service." *Naval Review* (1923): 201–14 [originally written in 1904].

Cox, Mary E. *War, Blockades, and Hunger: Nutritional Deprivation of German Children, 1914–1924.* University of Oxford Discussion Papers in Economic and Social History 110 (2013).

Craig, Gordon A. "Delbrück: The Military Historian." In *Makers of Modern Strategy from Machiavelli to the Nuclear Age*, ed. Peter Paret, pp. 326–53. Princeton: Princeton University Press, 1986.

David, W. G. "Our Merchant Marine: The Causes of Its Decline and the Means to Be Taken for Its Revival." U.S. Naval Institute *Proceedings* 8 (1882): 151–86.

Dull, Jonathan. "Mahan, Sea Power, and the War for American Independence." *International History Review* 10 (1988): 59–67.

Ferreiro, Larrie D. "Mahan and the 'English Club' of Lima, Peru: The Genesis of *The Influence of Sea Power upon History*." *Journal of Military History* 72 (2008): 901–6.

Field, James A. Jr. "The Origins of Maritime Strategy and the Development of Sea Power." In *War, Strategy, and Maritime Power*, ed. B. Mitchell Simpson III, pp. 77–94. New Brunswick: Rutgers University Press, 1977.

Fiennes, Gerard. *Sea Power and Freedom: A Historical Study.* Intro. Bradley Fiske. New York: G. P. Putnam's Sons, 1918.

Fiske, Bradley A. *From Midshipman to Rear-Admiral.* New York: Century, 1919.

———. *The Navy as a Fighting Machine.* 2nd ed. New York: Scribner's, 1918.

Freedman, Lawrence. *Strategy: A History.* New York: Oxford University Press, 2013.

Fuller, William C. "What Is a Military Lesson." In *Strategic Logic and Political Rationality: Essays in Honour of Michael I. Handel*, ed. Bradford A. Lee and Karl F. Walling, pp. 38–59. London: Frank Cass, 2003.

Gat, Azar. *The Development of Military Thought: The Nineteenth Century.* Oxford: Clarendon Press, 1992.

Gooch, John. "Maritime Command: Mahan and Corbett." In *Seapower and Strategy*, ed. Colin S. Gray and Roger W. Barnett, pp. 27–46. Annapolis: Naval Institute Press, 1989.

Gough, Barry M. "Maritime Strategy: The Legacies of Mahan and Corbett as Philosophers of Sea Power." *RUSI Journal* (winter 1988): 55–62.

Graham, Gerald S. *Politics of Naval Supremacy: Studies in British Maritime Ascendency.* London: Cambridge University Press, 1965.

Gray, Colin S. "Geography and Grand Strategy." *Comparative Strategy* 10 (1991): 311–29.

———. "History for Strategists: British Seapower as a Relevant Past." *Journal of Strategic Studies* 17 (1994): 7–32.

———. *The Leverage of Sea Power: The Strategic Advantage of Navies in War.* New York: Free Press, 1992.

Great Britain, Colonial Conference, 1902. "Memorandum on Sea Power and the Principles Involved in It." *Accounts and Papers: Colonies and British Possessions*, vol. 9. London: His Majesty's Stationary Office, 1903.

Grimes, Shawn T. *Strategy and War Planning in the British Navy, 1887–1918.* Woodbridge, Boydell Press, 2012.

Grotius, Hugo. *The Law of War and Peace: De Jure Belli ac Pacis Libri Tres.* Trans. Francis W. Kelsey. Indianapolis: Bobbs-Merrill, 1925.

H., H. "Naval History: Mahan and His Successors." *Military Historian and Economist* 3 (1918): 7–19.

Hamilton, C. I. "Anglo-French Seapower and the Declaration of Paris." *International History Review* 4 (1982): 166–90.

Hamley, Edward Bruce. *National Defence Articles and Speeches.* Edinburgh: William Blackwood, 1889.

———. *Operations of War: Explained and Illustrated.* Edinburgh: William Blackwood, 1866.

Handel, Michael I. *Masters of War: Classical Strategic Thought.* 3rd ed. London: Frank Cass, 2001.

Harrison, Benjamin. *Public Papers and Addresses of Benjamin Harrison, Twenty-Third President of the United States, March 4, 1889–March 4, 1893.* Washington: Government Printing Office, 1893.

Hattendorf, John B. "Alfred Thayer Mahan and His Strategic Thought." In *Maritime Strategy and the Balance of Power: Britain and America in the Twentieth Century*, ed. John B. Hattendorf and Robert S. Jordan, pp. 83–94. New York: St. Martin's Press, 1989.

———. "The Anglo-French Naval Wars (1689–1815) in Twentieth Century Naval Thought." *Journal for Maritime Research* 3 (2001): 41–69.

———. "The Idea of a 'Fleet in Being' in Historical Perspective." *Naval War College Review* 67 (2014): 43–60.

———, ed. and intro. *Mahan on Naval Strategy: Selections from the Writings of Rear Admiral Alfred Thayer Mahan.* Reprint. Annapolis: Naval Institute Press, 2015.

Henderson, G. F. R. *The Science of War: A Collection of Essays and Lectures, 1891–1903.* Ed. Neill Malcolm. 3rd ed. London: Longmans, Green, 1908.

Heuser, Beatrice. *The Evolution of Strategy: Thinking War from Antiquity to the Present.* Cambridge: Cambridge University Press, 2010.

———. "Regina Maris and the Command of the Sea: The Sixteenth Century Origins of Modern Maritime Strategy." *Journal of Strategic Studies* 40 (2017): 225–62.

———. *Strategy before Clausewitz: Linking Warfare and Statecraft, 1400–1830.* London: Routledge, 2018.

Hill, Richard. *The Prizes of War: The Naval Prize System in the Napoleonic Wars, 1793–1815.* Stroud, Gloucestershire, U.K.: Sutton, 1998.

Holmes, James R., and Toshi Yoshihara. "The Influence of Mahan upon China's Maritime Strategy." *Comparative Strategy* 24 (2005): 23–51.

Howard, Michael. *The British Way in Warfare: A Reappraisal.* London: Jonathan Cape, 1975.

Hunt, Barry D. "The Strategic Thought of Sir Julian S. Corbett." In *Maritime Strategy and the Balance of Power: Britain and America in the Twentieth Century*, ed. John B. Hattendorf and Robert S. Jordan, pp. 110–35. New York: St. Martin's Press, 1989.

Jomini, Antoine-Henri. *The Art of War.* Trans. G. H. Mendell and W. P. Craighill. Philadelphia: J. B. Lippincott, 1868.

———. *Summary of the Art of War; or A New Analytical Compend of the Principal Combinations of Strategy, of Grand Tactics and of Military Policy.* Trans. O. F. Winship and E. E. McLean. New York: G. P. Putnam, 1854.

Karsten, Peter. *The Naval Aristocracy: The Golden Age of Annapolis and the Emergence of Modern Navalism.* New York: Free Press, 1972.

Kennedy, Paul, ed. *Grand Strategies in Peace and War.* New Haven: Yale University Press, 1991.

———. "The Influence and Limitations of Sea Power." *International History Review* 10 (1988): 2–17.

———. *The Rise and Fall of British Naval Mastery.* London: Allen Lane, 1976. Reprint. London: Ashfield, 1983.

Lambert, Andrew. "Corbett and the Naval War Course." In *Dreadnought to Darling: 100 Years of Comment, Controversy and Debate in the* Naval Review, ed. Peter Hore, pp. 37–52. Barnsley: Seaforth, 2012.

———. "The Development of Education in the Royal Navy: 1854–1914." In *The Development of British Naval Thinking: Essays in Memory of Bryan McLaren Ranft*, ed. Geoffrey Till, pp. 34–59. London: Routledge, 2006.

———. *The Foundations of Naval History: John Knox Laughton, the Royal Navy and the Historical Profession.* London: Chatham, 1998.

———, ed. *Letters and Papers of Professor Sir John Knox Laughton, 1830–1915.* Aldershot: Ashgate for the Navy Records Society, 2002.

———. "Sir Julian Corbett, Naval History and the Development of Sea Power Theory." In *Strategy and the Sea: Essays in Honour of John B. Hattendorf*, ed. N. A. M. Rodger, J. Ross Dancy, Benjamin Darnell, and Evan Wilson, pp. 190–200. Woodbridge: Boydell Press, 2016.

———, ed. *21st Century Corbett: Maritime Strategy and Naval Policy for the Modern Era.* Annapolis: Naval Institute Press, 2017.

Lambert, Nicholas A. "Admiral Sir John Fisher and the Concept of Flotilla Defence, 1904–1909." *Journal of Military History* 59 (1995): 639–60.

———. "False Prophet?: The Maritime Theory of Julian Corbett and Professional Military Education." *Journal of Military History* 77 (2013): 1055–78.

Laughton, John Knox. "Captain Mahan on Maritime Power." *Edinburgh Review* 172 (1890): 420–53.

———. "Captain Mahan on Maritime Power." *Edinburgh Review* (1893): 484–518.

———. Review of *Drake and the Tudor Navy, The Successors of Drake*, and *Papers relating to the Navy during the Spanish War. Edinburgh Review* (1901): 1–27.

———. "The Scientific Study of Naval History." *Royal United Service Institution* 18 (1875): 508–27.

———. "The Study of Naval History." *Royal United Service Institution* 40 (1896): 795–820.

———. "Vice Admiral Baron von Tegetthoff." *Fraser's Magazine*, new ser. 17 (1878): 671–92.

Livezey, William E. *Mahan on Sea Power.* Rev. ed. Norman: University of Oklahoma Press, 1980.

Luce, Stephen B. "The Intellectual Focus: On the Study of Naval Warfare as a Science." In *The Writings of Stephen B. Luce*, ed. John D. Hayes and John B. Hattendorf, pp. 45–68. Newport: Naval War College Press, 1975.

———. "Tactics and History: On the Study of Naval History." In *The Writings of Stephen B. Luce*, ed. John D. Hayes and John B. Hattendorf, pp. 69–97. Newport: Naval War College Press, 1975.

Mahan, Alfred Thayer. *Admiral Farragut.* New York: D. Appleton, 1893.

———. "Appreciation of Conditions in the Russo-Japanese Conflict, Pt I." *Collier's Weekly* 32 (20 Feb 1904): 7–8.

———. "Appreciation of Conditions in the Russo-Japanese Conflict, Pt II." *Collier's Weekly*, 33 (30 Apr 1904): 10–13.

———. "Armaments and Arbitration." In *Armaments and Arbitration or the Place of Force in the International Relations of States*, pp. 15–35. New York: Harper and Brothers, 1912.

———. "Blockade in Relation to Naval Strategy." U.S. Naval Institute *Proceedings* 21 (1895): 851–66.

———. "Conditions Determining the Naval Expansion of the United States." In *Retrospect & Prospect: Studies in International Relations Naval and Political*, pp. 39–53. London: Sampson Low, Marston, 1902.

———. "Considerations Governing the Disposition of Navies." In *Retrospect & Prospect: Studies in International Relations Naval and Political*, pp. 139–205. London: Sampson Low, Marston, 1902.

———. "Current Fallacies upon Naval Subjects." In *Lessons of the War with Spain and Other Articles*, pp. 277–320. Boston: Little, Brown, 1899.

———. "The Effect of Asiatic Conditions upon World Policies." In *The Problem of Asia and Its Effect upon International Policies*, pp. 147–202. London: Sampson Low, Marston, 1900.

———. "The Engineer in Naval Warfare." *North American Review* 481 (1896): 648–54.

———. *From Sail to Steam: Recollections of Naval Life*. New York: Harper and Brothers, 1907.

———. "The Future in Relation to American Naval Power." In *The Interest of America in Sea Power, Present and Future*, pp. 137–72. Boston: Little, Brown, 1897.

———. *The Gulf and Inland Waters*. New York: Charles Scribner's Sons, 1883.

———. "The Hague Conference of 1907: The Question of Immunity for Belligerent Merchant Shipping." In *Some Neglected Aspects of War*, pp. 157–93. London: Sampson Low, Marston, 1907.

———. *The Harvest Within: Thoughts on the Life of the Christian*. Boston: Little, Brown, 1909.

———. "Hawaii and Our Future Sea Power." In *The Interest of America in Sea Power Present and Future*, pp. 31–55. Boston: Little, Brown, 1897.

———. "The Importance of the Command of the Sea." In *Scientific American Reference Book*, ed. Albert Hopkins and A. Russell Bond, pp. 412–13. New York: Munn, 1914.

———. *The Influence of Sea Power upon History, 1660–1783*. Boston: Little, Brown, 1890. Reprint. New York: Dover, 1987.

———. *The Influence of Sea Power upon the French Revolution and Empire, 1793–1812*. 9th ed. Boston: Little, Brown, 1898.

———. "The Influence of the South African War upon the Prestige of the British Empire." In *Retrospect & Prospect: Studies in International Relations Naval and Political*, pp. 57–86. London: Sampson Low, Marston, 1902.

———. *The Interest of America in International Conditions*. Boston: Little, Brown, 1910.

———. Introduction to *Ironclads in Action: A Sketch of Naval Warfare from 1855 to 1895*, by H. W. Wilson. London: Sampson Low, Marston, 1896.

———. "Lessons from the Yalu Fight." *Century Magazine* 50 (1895): 629–32.

———. *Lessons of the War with Spain and Other Articles*. Boston: Little, Brown, 1899.

———. *The Life of Nelson: The Embodiment of the Sea Power of Great Britain*. 2nd rev. ed. Boston: Little, Brown, 1899.

———. *The Major Operations of the Navies in the War of American Independence*. Boston: Little, Brown, 1913.

———. "The Military Rule of Obedience." In *Retrospect & Prospect: Studies in International Relations Naval and Political*, pp. 255–83. London: Sampson Low, Marston, 1902.

———. *Naval Administration and Warfare: Some General Principles with Other Essays*. Boston: Little, Brown, 1908.

———. "Naval Education." U.S. Naval Institute *Proceedings* 5 (1879): 345–76.

———. *Naval Strategy Compared and Contrasted with the Principles and Practice of Military Operations on Land.* Boston: Little, Brown, 1911.

———. "The Naval War College." In *Armaments and Arbitration or the Place of Force in the International Relations of States*, pp. 196–217. New York: Harper and Brothers, 1912.

———. "Navies as International Factors." In *Armaments and Arbitration or the Place of Force in the International Relations of States*, pp. 57–77. New York: Harper and Brothers, 1912.

———. "The Navy as a Career." *Forum* 20 (1895): 277–83.

———. "Objects of the United States Naval War College (an Address, August 1888)." In *Naval Administration and Warfare: Some General Principles with Other Essays*, pp. 177–213. Boston: Little, Brown, 1908.

———. "The Panama Canal and Sea Power in the Pacific." In *Armaments and Arbitration or the Place of Force in the International Relations of States*, pp. 155–80. New York: Harper and Brothers, 1912.

———. "The Panama Canal and the Distribution of the Fleet." *North American Review* 200 (1914): 406–17.

———. "The Persian Gulf and International Relations." In *Retrospect & Prospect: Studies in International Relations Naval and Political*, pp. 209–51. London: Sampson Low, Marston, 1902.

———. "The Place of Force in International Relations." In *Armaments and Arbitration or the Place of Force in the International Relations of States*, pp. 100–120. New York: Harper and Brothers, 1912.

———. "Possibilities of an Anglo-American Reunion." *North American Review* 159 (1894): 551–63.

———. "Preparedness for Naval War." *Harper's* 94 (1897): 579–88.

———. "Principles Involved in the War between Japan and Russia." In *Naval Administration and Warfare: Some General Principles with Other Essays*, pp. 89–129. Boston: Little, Brown, 1908.

———. "Principles of Naval Administration." In *Naval Administration and Warfare: Some General Principles with Other Essays*, pp. 3–48. Boston: Little, Brown, 1908.

———. *The Problem of Asia and Its Effect upon International Policies*. London: Sampson Low, Marston, 1900.

———. "The Problems that Rozhdestvensky and Togo Must Solve." *The Times* (London), 13 May 1905.

———. "Retrospect and Prospect." In *Retrospect & Prospect: Studies in International Relations Naval and Political*, pp. 3–35. London: Sampson Low, Marston, 1902.

———. "Retrospect upon the War between Japan and Russia." In *Naval Administration and Warfare: Some General Principles with Other Essays*, pp. 133–73. Boston: Little, Brown, 1908.

———. *Sea Power in Its Relations to the War of 1812*. 2 vols. Boston: Little, Brown, 1905.

———. *The Story of the War in South Africa 1899–1900.* 3rd ed. London: Sampson Low, Marston, 1901.

———. "The Strategic Features of the Gulf of Mexico and the Caribbean Sea." In *The Interest of America in Sea Power Present and Future*, pp. 271–314. Boston: Little, Brown, 1897.

———. "The Submarine and Its Enemies." *Collier's Weekly* 39 (6 Apr 1907): 19–21.

———. "The Subordination of Historical Treatment (President's Address to the American Historical Association, 1902)." In *Naval Administration and Warfare: Some General Principles with Other Essays*, pp. 245–72. Reprint. Boston: Little, Brown, 1908.

———. "Torpedo Craft vs. Battleships." *Collier's Weekly* 33 (21 May 1904): 16–17.

———. "A Twentieth Century Outlook." In *The Interest of America in Sea Power Present and Future*, pp. 217–68. Boston: Little, Brown, 1897.

———. *Types of Naval Officers: Drawn from the History of the British Navy.* London: Sampson Low, Marston, 1902.

———. "The United States Looking Outward." In *The Interest of America in Sea Power Present and Future*, pp. 3–27. Boston: Little, Brown, 1897.

———. "Why Fortify the Panama Canal." In *Armaments and Arbitration or the Place of Force in the International Relations of States*, pp. 181–95. New York: Harper and Brothers, 1912.

Mahan, D. H. *Advanced-Guard, Outpost, and Detachment Service of Troops with the Essential Principles of Strategy, and Grand Tactics for the Use of Officers of the Militia and Volunteers.* New ed. New York: John Wiley, 1870.

Marder, Arthur J., ed. *Fear God and Dread Nought: The Correspondence of Admiral of the Fleet Lord Fisher of Kilverstone.* 3 vols. London: Jonathan Cape, 1952–59.

Martin, Christopher. "The 1907 Naval War Plans and the Second Hague Peace Conference: A Case of Propaganda." *Journal of Strategic Studies* 28 (2005): 833–56.

Milevski, Lukas. *The Evolution of Modern Grand Strategic Thought.* Oxford: Oxford University Press, 2016.

Moll, Kenneth I. "A. T. Mahan: American Historian." *Military Affairs* 27 (autumn 1963): 131–40.

Murray, Stewart L. *The Reality of War: An Introduction to Clausewitz with a note by Spenser Wilkinson.* London: Hugh Rees, 1909.

Offer, Avner. *The First World War: An Agrarian Interpretation.* Oxford: Clarendon Press, 1989.

Parry, Clive, ed. *The Consolidated Treaty Series.* Vol. 115. Dobbs Ferry: Oceana Publications, 1969.

Petrie, Donald A. *The Prize Game: Lawful Looting on the High Seas in the Days of Fighting Sail.* New York: Berkley, 1999.

Posen, Barry. R. *Sources of Military Doctrine: France, Britain, and Germany between the World Wars.* Ithaca: Cornell University Press, 1986.

Puleston, W. D. *Mahan*. London: Jonathan Cape, 1939.

Quester, George H. "Mahan and American Naval Thought since 1914." In *The Influence of History on Mahan*, ed. John Hattendorf, pp. 177–95. Newport: Naval War College Press, 1991.

Ranft, Bryan. Foreword to *Some Principles of Maritime Strategy*, by Julian S. Corbett. London: Conway Maritime Press, 1972.

Reitzel, William. "Mahan on the Use of the Sea." *Naval War College Review* 25 (May–Jun 1973): 73–82.

Reynolds, Clark G. *Command of the Sea: The History and Strategy of Maritime Empires*. New York: William Morrow, 1974.

Richardson, John M. *A Design for Maintaining Maritime Superiority*, ver. 1.0. Jan 2016.

Richmond, Herbert. "The Late Sir Julian Corbett." *Naval Review* (1923): 14–21.

Rodger, N. A. M. *The Command of the Ocean: A Naval History of Britain, 1649–1815*. New York: W. W. Norton, 2004.

———. "The Significance of Trafalgar: Sea and Land Power in the Anglo-French Wars." In *Trafalgar in History: A Battle and Its Afterlife*, ed. David Cannadine, pp. 78–89. London: Palgrave, 2006.

Roksund, Arne. *The Jeune École: The Strategy of the Weak*. Leiden: Brill, 2007.

Roosevelt, Theodore. *The Naval War of 1812*. New York: G. P. Putnam's Sons, 1882.

Ropp, Theodore. *The Development of a Modern Navy: French Naval Policy 1871–1904*. Ed. Stephen S. Roberts. Annapolis: Naval Institute, 1987.

Rosinski, Herbert. "Mahan and World War II." In *The Development of Naval Thought: Essays of Herbert Rosinski*, ed. and intro. B. Mitchell Simpson III, pp. 20–40. Newport: Naval War College Press, 1977.

Rubel, Robert C. *Navies and Economic Prosperity—the New Logic of Sea Power*. Corbett Paper 11. Corbett Centre for Maritime Policy Studies, Oct 2012.

St. John, Ronald B. "European Naval Expansion and Mahan, 1889–1906." *Naval War College Review* 23 (Mar 1971): 74–83.

Schurman, Donald M. *The Education of a Navy: The Development of British Naval Strategic Thought, 1867–1914*. Reprint. Malabar, FL: Krieger, 1984.

———. "Historians and Britain's Imperial Strategic Stance in 1914." In *Perspectives of Empire: Essays Presented to Gerald S. Graham*, ed. John E. Flint and Glyndwr Williams, pp. 172–88. London: Longmans, 1973.

———. "Julian Corbett's Influence on the Royal Navy's Perception of Its Maritime Function." In *Mahan Is Not Enough: The Proceedings of a Conference on the Works of Sir Julian Corbett and Admiral Sir Herbert Richmond*, ed. James Goldrick and John Hattendorf, pp. 51–63. Newport: Naval War College Press, 1993.

———. *Julian S. Corbett: Historian of British Maritime Policy from Drake to Jellicoe*. London: Royal Historical Society, 1981.

———. "Mahan Revisited." In *Maritime Strategy and the Balance of Power: Britain and America in the Twentieth Century*, ed. John Hattendorf and Robert S. Jordan, pp. 95–109. New York: St. Martin's Press, 1989.

Seager, Robert II. "Alfred Thayer Mahan: Christian Expansionist, Navalist, and Historian." In *Admirals of the New Steel Navy: Makers of the American Naval Tradition, 1880–1930*, ed. James C. Bradford, pp. 24–72. Annapolis: Naval Institute Press, 1990.

———. *Alfred Thayer Mahan: The Man and His Letters*. Annapolis: Naval Institute Press, 1977.

———. "Ten Years before Mahan: The Unofficial Case for the New Navy, 1880–1890." *Mississippi Valley Historical Review* 40 (1953): 491–512.

Seager, Robert II, and Doris D. Maguire. *Letters and Papers of Alfred Thayer Mahan*. 3 vols. Annapolis: Naval Institute Press, 1975.

Semmel, Bernard. *Liberalism and Naval Strategy: Ideology, Interest, and Sea Power during the Pax Britannica*. Boston: Allen and Unwin, 1986.

Shy, John. "Jomini." In *Makers of Modern Strategy from Machiavelli to the Nuclear Age*, ed. Peter Paret, pp. 143–85. Princeton: Princeton University Press, 1986.

Sondhaus, Lawrence. "The Jeune École." In *Naval Warfare, 1815–1914*, pp. 139–59. New York: Routledge, 2001.

Sprout, Harold, and Margaret Sprout. *Rise of American Naval Power*. Reprint. Princeton: Princeton University Press, 2015.

Stanford, Peter M. "The Work of Sir Julian Corbett in the Dreadnought Era." U.S. Naval Institute *Proceedings* 77 (1951): 61–71.

Stoker, Donald. *Clausewitz: His Life and Work*. New York: Oxford, 2014.

Strachan, Hew. *Clausewitz's* On War: *A Biography*. New York: Atlantic Monthly, 2007.

———. *The Direction of War: Contemporary Strategy in Historical Perspective*. Cambridge: Cambridge University Press, 2013.

———. "The Lost Meaning of Strategy." *Survival* 47 (2005): 33–54.

Sumida, Jon Tetsuro. "Alfred Thayer Mahan, Geopolitician." *Journal of Strategic Studies* 22 (1999): 39–62.

———. *Decoding Clausewitz: A New Approach to* On War. Lawrence: University Press of Kansas, 2008.

———. "The Historian as Contemporary Analyst: Sir Julian Corbett and Admiral Sir John Fisher." In *Mahan Is Not Enough: The Proceedings of a Conference on the Works of Sir Julian Corbett and Admiral Sir Herbert Richmond*, ed. James Goldrick and John Hattendorf, pp. 125–40. Newport: Naval War College Press 1993.

———. *Inventing Grand Strategy and Teaching Command: The Classic Works of Alfred Thayer Mahan Reconsidered*. Washington: Woodrow Wilson Center Press, 1997.

———. "New Insights from Old Books: The Case of Alfred Thayer Mahan." *Naval War College Review* 54 (2001): 100–111.

Thucydides. *The Landmark Thucydides: A Comprehensive Guide to the Peloponnesian War.* Ed. Robert B. Strassler. New York: Simon and Schuster, 1996.

U.S. Senate. *The Executive Documents of the Senate of the United States for the Second Session of the Forty-Eighth Congress and the Special Session of the Senate Convened March 4, 1885.* Vol. 1. Washington: Government Printing Office, 1885.

Varacalli, Thomas F. X. "National Interest and Moral Responsibility in the Political Thought of Admiral Alfred Thayer Mahan." *Naval War College Review* 69 (2016): 108–27.

Weigley, Russell F. *The American Way of War: A History of United States Strategy and Policy.* Bloomington: Indiana University Press, 1973.

Widen, J. J. *Theorist of Maritime Strategy: Sir Julian Corbett and His Contribution to Military and Naval Thought.* Surrey: Ashgate, 2012.

JOURNALS, PERIODICALS, AND NEWSPAPERS

American Historical Review

Athenaeum

Atlantic

Daily Telegraph (London)

Edinburgh Review

Evening Standard (London)

Fortnightly Review

Johannesburg Star

Morning Post (London)

Naval and Military Record

Naval Review

New York Evening Post

New York Times

Observer (London)

Pall Mall Gazette (London)

Political Science Quarterly

Saturday Review (London)

Standard (London)

The Times (London)

United States Army and Navy Journal and Gazette

U.S. Naval Institute *Proceedings*

Western Mercury (Plymouth, U.K.)

INDEX

ABOUT THE AUTHOR

Kevin D. McCranie is the Philip A. Crowl Professor of Comparative Strategy at the U.S. Naval War College in Newport, Rhode Island. He is the author of *Admiral Lord Keith and the Naval War against Napoleon* and *Utmost Gallantry: The U.S. and Royal Navies at Sea in the War of 1812.*

THE NAVAL INSTITUTE PRESS is the book-publishing arm of the U.S. Naval Institute, a private, nonprofit, membership society for sea service professionals and others who share an interest in naval and maritime affairs. Established in 1873 at the U.S. Naval Academy in Annapolis, Maryland, where its offices remain today, the Naval Institute has members worldwide.

Members of the Naval Institute support the education programs of the society and receive the influential monthly magazine *Proceedings* or the colorful bimonthly magazine *Naval History* and discounts on fine nautical prints and on ship and aircraft photos. They also have access to the transcripts of the Institute's Oral History Program and get discounted admission to any of the Institute-sponsored seminars offered around the country.

The Naval Institute's book-publishing program, begun in 1898 with basic guides to naval practices, has broadened its scope to include books of more general interest. Now the Naval Institute Press publishes about seventy titles each year, ranging from how-to books on boating and navigation to battle histories, biographies, ship and aircraft guides, and novels. Institute members receive significant discounts on the Press' more than eight hundred books in print.

Full-time students are eligible for special half-price membership rates. Life memberships are also available.

For a free catalog describing Naval Institute Press books currently available, and for further information about joining the U.S. Naval Institute, please write to:

Member Services
U.S. NAVAL INSTITUTE
291 Wood Road
Annapolis, MD 21402-5034

Telephone: (800) 233-8764
Fax: (410) 571-1703
Web address: www.usni.org